COLLEGE WRITING SKILLS WITH READINGS

ATF

McGRAW-HILL BOOK COMPANY

New York   St. Louis   San Francisco   Auckland   Bogotá
Caracas   Colorado Springs   Hamburg   Lisbon   London
Madrid   Mexico   Milan   Montreal   New Delhi
Oklahoma City   Panama   Paris   San Juan
São Paulo   Singapore   Sydney   Tokyo   Toronto

COLLEGE WRITING SKILLS WITH READINGS

SECOND EDITION

JOHN LANGAN

Atlantic Community College

COLLEGE WRITING SKILLS WITH READINGS

1 2 3 4 5 6 7 8 9 0 DOCDOC 8 9 3 2 1 0 9 8

ISBN   0-07-036329-3

This book was set in Times Roman by Monotype Composition Company.
The editors were Susan Hurtt and Susan Gamer;
the designer was Rafael Hernandez;
the production supervisor was Diane Renda.
R. R. Donnelley & Sons Company was printer and binder.

Library of Congress Cataloging-in-Publication Data

Langan, John, (date).
    College writing skills, with readings.

    Includes index.
    1. English language—Rhetoric.   2. College readers.
I. Title.
PE1408.L3178   1989   808'.0427   88-13386
ISBN 0-07-036329-3

CONTENTS

PART TWO
OTHER IMPORTANT FACTORS IN WRITING

PART THREE
TYPES OF ESSAY DEVELOPMENT

PART FOUR
HANDBOOK OF SENTENCE SKILLS

PART FIVE
READINGS FOR WRITING

READINGS LISTED ACCORDING TO RHETORICAL MODE

Note: Some selections are cross-listed because they illustrate more than one rhetorical method of development.

COMPARISON-CONTRAST

DEFINITION

DIVISION AND CLASSIFICATION

DESCRIPTION

NARRATION

ARGUMENTATION AND PERSUASION

TO
THE
INSTRUCTOR

College Writing Skills with Readings is a rhetoric with readings that will help students master the writing of the traditional five-paragraph essay. It is a very practical book with a number of special features to aid teachers and their students.

- **Four principles are presented as keys to effective writing.** Four principles or standards—unity, support, coherence, and sentence skills—are highlighted on the inside front cover and reinforced throughout the book. Part One focuses on the first three standards; Part Four covers sentence skills, the fourth principle, by providing a brief handbook on grammar, punctuation, and usage. Part Two introduces students to important factors in writing that will help them achieve these four principles. In Part Three, students learn to use the four standards in different types of essay development. And then the reading selections in Part Five generate assignments which encourage students to apply the four principles in a variety of well-developed essays.

- **Activities, questions, and assignments are numerous and varied.** The more than one hundred activities in the book serve as an essential step between the explanation of a skill and a student's full understanding of that skill. Discussion questions follow all the student essays and the selections that make up the readings in the book; comprehension questions also follow the reading selections. Finally, a generous number of writing assignments are included in both the rhetoric and the reader parts of the book.

- **Clear thinking is stressed throughout.** This focus on logic starts with the introductory "To the Student" on pages xv–xvi. The book emphasizes that the essay is the result of a sustained reasoning process. Writing assignments provide direction in clear thinking and planning; a section in Part Two on outlining offers practice in grouping ideas and details in logical ways; many activities in the book require students to develop rigorous thinking skills; a form that will help students plan a well-thought-out essay appears on the inside back cover. In short, students learn that clear writing is inseparable from clear thinking.

- ■ *Writing is treated as a process.* Specific areas in Part Two concern prewriting, rewriting, and editing. In addition, most writing assignments are accompanied by ''Suggestions on How to Proceed'' that give step-by-step directions for the process of writing a paper.

- ■ *Lively models are provided.* One (though by no means the only) way that students learn is by imitation. *College Writing Skills with Readings* thus provides several high-interest essays with each assignment. Students read and evaluate these essays in terms of the standards of unity, support, and coherence, which have already been explained. Student essays appear along with professional ones written expressly for this book. Almost all the essays follow the 1-3-1 format and average about five hundred words, so that students have clear and realistic models for the essays they will be asked to write.

    The book assumes that students are especially interested in and challenged by the writing of their peers. After reading vigorous papers composed by other students and experiencing the power that good writing can have, students will be more encouraged to aim for similar honesty, realism, and detail in their own work.

- ■ *The book is versatile.* Since no two people use an English text in exactly the same way, the material has been organized in a highly accessible manner. Each of the five parts of the book deals with a distinct writing area. Instructors can therefore turn quickly and easily to the skills they want to present.

- ■ *A number of prose readings are included in Part Five.* These readings deal with many contemporary concerns and will stimulate lively class discussions as well as individual thought. They will serve as a rich source of material for a wide range of writing assignments.

    There are two special features of Part Five. First is the emphasis placed on helping students become stronger readers. A brief introductory section offers tips on good reading, and ten questions after each selection help students practice key skills in effective comprehension. A second special feature is the detailed guidelines provided with many of the writing assignments. Students are shown how to start thinking about an assignment, and they are often given specific ideas on how to proceed.

- ■ *Several learning aids are available.* Instructors will find useful the checklist of the four steps in essay writing on the inside front cover. Also helpful will be the form for planning an essay on the inside back cover and the list of correction symbols on the last page. A thorough Instructor's Manual includes a model syllabus, suggestions for using the book, a detailed answer key, and mastery tests for a number of key skills in essay writing. In addition, a set of twenty-five ditto master tests is provided free to those adopting the text. These tests offer practice in a wide range of skills covered in the book, from generating and narrowing a thesis to outlining essays to editing papers for such common mistakes as fragments, verb problems, and run-ons. Both the Instructor's Manual and the ditto masters are available from the local McGraw-Hill representative or by writing to the College English Editor, McGraw-Hill Book Company, 1221 Avenue of the Americas, New York, New York 10020.

DIFFERENCES BETWEEN THIS BOOK AND *COLLEGE WRITING SKILLS*

- Parts One to Three are essentially the same as the three rhetoric sections of *College Writing Skills*. There is one new feature: an additional writing assignment appears at the end of each chapter in Part Three. Titled "Writing about a Reading Selection," this assignment asks students to respond to one of the professional essays in Part Five by writing a paper using the mode of development in question.
- Part Four of *College Writing Skills,* "Special Skills," has been omitted to help create space for the twenty-five readings.
- Part Five of *College Writing Skills,* "Handbook of Sentence Skills," has been reduced somewhat—again, to create space for the readings. The editing tests, for example, have been shortened from ten to five.

CHANGES IN THE SECOND EDITION

Changes in the new edition of *College Writing Skills with Readings* include the following:

- The chapter titled "Reasons" in Part Three has been replaced by two chapters: "Cause and Effect" and "Argumentation and Persuasion." As a result, all the traditional modes of discourse are now represented in the book. The chapter on argumentation is completely new and features an extensive series of writing assignments. Four of these assignments approximate typical test-out exams used in a variety of English programs.

- Five of the readings are new: "Success Means Never Feeling Tired," by Mortimer Adler; "Smash Thy Neighbor," by John McMurtry; "An Adventure in the City," by Steve Lopez; "Drugs and Alcohol: A Continuing Threat to Health," by George Gallup, Jr.; and "College Lectures: Is Anybody Listening?" by David Daniels.

- Throughout the book, practice materials have been freshened. For example, there is a new essay activity on page 36. One of the outlining activities on pages 102–104 has been updated. There is a revised list of essay collections on page 124. A new final writing assignment appears on page 161. And five editing passages new to the book now appear on pages 298–303.

ACKNOWLEDGMENTS

I owe thanks to Phillip A. Butcher at McGraw-Hill, who first started me thinking about this book. My present editors, Susan Hurtt, Charlotte Smith, and Susan Gamer, have helped as well with their talented support.

Reviewers who have contributed through their helpful comments include Patricia Alexander, Charles S. Mott Community College; Joan Cronin, Miami Dade Community College; Brenda DoHarris, Brooklyn Technical College; Toni Empringham, El Camino College; Robert M. Esch, University of Texas at El Paso; Fred Fischer, Imperial Valley College; Jerry Fishman, Sacramento City College; Elaine M. Fitzpatrick, Massasoit Community College; M. Marie Foster, Florida A & M University; John J. S. Howe, Philadelphia Community College; Daniel Landau, Santa Monica College; Thomas Neuburger; Peter B. Ross, University of the District of Columbia; Dawn Scotland, Clark College; June W. Siegel, New York City College; Peggy M. Simmonds, Montgomery College; Joseph Szabo, Mercer County Community College; Bobby Truitt, Paine College; Walter F. Utroske, Eastern Montana College; and Charles F. Whitaker, Eastern Kentucky University.

Finally, I am grateful to Janet M. Goldstein and Carole Mohr, writers and colleagues who provided assistance with the second edition.

John Langan

TO THE STUDENT

The experience I had writing my first college essay has helped shape this book. I received a C− for the essay. Scrawled beside the grade was the comment, "Not badly written, but ill-conceived." I remember going to the instructor after class, asking about his comment as well as the word "Log" that he had added in the margin at various spots. "What are all these logs you put in my paper?" I asked, trying to make a joke of it. He looked at me a little wonderingly. "Logic, Mr. Langan," he answered, "logic." He went on to explain that I had not thought out my paper clearly. There were actually two ideas rather than one in my thesis, one supporting paragraph had nothing to do with either idea, another paragraph lacked a topic sentence, and so on. I've never forgotten his last words. "If you don't think clearly," he said, "you won't write clearly."

I was speechless, and I felt confused and angry. I didn't like someone telling me that I didn't know how to think. But I went back to my room and read over my paper several times. Eventually I decided that my teacher was right. "No more logs," I said to myself. "I'm going to get these logs out of my papers."

My instructor's advice was invaluable. I learned that if you plan and think through an essay first, you'll have completed a major stage of the work. *College Writing Skills with Readings* develops this idea by breaking down the writing process into a series of easily followed steps.

Part One of the book presents the four basic steps or principles you'll need to write strong essays:

1 Begin with a clearly stated point or thesis.
2 Provide logical, detailed support for your thesis.
3 Organize your supporting material effectively.
4 Revise and edit carefully so that the material is presented in clear, error-free sentences.

In Part Two, you'll learn a series of prewriting techniques that will help you generate and develop your ideas on paper. You'll also work through a series of outlining activities that will sharpen your ability to think clearly and logically. Other important factors in the writing process are presented as well.

Part Three describes a number of different ways you can organize and develop essays. Each chapter opens with a brief introduction followed by several essays written by students. Then comes a series of questions so that you can evaluate the essays in terms of the basic principles explained in Part One. Finally, a number of writing topics are presented, along with prewriting hints to help you plan and write an effective paper.

Part Four offers review and practice in skills needed to write clear, error-free, and varied sentences. The skills include writing complete and correctly joined sentences; making subjects, verbs, and pronouns agree; avoiding faulty modifiers; using parallel structure; observing all the rules of punctuation; choosing words effectively; varying sentence styles; and practicing correct manuscript form.

Finally, Part Five consists of a series of high-interest reading selections that will give you many ideas for writing. A special feature of Part Five is an introductory guide to effective reading. Each selection is then accompanied by comprehension questions that will give you practice in key reading skills. In addition, there are discussion questions and writing assignments that will help direct your thinking about each selection.

For your convenience, the book contains the following:

- On the inside front cover, a checklist of the four basic steps in effective writing.
- On the inside back cover, an essay outline form to use when planning an essay.
- On the last page, a list of correction symbols.

Get into the habit of referring to these guides on a regular basis; they can help ensure that you will produce clearly thought-out, well-written essays.

In summary, *College Writing Skills with Readings* will help you learn, practice, and apply the thinking and writing skills you need to communicate effectively. But your starting point must be the determination to do the work needed to become a strong writer. Remember that the ability to express yourself clearly and logically can open doors for you, both in school and in your career. If you decide—and only you can decide—that you want this kind of power, this book will help you reach that goal.

John Langan

PART ONE

BASIC PRINCIPLES OF ESSAY WRITING

INTRODUCTION
TO THE
ESSAY FORM

This chapter will explain:

- The importance of supporting a point in writing
- The difference between a paragraph and an essay
- The general structure of an essay

AN IMPORTANT DIFFERENCE
BETWEEN WRITING AND TALKING

In your everyday conversation, you make all kinds of points or assertions. You say, for example, "It's not safe to walk in our neighborhood after dark"; "My boss is a hard person to work for"; or "Poor study habits keep getting me into trouble." The points that you make concern personal matters as well as, at times, outside issues: "That trade will be a disaster for the team"; "Lots of TV commercials are degrading to women"; "Students should have to work for a year before attending college."

The people you are talking with do not always challenge you to give reasons for your statements. They may know why you feel as you do, or they may already agree with you, or they simply may not want to put you on the spot; and so they do not always ask, "Why?" The people who read what you write, however, may not know you, agree with you, or feel in any way obliged to you. So if you want to communicate effectively with them, you must provide solid evidence for any point you make. An important difference, then, between writing and talking is this: *In writing, any idea that you advance must be supported with specific reasons or details.*

Think of your readers as reasonable persons. They will not take your views on faith, but they are willing to accept what you say as long as you support it. So remember to support with specific evidence any statement that you make.

POINT AND SUPPORT IN A PARAGRAPH

In conversation you might say to a friend who has suggested a movie, "No thanks. Going to the movies is just too much of a hassle. Parking, people, everything." From shared past experiences, your friend may know what you are talking about, so that you will not have to explain your statement. But in writing, your point would have to be backed up with specific reasons and details. Below is a paragraph on why moviegoing is a hassle. A *paragraph* is a short paper of around 150 words. It consists of an opening point called a *topic sentence* followed by a series of sentences which support that point.

The Hazards of Moviegoing

Although I love movies, going to see them drives me slightly crazy. For one thing, getting to the theater means that I have a thirty-minute drive down a congested highway. Then, with a popular movie, I usually have to wait in a long line at the ticket booth. Another problem is that the theater itself is seldom a pleasant place to be. A musty smell suggests that there has been no fresh air in the theater since it was built. Half the seats seem to be falling apart. And the floor often has a sticky coating that gets on your shoes. The worst problem of all is some of the other moviegoers. Kids run up and down the aisle. Teenagers laugh and shout at the screen. People of all ages loudly drop soda cups and popcorn tubs, cough and burp, and elbow you out of the armrest on either side of your seat. All in all, I would rather stay home and wait for the latest movie hits to appear on TV in the safety and comfort of my own living room.

Notice what the details have done. They have provided you, the reader, with *the basis for understanding why* the writer makes the point that she does. Through specific evidence, she has explained and communicated successfully her idea that moviegoing can be a hassle.

Activity

The paragraph on moviegoing, like almost any piece of effective writing, has two essential parts: (1) a point is advanced and (2) that point is then supported. Taking a minute to outline the paragraph will help you understand these basic parts clearly. Write in the following space the point that has been advanced in the paragraph. Then add the words needed to complete the outline of the paragraph.

Point   _____

           _____

Support 1. *Getting to the theater* _____

           a. *Long drive* _____

           b. _____

        2. _____

           a. _____

           b. _____

           c. _____

        3. *Other moviegoers* _____

           a. _____

           b. _____

           c. *People of all ages* _____

              (1) _____

              (2) *Cough and burp* _____

              (3) _____

POINT AND SUPPORT IN AN ESSAY

Much of your college writing will be in the form of five-hundred-word essays—papers of several paragraphs that support a single point. An *essay* typically consists of an introductory paragraph, three supporting paragraphs, and a concluding paragraph. The central idea, or point, developed in an essay is called a *thesis statement* rather than, as in a paragraph, a topic sentence. A thesis appears in the introductory paragraph, and the specific support for the thesis appears in the paragraphs that follow. The supporting paragraphs allow for a fuller treatment of the reasons that back up the central point than would be possible in a single-paragraph paper.

Why Write Essays?

Mastering the essay form will help, first of all, on a practical level. For other courses, you will write specific forms of essays, such as the report and research paper. Many of your written tests will be in the form of essay exams. In addition, the basic structure of an essay will help in career-related writing, from a job application letter to the memos and reports that may become part of your work.

On a more abstract level, essay writing serves other valuable purposes. It will make you a better reader. You will become more aware of other writers' ideas and the evidence they provide (or fail to provide) to support those ideas. More important, essay writing will make you a better thinker. Writing an essay forces you to sort out and organize your ideas and think them through clearly. You will learn to identify just what your ideas are and what support exists to back them up. Essay writing, in short, will give you practice in the process of clear and logical reasoning. Your ability to recognize ideas and to measure their validity will help you make sound decisions not just in school and career but in all phases of your everyday life.

A Model Essay

The following model should help you understand clearly the form of an essay. The writer of the paragraph on moviegoing later decided to develop her subject more fully. Here is the essay that resulted.

The Hazards of Moviegoing

Introductory paragraph

I am a movie fanatic. When friends want to know what picture won the Oscar in 1980 or who played the police chief in *Jaws*, they ask me. My friends, though, have stopped asking me if I want to go out to the movies. The problems in getting to the theater, the theater itself, and the behavior of some patrons are all reasons why I often wait for a movie to show up on TV.

First supporting paragraph

For one thing, just getting to the theater presents difficulties. Leaving a home equipped with a TV and a video recorder isn't an attractive idea on a humid, cold, or rainy night. Even if the weather cooperates, there is still a thirty-minute drive to the theater down a congested highway, followed by the hassle of looking for a parking space. And then there are the lines. After hooking yourself to the end of a human chain, you worry about whether there will be enough tickets, whether you will get seats together, and whether many people will sneak into the line ahead of you.

Second supporting paragraph

Once you have made it to the box office and gotten your tickets, you are confronted with the problems of the theater itself. If you are in one of the run-down older theaters, you must adjust to the musty smell of seldom-cleaned carpets. Escaped springs lurk in the faded plush or cracked leather seats, and half the seats you sit in seem loose or tilted so that you sit at a strange angle. The newer twin and quad theaters offer their own problems. Sitting in an area only one-quarter the size of a regular theater, moviegoers often have to put up with the sound of the movie next door. This is especially jarring when the other movie involves racing cars or a karate war and you are trying to enjoy a quiet love story. And whether the theater is old or new, it will have floors that seem to be coated with rubber cement. By the end of a movie, shoes almost have to be pried off the floor because they have become sealed to a deadly compound of spilled soda, hardening bubble gum, and crushed Ju-Jubes.

Third
supporting
paragraph

Some of the other patrons are even more of a problem than the theater itself. Little kids race up and down the aisles, usually in giggling packs. Teenagers try to impress their friends by talking back to the screen, whistling, and making what they consider to be hilarious noises. Adults act as if they were at home in their own living rooms and comment loudly on the ages of the stars or why movies aren't as good anymore. And people of all ages crinkle candy wrappers, stick gum on their seats, and drop popcorn tubs or cups of crushed ice and soda on the floor. They also cough and burp, squirm endlessly in their seats, file out for repeated trips to the rest rooms or concession stand, and elbow you out of the armrest on either side of your seat.

Concluding
paragraph

After arriving home from the movies one night, I decided that I was not going to be a moviegoer anymore. I was tired of the problems involved in getting to the movies and dealing with the theater itself and other patrons. The next day I arranged to have cable TV service installed in my home. I may now see movies a bit later than other people, but I'll be more relaxed watching box office hits in the comfort of my own living room.

GENERAL STRUCTURE OF AN ESSAY

The essay just presented—"The Hazards of Moviegoing"—is a good example of the standard short essay you will write in college English. It is a composition of slightly over five hundred words that consists of a one-paragraph introduction, a three-paragraph body, and a one-paragraph conclusion. The roles of these paragraphs are described and illustrated below.

Introductory Paragraph of an Essay

The introductory paragraph of an essay should start with several sentences that attract the reader's interest. It should then advance the central idea or thesis that will be developed in the essay. Part of that thesis may include a plan of development—a "preview" of the major points that will support the thesis. These supporting points should be listed in the order in which they will appear in the essay. In some cases, the plan of development is presented in a sentence separate from the thesis; in other cases, it is omitted.

Activity

1. In "The Hazards of Moviegoing," which sentences are used to attract the reader's interest?
   a. First sentence
   b. First two sentences
   c. First three sentences

2. The thesis in "The Hazards of Moviegoing" is presented in the
   a. Third sentence
   b. Fourth sentence
3. The thesis contains a plan of development.
   a. Yes
   b. No
4. Write down the words in the thesis that announce the three major supporting points in the essay:

   a. _____

   b. _____

   c. _____

Supporting Paragraphs, or "Body," of an Essay

Most essays have three supporting points, developed at length over three separate paragraphs. (Some essays will have two supporting points, others four or more. For the purposes of this book, your goal will be three supporting points for each essay.) Each of the supporting paragraphs should begin with a *topic sentence* that states the point to be detailed in that paragraph. Just as the thesis provides a focus for the entire essay, the topic sentences provide a focus for each supporting paragraph.

Activity

1. What is the topic sentence for the first body paragraph? _____

   _____

   _____

2. The first topic sentence is then supported by details about (*fill in the missing words*):

   a. _____

   b. _____

   c. *Long ticket line* _____

3. What is the topic sentence for the second supporting paragraph? _____

_____

_____

4. The second topic sentence is then supported by details about (*fill in the missing words*):
    a. *Problems of old theaters (mustiness and* _____)
    b. *Problems of new theaters (* _____ *and sound of adjoining movie)*
    c. *Problem of old and new theaters (* _____

5. What is the topic sentence for the third body paragraph? _____

_____

_____

6. The third topic sentence is then supported by details about (*fill in the missing words*):
    a. *Patrons (kids,* _____ *, and* _____)
    b. *Distractions caused by people of all ages* _____

Concluding Paragraph of an Essay

The concluding paragraph often summarizes the essay by restating briefly the thesis and, at times, the main supporting points of the essay. In addition, the writer often presents a concluding thought about the subject of the paper.

Activity

1. Which two sentences in the concluding paragraph restate the thesis and supporting points of the essay?
    a. First and second
    b. Second and third
    c. Third and fourth
2. Which sentence contains the concluding thought of the essay?
    a. First
    b. Second
    c. Third
    d. Fourth

Diagram of an Essay

The following diagram shows you at a glance the different parts of a standard college essay.

Introduction

Opening remarks
Thesis
Plan of development (optional)

*Body
(supporting
paragraphs)*

Topic sentence (supporting point 1)
Specific evidence

Topic sentence (supporting point 2)
Specific evidence

Topic sentence (supporting point 3)
Specific evidence

Conclusion

Summary (optional)
General closing remarks

This diagram, along with the essay outline form on the inside back cover of the book, will serve as a helpful guide when you are writing or evaluating essays.

THE FIRST
AND SECOND
STEPS
IN ESSAY
WRITING

This chapter will show you how to:

- Start an essay with a point or thesis
- Support that point or thesis with specific evidence

Now that you have a sense of the general structure of an essay, it is time to consider the basic steps involved in writing such a paper. The four steps are as follows:

1 Begin with a point or thesis.
2 Support the thesis with specific evidence.
3 Organize the specific evidence.
4 Write clear, error-free sentences.

This chapter will describe the first two steps, and the chapter that follows (see page 39) will present the last two.

Step 1:
Begin with a Point or Thesis

Your first step in writing is to decide what point you want to make and to write out that point in a single sentence. Formulating your point or thesis right at the start will help in two ways. First, you will find out at once whether you have a clear and workable thesis. Second, you will be able to use the thesis as a guide while writing your essay. You will know what material to include by frequently asking yourself, "Does this support my thesis?" With the thesis as a guide, your chances of drifting away from the point of the essay are greatly reduced.

WRITING A GOOD THESIS

To write a good thesis, you must begin with a subject that is neither too broad nor too narrow. Suppose a teacher asks you to write a paper on some aspect of marriage. Such a topic is obviously too broad to cover in a five-hundred-word essay. You would have to write a book to support adequately any point you might make about the general subject of marriage. What you need to do, then, is to limit your subject. Narrow it down until you have a thesis that you can deal with specifically in four hundred to five hundred words. In the box that follows are examples of narrowed subjects.

General Subject	Limited Subject	Thesis
Marriage	Honeymoon	A honeymoon is perhaps the worst way to begin a marriage.
Family	Older sister	My older sister helped me overcome my shyness.
Television	TV preachers	TV evangelists use sales techniques to promote their messages.
Children	Disciplining of children	My husband and I have several effective ways of disciplining our children.
Sports	Players' salaries	High players' salaries are bad for the game, for the fans, and for the values our children are developing.

Activity

Sometimes a subject must go through several stages of limiting before it is narrow enough to write about. Below are four lists reflecting several stages that writers went through in moving from a general subject to a narrow thesis statement. Number the stages in each list from 1 to 5, with 1 marking the broadest stage and 5 the thesis.

List 1

_____ Teachers

_____ Education

_____ Math teacher

_____ My high school math teacher was incompetent.

_____ High school math teacher

List 2

_____ Bicycles

_____ Dangers of bike riding

_____ Recreation

_____ Recreational vehicles

_____ Bike riding in the city is a dangerous activity.

List 3

_____ Financial institutions

_____ Bank

_____ Dealing with customers

_____ Working in a bank

_____ I've learned how to handle unpleasant bank customers.

List 4

_____ Camping

_____ First camping trip

_____ Summer vacation

_____ My first camping trip was a disastrous experience.

_____ Vacations

Later in this chapter, you will get more practice in narrowing general subjects to thesis statements.

COMMON ERRORS IN WRITING A THESIS

When writing thesis statements, people often make one of several mistakes that undermine their chances of producing an effective essay. One mistake is to substitute an announcement of the subject for a true thesis idea. Other mistakes include writing theses that are too broad, too narrow, or too vague. A vague statement may be either one that is simply unclear or one that contains more than one idea. Following are examples of all four errors.

1   Announcements Rather Than Statements

> The subject of this paper will be my parents.
> I want to talk about the crime wave in our country.
> The "baby boom" generation is the concern of this essay.

2   Statements That Are Too Broad

> My parents have been the most influential people in my life.
> Crime is a major concern of everyone in our country.
> The "baby boom" generation has changed history.

3   Statements That Are Too Narrow

> My parents had only one child.
>
> In the last year there have been over twenty robberies in our neighborhood.
>
> The members of the post–World War II "baby boom" make up the largest single age group in America.

4   Statements That Are Too Vague

> My parents helped me grow in important ways, although in other respects I was limited.
>
> The problem of America's overcrowded prisons must be solved, and judges must start handing out tougher sentences.
>
> The "baby boom" generation has had many advantages, but it also faces many problems.

In the first group above, the sentences are not thesis statements but simple announcements of a topic idea. For instance, "The subject of this paper will be my parents" does not make a point but merely tells, in a rather weak and unimaginative way, the writer's general subject. A thesis statement must advance a point about a limited subject.

In the second group above, all the statements are too broad to be supported adequately. For example, "My parents have been the most influential people in my life" could not be supported with specific details in five hundred words or less. There are many autobiographies in which authors have devoted entire chapters to detailing the influence of their mothers or fathers on their lives.

In the third group above, there is no room in any of the three statements for support to be given. For instance, "My parents had only one child" is too narrow to be expanded into a paper. Such a statement is sometimes called a *dead-end statement*; there is no place to go with it. On the other hand, "My parents helped me grow in three important ways" is a point that you could go on to write about in an essay.

In the last group above, the statements are vague either in themselves or because they have more than one meaning. In "My parents helped me grow in important ways, although in other respects I was limited," there appear to be two separate ideas ("parents helped me grow" *and* "in other respects I was limited"). Also, it is not clear whether the writer was limited by his or her parents or by other unmentioned factors.

Activity

Put A beside sentences that are announcements rather than thesis statements. Put TB beside statements that are too broad to be covered in an essay. Put TN beside statements that are too narrow to be developed in an essay. Put V beside statements that contain more than one idea.

_____ 1. Clothing styles have changed a great deal since 1900.

_____ 2. Whole wheat bread is less fattening than white bread.

_____ 3. The hardest teacher I ever had taught me a lesson I will never forget.

_____ 4. The subject of this essay is the matter of daily prayer in our public schools.

_____ 5. The way our society treats its elderly is unbelievable.

_____ 6. My last car was dependable, but many American cars are poorly made.

_____ 7. Soap operas show many stereotyped characters, although they also portray real problems in American life.

_____ 8. I am going to write on my ideas concerning "F" grades.

_____ 9. Computers have changed our society.

_____ 10. The campus tutoring service operates all year round.

More practice in identifying these common errors will appear at the end of this chapter.

Step 2:
Support the Thesis
with Specific Evidence

The first essential step in writing a successful essay is to formulate a clearly stated thesis. The second basic step is to support the thesis with specific reasons or details.

To ensure that your essay will have adequate support, you may find an informal outline very helpful. Write down a brief version of your thesis idea and then work out and jot down the three points that will support that thesis.

Here is the informal outline that was prepared by the author of the essay on moviegoing:

Moviegoing is a problem.
1. Getting there
2. Theater itself
3. Patrons

An informal outline like this one looks simple, but achieving it often requires a great deal of careful thinking. The time spent, though, on developing a logical outline is invaluable. Once you have planned out the steps that logically support your thesis, you will be in an excellent position to go on to write an effective essay.

Activities in this chapter will give you practice in the crucial skill of clearly planning an essay.

Activity

Complete the following informal outlines by adding a third logical supporting point (*c*) that will parallel the two already provided (*a* and *b*).

1. The first day on a new job can be nerve-wracking.
   a. Meeting new people
   b. Finding your way around a new place

   c. _____

2. My stepmother has three qualities I admire.
    a. Patience
    b. Thoughtfulness

    c. _____

3. At our school, the library is the worst place to study.
    a. Uncomfortable chairs and tables
    b. Little privacy

    c. _____

4. College students should live at home.
    a. Stay in touch with family
    b. Avoid distractions of dorm or apartment life

    c. _____

THE IMPORTANCE OF SPECIFIC DETAILS

Just as a thesis must be developed with three supporting points, so those supporting points must be developed with specific details. Specific details have two key values. First of all, details excite the reader's interest. They make writing a pleasure to read, for we all enjoy learning particulars about people, places, and things. Second, details serve to explain a writer's points. They give the evidence needed for us to see and understand general ideas.

All too often, the body paragraphs in essays contain vague generalities rather than the specific supporting details that are needed to engage and convince a reader. Here is what one of the paragraphs in "The Hazards of Moviegoing" would have looked like if the writer had not vividly detailed her supporting evidence.

> Some of the other patrons are even more of a problem than the theater itself. Many people in the theater often show themselves to be inconsiderate. They make noises and create disturbances at their seats. Included are people in every age group, from the young to the old. Some act as if they were at home in their own living rooms watching the TV set. And people are often messy, so that you're constantly aware of all the food they're eating. People are also always moving around near you, creating a disturbance and interrupting your enjoyment of the movie.

The box below contrasts the vague support in the preceding paragraph with the specific support in the essay.

Vague Support	*Specific Support*
1. Many people in the theater show themselves to be inconsiderate. They make noises and create disturbances at their seats. Included are people in every age group, from the young to the old. Some act as if they were at home in their own living rooms watching the TV set.	1. Little kids race up and down the aisles, usually in giggling packs. Teenagers try to impress their friends by talking back to the screen, whistling, and making what they consider to be hilarious noises. Adults act as if they were at home in their own living rooms and comment loudly on the ages of the stars or why movies aren't as good anymore.
2. And people are often messy, so that you're constantly aware of all the food they're eating.	2. And people of all ages crinkle candy wrappers, stick gum on their seats, and drop popcorn tubs or cups of crushed ice and soda on the floor.
3. People are also always moving around near you, creating a disturbance and interrupting your enjoyment of the movie.	3. They also cough and burp, squirm endlessly in their seats, file out for repeated trips to the rest rooms or concession stand, and elbow you out of the armrest on either side of your seat.

The effective paragraph from the essay provides details that make vividly clear the statement that the patrons are a problem in the theater. The writer specifies the exact age groups (little kids, teenagers, and adults) and the offenses of each (giggling, talking and whistling, and loud comments). She specifies the various food excesses (crinkled wrappers, gum on seats, dropped popcorn and soda containers). Finally, she provides concrete details that enable us to see and hear other disturbances (coughs and burps, squirming, constant trips to bathroom, jostling for elbow room). The ineffective paragraph asks us to guess about these details; in the effective paragraph, we vividly see and hear them.

In the strong paragraph, then, the sharp details capture our interest and enable us to share in the writer's experiences. They provide pictures that make each of us feel, ''I am there.'' The particulars also enable us to understand clearly the writer's point that patrons are a problem. You should aim to make your own writing equally strong by providing detailed support in your papers.

Activity

Write S in front of the two selections below that provide specific evidence to support their opening points. Write X in front of the two selections that follow their opening points with vague, general, and wordy sentences.

_____   1.   Building a wooden deck can be an enjoyable project only if you take certain precautions.

Get a building permit before you start. If you don't have one, you may have to tear down everything you've built when the town's building inspector learns of your project. Also, purchase pressure-treated lumber for any posts that will be set into the ground. Ordinary wood, not treated with preservatives, will eventually rot from contact with soil and moisture.

_____   2.   My mother was a harsh disciplinarian.

When I did something wrong, no matter how small, she would inflict serious punishment. She made up a list of rules and regulations for me to follow, and she never bent the rules, no matter what circumstances came up. Rules not observed to the letter were dealt with severely, and there were no exceptions as far as my mother was concerned.

_____   3.   Some things are worse when they're ''improved.''

A good cheesecake, for one thing, is perfect. It doesn't need pineapple, cherries, blueberries, or whipped cream smeared all over it. Plain old American blue jeans, the ones with five pockets and copper rivets, are perfect too. Manufacturers only made them worse when they added flared legs, took away the pockets, tightened the fit, and plastered white logos and designers' names all over them.

_____   4.   Pets can be more trouble than children.

My dog, unlike my children, has never been completely housebroken. When he's excited or nervous, he still has an occasional problem somewhere in the house. My dog, unlike my children, has never learned how to take care of himself when we're away, despite the fact that we've given him plenty of time to do so gradually. We don't have to worry about our grown children anymore. However, we still have to hire a dog-sitter for him.

THE IMPORTANCE OF ADEQUATE DETAILS

One of the most common and serious problems in student writing is inadequate development. You must provide *enough* specific details to support fully the point in a body paragraph of an essay. You could not, for example, include a paragraph about a friend's unreliability and provide only a short example. You would have to add several other examples or provide an extended example showing your friend as an unreliable person. Without such additional support, your paragraph would be underdeveloped.

At times, students try to disguise an unsupported paragraph through repetition and wordy generalities. You should be careful not to fall into this "wordiness trap." Be prepared to do the plain hard work needed to ensure that each paragraph has full and solid support.

Activity

Both of the following body paragraphs were written on the same topic, and both have clear opening points. Which one is adequately developed? Which one, on the other hand, has only several particulars and uses mostly vague, general, wordy sentences to conceal the fact that it is starved for specific details?

Eternal Youth?--No Thanks

I wouldn't want to be a teenager again, first of all, because I wouldn't want to worry about talking to girls. I still remember how scary it was to call up a girl and ask her out. My heart would race, my pulse would pound, and perspiration would trickle down my face, adding to my acne by the second. I never knew whether my voice would come out deep and masculine, like Walter Cronkite's, or squeaky, like Tiny Tim's. Then there were the questions: Would she be at home? If she were, would she want to talk to me? And if she did, what would I say? The one time I did get up the nerve to take a girl in my homeroom to a movie, I was so tongue-tied that I stared silently at the box of popcorn in my lap until the feature finally started. Needless to say, I wasn't very interesting company.

Terrors of My Teenage Years

I wouldn't want to be a teenager again, first of all, because I wouldn't want to worry about talking to girls. Calling up a girl to ask her out was something that I completely dreaded. I didn't know what words to express or how to express them. I would have all the symptoms of nervousness when I got on the phone. I worried a great deal about how I would sound, and I had a lot of doubts about the girl's reaction. Once, I managed to call up a girl to go out, but the evening turned out to be a disaster. I was too unsure of myself to act in a confident way. I couldn't think of anything to say and just kept quiet. Now that I look back on it, I really made a fool of myself. Agonizing over my attempts at relationships with the opposite sex made adolescence a very uncomfortable time.

The first paragraph offers a series of well-detailed examples of the author's nerve-wracking experiences, as a teenager, with girls. The second paragraph, on the other hand, is underdeveloped. It speaks only of the "torture" of calling up a girl, whereas the first paragraph supplies such particulars as "My heart would race, my pulse would pound, and perspiration would trickle down my face." The second paragraph describes in a general way being "worried about my voice," whereas in the first paragraph, the author wonders if his voice will "come out deep and masculine, like Walter Cronkite's, or squeaky, like Tiny Tim's." And there is no specific description in the second paragraph of the evening that turned into a disaster. In summary, the second paragraph lacks the full detailed support needed to develop its opening point convincingly.

Practice in Advancing and Supporting a Thesis

You now know the two most important steps in competent essay writing: (1) advancing a point or thesis and (2) supporting that thesis. The purpose of this section is to expand and strengthen your understanding of these two basic steps. You will first work through a series of activities on developing a thesis:

1 Identifying the different parts of an essay
2 Evaluating thesis statements
3 Completing thesis statements
4 Writing a thesis statement
5 Limiting a topic and writing a thesis

You will then sharpen your understanding of how to *support* a thesis effectively by working through the following activities:

6 Making words and phrases specific
7 Making sentences specific
8 Providing specific evidence
9 Identifying adequate supporting evidence
10 Adding details to complete an essay

1   IDENTIFYING THE DIFFERENT PARTS OF AN ESSAY

Activity

This activity will sharpen your sense of the different parts of an essay. An essay titled "Coping with Old Age" appears below with no paragraph indentations. Read the essay carefully, and then double-underline the thesis and single-underline the topic sentence for each of the three supporting paragraphs and the first sentence of the conclusion. Then write the numbers of those sentences in the space provided at the end.

Coping with Old Age

[1]I recently read about an area of the Soviet Union where many people live to be well over a hundred years old. [2]Being 115 or even 125 isn't considered unusual there, and these old people continue to do productive work right up until they die. [3]America, however, isn't such a healthy place for older people. [4]Since I retired from my job, I've had to cope with the physical, mental, and emotional stresses of being "old." [5]For one thing, I've had to adjust to physical changes. [6]Now that I'm over sixty, the trusty body that carried me around for years has turned traitor. [7]Aside from the deepening wrinkles on my face and neck, and the wiry gray hairs that have replaced my brown hair, I face more frightening changes. [8]I don't have the energy I used to. [9]My eyes get tired. [10]Once in a while, I miss something that's said to me. [11]My once-faithful feet seem to have lost their comfortable soles, and I sometimes feel I'm walking on marbles. [12]In order to fight against this slow decay, I exercise whenever I can. [13]I walk, I stretch, and I climb stairs. [14]I battle constantly to keep as fit as possible. [15]I'm also trying to cope with mental changes. [16]My mind was once as quick and sure as a champion gymnast. [17]I never found it difficult to memorize answers in school or to remember the names of people I met. [18]Now, I occasionally have to search my mind for the name of a close neighbor or favorite television show. [19]Because my mind needs exercise, too, I challenge it as much as I can. [20]Taking a college course like this English class, for example, forces me to concentrate. [21]The mental gymnast may be a little slow and out of shape, but he can still do a backflip or turn a somersault when he has to. [22]Finally, I must deal with the emotional impact of being old. [23]Our society typecasts old people. [24]We're supposed to be unattractive, senile, useless leftovers. [25]We're supposed to be the crazy drivers and the cranky customers. [26]At first, I was angry and frustrated that I was considered old at all. [27]And I knew that people were wrong to stereotype me. [28]Then I got depressed. [29]I even started to think that maybe I <u>was</u> a cast-off, one of those old animals that slow down the rest of the herd. [30]But I have now decided to rebel against these negative

feelings. [31]I try to have friends of all ages and to keep up with what's going on in the world. [32]I try to remember that I'm still the same person who sat at a first-grade desk, who fell in love, who comforted a child, who got a raise at work. [33]I'm not "just" an old person. [34]Coping with the changes of old age has become my latest full-time job. [35]Even though it's a job I never applied for, and one for which I had no experience, I'm trying to do the best I can.

Thesis statement: _____

Topic sentence of first supporting paragraph: _____

Topic sentence of second supporting paragraph: _____

Topic sentence of third supporting paragraph: _____

First sentence of the conclusion: _____

2 EVALUATING THESIS STATEMENTS

As was explained on pages 14–15, some writers substitute announcements of a subject for a true thesis idea. Others write statements that are too narrow to need support or development. Contrasting with such dead-end statements are ones that are wide open—too broad to be adequately supported in the limited space of a five-hundred-word essay. Finally, some thesis statements are vague, often containing more than one idea. They suggest that a writer has not thought out his or her main point sufficiently.

Activity 1

Put A beside the sentences that are announcements rather than thesis statements. Put OK beside the statement in each pair that is a clear, limited point that could be developed in an essay.

1. _____ a. This essay will discuss the people you meet in exercise class.

   _____ b. The kinds of workout clothes worn by the members of my aerobics class identify the "jocks," the "strugglers," and the "princesses."

2. _____ a. I made several mistakes in the process of trying to win the respect and affection of my teenage stepson.

   _____ b. My thesis in this paper is relationships between stepparents and stepchildren.

3. _____ a. A period of loneliness can teach you to use your creativity, sort out your values, and feel empathy for others.

   _____ b. Loneliness is the subject of this paper.

4. _____ a. This paper will be about sharing housework.

_____ b. Deciding who will perform certain unpleasant household chores can be the crisis that makes or breaks a marriage.

5. _____ a. My concern here is to discuss the ''near-death'' experiences reported by some patients.

_____ b. There are several possible explanations for the similar ''near-death'' experiences reported by some patients.

Activity 2

Put TN beside statements that are too narrow to be developed in an essay. Put OK beside the statement in each pair that is a clear, limited point.

1. _____ a. I had squash, tomatoes, and corn in my garden last summer.

_____ b. Vegetable gardening can be a frustrating hobby.

2. _____ a. The main road into our town is lined with billboards.

_____ b. For several reasons, billboards should be abolished.

3. _____ a. There are more single-parent households in our country than ever.

_____ b. Organization is the key to being a successful single parent.

4. _____ a. In my first job, I learned that I had several bad work habits.

_____ b. Because I was late for work yesterday, I lost an hour's pay and was called in to see the boss.

5. _____ a. Americans abuse alcohol because liquor has become such an important part of our personal and public celebrations.

_____ b. Consumption of wine, beer, and hard liquor increases in the United States every year.

Activity 3

Put TB beside statements that are too broad to be developed in an essay. Put OK beside the statement in each pair that is a clear, limited point.

1. _____ a. In many ways, sports are an important part of American life.

_____ b. Widespread gambling has changed professional football for the worse.

2. _____ a. Modern life makes people suspicious and unfriendly.

_____ b. A succession of frightening news stories has made me lose my trust in strangers.

3. _____ a. Toy ads on television teach children to be greedy, competitive, and snobbish.

_____ b. Advertising has a bad influence on the values that children develop in life.

4. _____ a. Learning new skills can be difficult and frustrating.

_____ b. Learning a skill like writing takes work, patience, and a sense of humor.

5. _____ a. I didn't get along with my family, so I did many foolish things.

_____ b. Running away from home taught me that my parents weren't as terrible as I thought.

Activity 4

Put V beside statements that are too vague to be developed in an essay. Put OK beside the statement in each pair that is a clear, limited point.

1. _____ a. The new architecture on this campus is very unpleasant, despite the fact that the expansion was desperately needed.

_____ b. Our new college library building is ugly, intimidating, and inefficient.

2. _____ a. Working with old people changed my stereotyped ideas about the elderly.

_____ b. My life has moved in new directions since the rewarding job I had working with older people last summer.

3. _____ a. Among the most entertaining ads on TV today are those for mail-order products.

_____ b. Although ads on TV for mail-order products are often misleading, they can still be very entertaining.

4. _____ a. My roommate and I are compatible in most ways, but we still have conflicts at times.

_____ b. My roommate has his own unique systems for studying, writing term papers, and cleaning his room.

5. _____ a. Although some good movies have come out lately, I prefer to watch old movies because they're more interesting.

_____ b. Movies of the thirties and forties had better plots, sets, and actors than the ones made today.

3   COMPLETING THESIS STATEMENTS

Activity

Complete the following thesis statements by adding a third supporting point that will parallel the two already provided. You might want to check first the section on parallelism (pages 330–332) to make sure you understand parallel form.

1. Because I never took college preparatory courses in high school, I entered college deficient in mathematics, study skills, and _____ .

2. A good salesperson needs to like people, to be aggressive, and _____

   _____ .

3. Rather than blame myself for failing the course, I blamed the professor, my adviser, and even _____ .

4. Anyone who buys an old house planning to fix it up should be prepared to put in a lot of time, hard work, and _____ .

5. Our old car eats gas, makes funny noises, and _____ .

6. My mother, my boss, and my _____ are three people who are very important in my life right now.

7. Getting married too young was a mistake because we hadn't finished our education, we weren't ready for children, and _____

   _____ .

8. Some restaurant patrons seem to leave their honesty, their cleanliness, and their _____ at home.

9. During my first semester at college, I had to learn how to manage my time, how to manage my diet, and _____ .

10. Three experiences I wish I could forget are the time I fell off a ladder, the time I tried to fix my parents' lawn mower, and _____

    _____ .

4   WRITING A THESIS STATEMENT

Activity

This activity will give you practice in writing an effective thesis—one that is neither too broad nor too narrow for the supporting points in an essay. An added value of the activity is that sometimes you will construct your thesis after you have decided what your supporting points will be. You will need to know, then, how to write a thesis that will match exactly the points that you have developed.

1. Thesis: _____

    _____

   a. My first car was a rebellious-looking one which matched the way I felt and acted as a teenager.
   b. My next car reflected my more mature and practical adult self.
   c. My latest car seems to tell me that I'm aging; it shows my growing concern with comfort and safety.

2. Thesis: _____

    _____

   a. Going to a two-year college can save up to ten thousand dollars in tuition money.
   b. If the college is nearby, there are no room and board costs.
   c. All the course credits that are accumulated can be transferred to a four-year school.

3. Thesis: _____

    _____

   a. First, I tried simply avoiding the chips-and-munchies aisle of the supermarket.
   b. Then I started limiting myself to only five units of any given snack.
   c. Finally, in desperation, I began keeping the cellophane bags of snacks in a padlocked cupboard.

4. Thesis: _____

    _____

   a. The holiday can be frightening for little children and can encourage vandalism in older ones.
   b. Children can be struck by cars while wearing vision-obstructing masks and dark costumes.
   c. More and more incidents of deadly treats filled with razor blades or contaminated with poisons are occurring.

5. Thesis: _____

    _____

   a. First of all, I was a typical "type A" personality: anxious, impatient, and hard-driving.
   b. I also had a family history of relatives with heart trouble.
   c. My unhealthy lifestyle, though, was probably the major factor in the attack.

5   LIMITING A TOPIC AND WRITING A THESIS

The following two activities will give you practice in distinguishing general from limited subjects and in writing a thesis.

Activity 1

Look carefully at the ten general and limited subjects below. Then see if you can write a thesis for any five of them.

Hint: To create a thesis for a limited subject, ask yourself, "What point do I want to make about _____ (*my limited subject*)?"

General Subject	*Limited Subject*
1. Apartment	1. Sharing an apartment with a roommate
2. Self-improvement	2. Behavior toward others
3. Family	3. My mother
4. Eating out	4. Fast-food restaurants
5. Automobiles	5. Bad driving habits
6. Health	6. Regular exercise
7. Owning a house	7. Do-it-yourself repairs around the house
8. Baseball	8. Free-agent system
9. Parenthood	9. Being a single parent
10. Pollution	10. Noise pollution

Thesis statements for five of the limited subjects:

_____

_____

_____

_____

_____

Activity 2

Here is a list of ten general subjects. Limit all ten subjects. Then write a thesis about any five of the limited subjects.

General Subject	Limited Subject
1. Pets	_____
2. Teenagers	_____
3. Television	_____
4. Work	_____
5. College	_____
6. Doctors	_____
7. Vacations	_____
8. Cooking	_____
9. Money	_____
10. Shopping	_____

Thesis statements for five of the limited subjects:

_____

_____

_____

_____

_____

6   MAKING WORDS AND PHRASES SPECIFIC

To be an effective writer, you must use specific rather than general words. Specific words create pictures in the reader's mind. They help capture interest and make your meaning clear.

Activity

This activity will give you practice at changing vague, indefinite words into sharp, specific ones. Add three or more specific words to replace the general word or words italicized in each sentence. Make changes in the wording of a sentence as necessary.

Example   *Several of our appliances* broke down at the same time.

Our washer, refrigerator, and television broke down at the

same time.

1. *Salty snacks* are my diet downfall.

   _____

   _____

2. *Several sections* of the newspaper were missing.

   _____

   _____

3. *Various gifts for men* were displayed in the department-store window.

   _____

   _____

4. *Several items in my purse* had been crushed.

   _____

   _____

5. I swept aside the *things* on my desk in order to spread out the road map.

   _____

   _____

6. The waitress told us we could have *various types of potatoes.*

   _____

   _____

7. The doctor examined *various parts of my body* before diagnosing my illness
   as bronchitis.

   _____

   _____

8. The *food choices* in the cafeteria were unappetizing.

   _____

   _____

9. Terry threw all the *junk* from the bottom of her closet into a large cardboard
   carton.

   _____

   _____

10.   Our neighbor's family room has *a lot of electronic equipment.*

_____

_____

7   MAKING SENTENCES SPECIFIC

Again, you will practice changing vague, indefinite writing into lively, image-filled writing that helps capture your reader's interest and makes your meaning clear. Compare the following sentences:

General	*Specific*
She walked down the street.	Anne wandered slowly along Rogers Lane.
Animals came into the space.	Hungry lions padded silently into the sawdust-covered arena.
The man signed the paper.	The biology teacher hastily scribbled his name on the course withdrawal slip.

The specific sentences create clear pictures in our minds. The details *show* us exactly what has happened. Here are four ways to make your sentences specific.

1   Use exact names.

He sold his *camper.*
Vince sold his *Winnebago.*

2   Use lively verbs.

The flag *moved* in the breeze.
The flag *fluttered* in the breeze.

3   Use descriptive words (modifiers) before nouns.

A man strained to lift the crate.
A *heavyset, perspiring* man strained to lift the *heavy wooden* crate.

4 Use words that relate to the five senses of sight, hearing, taste, smell, and touch.

That woman jogs five miles a day.
That *fragile-looking, gray-haired* woman jogs five miles a day. (*sight*)
A noise told the crowd that there were two minutes left to play.
A *piercing whistle* told the *cheering* crowd that there were two minutes left to play. (*hearing*)
When he returned, all he found in the refrigerator was bread and milk.
When he returned, all he found in the refrigerator was *stale* bread and *sour* milk. (*taste*)
Neil stroked the kitten's fur until he felt its tiny claws on his hand.
Neil stroked the kitten's *velvety* fur until he felt its tiny, *needle-sharp* claws on his hand. (*touch*)
Fran placed a sachet in her bureau drawer.
Fran placed a *lilac-scented* sachet in her bureau drawer. (*smell*)

Activity

With the help of the methods described above, add specific details to any ten of the twelve sentences that follow. Use separate paper.

Examples The person got off the bus.
The teenage boy bounded down the steps of the shiny yellow school bus.

She worked hard all summer.
All summer, Eva sorted peaches and blueberries in the hot, noisy canning factory.

1. The car would not start.
2. The test was difficult.
3. The boy was tired.
4. My room needs cleaning.
5. The student was bored.
6. The game was exciting.
7. A fire started.
8. A vehicle blocked traffic.
9. A large rock fell.
10. The salesperson was obnoxious.
11. The child started to cry.
12. The lounge area was busy.

8   PROVIDING SPECIFIC EVIDENCE

Activity

Provide three details that logically support each of the following points. Your details can be drawn from your direct experience or they can be invented. In each case, the details should show in a specific way what the point expresses in only a general way. State your details briefly in several words rather than in complete sentences.

Example   Nick and Fran perform several chores before their guests arrive.

1. Hide toys and newspapers in spare closet

2. Vacuum pet hairs off sofa

3. Spray air freshener around living room

1.   The dinner was a disaster.

_____

_____

_____

2.   My seven-year-old nephew has some disgusting habits.

_____

_____

_____

3.   There are several things I hate about food shopping.

_____

_____

_____

4.   My parents never allowed me to think for myself.

_____

_____

_____

5. I have several ways in which I can earn extra cash.

    _____

    _____

    _____

6. My wardrobe is out of style.

    _____

    _____

    _____

7. My car needs repairs.

    _____

    _____

    _____

8. Friday evening, I didn't sit still for a minute.

    _____

    _____

    _____

9. Tony really knows how to relate easily to people.

    _____

    _____

    _____

10. Mrs. Attlee was the worst teacher I ever had.

    _____

    _____

    _____

9 IDENTIFYING ADEQUATE SUPPORTING EVIDENCE

Activity

The following body paragraphs were taken from student essays. Two of the paragraphs provide sufficient details to support convincingly their topic sentences. Write AD for *adequate development* beside those paragraphs. There are also three paragraphs that use vague, wordy, general, or irrelevant sentences as an excuse for real supporting details. Write U for *underdeveloped* beside those paragraphs.

_____   1. Another consideration in adopting a dog is the cost. Initial fees for shots and a license might add up to forty dollars. Annual visits to the vet for heartworm pills, rabies or distemper shots, and general checkups could cost fifty dollars or more. Then, there is the cost of food. A twenty-five-pound bag of dry food (the cheapest kind) costs around ten dollars. A large dog can eat that much in a couple of weeks.

_____   2. People can be cruel to pets simply by being thoughtless. They don't think about a pet's needs or simply ignore the needs. It never occurs to them that their pet can be experiencing a great deal of discomfort as a result of their failure to be sensitive. The cruelty is a result of the basic lack of attention and concern—qualities that should be there, but aren't.

_____   3. If I were in charge of the nighttime programming on a TV network, I would make several changes. I would completely eliminate some shows. In fact, all the shows that insult people's intelligence would be canceled. Commercials also would change, so that it would be possible to watch them without wanting to turn off the TV set. I would expand the good shows by lengthening their time periods. Network news would be made more interesting, and people would come away having learned more than they do now. My ideal network would be a lot better than the average lineup we see today on any of the major networks.

_____   4. A friend's rudeness is much more damaging than a stranger's. When a friend says sharply, "I don't have time to talk to you just now," you feel hurt instead of angry. When a friend shows up late for lunch or a shopping trip, with no good reason, you feel that you're being taken for granted. Worst, though, is a friend who pretends to be listening to you but whose wandering eyes reveal a lack of attention. Then you feel betrayed. Friends, after all, are supposed to make up for the thoughtless cruelties of strangers.

_____ 5. Giving my first shampoo and set to a real person, after weeks of practicing on wigs, was a nerve-wracking experience. The customer was an elderly woman who was very set in her ways. She tried to describe what she wanted, but she wasn't very clear. Every time I did something, she either made a strange noise or complained. I got more and more nervous as I worked on her hair, and the nervousness showed. The worst part of the ordeal happened when I did the comb-out. Nothing, to this woman, had turned out right.

10 ADDING DETAILS
TO COMPLETE AN ESSAY

Activity

The following essay needs specific details to back up the ideas in its supporting paragraphs. In the spaces provided, add a sentence or two of clear, convincing details for each idea. This activity will give you practice at supplying specific details and an initial feel for writing an essay.

Introduction

Life without Television

When my family's only television set went to the repair shop the other day, my parents, my sister, and I thought we would have a terrible week. How could we get through the long evenings in such a quiet house? What would it be like without all the shows to keep us company? We soon realized, though, that living without television for a while was a stroke of good fortune. It became easy for each of us to enjoy some activities alone, to complete some postponed chores, and to spend rewarding time with each other and friends.

*First
supporting
paragraph*

      First of all, with no television to compete for our time, we found plenty of hours for personal interests. We all read more that week than we had read during the six months before. _____

_____

_____

We each also enjoyed some hobbies we had ignored for ages. _____

_____

_____

In addition, my sister and I both stopped procrastinating with our

homework. _____

_____

_____

_____

*Second
supporting
paragraph*

      Second, we did chores that had been hanging over our heads for too long. There were many jobs around the house that had needed attention

for some time. _____

_____

_____

We also had a chance to do some long-postponed shopping. _____

_____

_____

And each of us also did some letter writing or other paperwork that was

long overdue. _____

_____

_____

_____

Third
supporting
paragraph

Finally, and probably most important, we spent time with each other. Instead of being in the same room together while we stared at a screen, we actually talked for many pleasant hours. _____

_____

_____

_____

Moreover, for the first time in years my family played some games together. _____

_____

_____

_____

And because we didn't have to worry about missing this or that show, we had some family friends over a couple of evenings and spent an enjoyable time with them. _____

_____

_____

_____

Conclusion

Once our television set returned, we were not prepared to put it in the attic. But we had a sense of how it can take over our lives if we are not careful. We are now more selective. We turn on the set for our favorite shows, certain sports events, and the news, but we don't leave it running all night. As a result, we find we can enjoy television and still have time left over for other activities and interests.

THE THIRD
AND FOURTH
STEPS
IN ESSAY
WRITING

This chapter will show you how to:

- Organize and connect the specific evidence in the body paragraphs of an essay
- Begin and end the essay with effective introductory and concluding paragraphs
- Write clear, error-free sentences

You know from the previous chapter that the first two steps in writing an effective essay are advancing a thesis and supporting it with specific evidence. The third step is to organize and connect the specific evidence, which appears in the body paragraphs of the essay. Most of this chapter will deal with the chief ways to organize and connect this supporting information in a paper. The chapter will also discuss how to start the essay smoothly with a suitable introductory paragraph and how to finish it effectively with a well-rounded concluding paragraph. Finally, the chapter will look briefly at the sentence skills that make up the fourth and final step in writing a successful paper.

Step 3:
Organize and Connect
the Specific Evidence

At the same time that you are generating the specific details needed to support a thesis, you should be thinking about ways to organize and connect those details. All the details in your essay must cohere, or stick together; in this way, your reader will be able to move smoothly and clearly from one bit of supporting information to the next. This section will discuss the following ways to organize and connect supporting details: (1) common methods of organization, (2) transitions, and (3) other connecting words.

COMMON METHODS OF ORGANIZATION

Time order and emphatic order are common methods used to organize the supporting material in an essay. (You will learn more specific methods of development in Part Three of this book.) *Time*, or *chronological, order* simply means that details are listed as they occur in time. *First* this is done; *next* this; *then* this; *after* that, this; and so on. Here is an outline of an essay in this book in which time order is used.

Thesis: However, for success in exercise, you should follow a simple plan consisting of arranging the time, making preparations, and following the sequence with care.

1. To begin with, set aside a regular hour for exercise.
2. Next, prepare for your exercise session.
3. If this is your first attempt at exercising, start slowly.

Fill in the missing word: The topic sentences in the essay use the words <u>To begin with</u> and _____ to help show time order.

Here is one supporting paragraph from the essay:

Next, prepare for your exercise session. You do this, first, by not eating or drinking anything for an hour before the session. Why risk an upset stomach? Then, dress comfortably in something that allows you to move freely. Since you'll be in your own home, there's no need to invest in a high-fashion dance costume. A loose T shirt and shorts are good. A bathing suit is great in summer, and in winter a set of long underwear is warm and comfortable. If your hair tends to flop in your eyes, pin it back or wear a headband or scarf. After dressing, prepare the exercise area. Turn off the phone and lock the door to prevent interruptions. Shove the coffee table out of the way so you won't bruise yourself on it. Finally, get out the simple materials you'll need to exercise on.

Fill in the missing words: The paragraph uses the following words to help show time order: _____*Next*_____, _____, _____, _____, and _____.

Emphatic order is sometimes described as "save-the-best-till-last" order. It means that the most interesting or important detail is placed in the last part of a paragraph or in the final body paragraph of an essay. (In cases where all the details seem equal in importance, the writer should impose a personal order that seems logical or appropriate to the details in question.) The last position in a paper is the most emphatic position because the reader is most likely to remember the last thing read. *Finally, last of all,* and *most important* are typical words showing emphasis. Here is an outline of an essay in the book that uses emphatic order:

Thesis: Celebrities lead very stressful lives; for, no matter how glamorous or powerful they are, they have too little privacy, too much pressure, and no safety.

1. For one thing, celebrities don't have the privacy an ordinary person does.
2. In addition, celebrities are under constant pressure.
3. Most important, celebrities must deal with the stress of being in constant danger.

Fill in the missing words: The topic sentences in the essay use the words *For one thing*_____, _____, and _____ to help show emphatic order.

Here is the third supporting paragraph from the essay:

Most important, celebrities must deal with the stress of being in constant danger. The friendly grabs, hugs, and kisses of enthusiastic fans can quickly turn into uncontrolled assaults on a celebrity's hair, clothes, and car. Also, celebrities often get strange letters from people who become obsessed with their idols or from people who threaten to harm them. Worst of all, threats can turn into deeds. The attempt to kill Ronald Reagan and the murder of John Lennon came about because two unbalanced people tried to transfer the celebrity's fame to themselves. Famous people must live with the fact that they are always fair game--and never out of season.

Fill in the missing words: The words _____ are used to mark the most emphatic detail in the paragraph.

Some essays use a combination of time order and emphatic order. For example, the essay on moviegoing in the first chapter includes a time order: The writer first talks of getting to the theater, then of the theater itself, and finally of the behavior of patrons during the movie. At the same time, the writer uses an emphatic order, ending with her most important reason for the dislike of moviegoing: "Some of the other patrons are even more of a problem than the theater itself."

Activity

Read the essays referred to below and identify whether they organize their details through time order, emphatic order, or a combination of both.

1. "My First Professional Performance" (page 194) _____

2. "A Vote for McDonald's" (page 148) _____

3. "Everyday Cruelty" (page 116) _____

The essay titled "My First Professional Performance" uses time order. The writer begins with the problems she experienced when she arrived at the carnival grounds, moves on to problems during the performance, and ends with the concert's rather abrupt finish. "A Vote for McDonald's" uses emphatic order. The writer presents three advantages of eating at McDonald's and ends with the most important one: reasonable prices. "Everyday Cruelty" uses a combination of time order and emphatic order. It moves from the beginning to the end of a particular workday. It also ends with "the worst incident of mean-spiritedness" that the writer witnessed that day.

TRANSITIONS

Transitions are signals that help readers follow the direction of the writer's thought. They are like signposts on the road that guide travelers. In the box that follows are some common transitional words and phrases, grouped according to the kind of signal they give to readers. Note that certain words provide more than one kind of signal.

Addition signals: one, first of all, second, the third reason, also, next, another, and, in addition, moreover, furthermore, finally, last of all

Time signals: first, then, next, after, as, before, while, meanwhile, now, during, finally

Space signals: next to, across, on the opposite side, to the left, to the right, above, below, nearby

Change-of-direction signals: but, however, yet, in contrast, otherwise, still, on the contrary, on the other hand

Illustration signals: for example, for instance, specifically, as an illustration, once, such as

Conclusion signals: therefore, consequently, thus, then, as a result, in summary, to conclude, last of all, finally

Activity

1. Underline the four *addition* signals in the following selection:

Another way that animals are abused is through their use in unnecessary lab and medical experiments. One instance is the use of rabbits in lab tests for cosmetic companies. The helpless animals are locked into neck restraints resembling the old-fashioned stocks used by the Puritans. Moreover, their eyes are pinned open with metal clamps. Solutions of experimental hair dye are dripped continuously into each rabbit's eyes to test the solution for possible irritation or cancer-causing effects. A second example of needless animal abuse involves the endless repetition of previously done experiments. Every year, science and medical students destroy thousands of monkeys, cats, dogs, and rabbits simply for practice. They repeat experiments whose results are well known and which they could learn from books and scientific reports. These are cases not of worthwhile advances in science but of the thoughtless destruction of life.

2. Underline the three *time* signals in the following selection:

Once you've snagged the job of TV sports reporter, you have to begin working on the details of your image. First, invest in two or three truly loud sports jackets. Look for gigantic plaid patterns in odd color combinations like purple and green or orange and blue. These should become familiar enough to viewers so that they will associate that crazy jacket with that dynamic sportscaster. Next, try to cultivate a distinctive voice that will be just annoying enough to be memorable. A nasal whine or a gravelly growl will do it. Be sure to speak only in tough, punchy sentences that seem to be punctuated with imaginary exclamation points. Finally, you must share lots of pompous, obnoxious opinions with your viewers. Your tone of voice must convey the hidden message, "I dare anyone to disagree with me." When the home teams lose, call them bums. When players strike, talk sarcastically about the good old days. When a sports franchise leaves town, say, "Good riddance."

3. Underline the three *space* signals in the following selection:

The vegetable bin of my refrigerator contained an assortment of weird-looking items. Next to a shriveled, white-coated lemon was a pair of oranges covered with blue fuzz. To the right of the oranges was a bunch of carrots that had begun to sprout points, spikes, knobs, and tendrils. The carrots drooped into U shapes as I picked them up with the tips of my fingers. Near the carrots was a net bag of onions; each onion had sent curling shoots through the net until the whole thing resembled a mass of green spaghetti. The most horrible item, though, was a head of lettuce that had turned into a pool of brown goo. It had seeped out of its bag and coated the bottom of the bin with a sticky, evil-smelling liquid.

4. Underline the two *change-of-direction* signals in the following selection:

Taking small children on vacation, for instance, sounds like a wonderful experience for the entire family. But vacations can be scary or emotionally overwhelming times for children. When children are taken away from their usual routine and brought to an unfamiliar place, they can become very frightened. That strange bed in the motel room or the unusual noises in Grandma's spare bedroom may cause nightmares. On vacations, too, children usually clamor to do as many things in one day as they can and to stay up past their usual bedtime. And, since it is vacation time, parents may decide to give in to the children's demands. A parental attitude like this, however, can lead to problems. After a sixteen-hour day of touring the amusement park, eating in a restaurant, and seeing a movie, children can experience sensory and emotional overload. They become cranky, unhappy, or even rebellious and angry.

5. Underline the two *illustration* signals in the following selection:

Supermarkets also use psychology to encourage you to buy. For example, in most supermarkets, the milk and the bread are either at opposite ends of the store or located far away from the first aisle. Even if you've stopped at the market only for staples like these, you must pass hundreds of items in order to reach them. The odds are that, instead of leaving with a quart of milk, you'll leave with additional purchases as well. Special displays, such as a pyramid of canned green beans in an aisle or a large end display of cartons of paper towels, also increase sales. Because you assume that these items are a good buy, you may pick them up. However, they may not even be on sale! Store managers know that customers are automatically attracted to these displays, and they will use them to move an overstocked product.

6. Underline the two *conclusion* signals in the following selection:

> Finally, my grandmother was extremely thrifty. She was one of those people who hoard pieces of used aluminum foil after carefully scraping off the cake icing or beef gravy. She had a drawer full of old eyeglasses that dated back at least thirty years. The lens prescriptions were no longer accurate, but Gran couldn't bear to throw away "a good pair of glasses." She kept them "just in case," but we could never figure out what horrible situation would involve a desperate need for a dozen pairs of old eyeglasses. We never realized the true extent of Gran's thriftiness, though, until after she died. Her house was to be sold, and therefore we cleaned out its dusty attic. In one corner was a cardboard box filled with two- and three-inch pieces of string. The box was labeled, in Gran's spidery hand, "String too short to be saved."

TRANSITIONAL SENTENCES

Transitions occur not only *within* the supporting paragraphs in an essay but also *between* the paragraphs. *Transitional*, or *linking*, *sentences* are used to help tie together the supporting paragraphs in an essay. They enable the reader to move smoothly and clearly from one idea and paragraph in an essay to the next idea and paragraph. Here are the two linking sentences in the essay on moviegoing:

> Once you have made it to the box office and gotten your tickets, you're confronted with the problems of the theater itself.

The words *made it to the box office* remind us of the point of the first supporting paragraph, while *confronted with the problems of the theater itself* presents the point to be developed in the second supporting paragraph.

> Some of the other patrons are even more of a problem than the theater itself.

The words *the theater itself* echo the point of the second supporting paragraph, while *some of the other patrons* announces the topic of the third supporting paragraph.

Activity

Given below is a brief sentence outline of an essay. In the outline, the second and third topic sentences serve as transitional or linking sentences. They both remind us of the point in the preceding paragraph and announce the point to be developed in the present paragraph. In the space provided, add the words needed to complete the second and third topic sentences.

Thesis   The most important values I learned from my parents are the importance of family support, of hard work, and of a good education.

First supporting paragraph

First, my parents taught me that family members should stick together, especially in times of trouble. . . .

Second supporting paragraph

In addition to teaching me about the importance of _____ _____ , my parents taught me the value of _____ _____. . . .

Third supporting paragraph

Along with the value of _____ , my parents emphasized the benefits of _____ _____. . . .

OTHER CONNECTING WORDS

In addition to transitions, there are three other kinds of connecting words that help tie together the specific evidence in a paper: repeated words, pronouns, and synonyms. Each will be discussed in turn.

Repeated Words

Many of us have been taught by English teachers—correctly so—not to repeat ourselves in our writing. On the other hand, repeating *key* words can help tie together the flow of thought in a paper. Below is a selection that uses repeated words to remind readers of the key idea on which the discussion is centered:

> One reason for studying psychology is to help you deal with your children. Perhaps your young daughter refuses to go to bed when you want her to and bursts into tears at the least mention of "lights out." A little knowledge of psychology comes in handy. Offer her a choice of staying up until 7:30 with you or going upstairs and playing until 8:00. Since she gets to make the choice, she does not feel so powerless and will not resist. Psychology is also useful in rewarding a child for a job well done. Instead of telling your ten-year-old son what a good boy he is when he makes his own bed, tell him how neat it looks, how happy you are to see it, and how proud of him you are for doing it by himself. The psychology books will tell you that being a good boy is much harder to live up to than doing one job well.

Pronouns

Pronouns (*he, she, it, you, they, this, that,* and others) are another way to connect ideas as you develop a paper. Using pronouns to take the place of other words or ideas can help you avoid needless repetition in a paper. (Note, however, that although pronouns are helpful, they should be used with care in order to avoid the unclear or inconsistent pronoun references described in this book on page 336–337.) Here is a selection that makes use of pronouns:

> Another way for people to economize at an amusement park is to bring their own food. If they pack a nourishing, well-balanced lunch of cold chicken, carrot sticks, and fruit, they will avoid having to pay high prices for hamburgers and hot dogs. They will also save on calories. Also, instead of filling up on soft drinks, they should bring a thermos of iced tea. It is more refreshing than soda, and it is a great deal cheaper. Every dollar that is not spent at a refreshment stand is one that can be spent on another ride.

Synonyms

Using synonyms (that is, words that are alike in meaning) also can help move the reader clearly from one step in the thought of a paper to the next. In addition, the use of synonyms increases variety and interest by avoiding needless repetition of the same words. Note the synonyms for *method* in the following selection:

There are several methods of fund-raising that work well with small organizations. One <u>technique</u> is to hold an auction, with everyone either contributing an item from home or obtaining a donation from a sympathetic local merchant. Because all the merchandise, including the services of the auctioneer, has been donated, the entire proceeds can be placed in the organization's treasury. A second fund-raising <u>procedure</u> is a car wash. Club members and their children get together on a Saturday and wash all the cars in the neighborhood for a few dollars apiece. A final, time-tested <u>way</u> to raise money is to give a bake sale, with each family contributing homemade cookies, brownies, layer cakes, or cupcakes. Sold by the piece or by the box, these baked goods will satisfyingly fill both the stomach and the pocketbook.

Activity

Read the selection below and then answer the questions about it that follow:

When I think about my childhood in the 1930s, today's energy crisis and lowered thermostats don't seem so bad. In our house, we had only a wood-burning cookstove in the kitchen to keep us warm. In the morning, my father would get up in the icy cold, go downstairs, and light a fire in the black iron range. When he called us, I would put off leaving my warm bed until the last 5 possible minute and then quickly grab my school clothes. The water pitcher and washing basin in my room would be layered with ice, and my breath would come out as white puffs as I ran downstairs. My sisters and I would all dress--as quickly as possible--in the chilly but bearable air of the kitchen. Our schoolroom, once we had arrived, didn't provide much relief from the 10 cold. Students wore woolen mitts which left their fingers free but covered their palms and wrists. Even with these, we occasionally suffered chilblains. The throbbing patches on our hands made writing a painful process. When we returned home in the afternoon, we spent all our indoor hours in the warm kitchen. We hated to leave it at bedtime in order to make the return 15 trip to those cold bedrooms and frigid sheets. My mother made up hot-water bottles and gave us hot bricks to tuck under the covers, but nothing could eliminate the agony of that penetrating cold when we first slid under the bedclothes.

1. How many times is the key word *cold* repeated? _____

2. Write here the pronoun that is used for *father* (line 3): _____;
    mitts (line 11): _____; *kitchen* (line 15): _____.

3. Write here the words that are used as synonyms for *cookstove* in line 3:
    _____; write in the words that are used as synonyms for
    chilblains in line 12: _____; write in the word that is used
    as a synonym for *cold* in line 16: _____.

INTRODUCTIONS AND CONCLUSIONS

So far, this chapter has been concerned with ways to organize the body paragraphs of an essay. A well-organized essay, however, should also have a strong introductory paragraph and an effective concluding paragraph.

Introductory Paragraph

A well-written introductory paragraph will perform several important roles:

1   It will attract the reader's interest, encouraging him or her to go on and actually read the essay. Using one of the methods of introduction described below can help draw the reader into your paper.

2   It will supply any background information needed to understand the essay. Such information is sometimes needed so that the reader has a context in which to understand the ideas presented in the essay.

3   It will present a thesis statement. This clear, direct statement of the main idea to be developed in the paper usually occurs near the end of the introductory paragraph.

4   It will indicate a plan of development. In this "preview," the major points that will support the thesis are listed in the order in which they will be presented in the essay. In some cases, the thesis and plan of development appear in the same sentence. In some cases, also, the plan of development may be omitted.

Common Methods of Introduction: Here are some common methods of introduction. Use any one method, or combination of methods, to introduce your subject in an interesting way to the reader.

1   ***Begin with a broad, general statement of your topic and narrow it down to your thesis statement.***   Broad, general statements ease the reader into your thesis statement by providing a background for it. In the example below, the writer talks generally about diets and then narrows down to comments on a specific diet.

> Bookstore shelves today are crammed with dozens of different diet books. The American public seems willing to try any sort of diet, especially the ones that promise instant, miraculous results. And authors are more than willing to invent new fad diets to cash in on this craze. Unfortunately, some of these fad diets are ineffective or even unsafe. One of the worst is the "Palm Beach diet." It is impractical, doesn't achieve the results it claims, and is a sure route to poor nutrition.

2 ***Start with an idea or situation that is the opposite of the one you will develop.*** This approach works because your readers will be surprised, and then intrigued, by the contrast between the opening idea and the thesis that follows it.

When I decided to return to school at age thirty-five, I wasn't at all worried about my ability to do the work. After all, I was a grown woman who had raised a family, not a confused teenager fresh out of high school. But when I started classes, I realized that those "confused teenagers" sitting around me were in much better shape for college than I was. They still had all their classroom skills in bright, shiny condition, while mine had grown rusty from disuse. I had totally forgotten how to locate information in a library, how to write a report, and even how to speak up in class discussions.

3 ***Explain the importance of your topic to the reader.*** If you can convince your readers that the subject in some way applies to them, or is something they should know more about, they will want to keep reading.

Diseases like scarlet fever and whooping cough used to kill more young children than any other cause. Today, however, child mortality due to disease has been almost completely eliminated by medical science. Instead, car accidents are the number one killer of our children. And most of the children fatally injured in car accidents were not protected by car seats, belts, or restraints of any kind. Several steps must be taken to remedy this serious problem.

4 ***Use an incident or brief story.*** Stories are naturally interesting. They appeal to a reader's curiosity. In your introduction, an anecdote will grab the reader's attention right away. The story should be brief and should be related to your main idea. The incident in the story can be something that happened to you, something you have heard about, or something you have read about in a newspaper or magazine.

Early Sunday morning the young mother dressed her little girl warmly and gave her a candy bar, a picture book, and a well-worn stuffed rabbit. Together, they drove downtown to a Methodist church. There the mother told the little girl to wait on the stone steps until children began arriving for Sunday school. Then the young mother drove off, abandoning her five-year-old because she couldn't cope with being a parent anymore. This incident is one of thousands of cases of child neglect and abuse that occur annually. Perhaps the automatic right to become a parent should no longer exist. Would-be parents, instead, should be forced to apply for licenses granting them the privilege of raising children.

5   *Ask one or more questions.*   But remember that questions need answers. You may simply want the reader to think about possible answers, or you may plan to answer the questions yourself later in the paper.

> What is love? How do we know that we are really in love? When we meet that special person, how can we tell that our feelings are genuine and not merely infatuation? And, if they are genuine, will these feelings last? Love, as we all know, is difficult to define. But most people agree that true and lasting love involves far more then mere physical attraction. It involves mutual respect, the desire to give rather than take, and the feeling of being wholly at ease.

6   *Use a quotation.*   A quotation can be something you have read in a book or article. It can also be something that you have heard: a popular saying or proverb (''Never give advice to a friend''); a current or recent advertising slogan (''Reach out and touch someone''); a favorite expression used by friends or family (''My father always says . . .''). Using a quotation in your introductory paragraph lets you add someone else's voice to your own.

> ''Fish and visitors,'' wrote Benjamin Franklin, ''begin to smell after three days.'' Last summer, when my sister and her family came to spend their two-week vacation with us, I became convinced that Franklin was right. After only three days, I was thoroughly sick of my brother-in-law's corny jokes, my sister's endless complaints about her boss, and their children's constant invasions of our privacy.

Activity

The box below summarizes the six kinds of introduction. Read the introductions that follow and, in the space provided, write the number of the kind of introduction used in each case.

1. General to narrow	4. Incident or story
2. Starting with an opposite	5. Questions
3. Stating importance of topic	6. Quotation

_____   The ad, in full color on a glossy magazine page, shows a beautiful kitchen with gleaming counters. In the foreground, on one of the counters, stands a shiny new food processor. Usually, a feminine hand is touching it lovingly. Around the main picture are other, smaller shots. They show mounds of perfectly sliced onion rings, thin rounds of juicy tomatoes, heaps of matchstick-sized potatoes, and piles of golden, evenly grated cheese. The ad copy tells you how wonderful, how easy, food preparation will be with a processor. Don't believe it. My processor turned out to be expensive, difficult to operate, and very limited in its use.

_____   People say, "You can't tell a book by its cover." Actually, you can. When you're browsing in the drugstore or supermarket and you see a paperback featuring an attractive young woman in a low-cut dress fleeing from a handsome dark figure in a shadowy castle, you know exactly what you're getting. Every romance novel has the same elements: an innocent heroine, an exotic setting, and a cruel but fascinating hero.

_____   We Americans are incredibly lazy. Instead of cooking a simple, nourishing meal, we pop a frozen dinner into the oven. Instead of studying a daily newspaper, we are contented with the capsule summaries on the network news. Worst of all, instead of walking even a few blocks to the local convenience store, we jump into our cars. This dependence on the automobile, even for short trips, has robbed us of a valuable experience— walking. If we drove less and walked more, we would save money, become healthier, and discover fascinating things about our surroundings.

Concluding Paragraph

A concluding paragraph is your chance to remind the reader of your thesis idea. Also, the conclusion brings the paper to a natural and graceful end, sometimes leaving the reader with a final thought on the subject.

Common Methods of Conclusion: Any one of the methods below, or a combination of methods, may be used to round off your paper.

1   ***End with a summary and final thought.***   When Army instructors train new recruits, each of their lessons follows a three-step formula:
   a   Tell them what you're going to tell them.
   b   Tell them.
   c   Tell them what you've told them.

An essay that ends with a summary is not very different. After you have stated your thesis ("Tell them what you're going to tell them") and supported it ("Tell them"), you restate the thesis and supporting points ("Tell them what you've told them"). Don't, however, use the exact wording you used before. Here is a summary conclusion:

Catalog shopping at home, then, has several advantages. Such shopping is convenient, saves you money, and saves you time. It is not surprising that growing numbers of devoted catalog shoppers are welcoming those full-color mail brochures that offer everything from turnip seeds to televisions.

Note that the summary is accompanied by a final comment that "rounds off" the paper and brings the discussion to a close. This combination of a summary and a final thought is the most common method of concluding an essay.

2   ***Include a thought-provoking question or short series of questions.***   A question grabs the reader's attention. It is a direct appeal to your reader to think further about what you have written. A question should follow logically from the points you have already made in the paper. A question must deal with one of these areas:

a   Why the subject of your paper is important
b   What might happen in the future
c   What should be done about this subject
d   Which choice should be made

You may provide an answer to your question in the conclusion. Be sure, though, that your question is closely related to your thesis. Here is an example:

> What, then, will happen in the twenty-first century when most of the population will be over sixty years old? Retirement policies could change dramatically, with the age-sixty-five testimonial dinner and gold watch postponed for five or ten years. Even television would change as the Geritol generation replaces the Pepsi generation. Glamorous gray-haired models would sell everything from toilet paper to televisions. New soap operas and situation comedies would reveal the secrets of the "sunset years." It will be a different world indeed when the young finally find themselves outnumbered.

3   ***End with a prediction or recommendation.***   Like questions, predictions and recommendations also involve your readers. A prediction states what will or may happen in the future:

> If people stopped to think before acquiring pets, there would be fewer instances of cruelty to animals. Many times, it is the people who adopt pets without considering the expense and responsibility involved who mistreat and neglect their animals. Pets are living creatures. They do not deserve to be acquired as carelessly as one would acquire a stuffed toy.

A recommendation suggests what should be done about a situation or problem:

> Stereotypes such as the helpless homemaker, harried executive, and dotty grandparent are insulting enough to begin with. Placed in magazine ads or television commercials, they become even more insulting. Now these unfortunate characters are not just being laughed at; they are being turned into hucksters to sell products to an unsuspecting public. Consumers should boycott companies whose advertising continues to use such stereotypes.

Activity

Read the concluding paragraph below and answer the question that follows:

> You may never need surgery. But if you do, you can prepare for it by getting as much information as you can, keeping your body as strong as possible, and maintaining a positive, relaxed attitude. Such thorough preparation can make a difficult experience bearable.

Which method of concluding a paper is illustrated by the paragraph?

_____

Step 4: Write Clear, Error-Free Sentences

The fourth step in writing an effective paper is to follow the agreed-upon rules or conventions of written English. These conventions—or, as they are called in this book, *sentence skills*—must be followed if your sentences are to be clear and error-free. Here are the most common of these conventions.

1 Write complete sentences rather than fragments.
2 Do not write run-on sentences.
3 Use verb forms correctly.
4 Make sure that subject, verbs, and pronouns agree.

5   Eliminate faulty parallelism and faulty modifiers.

6   Use pronoun forms correctly.

7   Use capital letters where needed.

8   Use correctly the following marks of punctuation: apostrophe, quotation marks, comma, semicolon, colon, hyphen, dash, parentheses.

9   Use correct paper format.

10   Eliminate wordiness.

11   Choose words carefully.

12   Check for possible spelling errors.

13   Eliminate careless errors.

14   Vary your sentences.

Space will not be taken here to explain and offer activities in all the sentence skills. Rather, they will be treated in detail in Part Five of this book, where they can be referred to easily as needed. Note that both the list of sentence skills on the inside front cover (item 4) and the correction symbols on the last page of the book contain page references, so that you can turn quickly to those skills which give you problems.

Practice in Organizing and Connecting Specific Evidence

You now know the third step in effective writing: organizing the specific evidence used to support the thesis of a paper. You also know that the fourth step— writing clear, error-free sentences—will be treated in detail in Part Five. This closing section will expand and strengthen your understanding of the third step in writing. You will work through the following series of activities:

1   Organizing through time or emphatic order

2   Providing transitions

3   Identifying transitions and other connecting words

4   Completing transitional sentences

5   Identifying introductions and conclusions

1   ORGANIZING THROUGH TIME OR EMPHATIC ORDER

Activity 1

Use time order to organize the scrambled lists of supporting ideas below. Put 1 beside the supporting idea that should come first in time, 2 in front of the idea that logically follows, and 3 in front of the idea that comes last in time.

1. **Thesis:**   When I was a child, Disney movies frightened me more than any other kind.

   _____   As a five-year-old, I found the story of *Pinocchio*, a boy transformed into a puppet, terrifying.

   _____   Although I saw *Bambi* when I was old enough to begin poking fun at "baby movies," the scene during which Bambi's mother is killed has stayed with me to this day.

   _____   About a year after *Pinocchio*, I gripped my seat in fear as the witches and goblins of *Fantasia* flew across the screen.

2. **Thesis:**   Beware of these pitfalls if you want to make the perfect cheesecake.

   _____   There's only one way to remove the cake cleanly and easily from its pan.

   _____   Plan in advance to have your equipment ready and the ingredients at room temperature.

   _____   Remember to time the baking process and regulate the oven temperature while the cake is baking.

3. **Thesis:**   Applying for unemployment benefits was a confusing, frustrating experience.

   _____   It was difficult to find both the office and a place to park.

   _____   When I finally reached the head of the line after four hours of waiting, the clerk had problems processing my claim.

   _____   There was no one to direct or help me when I entered the large office, which was packed with people.

Activity 2

Use emphatic order (order of importance) to arrange the following scrambled list of supporting ideas. Put 1 beside the point that is perhaps less important or interesting than the other two, 2 beside the point that appears more important or interesting, and 3 beside the point that should be most emphasized.

1. Thesis: My after-school job has been an invaluable part of my life this year.

   _____   It has taught me how to get along with many kinds of people.

   _____   It has shown me the value of accurate record keeping.

   _____   Without it, I would have had to drop out of school.

2. Thesis: We received some odd gifts for our wedding.

   _____   The winner in the odd-gift category was a large wooden box with no apparent purpose or function.

   _____   There were several unusual homemade presents sent by well-intentioned relatives.

   _____   A few people sent things that seem to have been meant for some other couple.

3. Thesis: Donna is my most loyal friend.

   _____   She's there in real emergencies or emotional crises.

   _____   On a daily basis, she helps me out with minor problems.

   _____   She's willing to do special favors for me when I need them.

2 PROVIDING TRANSITIONS

Activity

In the spaces provided, add appropriate transitions to tie together the sentences and ideas in the following essay. Draw from the words given in the box below.

and	second	last of all
then	after	on the contrary
too	however	otherwise
but	another	as a result
or	for example	first of all

Annoying People

President Richard Nixon used to keep an "enemies list" of all the people he didn't especially like. I'm ashamed to confess it, but I, too, have an enemies list--a mental one. On this list are all the people I would gladly live without, the ones who cause my blood pressure to rise to the boiling point.

The top three places on the list go to people with annoying nervous habits, people who talk in movie theaters, and people who smoke in restaurants.

_____, there are the people with nervous habits. _____, there are the ones who make faces. When in deep thought, they twitch, squint, and frown, and they can be a real distraction when I'm trying to

concentrate during an exam. _____ type of nervous character makes useless designs. These people bend paper clips into abstract sculptures

as they talk or string the clips into necklaces. _____, neither of these groups is as bad as the people who make noises. These individuals, when they are feeling uncomfortable, bite their fingernails or crack their knuckles. If they have a pencil in their hands, they tap it rhythmically against whatever surface is handy--a desk, a book, a head. Lacking a pencil to play with, they jingle the loose change or keys in their pockets. These people make me wish I were hard of hearing.

_____ category of people I would gladly do away with is the ones who talk in movie theaters. These people are not content to sit

back, relax, and enjoy the film they have paid to see. _____, they feel compelled to comment loudly on everything from the hero's

hairstyle to the appropriateness of the background music. _____,

no one hears a word of any dialog except theirs. _____ they

have been in the theater for a while, their interest in the movie may fade.

_____ they will start discussing other things,

_____ the people around them will be treated to an instant replay of the last family scandal or soap opera episode. These stories may be entertaining, but they don't belong in a movie theater.

_____, there are the restaurant smokers. If I have ordered an expensive dinner, I don't appreciate having another diner's smelly cigar smoke compete with the aroma of my sirloin steak. Even the appetizing smell of a Big Mac or Whopper can be spoiled by the sharp fumes sent out by a nearby cigarette smoker. Often, I have to lean over to the next table and ask

the offender to stop smoking. _____, it is impossible for me to taste my food.

So long as murder remains illegal, the nervous twitchers, movie talkers,

and restaurant smokers of the world are safe from me. _____, if ever I am granted the power of life or death, these people had better think twice about annoying me. They might not have long to live.

3   IDENTIFYING TRANSITIONS AND OTHER CONNECTING WORDS

Activity

The following selections use transitions, repeated words, synonyms, and pronouns to help tie together ideas. The connecting words you are to identify have been set off in italics. In the space provided, write T for *transition*, RW for *repeated word*, S for *synonym*, and P for *pronoun*.

_____   1.   Kate wears a puffy, quilted, down-filled jacket. In this *garment*, she resembles a stack of inflated inner tubes.

_____   2.   Christmas plants like poinsettias and mistletoe are pretty. *They* are also poisonous.

_____   3.   A strip of strong cloth can be used as an emergency fan-belt replacement. *In addition*, a roll of duct tape can be used to patch a leaky hose temporarily.

_____   4.   Newspapers may someday be brought to your home, not by paper carriers, but by computers. Subscribers will simply punch in a code, and the *machines* will display the desired pages.

_____   5.   I'm always losing my soft contact lenses, which resemble little circles of thick Saran Wrap. One day I dropped both of *them* into a cup of hot tea sitting on the sink.

_____   6.   The molded plastic chairs in the classrooms are hard and uncomfortable. Every time I sit in one of these *chairs*, I feel as if I were trying to sit in a bucket

_____   7.   One way to tell if your skin is aging is to pinch a fold of skin on the back of your hand. If *it* doesn't smooth out quickly, your skin is losing its youthful tone.

_____   8.   I never eat sloppy joe sandwiches. *They* look as if they've already been eaten.

_____   9.   Clothing intended just for children seems to have vanished. *Instead*, children wear scaled-down versions of everything adults wear.

_____   10. Some successful salespeople use voice tones and hand gestures that are almost hypnotic. Customers are not conscious of this *hypnotic* effect but merely feel the urge to buy.

_____   11. The giant cockroaches in Florida are the subject of local legends. A visitor, according to one tale, saw one of the *insects*, thought it was a Volkswagen, and tried to drive it away.

_____   12. Some thieves scour garbage cans for credit-card receipts. *Then*, they use the owner's name and card number to order merchandise by phone.

_____ 13. When the phone rang, I dropped the garden hose. *It* whipped around crazily and squirted water through the kitchen screen door.

_____ 14. There are many phobias other than the ones described in psychology textbooks. I have *phobias*, for instance, about toasters and lawn mowers.

_____ 15. My mother believes that food is love. *Therefore*, when she passes around the homemade cookies or cupcakes, I hate to hurt her feelings by refusing them.

4   COMPLETING TRANSITIONAL SENTENCES

Activity

Following are brief sentence outlines from two essays. In each outline, the second and third topic sentences serve as transitional, or linking, sentences. They both remind us of the point in the preceding paragraph and announce the point to be developed in the present paragraph. In the space provided, add the words needed to complete the second and third topic sentences.

Thesis 1   Cheaper cost, greater comfort, and superior electronic technology make watching football at home more enjoyable than attending a game at the stadium.

First supporting paragraph

For one thing, watching the game on TV eliminates the cost of attending the game. . . .

Second supporting paragraph

In addition to saving me money, watching the game at home is more _____ than sitting in a stadium. . . .

Third supporting paragraph

Even more important than _____ and _____, though, is the _____ which makes a televised game better than the "real thing." . . .

Thesis 2   In order to set up a day-care center in your home, you must make sure your house will conform to state regulations, obtain the necessary legal permits, and advertise your service in the right places.

First supporting paragraph

First of all, as a potential operator of a home day-care center, you must make sure your house will conform to state regulations. . . .

Second supporting paragraph

After making certain that _____

_____ ,

you must obtain _____. . . .

Third supporting paragraph

Finally, once you have the necessary _____

you can begin to _____ .

---

5   IDENTIFYING INTRODUCTIONS AND CONCLUSIONS

Activity

The box below lists six common kinds of introductions and three common kinds of conclusions. Read the three sets of introductory and concluding paragraphs that follow. Then, in the space provided, write the number of the kind of introduction or conclusion used in each case.

Introductions	*Conclusions*
1. General to narrow	1. Summary and final thought
2. Starting with an opposite	2. Question(s)
3. Stating importance of topic	3. Prediction or recommendation
4. Incident or story	
5. Question(s)	
6. Quotation	

—————— Shortly before Easter, our local elementary school sponsored a fund-raising event at which classroom pets and their babies--hamsters, guinea pigs, and baby chicks--were available for adoption. Afterward, as I was driving home, I saw a hand drop a baby hamster out of the car ahead of me. I couldn't avoid running over the tiny creature. One of the parents had taken the pet, regretted the decision, and decided to get rid of it. Such people have never stopped to consider the real obligations involved in owning an animal. . . .

—————— A pet cannot be thrown onto a trash heap when it is no longer wanted or tossed into a closet if it begins to bore its owner. A pet, like us, is a living thing that needs physical care, affection, and respect. Would-be owners, therefore, should think seriously about their responsibilities before they acquire a pet.

—————— What would life be like if we could read each other's minds? Would communications be instantaneous and perfectly clear? These questions will never be answered unless mental telepathy becomes a fact of life. Until then, we will have to make do with less-perfect means of communication, such as letters, telephone calls, and face-to-face conversations. Each of these has its drawbacks. . . .

—————— Neither letters, phone calls, nor conversations guarantee perfect communication. With all our sophisticated skills, we human beings often communicate less effectively than howling wolves or chattering monkeys. Even if we <u>were</u> able to read each other's minds, we'd probably still find some way to foul up the message.

—————— "Few things are harder to put up with," said Mark Twain, "than the annoyance of a good example." Twain obviously knew the problems faced by siblings cursed with older brothers or sisters who are models of perfection. All our lives, my older sister Shelley and I have been compared. Unfortunately, my looks, talents, and accomplishments always ended up on the losing side. . . .

—————— Although our looks, talents, and accomplishments were constantly compared, Shelley and I have somehow managed not to turn into deadly enemies. Feeling like the Edsel of the family, in fact, helped me to develop a drive to succeed and a sense of humor. In our sibling rivalry, we both managed to win.

THE FOUR BASES FOR EVALUATING ESSAY WRITING

This chapter will show you how to evaluate an essay for:

- Unity
- Support
- Organization
- Sentence skills

In the preceding chapters, you learned the four essential steps in writing an effective paper. The box below shows how the steps lead to four standards, or bases, you can use in evaluating an essay.

Four Steps ⟶	*Four Bases*
1 If you advance a single point and stick to that point,	you will have *unity* in your paper.
2 If you support the point with specific evidence,	you will have *support* in your paper.
3 If you organize and connect the specific evidence,	you will have *coherence* in your paper.
4 If you write clear, error-free sentences,	you will have effective *sentence skills* in your paper.

This chapter will discuss the four bases of unity, support, coherence, and sentence skills and will show how these four bases can be used to evaluate a paper.

Base 1: Unity

Activity

The following student essays were written on the topic "Special Problems or Pleasures of My Teenage Years." Read them and decide which one more clearly and effectively makes its point, and why.

Teenage Pranks

Looking back at some of the things that I did as a teenager makes me break out in a cold sweat. The purpose of each adventure was always fun, but occasionally things got out of hand. In my search for good times, I was involved in three notable pranks, ranging from fairly harmless to fairly serious.

The first prank proved that good, clean fun does not have to be dull. As a high school student, I was credited with making the world's largest dessert. Together with several friends, we spent an entire year collecting boxes of Jell-O. Entering our school's indoor pool late one night, we turned the water temperature up as high as it would go and poured in box after box of the strawberry powder. The next morning, school officials arrived to find the pool filled with thirteen thousand gallons of the quivering, rubbery stuff. No one was hurt by the prank, but we did suffer through three days of a massive cleanup.

Not all my pranks were harmless, and one involved risking my life. As soon as I got my driver's license, I wanted to join the "Fliers' Club." Membership in this club was limited to those who could make their cars fly a distance of at least ten feet. The qualifying site was an old quarry field where friends and I had built a ramp made of dirt. I drove my battered Ford Pinto up this ramp as fast as it would go. The Pinto flew ten feet, but one of the tires exploded when I landed. The car rolled on its side, and I luckily escaped with only a bruised arm.

Risking my own life was bad enough, but there was another prank where other people could have been hurt, too. On this occasion, I accidentally set a valley on fire. Two of my friends and I were sitting on a hill sharing a few beers. It was a warm summer night, and there was absolutely nothing to do.

The idea came like a thunderclap. We collected a supply of large plastic trash bags, emergency highway flares, and the half tank of helium left over from a science-fair experiment. Then we began to construct a fleet of UFOs. Filling the bags with helium, we tied them closed with wire and suspended several burning flares below each bag. Our UFOs leaped into the air like an army of invading Martians. Rising and darting in the blackness, they convinced even us. Our fun turned into horror, though, as we watched the balloons begin to drop onto the wooded valley of expensive homes below. Soon, a brush fire started and, quickly sobered, we hurried off to call the fire department anonymously.

Every so often, I think back on the things that I did as a teenager. I chuckle at the innocent pranks and feel lucky that I didn't harm myself or others with the not-so-innocent ones. Those years were filled with wild times. Today I'm older, wiser--and maybe just a little more boring.

Problems of My Adolescence

In the unreal world of television situation comedies, teenagers are carefree, smart, funny, wisecracking, secure kids. In fact, most of them are more "together" than the adults on the shows. This, however, isn't how I recall my teenage years at all. As a teen, I suffered. Every day, I battled the terrible physical, family, and social troubles of adolescence.

For one thing, I had to deal with a demoralizing physical problem--acne. Some days, I would wake up in the morning with a red bump the size of a taillight on my nose. Since I worried constantly about my appearance anyway, acne outbreaks could turn me into a crying, screaming maniac. Plastering on a layer of orange-colored Clearasil, which didn't fool anybody, I would slink into school, hoping that the boy I had a crush on would be absent that day. Within the last few years, however, treatments for acne have improved. Now, skin doctors prescribe special drugs that clear up pimples almost immediately. An acne attack could shatter whatever small amount of self-esteem I had managed to build up.

In addition to fighting acne, I felt compelled to fight my family. As a teenager, I needed to be independent. At that time, the most important thing in life was to be close to my friends and to try out new, more adult experiences. Unfortunately, my family seemed to get in the way. My little brother, for instance, turned into my enemy. We're close now, though. In fact, Eddie recently painted my new apartment for me. Eddie used to barge into my room, listen to my phone conversations, and read my secret letters. I would threaten to tie him up and leave him in a garbage Dumpster. He would scream, my mother would yell, and all hell would break loose. My parents, too, were enemies. They wouldn't let me stay out late, wear the clothes I wanted to wear, or hang around with the friends I liked. So I tried to get revenge on them by being miserable, sulky, and sarcastic at home.

Worst of all, I had to face the social traumas of being a teenager. Things that were supposed to be fun, like dates and dances, were actually horrible. On the few occasions when I had a real date, I agonized over everything-- my hair, my weight, my pimples. After a date, I would come home, raid the kitchen, and drown my insecurities in a sea of junk food. Dances were also stressful events. My friends and I would sneak a couple of beers just to get up the nerve to walk into the school gym. Now I realize that teenage drinking is dangerous. I read recently that the number one killer of teenagers is drunk driving. At dances, I never relaxed. It was too important to look exactly right, to act really cool, and to pretend I was having fun.

I'm glad I'm not a teenager anymore. I wouldn't ever want to feel so unattractive, so confused, and so insecure again. I'll gladly accept the crow's-feet and stomach bulge of adulthood in exchange for a little peace of mind.

The _____ essay makes its point more clearly and effectively because

_____

_____

UNDERSTANDING UNITY

The first essay is more effective because it is unified. All the details in the essay are on target; they support and develop each of the essay's three topic sentences ("The first prank proved that good, clean fun does not have to be dull"; "Not all my pranks were harmless, and one involved risking my life"; and, "Risking my own life was bad enough, but there was another prank where other people could have been hurt, too"). On the other hand, the second essay contains some details irrelevant to the essay's topic sentences. In the first supporting paragraph, the sentences, "Within the last few years, however, treatments for acne have improved. Now, skin doctors prescribe special drugs that clear up pimples almost immediately," do not support the writer's topic statement that she had to deal with the physical problem of acne. Such details should be left out in the interest of unity. Go back to the second essay and cross out the two sentences in the second supporting paragraph and the two sentences in the third supporting paragraph that are off target and do not help support their topic sentences.

You should have crossed out the following sentences: "We're close now . . . apartment for me" and "Now I realize . . . drunk driving."

The difference between the first two essays leads us to the first base or standard of effective writing: *unity*. To achieve unity is to have all the details in your paper related to your thesis and three supporting topic sentences. Each time you think of something to put into your paper, ask yourself whether it relates to your thesis and supporting points. If it does not, leave it out. For example, if you were writing a paper about the problems of being unemployed and then spent a couple of sentences talking about the pleasures of having a lot of free time, you would be missing the first and most essential base of good writing. The pages ahead will consider the other three bases that you must touch in order to succeed in your writing.

Base 2: Support

Activity

The following essays were written on the topic "Dealing with Disappointment." Both are unified, but one communicates more clearly and effectively. Which one, and why?

Dealing with Disappointment

One way to look at life is as a series of disappointments. Life can certainly appear that way because disappointment crops up in the life of everyone more often, it seems, than satisfaction. How disappointments are handled can have a great bearing on how life is viewed. People can react negatively by sulking or by blaming others, or they can try to understand the reasons behind the disappointment.

Sulking is one way to deal with disappointment. This "Why does everything always happen to me?" attitude is common because it is an easy attitude to adopt, but it is not very productive. Everyone has had the experience of meeting people who specialize in feeling sorry for themselves. A sulky manner will often discourage others from wanting to lend support, and it prevents the sulker from making positive moves toward self-help. It becomes easier just to sit back and sulk. Unfortunately, feeling sorry for oneself does nothing to lessen the pain of disappointment. It may, in fact, increase the pain. It certainly does not make future disappointments easier to bear.

Blaming others is another negative and nonproductive way to cope with disappointment. This all-too-common response of pointing the finger at someone else doesn't help one's situation. This posture will lead only to anger, resentment, and, therefore, further unhappiness. Disappointment in another's performance does not necessarily indicate that the performer is at fault. Perhaps expectations were too high, or there could have been a misunderstanding as to what the performer actually intended to accomplish.

A positive way to handle disappointment is to try to understand the reasons behind the disappointment. An analysis of the causes for disappointment can have an excellent chance of producing desirable results. Often understanding alone can help alleviate the pain of disappointment and can help prevent future disappointments. Also, it is wise to try to remember that what would be ideal is not necessarily what is reasonable to expect in any given situation. The ability to look disappointment squarely in the face and then go on from there is the first step on the road back.

Continuous handling of disappointment in a negative manner can lead to a negative view of life itself. Chances for personal happiness in such a state of being are understandably slim. Learning not to expect perfection in an imperfect world and keeping in mind those times when expectations were actually surpassed are positive steps toward allowing the joys of life to prevail.

Reactions to Disappointment

Ben Franklin said that the only sure things in life are death and taxes. He left something out, however: disappointment. No one gets through life without experiencing many disappointments. Strangely, though, most people seem unprepared for disappointment and react to it in negative ways. They feel depressed or try to escape their troubles instead of using disappointment as an opportunity for growth.

One negative reaction to disappointment is depression. A woman trying to win a promotion, for example, works hard for over a year in her department. Helen is so sure she will get the promotion, in fact, that she has already picked out the car she will buy when her salary increase comes through. However, the boss names one of Helen's coworkers to the spot. The fact that all the other department employees tell Helen that she is the one who really deserved the promotion doesn't help her deal with the crushing disappointment. Deeply depressed, Helen decides that all her goals are doomed to defeat. She loses her enthusiasm for her job and can barely force herself to show up every day. Helen tells herself that she is a failure and that doing a good job just isn't worth the work.

Another negative reaction to disappointment, and one that often follows depression, is the desire to escape. Kevin fails to get into the college his brother is attending, the college that was the focus of all his dreams, and decides to escape his disappointment. Why worry about college at all? Instead, he covers up his real feelings by giving up on his schoolwork and getting completely involved with friends, parties, and "good times." Or Linda doesn't make the varsity basketball team--something she wanted very badly--and so refuses to play sports at all. She decides to hang around with a new set of friends who get high every day; then she won't have to confront her disappointment and learn to live with it.

The positive way to react to disappointment is to use it as a chance for growth. This isn't easy, but it's the only useful way to deal with an inevitable part of life. Helen, the woman who wasn't promoted, could have handled her disappointment by looking at other options. If her boss doesn't recognize talent and hard work, perhaps she could transfer to another department. Or she could ask the boss how to improve her performance so that she would be a shoo-in for the next promotion. Kevin, the boy who didn't get into the college of his choice, should look into other schools. Going to another college may encourage him to be his own person, step out of his brother's shadow, and realize that being turned down by one college isn't a final judgment on his abilities or potential. Rather than escape into drugs, Linda could improve her basketball skills for a year or pick up another sport--like swimming or tennis--that would probably turn out to be more useful to her as an adult.

Disappointments are unwelcome, but regular, visitors to everyone's life. We can feel depressed about them or we can try to escape from them. The best thing, though, is to accept a disappointment and then try to use it somehow: step over the unwelcome visitor on the doorstep and get on with life.

The _____ essay makes its point more clearly and effectively because

_____

_____

UNDERSTANDING SUPPORT

The second essay is more effective, for it offers specific examples of the ways people deal with disappointment. We see for ourselves the kinds of reactions people have to disappointment. The first essay, on the other hand, gives us no specific evidence. The writer tells us repeatedly that sulking, blaming others, and trying to understand the reasons behind the disappointment are the reactions people have to a letdown. However, the writer never *shows* us these responses in action. Exactly what kinds of disappointments is the writer talking about? And how, for instance, does someone analyze the causes of disappointment? Would a person make up a list of causes on a piece of paper, or review the causes with a concerned friend, or speak to a professional therapist? We want to see *examples* of how sulking and blaming others are negative ways of dealing with disappointment.

Consideration of the two essays leads us to the second base of effective writing: *support*. After realizing the importance of specific supporting details, one student writer revised a paper she had done on being lost in the woods as the worst experience of her childhood. In the revised paper, instead of talking about "the terror of being separated from my parents," she referred to such specifics as "tears streamed down my cheeks as I pictured the faces I would never see again" and "I clutched the locket my parents had given me as if it were a lucky charm that could help me find my way back to the campsite." All your papers should include many vivid details!

Base 3: Coherence

Activity

The following two essays were written on the topic "Positive or Negative Effects of Television." Both are unified and both are supported. However, one communicates more clearly and effectively. Which one, and why?

Harmful Effects of Watching Television

In a recent cartoon, one character said to another, "When you think of the awesome power of television to educate, aren't you glad it doesn't?" It's true that television has the power to educate and to entertain, but unfortunately, these benefits are outweighed by the harm it does to dedicated viewers. Television is harmful because it creates passivity, discourages communication, and presents a false picture of reality.

Television makes viewers passive. Children who have an electronic baby-sitter spend most of their waking hours in a semiconscious state. Older viewers watch tennis matches and basketball games with none of the excitement of being in the stands. Even if children are watching Sesame Street or The Electric Company, they are being educated passively. The child actors are going on nature walks, building crafts projects, playing with animals, and participating in games, but the little viewers are simply watching. Older viewers watch members of a studio audience discuss vital issues with Phil Donahue, but no one will turn to the home viewers to ask their opinion.

Worst of all is that TV presents a false picture of reality that leaves viewers frustrated because they don't have the beauty or wealth of characters on television. Viewers begin to absorb the idea that everyone else in the United States owns a lavishly decorated apartment, suburban house, sleek car, and expensive wardrobe. Every detective, police officer, oil baron, and lawyer, whether male or female, is suitable for a pinup poster. The material possessions on TV shows and commercials contribute to the false image of reality. News anchors and reporters, with their perfect hair and makeup, must fit television's standard of beauty. From their modest homes or cramped apartments, many viewers tune in daily to the upper-middle-class world that TV glorifies.

Television discourages communication. Families watching television do very little talking except for brief exchanges during commercials. If Uncle Bernie or the next-door neighbors drop in for a visit, the most comfortable activity for everyone may be not conversation but watching Wide World of Sports. The family may not even be watching the same set; instead, in some households, all the family members head for their own rooms to watch their own sets. At dinner, plates are plopped on the coffee table in front of the set, and the meal is wolfed down during the CBS Nightly News. During commercials, the only communication a family has all night may consist of questions like "Do we have any popcorn?"and "Where's the TV Guide?"

Television, like cigarettes or saccharine, is harmful to our nation's health. We are becoming isolated, passive, and frustrated. And the most frightening part of the problem is that the average viewer spends more time watching television than ever.

The Benefits of Television

We hear a lot about the negative effects of television on the viewer. Obviously, television can be harmful if it is watched constantly to the exclusion of other activities. It would be just as harmful to listen to records or to eat constantly. However, when television is watched in moderation, it is extremely valuable, as it provides relaxation, entertainment, and education.

First of all, watching TV has the value of sheer relaxation. Watching television can be soothing and restful after an eight-hour day of pressure, challenges, or concentration. After working hard all day, people look forward to a new episode of a favorite show or yet another showing of Casablanca or Red River. This period of relaxation leaves viewers refreshed and ready to take on the world again. Watching TV also seems to reduce stress in some people. This benefit of television is just beginning to be recognized. One doctor, for example, advises his patients with high blood pressure to relax in the evening with a few hours of television.

In addition to being relaxing, television is entertaining. Along with the standard comedies, dramas, and game shows that provide enjoyment to viewers, television offers a variety of movies and sports events. Moreover, in many areas, viewers can pay a monthly fee and receive special cable programming. With this service, viewers can watch first-run movies, rock and classical music concerts, and specialized sports events, like European soccer and Grand Prix racing. Viewers can also buy or rent movies to show on their television sets through videodisc players or videocassette players. Still another growing area of TV entertainment is video games. Cartridges are available for everything from electronic baseball to Pac-man, allowing the owner to have a video game arcade in the living room.

Most important, television is educational. Preschoolers learn colors, numbers, and letters from public television programs, like Sesame Street, that use animation and puppets to make learning fun. Science shows for older children, like 1-2-3 Contact, go on location to analyze everything from volcanoes to rocket launches. Adults, too, can get an education (college credits included) from courses given on television. Also, television widens our knowledge by covering important events and current news. Viewers can see and hear presidents' speeches, state funerals, natural disasters, and election results as they are happening. Finally, a television set hooked up to a home computer can help its owner learn how to manage the household budget, invest in the stock market, or master a foreign language.

Perhaps because television is such a powerful force, we like to criticize it and search for its flaws. However, the benefits of television should not be ignored. We can use television to relax, to have fun, and to make ourselves smarter. This electronic wonder, then, is a servant, not a master.

The _____ essay makes its point more clearly and effectively because

_____

_____

_____

UNDERSTANDING COHERENCE

The second essay is more effective because the material is organized clearly and logically. Using emphatic order, the writer develops three positive uses of television, ending with the most important use: television as an educational tool. The writer also includes transitional words that act as signposts, making movement from one idea to the next easy to follow. The major transitions include *First of all*, *In addition*, and *Most important;* transitions within paragraphs include such words as *Moreover, Still another, too, Also,* and *Finally*. And the writer of the second essay uses a linking sentence ("In addition to being relaxing, television is entertaining") to tie together clearly the first and second supporting paragraphs.

Although the first essay is unified and supported, the writer does not have any clear and consistent way of organizing the material. The most important idea to be developed (signaled by the phrase *Worst of all*) is discussed in the second supporting paragraph instead of being saved for last. None of the supporting paragraphs organizes its details in a logical fashion. The first supporting paragraph, for example, discusses older viewers, then younger viewers, then jumps back to older people again. The third supporting paragraph, like the first, leaps from an opening idea (families talking only during commercials), to several intervening ideas, back to the original idea (talking during commercials). In addition, this essay uses practically no transitional devices to guide the reader.

These two essays lead us to the third base of effective writing: *coherence*. The supporting ideas and sentences in a paper must be organized so that they cohere, or ''stick together.'' As has already been mentioned, key techniques for tying together the material in a paper include a clear method of organization (such as time order or emphatic order), transitions, and other connecting words.

Base 4: Sentence Skills

Activity

Following are two versions of an essay. Both are unified, supported, and organized, but one version communicates more clearly and effectively. Which one, and why?

''revenge''

[1]Revenge is one of those things that everyone enjoy. [2]People don't like to talk about it, though. [3]Just the same, there is nothing more tempting, more satisfying, or more rewarding than revenge. [4]The purpose is not to harm your victims. [5]But to let them know that I am upset about something they are doing. [6]Careful plotting can provide you with relief from bothersom coworkers, gossiping friends, or nagging family members.

[7]Coworkers who make comments about the fact that you are always fifteen minutes late for work can be taken care of very simply. [8]All you have to do is get up extra early one day. [9]Before the sun comes up, drive to each coworker's house, reach under the hood of his car, and disconnected the center wire that leads to the distrib. cap. [10]The car will be unharmed, but it will not start, and your friends at work will all be late for work on the same day. [11]If youre lucky, your boss might notice that you are the only one there and will give you a raise. [12]Later if you feel guilty about your actions you can call each person anonymously and tell them how to get the car running again.

[13]Gossiping friends at school are also perfect targets for a simple act of revenge. [14]A way to trap either male or female friends are to leave phony messages on their lockers. [15]If the friend that you want to get is male, leave a message that a certain girl would like him to stop by her house later that day. [16]With any luck, her boyfriend will be there. [17]The girl won't know what's going on, and the victim will be so embarrassed that he probably won't leave his home for a month. [18]The plan works just as well for female friends, too.

[19]When Mom and Dad and your sisters and brothers really begin to annoy you, harmless revenge may be just the way to make them quite down for a while. [20]The dinner table, where most of the nagging probably happens,

is a likely place. [21]Just before the meal begins, throw a handful of raisins into the food. [22]Wait about 5 minutes and, after everyone has began to eat, clamp your hand over your mouth and begin to make odd noises. [23]When they ask you what the matter is, point to a raisin and yell, Bugs. [24]Dumping the food in the disposal, the car will make a bee-line for mcdonald's. [25]That night, you'll have your first quiet, peaceful meal in a long time.

[26]A well-planned revenge does not have to hurt anyone. [27]The object is simply to let other people know that they are beginning to bother you. [28]You should remember, though, to stay on your guard after completing your revenge. [29]The reason for this is simple, coworkers, friends, and family can also plan revenge on you.

Revenge

Revenge is one of those things that everyone enjoys. People don't like to talk about it, though. Just the same, there is nothing more tempting, more satisfying, or more rewarding than revenge. The purpose is not to harm your victims but to let them know that you are upset about something that they are doing to you. Careful plotting can provide you with relief from bothersome coworkers, gossiping friends, or nagging family members.

Coworkers who make comments about the fact that you are always fifteen minutes late for work can be taken care of very simply. All you have to do is get up extra early one day. Before the sun comes up, drive to each coworker's house. Reach under the hood of your coworker's car and disconnect the center wire that leads to the distributor cap. The car will be unharmed, but it will not start, and your friends at work will all be late for work on the same day. If you're lucky, your boss might notice that you are the only one there and will give you a raise. Later, if you feel guilty about your actions, you can call your coworkers anonymously and tell them how to get their cars running again.

Gossiping friends at school are also perfect targets for a simple act of revenge. A way to trap either male or female friends is to leave phony messages on their lockers. If the friend that you want to get is male, leave a message that a certain girl would like him to stop by her house later that day. With any luck, her boyfriend will be there. The girl won't know what's going on, and the victim will be so embarrassed that he probably won't leave his home for a month. The plan works just as well for female friends, too.

When Mom and Dad and your sisters and brothers really begin to annoy you, harmless revenge may be just the way to make them quiet down for a while. The dinner table, where most of the nagging probably happens, is a likely place. Just before the meal begins, throw a handful of raisins into the food. Wait about five minutes and, after everyone has begun to eat, clamp your hand over your mouth and begin to make odd noises. When they ask you what the matter is, point to a raisin and yell, "Bugs!" They'll all dump their food in the disposal, jump into the car, and head for McDonald's. That night, you'll have your first quiet, peaceful meal in a long time.

A well-planned revenge does not have to hurt anyone. The object is simply to let other people know that they are beginning to bother you. You should remember, though, to stay on your guard after completing your revenge. The reason for this is simple. Coworkers, friends, and family can also plan revenge on you.

The _____ essay makes its point more clearly and effectively because

_____

_____

_____

UNDERSTANDING SENTENCE SKILLS

The second essay is more effective because it properly uses *sentence skills*, the fourth base of competent writing. See now if you can find and explain briefly the twenty sentence-skills mistakes made in the first essay. Use the space provided. The first mistake is described for you as an example. Note that comparing the first essay with the corrected essay will help you locate the mistakes.

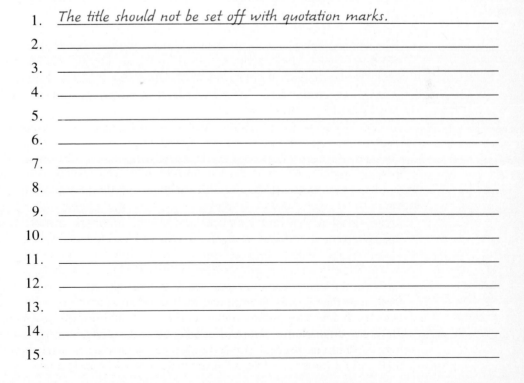

1. *The title should not be set off with quotation marks.*

2. _____

3. _____

4. _____

5. _____

6. _____

7. _____

8. _____

9. _____

10. _____

11. _____

12. _____

13. _____

14. _____

15. _____

16. _____

17. _____

18. _____

19. _____

20. _____

Practice in Using the Four Bases

You are now familiar with the four standards, or bases, of effective writing: unity, support, coherence, and sentence skills. In this section you will expand and strengthen your understanding of the four bases as you work through the following activities:

1 Evaluating essays for unity
2 Evaluating essays for support
3 Evaluating essays for coherence
4 Evaluating essays for all four bases: unity, support, coherence, and sentence skills

1 EVALUATING ESSAYS FOR UNITY

Activity

Both of the essays below contain irrelevant sentences that do not relate to the thesis of the essay or support the topic sentence of the paragraph in which they appear.

Cross out the irrelevant sentences and put the numbers of those sentences in the spaces provided.

Playing on the Browns

¹For the past three summers, I have played first base on a softball team known as the Browns. ²We play a long schedule, including play-offs, and everybody takes the games pretty seriously. ³In that respect, we're no different from any other of the thousand or so teams in our city. ⁴But in one respect, we are different. ⁵In an all-male league, we have a woman on the team--me.

⁶Thus I've had a chance to observe something about human nature by seeing how the men have treated me. ⁷Some have been disbelieving; some have been patronizing; and fortunately, some have simply accepted me.

⁸One new team in the league was particularly flabbergasted to see me start the game at first base. ⁹Nobody on the Comets had commented one way or the other when they saw me warming up, but playing in the actual game was another story. ¹⁰The Comet first-base coach leaned over to me with a disbelieving grin and said, "You mean, you're starting, and those three guys are on the bench?" ¹¹I nodded and he shrugged, still amazed. ¹²He probably thought I was the manager's wife. ¹³When I came up to bat, the Comet pitcher smiled and called to his outfielders to move way in on me. ¹⁴Now, I don't have a lot of power, but I'm not exactly feeble. ¹⁵I used to work out on the exercise machines at a local health club until it closed, and now I lift weights at home a couple of times a week. ¹⁶I wiped the smirks off their faces with a line drive double over the left fielder's head.

The number of the irrelevant sentence: _____

¹⁷The next game, we played another new team, and this time their attitude was a patronizing one. ¹⁸The Argyles had seen me take batting practice, so they didn't do anything so rash as to draw their outfield way in. ¹⁹They had respect for my ability as a player. ²⁰However, they tried to annoy me with phony concern. ²¹For example, a redheaded Argyle got on base in the first inning and said to me, "You'd better be careful, Hon. ²²When you have your foot on the bag somebody might step on it. ²³You can get hurt in this game." ²⁴I was mad, but I have worked out several mental techniques to control my anger because it interferes with my playing ability. ²⁵Well, this delicate little girl survived the season without injury, which is more than I can say for some of the "he-men" on the Argyles.

The number of the irrelevant sentence: _____

²⁶Happily, most of the teams in the league have accepted me, just as the Browns did. ²⁷The men on the Browns coached and criticized me (and occasionally cursed me) just like anyone else. ²⁸Because I'm a religious person, I don't approve of cursing, but I don't say anything about it to my teammates. ²⁹They are not amazed when I get a hit or stretch for a wide throw. ³⁰My average this year was higher than the averages of several of my teammates, yet none of them acted resentful or threatened. ³¹On several occasions I was taken out late in a game for a pinch runner, but other slow players on the team were also lifted at times for pinch runners. ³²Every woman should have a team like the Browns!

The number of the irrelevant sentence: _____

[33]Because I really had problems only with the new teams, I've concluded that it's when people are faced with an unfamiliar situation that they react defensively. [34]Once a rival team has gotten used to seeing me on the field, I'm no big deal. [35]Still, I suspect that the Browns secretly feel that we're a little special. [36]After all, we won the championship with a woman on the team.

How to Con a Teacher

[1]Enter college, and you'll soon be reminded of the truth of an old saying: "The pen is mightier than the sword." [2]That person behind the teacher's desk holds your future in his or her ink-stained hands. [3]So your first important assignment in college has nothing to do with required readings, examinations, or even the hazards of registration. [4]It is, instead, how to con a teacher.

[5]The first step in conning a teacher is to use body language. [6]You may be able to convince your instructor you are special without even saying a word. [7]When you enter the classroom, be sure to sit in the front row. [8]That way, the instructor can't possibly miss you. [9]Then, as your teacher lectures, take notes frantically. [10]The teacher will be flattered that you think so much of his or her words that you want to write them all down. [11]Using a felt-tip pen is superior to a pen or pencil; it will help you write faster and prevent aching wrists. [12]While you are writing, be sure to smile at the teacher's jokes and nod violently in agreement with every major point. [13]Most important of all, as class continues, sit with your body pitched forward and your eyes wide open, fixed firmly, as if hypnotized, on your teacher's face. [14]Make your whole body suggest that you are watching a star.

The number of the irrelevant sentence: _____

[15]Once you have mastered body language, it is time to move on to the second phase of teacher conning: class participation. [16]Everyone knows that the student who is most eager to learn is the one who responds to the questions that are asked and even comes up with a few more. [17]Therefore, be sure to be responsive. [18]Questions such as "How does this affect the future of the United States?" or "Don't you think that someday all of this will be done by computer?" can be used in any class without prior knowledge of the subject matter. [19]Many students, especially in large classes, get lost in the crowd and never do anything to make themselves stand out. [20]Another good participation technique is to wait until the instructor has said something that sounds profound and then ask him or her to repeat it slowly so you can get it down word for word in your notes. [21]No teacher can resist this kind of flattery.

The number of the irrelevant sentence: _____

[22]However, the most advanced form of teacher conning happens after class is over. [23]Don't be like the others who slap their notebooks closed, pick up their books, and rush out the door before the echoes of the final bell have died away. [24]Did you ever notice how students begin to get restless about five minutes before class ends, even if there's no clock on the wall? [25]Instead, be reluctant to leave. [26]Approach the instructor's desk hesitantly, almost reverently. [27]Say that you want to find out more about the topic. [28]Is there any extra reading you can do? [29]Even better, inquire if the instructor has written anything on the topic--and whether you could borrow it. [30]Finally, compliment your teacher by saying that this is the most interesting course you've ever taken. [31]Nothing beats the personal approach for making a teacher think you care.

The number of the irrelevant sentence: _____

[32]Body language, questions, after-class discussions--these are the secrets of teacher conning every college student should know. [33]These kinds of things go on in high school, too, and they're just as effective on that level. [34]Once you master these methods, you won't have to worry about a thing-- until the final exam.

The number of the irrelevant sentence: _____

2   EVALUATING ESSAYS FOR SUPPORT

Activity

Both of the essays below lack supporting details at certain key points. Identify the spots where details are needed in each essay.

Formula for Happiness

[1]Everyone has his or her own formula for happiness. [2]As we go through life, we discover the kinds of activities that make us feel best. [3]I've already discovered three keys for my happiness. [4]In order to be at my peak, I depend on karate, music, and self-hypnosis.

[5]An activity which helps me to feel good physically is karate. [6]Before taking karate lessons, I was tired most of the time, my muscles felt like foam rubber, and I was also about twenty pounds overweight. [7]After about three months of these lessons, I began to notice a marked improvement in my physical condition. [8]I have also noticed that my endurance has increased.

[9]At the end of my work day, I used to drag myself home to eat and watch television all night. [10]Now, I still have enough energy to play with my children, go shopping, or see a movie. [11]My karate lessons have made me feel healthy, strong, and happy.

The spot where supporting details are needed occurs after sentence _____.

[12]Singing with a choral group has helped me to achieve emotional well-being through the expression of my feelings. [13]In common situations where other people would reveal their feelings, I would remain quiet. [14]Since joining the chorus, however, I have had an outlet for my feelings of joy, anger, or sadness. [15]When I sing, I pour my emotions into the music and don't have to feel shy about expressing myself. [16]For this reason, I enjoy singing certain kinds of music the most, since they demand real depth of feeling.

The first spot where supporting details are needed occurs after sentence _____.

The second spot occurs after sentence _____.

[17]A very important activity which gives me peace of mind is self-hypnosis. [18]This is a total relaxation technique which I learned from a hypnotist several years ago. [19]Essentially I breathe deeply and concentrate on relaxing all the muscles of my body. [20]I then repeat a key suggestion to myself. [21]Because I practice self-hypnosis, I have gained control over several bad habits that have long been haunting me.[22]I have also learned to reduce the stress that goes along with my secretarial job. [23]Now I can handle the boss's demands or unexpected work without feeling tense.

The first spot where supporting details are needed occurs after sentence _____.

The second spot occurs after sentence _____.

[24]In short, my physical, emotional, and mental well-being have been greatly increased through my interests in karate, music, and self-hypnosis. [25]These activities have become the most important elements in my formula for happiness.

Problems of a Foreign Student

[1]About ten months ago I decided to leave my native country and come to the United States to study. [2]When I got here, I suddenly turned into someone labeled "foreign student." [3]A foreign student, I discovered, has problems. [4]Whether from Japan, like me, or from some other country, a foreign student has to work twice as hard as Americans do to succeed in college.

[5]First of all, there is the language problem. [6]American students have the advantage of comprehending English without working at it. [7]But even they complain that some professors talk too fast, mumble, or use big words. [8]As a result, they can't take notes fast enough to keep up, or they misunderstand what was said. [9]Now consider my situation. [10]I'm trying to cope with a language that is probably one of the hardest in the world to learn. [11]Dozens of English slang phrases--"mess around," "hassle," "get into"--were totally new to me. [12]Other language problems gave me trouble, too.

The spot where supporting details are needed occurs after sentence _____.

[13]Another problem I face has to do with being a stranger to American culture. [14]For instance, the academic world is much different in Japan. [15]In America, professors seem to treat students as equals. [16]Many classes are informal, and the relationship between teacher and student is friendly; in fact, students call some teachers by their first names. [17]In Japan, however, the teacher-student relationship is different. [18]Lectures, too, are more formal, and students show respect by listening quietly and paying attention at all times. [19]This more casual atmosphere occasionally makes me feel uncomfortable in class.

The spot where supporting details are needed occurs after sentence _____.

[20]Perhaps the most difficult problem I face is a social one. [21]American students may have some trouble making new friends or may feel lonely at times.[22]However, they usually manage to find other people with the same backgrounds, interests, or goals. [23]It is twice as hard to make friends, though, if a person has trouble making the small talk that can lead to a relationship. [24]I find it difficult to become friends with other students because I don't understand some aspects of American life. [25]Students would rather talk to someone who is familiar with these things.

The spot where supporting details are needed occurs after sentence _____.

[26]Despite all the handicaps that I, as a foreign student, have to overcome, I wouldn't give up this chance to go to school in the United States. [27]Each day, the problems seem a little bit less overwhelming. [28]Like a little child who is finally learning to read, write, and make sense of things, I am starting to enjoy my experience of discovering a brand-new world.

3 EVALUATING ESSAYS FOR COHERENCE

Activity

Both of the essays that follow could be revised to improve their coherence. Answer the questions about coherence that come after each essay.

Noise Pollution

Paragraph a ¹Natural sounds--waves, wind, bird songs--are so soothing that companies sell tapes of them to anxious people seeking a relaxing atmosphere in their homes or cars. ²One reason why "environmental sounds" are big business is the fact that ordinary citizens--especially city dwellers--are bombarded by noise pollution. ³On the way to work, on the job, and on the way home, the typical urban resident must cope with a continuing barrage of unpleasant sounds.

Paragraph b ⁴The noise level in an office can be unbearable. ⁵From nine o'clock to five, phones ring, typewriters clack and clatter, intercoms buzz, and Xerox machines thump back and forth. ⁶Every time the receptionists can't find people, they resort to a nerve-shattering public address system. ⁷And because the managers worry about the employees' morale, they graciously provide the endless droning of canned music. ⁸This effectively eliminates any possibility of a moment of blessed silence.

Paragraph c ⁹Traveling home from work provides no relief from the noisiness of the office. ¹⁰The ordinary sounds of blaring taxi horns and rumbling buses are occasionally punctuated by the ear-piercing screech of car brakes. ¹¹Taking a shortcut through the park will bring the weary worker face to face with chanting religious cults, free-lance musicians, screaming children, and barking dogs. ¹²None of these sounds can compare with the large radios many park visitors carry. ¹³Each radio blasts out something different, from heavy-metal rock to baseball, at decibel levels so strong that they make eardrums throb in pain. ¹⁴If there are birds singing or wind in the trees, the harried commuter will never hear them.

Paragraph d ¹⁵Even a trip to work at 6 or 7 A. M. isn't quiet. ¹⁶No matter which route a worker takes, there is bound to be a noisy construction site somewhere along the way. ¹⁷Hard hats will shout from third-story windows to warn their coworkers below before heaving debris out and sending it crashing to earth. ¹⁸Huge front-end loaders will crunch into these piles of rubble and back up, their warning signals letting out loud, jarring beeps. ¹⁹Air hammers begin an ear-splitting chorus of rat-a-tat-tat sounds guaranteed to shatter sanity as well as concrete. ²⁰Before reaching the office, the worker is already completely frazzled.

Paragraph e ²¹Noise pollution is as dangerous as any other kind of pollution. ²²The endless pressure of noise probably triggers countless nervous breakdowns, vicious arguments, and bouts of depression. ²³And imagine the world problems we could solve, if only the noise stopped long enough to let us think.

1. What is the number of the sentence to which the transition word *Also* could be added in paragraph *a*? _____

2. In the last sentence of paragraph *a*, to what does the pronoun *This* refer?

   _____

3. What is the number of the sentence to which the transition word *But* could be added in paragraph *b*? _____

4. What is the number of the sentence to which the transition word *Then* could be added in paragraph *c*? _____

5. What is the number of the sentence to which the transition word *Meanwhile* could be added in paragraph *c*? _____

6. What word is used as a synonym for *debris* in paragraph *c*?

   _____

7. How many times is the key word *sounds* repeated in the essay? _____

8. The time order of the three supporting paragraphs is confused. Which supporting paragraph should come first? _____ Second? _____ Third?

   _____

Weight Loss

Paragraph a   ¹The big fraternity party turned out to be the low point of my freshman year. ²I was in heaven until I discovered that my date with handsome Greg, the fraternity vice president, was a hoax: he had used me to win the "ugliest date" contest. ³I ran sobbing back to the dorm, wanting to resign from the human race. ⁴Then I realized that it was time to stop kidding myself about my weight. ⁵Within the next two years, I lost forty-two pounds and turned my life around. ⁶Losing weight gave me self-confidence socially, emotionally, and professionally.

Paragraph b   ⁷I am more outgoing socially. ⁸Just being able to abandon dark colors, overblouses, and tent dresses in favor of bright colors, T shirts, and designer jeans made me feel better in social situations. ⁹I am able to do more things. ¹⁰I once turned down an invitation for a great camping trip with my best friend's family, making up excuses about sun poisoning and allergies. ¹¹Really, I was too embarrassed to tell them that I couldn't fit in the bathroom in their Winnebago! ¹²I made up for it last summer when I was one of the organizers of a college backpacking trip through the Rockies.

Paragraph c   ¹³Most important, losing weight helped me seek new professional goals. ¹⁴When I was obese, I organized my whole life around my weight, as if it were a defect I could do nothing about. ¹⁵With my good grades, I could have chosen almost any major the college offered, but I had limited my goal to kindergarten teaching because I felt that little children wouldn't judge how I looked. [16]Once I was no longer fat, I realized that I love working with all sorts of people. [17]I became a campus guide and even had small parts in college theater productions. [18]As a result, last year I changed my major to public relations. [19]The area fascinates me, and I now have good job prospects there.

Paragraph d   [20]I have also become more emotionally honest. [21]Rose, at the college counseling center, helped me see that my "fat and jolly" personality had been false. [22]I was afraid others would reject me if I didn't always go along with their suggestions. [23]I eventually put Rose's advice to the test. [24]My roommates were planning an evening at a Greek restaurant. [25]I loved the restaurant's atmosphere, but there wasn't much I liked on the menu. [26]Finally, in a shaky voice I said, "Actually, I'm not crazy about lamb. [27]How about Italian or Chinese food?" [28]They scolded me for not mentioning it before, and we had dinner at a Chinese restaurant and ended with coffee, dessert, and entertainment at the Greek restaurant. [29]We all agreed it was one of our best evenings out.

Paragraph e   [30]Fortunately, the low point of my freshman year turned out to be the turning point leading to what promises to be an exciting senior year. [32]Greg's cruel joke became a strange sort of favor, and I've gone from wanting to resign from the human race to welcoming each day as a source of fresh adventure and self-discovery.

1. What is the number of the sentence to which the transition words *For one thing* could be added in paragraph *a*? _____

2. What is the number of the sentence to which the transition word *Also* could be added in paragraph *a*? _____

3. What is the number of the sentence to which the transition word *But* could be added in paragraph *a*? _____

4. In sentence 11, to what does the pronoun *them* refer? _____

5. What is the number of the sentence to which the transition word *However* could be added in paragraph *b*? _____

6. What word is used as a synonym for *obese* in paragraph *c*? _____

7. How many times is the key word *weight* repeated in the essay? _____

8. Which supporting paragraph should be placed in the emphatic final position? _____

4   EVALUATING ESSAYS FOR ALL FOUR BASES: UNITY, SUPPORT, COHERENCE, AND SENTENCE SKILLS

Activity

In this activity, you will evaluate two essays in terms of the four bases of unity, support, coherence, and sentence skills. Evaluative comments follow each supporting paragraph in the essays below. Circle the letter of the *one* statement that applies in each case.

Chiggers

I had lived my whole life not knowing what chiggers are. I thought they were probably a type of insect Humphrey Bogart encountered in The African Queen. I never had any reason to really care, until one day last summer. Within twenty-four hours, I had vividly experienced what chigger bites are, learned how to treat them, and learned how to prevent them.

First of all, I learned that chiggers are the larvae of tiny mites found in the woods and that their bites are always multiple and cause intense itching. A beautiful summer day seemed perfect for a walk in the woods. I am definitely not a city person, for I couldn't stand to be surrounded by people, noise, and concrete. As I walked through the ferns and pines, I noticed what appeared to be a dusting of reddish seeds or pollen on my slacks. Looking more closely, I realized that each speck was a tiny insect. I casually brushed off a few and gave them no further thought. I woke up the next morning feeling like a settler staked to an ant hill by an Indian wise in the ways of torture. Most of my body was speckled with measlelike bumps that at the slightest touch burned and itched like a mosquito bite raised to the twentieth power. When antiseptics and calamine lotion failed to help, I raced to my doctor for emergency aid.

a.   The paragraph contains an irrelevant sentence.

b.   The paragraph lacks supporting details at one key spot.

c.   The time order in the paragraph is confused.

d.   The paragraph contains two run-on sentences.

Healing the bites of chiggers, as the doctor diagnosed them to be, is not a simple procedure. It seems there is really no wonder drug or commercial product to help the cure. The victim must rely on a harsh and primitive home remedy and mostly wait out the course of the painful bites. First, the doctor explained, the skin must be bathed carefully in alcohol. An antihistamine spray applied several hours later will soothe the intense itching and help prevent infection. Before using the spray, I had to saturate each bite with gasoline or nail polish to kill any remaining chiggers. A few days after the treatment, the bites finally healed. Although I was still in pain, and desperate for relief, I followed the doctor's instructions. I carefully applied gasoline to the bites and walked around for an hour smelling like a filling station.

a. The paragraph contains an irrelevant sentence.
b. The paragraph lacks supporting details at one key spot.
c. The time order in the paragraph is confused.
d. The paragraph contains one sentence fragment.

Most important of all, I learned what to do to prevent getting chigger bites in the future. Mainly, of course, stay out of the woods in the summertime. But if the temptation is too great on an especially beautiful day, I'll be sure to wear the right type of clothing, like a long-sleeved shirt, long pants, knee socks, and closed shoes. In addition, I'll cover myself with clouds of superstrength insect repellent. I will then shower thoroughly as soon as I get home, I also will probably burn all my clothes if I notice even one suspicious red speck.

a. The paragraph contains an irrelevant sentence.
b. The paragraph lacks supporting details at one key spot.
c. The paragraph lacks transitional words.
d. The paragraph contains a run-on and a fragment.

I will never forget my lessons on the cause, cure, and prevention of chigger bites. I'd gladly accept the challenge of rattlesnakes and scorpions in the wilds of the West but will never again confront a siege of chiggers in the pinewoods.

The Hazards of Being an Only Child

Many people who have grown up in multichild families think that being an only child is the best of all possible worlds. They point to such benefits as the only child's annual new wardrobe and lack of competition for parental love. But single-child status isn't as good as people say it is. Instead of having everything they want, only children are sometimes denied certain basic human needs.

Only children lack companionship. An only child can have trouble making friends, since he or she isn't used to being around other children. Often, the only child comes home to an empty house; both parents are working, and there are no brothers or sisters to play with or to talk to about the day. At dinner, the single child can't tell jokes, giggle, or throw food while the adults discuss boring adult subjects. An only child always has his or her own room but never has anyone to whisper to half the night when sleep doesn't come.

Some only children thrive on this isolation and channel their energies into creative activities like writing or drawing. Owing to this lack of companionship, an only child sometimes lacks the social ease and self-confidence that come from being part of a closely knit group of contemporaries.

a. The paragraph contains an irrelevant sentence.
b. The paragraph lacks supporting details at one key spot.
c. The paragraph lacks transitional words.
d. The paragraph contains one fragment and one run-on.

Second, only children lack privacy. An only child is automatically the center of parental concern. There's never any doubt about which child tried to sneak in after midnight on a weekday. And who will get the lecture the next morning. Also, whenever an only child gives in to a bad mood, runs into his or her room, and slams the door, the door will open thirty seconds later, revealing an anxious parent. Parents of only children sometimes don't even understand the child's need for privacy. For example, they may not understand why a teenager wants a lock on the door or a personal telephone. After all, the parents think, there are only the three of us, there's no need for secrets.

a. The paragraph contains an irrelevant sentence.
b. The paragraph lacks supporting details at one key spot.
c. The paragraph lacks transition words.
d. The paragraph contains one fragment and one run-on.

Most important, only children lack power. They get all the love; but if something goes wrong, they also get all the punishment. When a bottle of perfume is knocked to the floor or the television is left on all night, there's no little sister or brother to blame it on. Moreover, an only child has no recourse when asking for a privilege of some kind, such as permission to stay out to a late hour or to take an overnight trip with friends. There are no older siblings to point to and say, "You let them do it. Why won't you let me?" With no allies their own age, only children are always outnumbered, two to one. An only child hasn't a chance of influencing any major family decisions, either.

a. The paragraph contains an irrelevant sentence.
b. The paragraph lacks supporting details at one key spot.
c. The paragraph lacks transitional words.
d. The paragraph contains one fragment and one run-on.

Being an only child isn't as special as some people think. It's no fun being without friends, without privacy, and without power in one's own home. But the child who can triumph over these hardships grows up self-reliant and strong. Perhaps for this reason alone, the hazards are worth it.

PART TWO

OTHER IMPORTANT FACTORS IN WRITING

KEY
FACTORS
IN WRITING

This chapter will discuss the importance of:

- Having the right attitude about writing
- Knowing your subject
- Prewriting
- Outlining
- Rewriting and proofreading

Having the Right Attitude

One sure way to wreck your chances of learning how to write competently is to believe that writing is a natural gift. People with this attitude think that they are the only ones for whom writing is an unbearably difficult activity. They feel that everyone else finds writing easy or at least tolerable. Such people typically say, "I'm not any good at writing" or "English was not one of my good subjects." They imply that they simply do not have a talent for writing, while others do. The result of this attitude is that people do not do their best when they write, or even worse, that they hardly try at all. Their self-defeating attitude becomes a reality; their writing fails chiefly because they have brainwashed themselves into thinking that they don't have the natural talent needed to write. Until their attitude is changed, they probably will not learn how to write effectively.

A realistic attitude about writing, rather than the mistaken "natural gift" attitude, should build on the following two ideas.

1   ***Writing is hard work for almost everyone.*** It is painful to do the intense and active thinking that clear writing demands. (Perhaps television has made us all so passive that the active thinking necessary in both writing and reading now seems doubly hard.) It is scary to sit down before a blank sheet of paper and know that an hour later, nothing on it may be worth keeping. It is frustrating to discover how difficult it is to transfer thoughts and feelings from one's head onto a sheet of paper. It is upsetting to find how an apparently simple writing subject often turns out to be complicated. But writing is not an automatic process; we will not get something for nothing; and we cannot expect something for nothing. Competent writing results only through plain hard work—through determination, sweat, and head-on battle.

2   ***Writing is a skill.*** Writing is a skill like driving, typing, or even preparing a good meal. Like any skill, it can be learned—*if* you decide that you are going to learn and then really work at it. This book will give you the extensive practice needed to develop your writing skills.

Activity

Answering the following questions will help you evaluate your attitude about writing.

1. How much practice were you given writing compositions in high school?

    _____ Much   _____ Some   _____ Little

2. How much feedback (positive or negative comments) from teachers were you given on your compositions?

    _____ Much   _____ Some   _____ Little

3. How did your teachers seem to regard your writing?

    _____ Good   _____ Fair   _____ Poor

4. Do you feel that some people simply have a gift for writing and others do not?

    _____ Yes   _____ Sometimes   _____ No

Many people who answer *Little* to questions 1 and 2 also answer *Poor* and *Yes* to the other questions. On the other hand, people who can answer positively to questions 1 and 2 also tend to have more favorable responses to the other questions. The point is that people with little practice in the skill of writing often have understandably negative feelings about their writing ability. They need not have such feelings, however, because writing is a skill that they can learn with practice.

Knowing Your Subject

Whenever possible, try to write on a subject which interests you. You will find it easier to put more time into your work. Even more important, try to write on a subject that you know about. If you do not have direct experience with the subject, you should at least have indirect experience—knowledge gained through thinking, reading, or talking about the subject. Without direct or indirect experience, or both, you will not be able to provide the specific evidence needed to support whatever points you make. Your writing will be starved for specifics.

When you are writing supporting paragraphs in an essay, you can take any one of three different approaches.

1   *Use the first-person approach.*   Draw on your own experience, and speak to your audience in your own voice. For example, here is a first-person supporting paragraph from an essay on camping:

> First of all, I like comfort when I'm camping. My GMC motor home, with its completely equipped kitchen, shower stall, toilet, double bed, and color television, resembles a mobile motel room. I can sleep on a real mattress, clean sheets, and fluffy pillows. Next to my bed are devices that make me feel at home: a radio, alarm clock, and TV remote-control unit. Unlike the poor campers huddled in tents, I don't have to worry about cold, rain, heat, or annoying insects. After a hot shower, I can slide into my best nightgown, sit comfortably on my down-filled quilt, and read the latest best-seller while a thunderstorm booms outside.

Note the use of the first-person pronouns *I*, *my*, and *me* in the preceding paragraph.

2   *Use the third-person approach.*   Draw on information you have gotten through observation or research and speak about the subject to your audience. Here is the same supporting paragraph recast in the third person:

> First of all, modern campers bring complete bedrooms with them. Like mobile motel rooms, the Winnebagoes, GMC motor homes, and Airstream trailers lumber into America's campgrounds every summer. All the comforts of home are provided inside. Campers sleep on real mattresses with clean sheets and fluffy pillows. Next to their beds are the same gadgets that litter their night tables at home--radios, alarm clocks, and TV remote-control units. It's not necessary for them to worry about annoyances like cold, heat, rain, or buzzing insects, either. They can sit comfortably in bed and read the latest best-sellers while a thunderstorm booms outside.

Note the use of the third-person pronouns *their*, *them*, and *they*, which all refer to *campers* in the preceding paragraph.

3   *Use the third-person approach with hypothetical examples.*   This is the kind of writing you'll find in many magazine and newspaper articles. Create examples based on information you have heard about or researched, and use the examples to support your points. In the following paragraph, "the Watsons" are fictional people who represent a certain kind of modern-day camper.

> Campgrounds are rapidly being taken over by people who refuse to abandon the comforts of home. Take the Watsons, for example. They pull their motor home into a large campsite and hook up to the park's electricity and water lines. After the day's activities, they make up their beds with real mattresses, clean sheets, and fluffy pillows. Before falling asleep, Harvey and Ruth may watch television on their color set; their son Eddie may listen to rock music on his stereo. The Watsons don't worry about cold, heat, rain, or buzzing insects, either. They have an air conditioner, a heater, and a metal shell to protect them. During the worst storms, they stay snug and dry.

Activity

Here are three more paragraphs, each of which could have been used in the essays on camping. Put 1 before the first-person selection, 3 before the third-person selection, and 3-H beside the third-person selection with hypothetical examples.

_____

> Today's campers like their food to be familiar, too. The days of landing a trout and pan-frying it over a wood fire are long gone. Now, campers simply travel with plenty of supplies from home stocked in the motor home's minikitchen. Frozen meats, vegetables, and TV dinners are brought along, making it possible to spend an entire vacation eating nothing but food from the hometown supermarket. If campers do feel like sampling the local fare, however, they usually go no farther than the McDonald's or Burger King in the nearest town. A fast-food outlet is safe and reassuring. The burgers, shakes, prices, and employees will all resemble the ones at home.

_____

> When they're camping, the Watsons want their food to be familiar, too. Harvey has no intention of landing and cleaning a trout for breakfast. Instead, he sleeps on in one of the motor home's bunks while Ruth pulls a couple of Swanson's frozen pancake-and-sausage breakfasts out of the fridge, preheats the oven, and mixes up some instant orange juice. While she waits for the coffee to perk, Ruth checks her stocks of beef cuts, chickens, frozen vegetables, and TV dinners--all purchased ahead of time from the hometown

Shop 'n' Bag. Tonight, however, the Watsons have decided to sample some of the local fare in a nearby village. Around six o'clock, they will detach the Chevette from the Winnebago's trailer hitch, head into town, and stop at McDonald's for Big Macs, fries, and shakes.

_____

When I'm camping, I want to eat as well as I do at home. I certainly don't want to catch my food, and I don't want to buy it from dusty little general stores or unfamiliar restaurants, either. Instead, before the trip I stock my camper with plenty of supplies from my local supermarket--frozen meat, boxes of vegetables, dried fruit, and canned juices. I even prepare homemade casseroles and stews to store in the motor home's freezer compartment. When I do want a change of pace from home cooking, however, I go no farther than the closest McDonald's. There, I can count on getting the same product that I would expect from my hometown branch of the fast-food chain.

Prewriting

If you are like many people, you may sometimes have trouble getting started with your writing. A mental block may develop when you sit down before a blank sheet of paper. Or after you have started a paper, you may hit snags or moments of "Where to go next?" The following pages describe four techniques that will help you think about your topic and get words down on paper. The techniques are often called _prewriting techniques_ because they come before the actual writing of a paper. They are (1) brainstorming, (2) freewriting, (3) making a list, and (4) making a scratch outline.

TECHNIQUE 1: BRAINSTORMING

In _brainstorming_ you generate ideas and details by asking as many questions as you can think of about your subject. Such questions include _What? When? Why? How? Where?_ and _Who?_

On the next page is an example of how one person, Tim, used the brainstorming technique to generate material for a paper. Tim felt he could write about a lonely diner he had visited, but he was having trouble getting started. So he asked himself a series of brainstorming questions about the experience and, as a result, he accumulated a series of details that provided the basis for the paper he finally wrote.

Here are the questions Tim asked and the answers he wrote:

<u>Why</u> did I stop at the diner?	I was coming home from an all-day car trip, and I was tired and sleepy. I decided to get a cup of coffee at the next diner.
<u>How</u> do I feel about diners?	I've always liked diners. I was looking forward to a friendly waitress and some discussion with the customers at the counter.
<u>What</u> was the diner like?	It was lonely. There were only a few people, and it was very quiet. There was only one waitress on duty. Even the parking lot looked lonely--trash was blowing around and it was raining.
<u>Who</u> was in the diner?	Two workingmen were sitting at the counter. There was a young man sitting by himself at the far end of the counter. He looked depressed. There was one middle-aged couple in a booth. They weren't talking to each other--one was doodling, the other staring.
<u>What</u> happened at the diner?	I got out of there as fast as possible. I just wanted to get away from that lonely place and reach my home.

After brainstorming, Tim's next step was to prepare a scratch outline. He then prepared several drafts of the paper. The effective essay that eventually resulted from Tim's prewriting techniques appears on page 180.

TECHNIQUE 2: FREEWRITING

When you do not know what to write about a particular subject or when you are blocked in a composition, freewriting sometimes helps. In freewriting you write as fast as you can for ten minutes. You do not worry about spelling, punctuation, erasing mistakes, or finding exact words. You just write without stopping. If you get stuck for words, you write, ''I am looking for something to say,'' or repeat words until something comes. There is no need to feel inhibited, for mistakes do not count and you do not have to hand in your paper.

Freewriting will limber up your writing muscles and make you familiar with the act of writing. It is a way to break through mental blocks about writing and the fear of making errors. As you do not have to worry about making mistakes, you can concentrate on discovering what you want to say about a subject. Your initial ideas and impressions will often become clearer after you have gotten them down on paper. Through continued practice in freewriting, you will develop the habit of thinking as you write. And you will learn a technique that is a helpful way to get started on almost any paper that you write.

Here is the freewriting that one student did to accumulate details for a paper on why she decided to put her mother in a nursing home.

> I'm still upset about the whole thing, but seeing everything going downhill really forced the decision. Mom just needed so much help with all the pills and dressing and bathing. She needed more help than Daddy could handle by himself. Hospital bills in this country are outrageous and Medicare doesn't pay for everything. Mom needed someone to work out that special diet because it was so complicated. The wheelchair rental was expensive. The hardest thing was the fact that she was breaking down emotionally, saying things like "You don't care about me." We cared, but we worried about Dad. What an enormous strain he was under in all this. Mom really acted emotionally disturbed at times. She would call for an ambulance and tell them she was dying. Dad started to lose weight. The bills coming in started to fill an entire shopping bag. Some people think we were cruel, but we didn't have any other choice. My father doesn't drive, so he was walking all over town to get medicine and food.

The writer's next step was to use the freewriting as the basis for a scratch outline. The effective paper that eventually resulted from the author's freewriting, a scratch outline, and a good deal of rewriting appears on page 126.

TECHNIQUE 3: MAKING A LIST

Write out a list of as many different items as you can think of concerning your topic. Do not worry about repeating yourself, about sorting out major details from minor ones, or about spelling or punctuating correctly. Simply make a list of everything about your subject that occurs to you. Your aim is to generate details and to accumulate as much raw material for writing as possible.

Following is a list prepared by one person, Jan, who was gathering details for an essay called "The Benefits of Television." Her first stage in doing the paper was simply to make a list of thoughts and details about the topic that occurred to her. Here is her list:

Entertainment
Movies and sports events
Video games
Educational (important--save for last)

> Relaxing after work
> Covers major world events
> Can be used with computers
> Reduce stress (used for high-blood-pressure patients)
> Rent videocassettes
> Shows for children (Sesame Street)
> Special cable services (sports, concerts)
> College courses on TV

Notice that partway down the list Jan puts in parentheses a note to herself that one thought (about the educational benefits of television) seems most important and should be saved for last. Very often as you make a list, ideas about how to develop and organize a paper will occur to you. Jot them down.

Making a list is an excellent way to get started. Often you then can go on to make a scratch outline and write the first draft of your paper. A scratch outline for Jan's list is shown below.

TECHNIQUE 4: PREPARING A SCRATCH OUTLINE

A scratch outline can often be the *most helpful single technique* for writing a good paper. It is an excellent follow-up to the prewriting techniques already mentioned: brainstorming, freewriting, and making a list. In a scratch outline, you think carefully about the exact point you are making, about the exact items that you want to support that point, and about the exact order in which you want to arrange those items. The scratch outline is, then, a plan or blueprint that will help you achieve a unified, supported, and organized composition.

Here is the scratch outline that the student Jan prepared for her general list above:

> Television can have real benefits.
>
> 1. Relaxation
>   a. After work
>   b. Reduce stress
> 2. Entertainment
>   a. Network programming
>   b. Cable programming
>   c. Videodiscs and videocassettes
>   d. Video games

3. Education
   a. Children's shows
   b. College courses
   c. World events
   d. Computer capability

This scratch outline enabled Jan to think about her paper—to decide exactly what to put into the paper and in what order. Without having to write a number of sentences, she has taken a giant step toward a paper that is unified (she has left out items that are not related), supported (she has added items that develop her point), and organized (she has arranged the items in a logical way—here, using emphatic order). The effective essay that eventually resulted from Jan's list and scratch outline is on page 71.

COMBINED USE OF THE FOUR TECHNIQUES

Very often the scratch outline follows brainstorming, freewriting, or making a list. At other times, the scratch outline may substitute for the other three techniques. Also, you may use several techniques almost simultaneously when writing a paper. You may, for example, ask questions while making a list; you may organize and outline the list as you write it; you may ask yourself questions and then freewrite answers to them. The four techniques are all ways to help you go about writing a paper.

Activity 1

Answer the following questions.

1. Which of the prewriting techniques do you already practice?

   _____ Brainstorming   _____ Freewriting   _____ Making a list

   _____ Making a scratch outline

2. Which prewriting technique involves asking questions about your topic?

   _____

3. Which prewriting technique involves writing quickly about your topic without being concerned about grammar or spelling? _____

4. Which prewriting technique is almost always part of doing an essay?

   _____

5. Which techniques do you think are the ones that will work best for you?

   _____

Activity 2

Given below are examples of the four prewriting techniques used to develop the topic "Problems of Combining Work and College." Put B before the brainstorming selection, F before the freewriting, L before the list, and SO before the scratch outline.

_____

Never enough time
Miss campus parties
Had to study (only two free hours a night)
Give up activities with friends
No time to rewrite papers
Can't stay at school to play video games or talk to friends
Friends don't call me to go out anymore
Sunday no longer relaxed day--have to study
Missing sleep I should be getting
Grades aren't as good as they could be
Can't watch favorite TV shows
Really need the extra money
Tired when I sit down to study at nine o'clock

_____

What are some of the problems of combining work and school?

Schoolwork suffers because I don't have time to study or rewrite papers. I've had to give up things I enjoy, like sleep or playing touch football with my friends. I can't get into the social life at college, because I have to leave for work right after class.

How have these problems changed my life?

My grades aren't as good as they were when I didn't work. Some of my friends have stopped calling me. My relationship with a girl I liked fell apart because I couldn't spend much time with her. I miss all the TV shows I used to enjoy.

What do I do in a typical day?

I get up at 7 to make an 8 A.M. class. I have classes till 1:30, and then I drive to the supermarket where I work. I work till 7 P.M., and then I drive home and eat dinner. After I take a shower and relax for a half hour, it's about 9. This gives me only a couple of hours to study—read textbooks, do math exercises, write essays. My eyes start to close well before I go to bed at 11.

<u>Why</u> do I keep up this schedule?   I can't afford to go to school without working, and I need a degree to get the accounting job I want. If I invest my time now, I'll have a better future.

_____   Juggling a job and a full load of college courses has created some major difficulties in my life.

1. Little time for studying
   a. Not reading textbooks
   b. Not rewriting papers
   c. Little studying for tests
2. Little time for enjoying social side of college
   a. During school
   b. After school
3. No time for personal pleasures
   a. Favorite TV shows
   b. Sunday football games
   c. Sleeping late

_____   It's hard working and going to school at the same time. I never realized how much I'd have to give up. I won't be quitting my job because I need the money and the people are friendly at the place where I work. I've had to give up a lot more than I thought. We used to play touch football games every Sunday. They were fun and we'd go out for drinks afterwards. Sundays now are for catch-up work with my courses. I have to catch up because I don't get home every day until 7, and I have to eat dinner first before studying. Sometimes I'm so hungry I just eat cookies or chips. Anyway, by the time I take a shower it's 9 P.M. or later and I'm already feeling tired. I've been up since 7 A.M. Sometimes I write an English paper in twenty minutes and don't even read it over. I feel that I'm missing out on a lot in college. The other day some people I like were sitting in the cafeteria listening to music and talking. I would have given anything to stay and not have to go to work. I almost called in sick. I used to get invited to parties but I don't much anymore. My friends know I'm not going to be able to make it, so they don't bother. I can't even sleep late on weekends or watch my favorite shows during the week.

Outlining

An effective piece of writing rests on a strong foundation: logical thinking. Any paper that you write must be completely thought out and planned. The goal of planning is to produce an essay with a thesis idea that is fully and logically supported by the three body paragraphs.

In planning an essay, you should make an outline. Outlining is an organizational skill that will develop your ability to think in a clear and logical manner. An outline lets you work on, and see, the bare bones of your paper, without the distraction of a clutter of words and sentences. A sound outline guarantees a paper that is, at the very least, well organized.

The following series of exercises will help you develop the outlining skills so important to planning a solid essay.

Activity 1

One key to effective outlining is the ability to distinguish between major ideas and details that fit under those ideas. The exercise below will develop your ability to generalize from a list of details and to determine a major thought.

Examples *Writing instruments*   *Outer garments*

Pencil   Coat
Ball-point pen   Shawl
Crayon   Jacket
Felt-tip marker   Cape

1. _____   2. _____

Spiderman   Gas
Superman   Electricity
Wonder Woman   Water
Batman   Phone

3. _____   4. _____

Boston Globe   Tinsel
The New York Times   Mistletoe
Washington Post   Lights
Philadelphia Inquirer   Wreaths

5. _____   6. _____

Chicken   Dictionary
Turkey   Almanac
Cornish game hen   Encyclopedia
Duck   Atlas

7. _____   8. _____

Chain   Loans
Handlebars   Checking accounts
Gearshift   Savings accounts
Wheel spokes   Check cashing

9. _____   10. _____

    Wrinkles   Crutch

    Hearing loss   Cane

    Brittle bones   Metal walker

    Thinning hair   Artificial leg

    Weakened eyesight

Activity 2

Major and minor ideas are mixed together in the two lists below. Put the ideas into logical order by filling in the outlines that follow.

1. Thesis: My high school had three problem areas.

    Involved with drugs   a. _____

    Leaky ceilings   (1) _____

    Students   (2) _____

    Unwilling to help after class

    Formed cliques   b. _____

    Teachers   (1) _____

    Buildings   (2) _____

    Ill-equipped gym   c. _____

    Much too strict   (1) _____

                            (2) _____

2. Thesis: Working as a dishwasher in a restaurant was my worst job.

    Ten-hour shifts   a. _____

    Heat in kitchen   (1) _____

    Working conditions   (2) _____

    Minimum wage

    Hours changed every week   b. _____

    No bonus for overtime   (1) _____

    Hours   (2) _____

    Pay   c. _____

    Noisy work area   (1) _____

                            (2) _____

Activity 3

Again, major and minor ideas are mixed together. In addition, in each outline one of the three major ideas is missing and must be added. Put the ideas into a logical order by filling in the outlines that follow and adding a third major idea.

1. Thesis: Joining an aerobics class has many benefits.

Make new friends

Reduce mental stress

Social benefits

Strengthens heart

Improves self-image

Mental benefits

Tones muscles

Meet interesting instructors

a. _____

   (1) _____

   (2) _____

b. _____

   (1) _____

   (2) _____

c. _____

   (1) _____

   (2) _____

2. Thesis: My favorite times in school were the days before holiday vacations.

Lighter workload

Teachers more relaxed

Pep rallies

Less work in class

Friendlier atmosphere

Less homework

Holiday concerts

Students happy about vacation

a. _____

   (1) _____

   (2) _____

b. _____

   (1) _____

   (2) _____

c. _____

   (1) _____

   (2) _____

Activity 4

Read the following two essays. Then outline each one in the space provided. Write out the theses and topic sentences and summarize in a few words the supporting material that fits under each topic sentence.

Losing Touch

Steve, a typical American, stays home on workdays. He plugs into his personal computer terminal in order to hook up with the office. After work, he puts on his stereo headphones, watches a movie on his home video recorder, or challenges himself to a game of electronic baseball. On many days, Steve doesn't talk to any other human beings, and he doesn't see any people except the ones on television. Steve is imaginary, but his lifestyle is very possible. The inventions of modern technology seem to be cutting us off from contact with our fellow human beings.

The world of business is one area in which technology is isolating us. Experts predict, for example, that many people will soon be able to work at home. With access to a large central computer, employees such as secretaries, insurance agents, and accountants could do their jobs at display terminals in their own homes. They would never actually have to see the people they're dealing with. In addition, the way employees are paid will change. Workers' salaries will automatically be credited to their bank accounts, eliminating the need for paper checks or pay stubs. No workers will stand in line to receive their pay or cash their checks. Personal banking will change, too. Customers will deal with machines to deposit or withdraw money from their accounts. Bank loans will be approved or rejected, not in an interview with a loan officer, but through a display on a computer screen.

Another area that technology is changing is entertainment. Music, for instance, was once a group experience. People listened to music at concert halls or in small social gatherings. For many people now, however, music is a solitary experience. Walking along the street or sitting in their living rooms, they wear headphones to build a wall of music around them. Movie entertainment is changing, too. Movies used to be social events. Now, fewer people are going out to see a movie. Many more are choosing to wait for a film to appear on cable television. Instead of being involved with the laughter, applause, or hisses of the audience, viewers watch movies in the isolation of their own living rooms.

Education is a third important area in which technology is separating us from others. From elementary schools to colleges, students spend more and more time sitting by themselves in front of computers. The computers give them feedback, while teachers spend more time tending the computers and less time interacting with their classes. A similar problem occurs in homes. As more families buy computers, increasing numbers of students practice their math and reading skills with software programs instead of with their friends, brothers and sisters, and parents. Last, alienating results are occurring as a result of another high-tech invention, videotapes. People are buying videocassette tapes on subjects such as cooking, real estate investment, speaking, and speed-reading. They then practice their skills at home rather than by taking group classes in which a rich human interaction can occur.

Technology, then, seems to be driving human beings apart. Soon, we may no longer need to communicate with other human beings in order to do our work, entertain ourselves, or play the games we enjoy. Machines will be the coworkers and companions of the future.

Thesis: _____

_____

First topic sentence: _____

_____

Support: 1.   _____

2.   _____

3.   _____

a.   _____

b.   _____

Second topic sentence: _____

_____

Support: 1.   _____

2.   _____

Third topic sentence: _____

_____

Support: 1.   _____

2.   _____

3.   _____

Coming to State College

On my first day here at State College, I was handed a questionnaire called "Motivational Survey." The college wanted to know exactly why I was here. Four pages and sixty questions later, I handed the sheets back to the woman at the orientation desk. However, I could have told her in about a dozen words why I had decided to attend State College. I'm here because this school is economical, convenient, and right for my needs.

I chose State College, first, because it's an inexpensive place to get a good education. Tuition for a full course load is only $950 per semester, so I can save enough money for my tuition while I'm working at my summer job in a plastics factory. I can also earn enough money to live on during the year from my part-time job in a nearby drugstore. Finally, State College is only fifteen miles from my home, so I don't have to pay two or three thousand dollars a year to live in a dormitory. Instead, I keep my Ford Escort on the road for about twenty-five dollars a week.

In addition, I chose State College because its location is convenient. Since my mother died a year ago, I've kept house for my father, my ten-year-old brother, and my eight-year-old sister. I've scheduled all my classes in the morning so that I can be home by one o'clock to clean the house and get something simple, like hamburgers or stew, ready for dinner. Commuting to State College also allows me to be with my old friends from high school. With all the responsibilities in my life just now, I didn't want the added strain of moving away from the friends I like and care about. Last of all, I can be with my boyfriend almost every day. He gives me the emotional support I need to achieve my goals.

Most important, State College has the academic program I want. At the end of four years, not only will I have my bachelor's degree, but I will also be certified as a registered nurse. With these double qualifications, I shouldn't have any trouble getting a job in the booming health field. State College also grants academic credits for course-related internships, so there is a possibility that I can complete my studies even faster if I am accepted for training by a local hospital. And, since nursing degrees from State College are well respected, I might be able, someday, to enter a graduate program and specialize in a field like cardiac nursing.

By attending State College, I am getting a quality education at a bargain price. I am also able to take care of my family while I take care of my future. I didn't need a "motivational survey" to figure out why I made the choice I did.

Thesis: _____

_____

First topic sentence: _____

_____

    Support: 1. _____

             2. _____

             3. _____

Second topic sentence: _____

    Support: 1. _____

             2. _____

             3. _____

Third topic sentence: _____

_____

Support: 1. _____

2. _____

3. _____

Rewriting and Proofreading

Writing an effective paper is almost never done all at once. Rather, it is a step-by-step process in which you take your paper through a series of stages—prewriting, first draft, added drafts, and final draft.

In the first stage, you *go over, change, improve, add to,* and perhaps *subtract* from your material as you take your paper through several rough drafts. Many people, especially those who feel uneasy or insecure about writing, dread the rewriting stage. The act of writing a *first* draft is often so painful that the writer has no desire to revise the work. However, simply writing a first draft, in order to be done with a paper, is a great mistake—rather like thinking you've made a stew if all you've done is throw raw vegetables into a pot. It takes work to create a paper with a clear thesis and strong supporting details. With each draft, you can tighten the organization of your paper and make the writing flow more smoothly. For example, in the second draft you may spot some details that do not clearly relate to the main point of a paragraph. You may also spot areas where more details are needed. In the next draft, you may work on inserting transitional devices to bridge the gaps between ideas.

In the last stage, you *proofread* the next-to-final draft. Proofreading is another essential step that some people avoid, often because they have worked so hard on the previous stages. It may be better to set your paper aside for a while and then proofread with a fresh, rested mind. Proofreading for sentence-skills mistakes can turn an average paper into a better one and a good paper into an excellent one. Proofreading to strengthen your sentence skills is a basic part of clear and effective writing. A later section of this book (page 431) will give you practice in the important skill of proofreading.

Activity 1

Answering the questions below will help you evaluate your attitude about rewriting and proofreading.

1. When do you typically start work on a paper?

    _____ Several nights before it's due   _____ Night before it's due

    _____ Day it's due

2. How many drafts do you typically write when doing a paper?

    _____ One   _____ Two   _____ Three   _____ Four or more

3. How would you describe your proofreading?

    _____ Do not look at paper again after the last word is written

    _____ May glance quickly at paper for obvious errors

    _____ Read paper over carefully to find mistakes

4. Do you ever get back papers marked for obvious errors?

    _____ Frequently   _____ Sometimes   _____ Almost never

    _____ Never

Activity 2

Following is a supporting paragraph from an essay called "Problems of Combining School and Work." You saw prewriting material for this essay on pages 97–99. The paragraph below is shown in four different stages of development: first draft, second draft, third draft, and final draft. Place the number 1 in front of the first draft and number in sequence the remaining drafts.

_____   I have also given up some special personal pleasures in my life. On Sundays, for example, I used to play softball or football, now I use the entire day to study. Another pleasure Ive had to give up is good old-fashioned sleep. I never get as much as I like because their just isnt time. Finally I miss having the chance to just sit in front of the TV, on weeknights. In order to watch the whole lineup of movies and sports that I used to watch regularly. These sound like small pleasures, but you realize how important they are when you have to give them up.

_____   I've had to give up special personal pleasures in my life. I use to spend Sundays playing pick-up games, now I have to study. Im the sort of person who needs alot of sleep, but I dont have the time for that either. Sleeping nine or ten hours a night woul'dnt be unusual. Psychologists have shown that each individual need a different amount of sleep, some people as little as five hours, some as much as nine or ten. so I'm not unusual in that. But I've given up that pleasure too. The third thing is that I can't watch the TV shows I use to enjoy. This is another personal pleasure I've had to give up trying to balence work and school. These sound like small pleasures, but you realize how important they are when you have to give them up.

_____   Besides missing the social side of college life, I've also had to give up some of my special personal pleasures. I used to spend Sunday afternoons, for example, playing lob-pitch softball or touch football, depending on the season. Now, I use Sunday as a catch-up day for my studies. Another pleasure I've lost is sleeping late on days off and weekends. I once loved mornings when I could check the clock, bury my head in the pillow, and drift off for another hour. These days I'm forced to crawl out of bed the minute the alarm lets out its piercing ring. Finally, I no longer have the chance to just sit, for three or four hours at a time, watching the movies and sports programs I enjoy. A leisurely night of Monday Night Football or a network premiere of a Clint Eastwood movie is a pleasure of the past for me now.

_____   Besides missing the social side of college life, I've also had to give up some of my special personal pleasures. I used to spend Sunday afternoons, for example, playing lob-pitch softball or touch football, depending on the season. Now I use Sunday as a day for my studies. Another pleasure I've had to give up is sleeping late on days off and weekends. I once loved mornings when I could check the clock, bury my head in the pillow, and drifting off for another hour. These days I'm forced to get out of bed the minute the alarm lets out it's piercing ring. Finally, I no longer have the chance to just sit watching the movies and sports programs I enjoy. A liesurely night of Monday Night Football or a network premere of a Clint Eastwood movie is a pleasure of the past for me now.

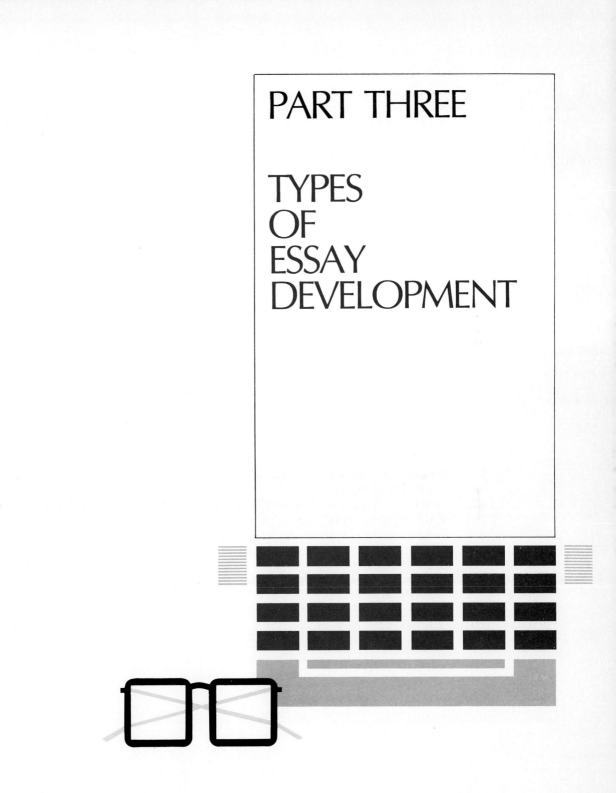

PART THREE

TYPES
OF
ESSAY
DEVELOPMENT

INTRODUCTION TO ESSAY DEVELOPMENT

THE FOUR TRADITIONAL MODES OF WRITING

Traditionally, all writing has been divided into four major forms or modes. They are as follows:

- Exposition

  Examples   Comparison-contrast
  Cause-effect   Definition
  Process   Division and classification
- Description
- Narration
- Persuasion or argumentation

In *exposition*, the writer provides information about a particular subject. The methods of development in exposition include (1) giving examples, (2) presenting causes or effects, (3) explaining a process, (4) comparing or contrasting, (5) defining, and (6) dividing and classifying. A *description* is a verbal picture of a person, place, or object. In a *narration*, a writer tells the story of something that happened. *Persuasion* or *argumentation* is an attempt to prove a point or defend an opinion.

In this part of the book, each of the six types of expository development is presented in a separate chapter. There are also individual chapters devoted to description, narration, and argument.

WRITING AS A FORM OF PERSUASION

Although persuasion or argumentation is one of the modes of writing, actually most of the essays you write in any mode will probably involve some form of persuasion. You will advance a thesis and then support it in a variety of ways. To convince the reader that your thesis is valid, you may use description or narration or some method of exposition. In the essays you will read in Part Three, for example, one writer supports the point that a certain diner is lonely by providing a number of descriptive details. Another writer labels a certain experience in her life as embarrassing and then uses a narrative to demonstrate the truth of this statement. A third writer advances the opinion that a fast-food restaurant can be preferable to a fancy one and then supplies comparative information about both to support his claim. All your writing, in short, has the purpose of persuading your reader that the idea you have advanced is a valid one.

THE ORDER OF EACH CHAPTER

After each type of essay development is explained, student papers illustrating that type are presented, followed by questions about the papers. The questions relate to unity, support, and coherence, the principles of effective writing explained earlier in the book. You are then asked to write your own essay. In most cases, the first assignment is fairly structured and provides a good deal of guidance for the writing process. The other assignments offer a wide and interesting choice of writing topics. In three instances (examples, cause-effect, and comparison-contrast), the final assignments require outside reading of literary works; a student model is provided for each of these assignments.

EXAMPLES

In our daily conversations, we often provide *examples*—that is, details, particulars, specific instances—to explain statements that we make. Here are several statements and supporting examples:

The first day of school was frustrating.	My sociology course was cancelled. Then, I couldn't find the biology lab. And the lines at the bookstore were so long that I went home without buying my textbooks.
That washing machine is unreliable.	The water temperature can't be predicted; it stops in midcycle; and it sometimes shreds my clothing.
My grandfather is a thrifty person.	He washes and reuses aluminum foil. He wraps gifts in newspaper. And he's worn the same Sunday suit for twenty years.

In each case, the examples help us see for ourselves the truth of the statement that has been made. In essays, too, explanatory examples help your audience fully understand your point. Lively, specific examples also add interest to your paper.

In this section, you will be asked to provide a series of examples to support your thesis. First read the essays ahead; they all use examples to develop their points. Then answer the questions that follow.

ESSAYS TO CONSIDER

Everyday Cruelty

Last week, I found myself worrying less about problems of world politics and national crime and more about smaller evils. I came home one day with a bad taste in my mouth, the kind I get whenever I witness the little cruelties that people inflict on each other. On this particular day, I had seen three especially mean-spirited things happen.

I first thought about mean-spirited people as I walked from the bus stop to the office where I work. I make this walk every day, and it's my first step away from the comforts of home and into the tensions of the city. For me, a landmark on the route is a tiny patch of ground that was once strewn with rubbish and broken glass. The city is trying to make a "pocket park" out of it by planting trees and flowers. Every day this spring, I watched the skinny saplings put out tiny leaves. When I walked past, I always noted how big the tulips were getting and made bets with myself on when they would bloom. But last Wednesday, as I reached the park, I felt sick. Someone had knocked the trees to the ground and trampled the budding tulips into the dirt. Someone had destroyed a bit of beauty for no reason.

At lunchtime on Wednesday, I witnessed more meanness. Along with dozens of other hungry, hurried people, I was waiting in line at McDonald's. Also in line was a young mother with two tired, impatient children clinging to her legs. The mother was trying to calm the children, but it was obvious that their whining was about to give way to full-fledged tantrums. The lines barely moved, and the lunchtime tension was building. Then, one of the children began to cry and scream. The little boy's bloodcurdling yells resounded through the restaurant, and people stared angrily at the helpless mother. Finally, one man turned to her and said, "Lady, you shouldn't bring your kids to a public place if you can't control them." The woman was exhausted and hungry. Someone in line could have helped her with her problem. Instead, even though many of the customers in the restaurant were parents themselves, they treated her like a criminal.

The worst incident of mean-spiritedness that I saw that day happened after I left work. As I walked to the bus stop, I approached an old woman huddled in a doorway. She was wrapped in a dirty blanket and clutched a cheap vinyl bag packed with her belongings. She was one of the "street people" our society leaves to fend for themselves. The United States, the richest country on earth, should not allow such suffering. Some of these victims even live in cardboard boxes during the coldest winters. Approaching the woman from the opposite direction were three teenagers who were laughing and talking in loud voices. When they saw the old woman, they began to shout crude remarks at her. One of them grabbed her shopping bag and pretended to throw it out into the street. The woman stared helplessly at them, like a wounded animal surrounded by hunters. Then, having had their fun, the teenagers went on their way.

I had seen enough of the world's coldness that day and wanted to leave it behind. At home, I huddled in the warmth of my family. I wondered why we all contribute to the world's supply of petty cruelty. There's enough of it already.

Altered States

Most Americans are not alcoholics. Most of us do not smoke marijuana to get high. LSD trips went out of style along with the flower children of the sixties. Nevertheless, many Americans <u>are</u> walking and driving around with their minds slightly out of kilter. In its attempt to cope with modern life, the human mind seems to have evolved some defense strategies. When confronted with inventions like the automobile, the television, and the shopping center, for example, the mind will slip--all by itself--into an altered state.

First of all, the mind must now cope with the automobile. In the past, no human being ever sat for hours at a time, in the same position, staring at endless white lines and matched pairs of small red lights. In order to deal with this unnatural situation, the mind goes on automatic pilot. A primitive, less-developed region of the brain takes over the actual driving. It tells the foot when to apply pressure to the brake and gas pedal and directs the eyes to stay open. Meanwhile, the rest of the brain continues on with higher functions. It devises excuses for being late for work. It replays, better than any video system, yesterday's Cowboys game. Or, it creates a pleasant imaginary world where its owner wins all arguments, tells hilarious jokes, and attracts the opposite sex like a magnet. By splitting into two halves, the mind deals with the boredom of driving.

The mind has defenses not only against the auto but also against television. Since too much staring at flickering images of police officers, detectives, and talk-show hosts can be dangerous to human sanity, the mind automatically goes into a TV hypnosis state. The eyes see the sitcom or the dog food commercial, but the mind goes into a holding pattern. None of the televised images or sounds actually enters the brain. This is why, when questioned, people cannot remember commercials they have seen five seconds before or why the TV cops are chasing a certain suspect. During this hypnotic, trancelike state, the mind resembles an armored armadillo. It rolls up in self-defense, allowing the stream of televised information to pass it by harmlessly.

Perhaps the most dangerous threat to the mind, however, is the shopping center. In the modern mall, dozens of stores, restaurants, and movie theaters compete for the mind's attention. There are hundreds of questions to be answered. Should I start with the upper or lower mall level? Which stores should I look in? Should I bother with the sweater sale at J. C. Penney? Should I eat fried chicken or a burger for lunch? Where is my car parked? To combat this mental overload, the mind goes into a state resembling the white-out experienced by mountain climbers trapped in a blinding snowstorm.

Suddenly, everything looks the same. The shopper is unsure where to go next and cannot remember what he or she came for in the first place. The mind enters this state deliberately, so that the shopper has no choice but to leave.

Therefore, the next time you see drivers, TV viewers, or shoppers with eyes as glazed and empty as polished doorknobs, you'll know these people are in a protective altered state. Be gentle with them. They are merely trying to cope with the mind-numbing inventions of modern life.

Childhood Fears

I remember my childhood as being generally happy and can recall experiencing some of the most carefree times of my life. But I can also remember, even more vividly, moments of being deeply frightened. As a child, I was truly terrified of the dark and of getting lost; these fears were very real and caused me some extremely uncomfortable moments.

Maybe it was the strange way things looked and sounded in my familiar room at night that scared me so much. There was never total darkness, but a streetlight or passing car lights made clothes hung over a chair take on the shape of an unknown beast. Out of the corner of my eye, I saw curtains seem to move when there was no breeze. A tiny creak in the floor would sound a hundred times louder than in the daylight, and my imagination would take over, creating burglars and monsters on the prowl. Darkness always made me feel so helpless, too. My heart would pound, and I would lie very still so that the "enemy" wouldn't discover me.

Another of my childhood fears was that I would get lost, especially on the way home from school. Every morning I got on the school bus right near my home--that was no problem. After school, though, when all the buses were lined up along the curb, I was terrified that I'd get on the wrong one and be taken to some unfamiliar neighborhood. I would scan the bus for the faces of my friends, make sure the bus driver was the same one that had been there in the morning, and even then ask the others over and over again to be sure I was on the right bus. On school or family trips to an amusement park or a museum, I wouldn't let the leaders out of my sight. And of course, I was never very adventurous when it came to taking walks or hikes, because I would go only where I was sure I could never get lost.

Perhaps one of the worst fears of all I had as a child was that of not being liked or accepted by others. First of all, I was quite shy. Second, I worried constantly about my looks, thinking people wouldn't like me because I was too fat or wore braces. I tried to wear the "right" clothes and even had intense arguments with my mother over the importance of wearing "flats" instead of saddle shoes to school. I'm sorry that we had these arguments now, especially since my mother is quite sickly and has spent the last year in and out of the hospital. Being popular was so important to me then, and the fear of not being liked was a powerful one.

One of the processes of evolving from a child to an adult is being able to recognize and overcome or outgrow our fears. I've learned that darkness does not have to take on a life of its own, that others can help me when I'm lost, and that friendliness and sincerity will encourage people to like me. Understanding the things that scared us as children helps us to cope with our lives as adults.

■ Questions

About Unity

1. Which sentence in the third supporting paragraph of "Childhood Fears" should be omitted in the interest of paragraph unity?

_____

2. Which two sentences in the third supporting paragraph of "Everyday Cruelty" should be omitted in the interest of paragraph unity?

_____

3. Which thesis statement fails to mention all three of its supporting points in its plan of development?

_____

About Support

4. After which sentence in the third supporting paragraph of "Childhood Fears" are more supporting details needed?

_____

5. Which essay uses a single extended example in each of its supporting paragraphs?

_____

About Coherence

6. Which words in the third supporting paragraph of "Altered States" signal that the most important idea was saved for last?

_____

7. What are the two transition words in the third supporting paragraph of "Childhood Fears"?

_____

8. Which topic sentence in "Altered States" functions as a linking sentence between paragraphs?

_____

About the Introduction and Conclusion

9. Circle below the kind of introduction used in "Childhood Fears."
   a. Broad, general statement narrowing to thesis
   b. Idea that is the opposite of the one to be developed
   c. Quotation
   d. Anecdote
   e. Questions

10. Which transition word signals the conclusion of "Altered States"?

_____

WRITING THE ESSAY

■ **Writing Assignment 1**

For this assignment, you will complete an unfinished essay by adding appropriate supporting examples. Here is the incomplete essay:

Problems with My Apartment

> They say there's no place like home. In my case, that is probably a good thing. My apartment has given me nothing but headaches. From the day I signed the lease, I've had to deal with an uncooperative landlord, an incompetent janitor, and inconsiderate neighbors.

> First of all, my landlord has been uncooperative. . . .

> I've had a problem not only with my landlord but also with an incompetent janitor. . . .

> Perhaps the worst hassle of all has been with the inconsiderate neighbors who live in the apartment above me. . . .

> Sometimes, my apartment seems like a small, friendly oasis surrounded by hostile enemies. I never know what side trouble is going to come from next: the landlord, the janitor, or the neighbors. Home may be where the heart is, but my sanity is thinking about moving out.

How to Proceed

a   Brainstorm the assignment by making up answers to the following questions. Use separate paper.

How has the landlord been uncooperative?
In what ways have you been inconvenienced?
Has he been uncooperative more than once?
What has been your reaction?
What has been the landlord's reaction?
What kinds of things have you said to each other?

Who is the janitor?
What has he tried to fix in the apartment?
In what ways has he been incompetent?
How has he inconvenienced you?
Has the janitor's incompetence cost you money?
What is the worst example of the janitor's incompetence?

Who are the neighbors?
How long have they lived upstairs?
What kinds of hassles have you had?
Have these incidents happened several times?
If you have spoken to the neighbors, what did they say?
What is the worst problem with these neighbors?

The answers to these questions should serve as an excellent source of details for the essay.

b Keep in mind that you may use one extended example in each paragraph (as in the essay ''Everyday Cruelty'') or two or three short examples (as in ''Childhood Fears'').

c As you are writing drafts of your three supporting paragraphs, ask yourself repeatedly:

Do my examples truly show my landlord as *uncooperative?*
Do my examples truly show the janitor as *incompetent?*
Do my examples truly show my neighbors as *inconsiderate?*

Your aims in this assignment are twofold: (1) to provide *adequate* specific details for the three qualities in question and (2) to provide *enough* specific details so that you solidly support each quality.

d When you are satisfied that you have provided effective examples, proofread your paragraphs carefully for the sentence-skills mistakes listed on the inside front cover. Then write out the full essay on separate paper and submit it to your instructor.

■ Writing Assignment 2

Write an essay on the good or bad qualities (or habits) of a person you know well. The person might be a member of your family, a friend, a roommate, a boss or supervisor, a neighbor, a teacher, or someone else. Listed below are some descriptive words that can be applied to people. They are only suggestions; you can write about other qualities as well.

Honest	Hardworking	Jealous
Bad-tempered	Supportive	Modest
Ambitious	Suspicious	Sarcastic
Bigoted	Open-minded	Self-centered
Considerate	Lazy	Spineless
Argumentative	Independent	Good-humored
Softhearted	Stubborn	Cooperative
Energetic	Flirtatious	Disciplined
Patient	Irresponsible	Sentimental
Reliable	Stingy	Defensive
Generous	Trustworthy	Dishonest
Persistent	Aggressive	Insensitive
Shy	Courageous	Unpretentious
Sloppy	Compulsive	Neat

You may want to write about three related qualities of one person (for example, "My brother is stubborn, bad-tempered, and suspicious") or about one quality that is apparent in different aspects of a person's life (for example, "My wife's sensitivity is apparent in her relationships with her friends at work, my parents, and our teenage son").

■ Writing Assignment 3

Write an essay that uses examples to develop one of the following statements or a related statement of your own.

> If you look hard enough, you can see complete strangers being kind to one another.
>
> The gossip tabloids sold at supermarket checkouts use several techniques to lure consumers into buying them.
>
> The Super Bowl is superhype, not supersport.
>
> The best things in life are definitely not free.
>
> Living with a roommate teaches you tolerance, adaptability, and patience.
>
> There's more joy in simple pleasures than in life's great events.
>
> Looking for a job is a demeaning process.
>
> Pets in the United States are treated like surrogate children.
>
> Our lives would be improved without the automobile.
>
> American culture is infatuated with violence.

Be sure to choose examples that actually support your thesis. They should be relevant facts, statistics, personal experiences, or incidents you have heard or read about.

Organize each paragraph by grouping several examples that support a particular point. Or use one extended example—an incident or story that may take up a full paragraph.

Save the paragraph containing the most vivid, convincing, or important examples for last.

■ Writing Assignment 4

Write an essay based on an outside reading. It might be a selection in one of the following books (many should be available in your college library) or another selection recommended by your instructor.

Walter Anderson, *Courage Is a Three-Letter Word*

Dave Barry, *Bad Habits*

Nora Ephron, *Crazy Salad*

Ellen Goodman, *Keeping in Touch* (or another collection of essays)

Bob Greene, *American Beat* or *Cheeseburgers*

Maxine Hong Kingston, *The Woman Warrior*

Harold S. Kushner, *When All You've Ever Wanted Isn't Enough*

Anne Morrow Lindbergh, *Gift from the Sea*

Alison Lurie, *The Language of Clothes*

Jessica Mitford, *The American Way of Death*

James Moffett, Ed., *Points of Departure*

Willliam Least Heat Moon, *Blue Highways*

Nancy R. Newhouse, Ed., *Hers*

Vance Packard, *Our Endangered Children* (or another book)

Richard Rodriguez, *The Hunger of Memory*

Andrew A. Rooney, *Word for Word* (or another collection of essays)

Berton Roueche, *The Medical Detectives*

Mike Royko, *Sez Who? Sez Me* (or another collection of essays)

Gloria Steinem, *Outrageous Acts and Everyday Rebellions*

Jim Trelease, *The Read-Aloud Handbook*

Marie Winn, *The Plug-In Drug* or *Children without Childhood*

Base your essay on some idea in the selection you have chosen and provide a series of examples to back up your idea. A student model follows.

The Victims in "Shooting an Elephant"

In "Shooting an Elephant," George Orwell describes how, as an English policeman in Burma, he was forced to destroy an animal that had killed a man. But the man the elephant crushes--a man who had died in "unendurable agony"--is only one of many victims in the story. The elephant, the Burmese natives, and Orwell himself are all, in some way, victims of their surroundings.

The elephant, first of all, is most obviously a victim. Although it knocks down a bamboo hut, raids a fruit stall, and finally kills a man, the animal does not deserve its fate--a long, painful death of "tortured gasps" and "shot after shot" poured "into his heart and down his throat." As Orwell makes clear, the elephant is a tame one that escapes while it is in a state of sexual heat. When Orwell finds the elephant, it is already beginning to calm down.

In fact, it is cleaning bunches of grass to eat by beating them against its knees with a "preoccupied grandmotherly air." The elephant should have been allowed to live, but it becomes a victim of Orwell and the crowd that is following him. The crowd wants "a bit of fun" in seeing the animal shot; the people also want the elephant meat. Orwell, who feels pressured by the crowd to act as the authority with the "magical rifle," shoots the elephant despite doubts about the rightness of his action. The elephant falls victim to the humans' cruelty and confusion.

The Burmese people are also victims. Orwell vividly describes the treatment some of them receive at the hands of the British authorities. Prisoners are penned in "stinking cages" and men who have been "flogged with bamboos" bear terrible scars. The Burmese people are victims, too, of poverty and powerlessness. As Orwell says, they have no weapons and are so "helpless" against the elephant. They live in flimsy huts, their children run naked, and they are hungry for the elephant's meat. Worst of all, the native people are victims of the English authorities' racism and prejudice. Some Europeans later criticize Orwell for shooting the elephant because "an elephant was worth more than any damn . . . coolie." Orwell himself begins to see the people only as "sneering yellow faces" and "evil-spirited little beasts" ready to humiliate him "with hideous laughter."

Finally, Orwell is a victim of his job and of his own ego. As a police officer, Orwell is resented by the Burmese people; he is jeered, hooted at, and tripped up on the football field. Orwell feels some sympathy for the Burmese, but in his job of doing the "dirty work" of the English authorities, he must keep silent. When Orwell is confronted with the problem of the elephant--should he shoot the creature, as the crowd wants, or allow the animal to live, as he knows is right?--he becomes a victim of the need to protect his own ego. In front of the crowd, Orwell puts on the "mask" of authority; as he says, "The people expected it of me and I had got to do it." If Orwell walks "feebly" away from the elephant, the crowd will laugh at him and embarrass him. So he acts--and kills.

In summary, "Shooting an Elephant" is an essay filled with victims. The elephant, the Burmese, and Orwell are all pushed along toward their destinies by forces they cannot control. Tragically, none can understand or communicate with the others; they are all victims in a drama of death.

■ Writing Assignment 5: Writing about a Reading Selection

Read the selection titled "The Thin Grey Line" on pages 402–404. Then write an essay with a thesis that rejects Marya Mannes' idea that dishonesty is on the upswing. Your thesis could be similar to this one: "Honesty is more characteristic of this society than dishonesty." In your introduction, refer to Mannes' essay and state that you disagree with her ideas. Here is a model introduction you might use:

> In "The Thin Grey Line," Marya Mannes argues that dishonesty and corruption are on the rise. She believes that the barrier between good and evil is breaking down because we have convinced ourselves that small dishonesties don't matter. But this point of view is inaccurate. Honesty is more characteristic of our society than dishonesty.

You might organize the essay by discussing, in separate paragraphs, any three of the following:

Honesty in school
Honesty on the job
Honesty toward government and other authorities
Honesty in public places

Support each of your topic sentences with specific examples. A person writing about "honesty in public places" might, for instance, flesh out the following incidents as examples supporting the topic sentence, "In public places, most people are honest, even if they are not being watched."

1. Each person buying a paper from a newspaper "honor box" takes only one.
2. A person finds a valuable watch in a rest room and turns it in to Lost and Found.
3. A waitress runs after a customer who has mistakenly left a large bill on the table.

Your examples should be as specific and vivid as you can make them in order to be convincing.

Write an outline for your essay by listing the areas you plan to cover and the examples you will use in the order that seems best to you.

In your conclusion, you might state that most people still seem to have a clear idea of the difference between right and wrong.

Note: As an alternative assignment, you may want to write an essay supporting Mannes' idea that dishonesty has increased in our society.

CAUSE
AND
EFFECT

Why did Janet decide to move out of her parents' house? What made you quit a well-paying job? Why are horror movies so popular? Why has Ben acted so depressed lately? Why did our team fail to make the league play-offs?

Every day we ask questions similar to those above and look for answers. We realize that many actions do not occur without causes, and we realize also that a given action can have a series of effects—for good or bad. By examining the causes or effects of an action, we seek to understand and explain things that happen in our lives.

You will be asked in this section to do some detective work by examining the cause of something or the effects of something. First read the three essays that follow and answer the questions about them. All three essays support their thesis statements by explaining a series of causes or a series of effects.

ESSAYS TO CONSIDER

A Necessary Decision

Have you ever seen a supermarket bag crammed full of medical bills for just one person? Well, I have. I had known that my mother was sick as a result of a failing kidney, but I had not realized how much trouble my parents were having in dealing with that sickness. Only when I had saved enough money to visit them in Florida did I discover just how critical the situation had become. The problems were so serious, in fact, that I had to make the decision to put my mother in a nursing home.

First, there were countless bills. Many were for drugs, since Mother was taking about twenty-four pills a day along with receiving insulin injections.

Then there were hospital bills for the initial diagnosis, for batteries of tests, and for the operation that prepared her for kidney dialysis. Next, there were the ambulance bills for my mother's trips three times a week to the dialysis clinic. And finally, there were clinic bills for $350 for each of the dozen or so treatments she had already had. Unable to contend with the insurance paperwork needed to pay for the bills, my father had stuffed all incoming bills into a Winn-Dixie shopping bag in the closet.

She was confined to a wheelchair and needed help moving around. She had to have assistance in getting dressed and undressed, going to the bathroom, and getting into and out of bed. She also needed a very specialized diet involving a combination of foods for renal, diabetic, and gallbladder patients. In addition, she required emotional support. Sometimes she was so depressed, she wouldn't eat unless she was urged to. "I'm going to die; just let me die in peace," she would say, or "You don't love me anymore now that I'm sick." These constant needs, I concluded, would benefit from professional care.

Finally, I was concerned not only with my mother's needs but also with my father's welfare. He assumed total responsibility for my mother. Since he doesn't drive, he walked everywhere, including to the grocery store, drugstore, laundromat, hospital, and clinic. Also, he did all the housework; he fed, dressed, bathed, and medicated my mother; and he prepared her special meals and snacks. In addition, her behavior was a strain on him. She would wait until he was in the kitchen, and then she would call the police or ambulance to say she was dying. Or she would wait until 3 A.M. and telephone each of her children to say good-bye. Never robust, my father dropped from 125 pounds to 98 pounds under the strain, caught a bad cold, and finally telephoned me for help.

I conferred with a social worker, found a nursing home, and signed my mother in. My father is able to get a bus that takes him, within twenty minutes, right to the nursing home door. He has gained weight and has gotten back in control of things to the point where he can handle the paperwork again. Even my mother has recovered to the extent that she is making my daughter a quilt. My decision was not easy, but it has turned out to be the best one for both my parents.

The Joys of an Old Car

Some of my friends can't believe my car still runs. Others laugh when they see it parked outside the house and ask if it's an antique. But they aren't being fair to my fourteen-year-old Datsun. In fact, my "antique" has opened my eyes to the rewards of owning an old car.

One obvious reward is economy. Fourteen years ago, when my husband and I were newly married and nearly broke, we bought the car--a shiny, red, year-old leftover--for a mere $1800. Today it would cost five times as much.

We save money on insurance, since it's no longer worthwhile for us to have collision coverage. Old age has even been kind to the Datsun's engine, which required only three major repairs in the last several years. And it still delivers twenty-six miles per gallon in the city and thirty-eight on the highway--not bad for a senior citizen.

The second benefit is dependability. If a Datsun passes the twenty-thousand-mile mark with no major problems, it will probably go on forever. Our Datsun breezed past that mark many years ago and has run almost perfectly ever since. Even on the coldest, snowiest mornings, I can count on my car to sputter to life and roll surefootedly down the driveway. The only time it didn't start, unfortunately, was the day I had a final exam. The Datsun may have the body of an old car, but beneath its elderly hood hums the engine of a teenager.

Last of all, there is the advantage of familiarity. When I open the door and slide into the driver's seat, the soft vinyl envelops me like a well-worn glove. I know to the millimeter exactly how much room I have when I turn a corner or back into a streetside parking space. When my gas gauge is on empty, I know that 1.3 gallons are still in reserve and I can plan accordingly. The front wheels invariably begin to shake when I go more than fifty-five miles an hour, reminding me that I am exceeding the speed limit. With the Datsun, the only surprises I face are the ones from other drivers.

I prize my fourteen-year-old Datsun's economy and dependability, and most of all, its familiarity. It is faded, predictable, and comfortable, like a well-worn pair of jeans. And, like a well-worn pair of jeans, it will be difficult to throw away.

Stresses of Being a Celebrity

Last week, a woman signing herself "Want the Truth in Westport" wrote to Ann Landers with a question she just had to have answered. "Please find out for sure," she begged the columnist, "whether or not Lena Horne has had a face-lift." Fortunately for Ms. Horne's privacy, Ann Landers refused to answer the question. But the incident disturbed me. How awful it would be to be a celebrity, I thought, and always be in the public eye. Celebrities lead very stressful lives, for no matter how glamorous or powerful they are, they have too little privacy, too much pressure, and no safety.

For one thing, celebrities don't have the privacy an ordinary person has. The most personal details of their lives are splashed all over the front pages of the National Enquirer and the Globe so that bored supermarket shoppers can read about "Liz and Her New Love" or "Burt's Deepest Fear." Even a celebrity's family is hauled into the spotlight. A teenage son's arrest for pot possession or a wife's drinking problem becomes the subject of glaring headlines. Photographers hound celebrities at their homes, in restaurants, and on the street, hoping to get a picture of a Jackie Onassis in curlers or a Burt Reynolds in a fistfight. When celebrities try to do the things that normal people do, like eat out or attend a football game, they run the risk of being interrupted by thoughtless autograph hounds or mobbed by aggressive fans.

In addition, celebrities are under constant pressure. Their physical appearance is always under observation. Famous women, especially, suffer from the "she really looks old" or the "boy, has she put on weight" spotlight. Unflattering pictures of celebrities are photographers' prizes to be sold to the highest bidder; this increases the pressure on celebrities to look good at all times. Famous people are also under pressure to act calm and collected under any circumstances. There's no freedom to blow off steam or to do something just a little crazy. Therefore, people who forget this must suffer the consequences.

Most important, celebrities must deal with the stress of being in constant danger. The friendly grabs, hugs, and kisses of enthusiastic fans can quickly turn into uncontrolled assaults on a celebrity's hair, clothes, and car. Celebrities often get strange letters from people who become obsessed with their idols or from people who threaten to harm them. The attempt to kill Ronald Reagan and the murder of John Lennon came about because two unbalanced people tried to transfer the celebrity's fame to themselves. Famous people must live with the fact that they are always fair game--and never out of season.

Some people dream of starring roles, their names in lights, and their pictures on the cover of People magazine. I'm not one of them, though. A famous person gives up private life, feels pressured all the time, and is never completely safe. So let someone else have that cover story. I'd rather lead an ordinary, but calm, life than a stress-filled public one.

■ Questions

About Unity

1. Which supporting paragraph in "A Necessary Decision" lacks a topic sentence?

   _____

2. Which sentence in the second supporting paragraph of "The Joys of an Old Car" should be omitted in the interest of paragraph unity?

   _____

3. Rewrite the thesis statement of "The Joys of an Old Car" to include a plan of development.

   _____

   _____

About Support

4. How many effects are given to develop the thesis in ''Stresses of Being a Celebrity''?

    _____ 1   _____ 2   _____ 3   _____ 4

    How many are given in ''The Joys of an Old Car''?

    _____ 1   _____ 2   _____ 3   _____ 4

5. After which sentence in the second supporting paragraph of ''Stresses of Being a Celebrity'' are more specific details needed?

    _____

6. How many examples are given to support the topic sentence ''One obvious reward is economy'' in ''The Joys of an Old Car''?

    _____

About Coherence

7. Which topic sentence in ''A Necessary Decision'' functions as a linking sentence between paragraphs?

    _____

8. What are the three main transition words in the second supporting paragraph of ''Stresses of Being a Celebrity''?

    _____   _____   _____

9. What are the three transition words in ''The Joys of an Old Car'' that signal the three major points of support for the thesis?

    _____   _____   _____

About the Introduction

10. Select from below the two methods of introduction that combine to form the first paragraph of ''Stresses of Being a Celebrity.''
    a. Broad, general statement narrowing to thesis
    b. Idea that is the opposite of the one to be developed
    c. Quotation
    d. Anecdote
    e. Questions

Activity 1

Complete the following outline of the essay titled ''A Necessary Decision.'' The effect is the author's decision to put her mother in a nursing home; the causes of that decision are what make up each supporting paragraph. Summarize each cause in a few words. The first cause and one detail are given for you as an example.

Thesis: The problems were so serious, in fact, that I had to make the decision to put my mother in a nursing home.

1. *Countless bills* _____
    a. *Bills for drugs* _____
    b. _____
    c. _____
    d. _____
2. _____
    a. _____
    b. _____
    c. _____
3. _____
    a. _____
    b. _____
    c. _____

Activity 2

In scratch-outline form on separate paper, provide brief causes or effects for at least four of the ten statements below. Note the example. Make sure that you have three *separate* and *distinct* items for each statement. Also, indicate whether you have listed three causes or three effects.

Example   Many youngsters are terrified of school.

    1. *Afraid of not being liked by other students* ⎫
    2. *Fearful of failing tests*   ⎬ *Causes*
    3. *Intimidated by teachers*   ⎭

1. The availability of fast-food outlets has changed the eating habits of many Americans.

2. I would recommend (*or* not recommend) _____ (*name a certain course*) to other students.

3. The women's movement has had an enormous impact on women's lives.

4. There are several steps Congress should take to make automobile driving a safer matter.

5. Exercise has changed my life.

6. Students often have trouble adjusting to college for several reasons.

7. Videocassette recorders have changed the way we watch television.

8. _____ is a popular sport for several reasons.

9. Computers have begun to affect the lives of many families.

10. There are several advantages (*or* drawbacks) to living at home while going to school.

WRITING THE ESSAY

■ Writing Assignment 1

Decide, perhaps through discussion with your instructor or classmates, which of the outlines prepared in Activity 2 (page 131) would be most promising to develop into an essay. Make sure that your supporting reasons are logical ones that actually back up your thesis statement. Ask yourself in each case, "Does this reason truly support my thesis idea?"

How to Proceed

a   On separate paper, make a list of details that might go under each of the supporting points. Provide more details than you can possibly use. Here, for example, are the details generated by the writer of "The Joys of an Old Car" when she was working on her third supporting paragraph:

Car's familiarity:

Know how much space I have to park
Front wheels shake at fifty-five miles per hour
Know what's in glove compartment
Worn seat--comfortable
Know tire inflation (pounds of pressure)
Can turn corners expertly (space)

Gas tank has reserve
Radio push buttons are set for favorite stations
Know how hard to press brake
Know that reverse gear is over, <u>then</u> down

b Decide which details you will use to develop each of your supporting paragraphs. Also, number the details in the order in which you will present them. Here is how the writer of "The Joys of an Old Car" made decisions about the details in her final supporting paragraph:

2 Know how much space I have to park
4 Front wheels shake at fifty-five miles per hour
~~Know what's in glove compartment~~
1 Worn seat--comfortable
~~Know tire inflation (pounds of pressure)~~
2 Can turn corners expertly (space)
3 Gas tank has reserve
~~Radio push buttons are set for favorite stations~~
~~Know how hard to press brake~~
~~Know that reverse gear is over, then down~~

c As you are working on the drafts of your paper, refer to the checklist on the inside front cover. Make sure that you can answer *Yes* to the questions about unity, support, and coherence.

d You may also want to refer to pages 49–54 for suggestions on writing an effective introduction and conclusion to your essay.

e Finally, use the checklist on the inside front cover when you are proofreading the next-to-final draft of your paper for sentence-skills mistakes, including spelling.

■ **Writing Assignment 2**

Below are six possible thesis statements for a "cause" paper and six for an "effect" paper. In scratch-outline form, provide brief supporting points for four of the twelve statements.

List the Causes

1. Americans tend to get married later in life than they used to.
2. Childhood is the unhappiest time of life.
3. Being young is better than being old. *Or:* Being old is better than being young.
4. _____ is the most difficult course I have ever taken.

5. My relationship with _____ (name a relative, employer, or friend) is better than ever.

6. It is easy to fall into an unhealthy diet in our society.

List the Effects

7. Punishment for certain crimes should take the form of community service.

8. Growing up in the family I have has influenced my life in important ways.

9. The average workweek should be no more than thirty hours long.

10. A bad (*or* good) teacher can affect students in significant ways.

11. The drinking age should be raised to twenty-one in every state.

12. The fact that both parents often work has led to a number of changes in the typical family household.

■ Writing Assignment 3

If friendly aliens from a highly developed civilization decided to visit our planet, they would encounter a contradictory race of beings—us. We human beings would have reasons to feel both proud and ashamed of the kind of society the aliens would encounter. Write an essay explaining whether you would be proud or ashamed of the state of the human race today. Give reasons for your feeling.

■ Writing Assignment 4

Write an essay in which you advance an idea about a poem, story, play, literary essay, or novel. The work you choose may be assigned by your instructor or require your instructor's approval. Use a series of two or more reasons and specific supporting evidence for each reason to develop your idea. A student model follows.

Paul's Suicide

Paul, the main character in Willa Cather's short story "Paul's Case," is a young man on a collision course with death. As Cather reveals Paul's story, we learn about elements of Paul's personality that inevitably come together and cause his suicide. Paul takes his own life as a result of his inability to conform to his society, his passive nature, and his emotional isolation.

First of all, Paul cannot conform to the standards of his own society. At school, Paul advertises his desire to be part of another, more glamorous world by wearing fancy clothes that set him apart from the other students. At home on Cordelia Street, Paul despises everything about his middle-class neighborhood. He hates the houses "permeated by kitchen odors," the "ugliness and commonness of his own home," and the respectable neighbors sitting on their front stoops every Sunday, "their stomachs comfortably protruding." Paul's father hopes that Paul will settle down and become like the young man next door, a nearsighted clerk who works for a corporate steel magnate. Paul, however, is repelled by the young man and all he represents. It seems inevitable, then, that Paul will not be able to cope with the office job his father obtains for him at the firm of Denny & Carson; and this inability to conform will, in turn, lead to Paul's theft of a thousand dollars.

Paul's suicide is also due, in part, to his passive nature. Throughout his life, Paul has been an observer and an onlooker. Paul's only escape from the prison of his daily life comes from his job as an usher at Pittsburgh's Carnegie Hall; he lives for the moments when he can watch the actors, singers, and musicians. However, Paul has no desire to be an actor or musician. As Cather says, ". . . What he wanted was to see, to be in the atmosphere, float on the wave of it, to be carried out . . . away from everything." Although Paul steals the money and flees to New York, these uncharacteristic actions underscore the desperation he feels. Once at the Waldorf in New York, Paul is again content to observe the glamorous world he has craved for so long: "He had no especial desire to meet or to know any of these people; all he demanded was the right to look on and conjecture, to watch the pageant." During his brief stay in the city, Paul enjoys simply sitting in his luxurious rooms, glimpsing the show of city life through a magical curtain of snow. At the end, when the forces of ordinary life begin to close in again, Paul kills himself. But it is typical that he does not use the gun he has bought. Rather, more in keeping with his passive nature, Paul lets himself fall under the wheels of a train.

Finally, Paul ends his life because he is emotionally isolated. Throughout the story, not one person makes any real contact with Paul. His teachers do not understand him and merely resent the attitude of false bravado that he uses as a defense. Paul's mother is dead; he cannot even remember her. Paul is completely alienated from his father, who obviously cares for him but who cannot feel close to his withdrawn, unhappy son. To Paul, his father is only the man waiting at the top of the stairs, "his hairy legs sticking out of his nightshirt," who will greet him with "inquiries and reproaches." When Paul meets a college boy in New York, they share a night on the town. But the "champagne friendship" ends with a "singularly cool" parting. Paul is not the kind of person who can let himself go or confide in one of his peers. For the most part, Paul's isolation is self-imposed. He has drifted so far into his fantasy life that people in the "real" world are treated like invaders. As he allows no one to enter his dream, there is no one Paul can turn to for understanding.

The combination of these personality factors--inability to conform, passivity, and emotional isolation--makes Paul's tragic suicide inevitable. Before he jumps in front of the train, Paul scoops a hole in the snow and buries the carnation that he has been wearing in his buttonhole. Like a hothouse flower in the winter, Paul has a fragile nature that cannot survive its hostile environment.

■ **Writing Assignment 5:**
Writing about a Reading Selection

Read the essay titled "The Plug-In Drug" on pages 457–463. Then write an essay that develops *either* of the following statements:

■ There are three reasons why people watch so much television.

■ There are three reasons why people should not watch as much television as they do.

Use specific examples to support each reason—either examples based on your observations of real households or hypothetical examples using fictionalized typical households. (See page 94 on how to use hypothetical examples.)

To get started, you may find it helpful to freewrite for several minutes on the topic of television: the needs it satisfies, the pleasures it gives us, the problems it hides, the purpose it serves in the household.

PROCESS

Every day we perform many activities that are *processes*, that is, series of steps carried out in a definite order. Many of these processes are familiar and automatic: for example, loading film in a camera, diapering a baby, or making an omelet. We are thus seldom aware of the sequence of steps that makes up each activity. In other cases, such as when a person asks us for directions to a particular place or when we try to read and follow the directions for a new table game that someone has given us, we may be painfully conscious of the whole series of steps involved in the process.

In this section, you will be asked to write a *process essay*—one that explains clearly how to do or make something. To prepare for this assignment, you should first read the student process papers below and then respond to the questions that follow.

ESSAYS TO CONSIDER

Successful Exercise

Regular exercise is something like the weather--we all talk about it, but we tend not to do anything about it! Television exercise classes, records and tapes, and new videocassettes and disks, as well as the instructions in books, magazines, and pamphlets, now make it easy to have a personal, low-cost exercise program without leaving home. However, for success in exercise, you should follow a simple plan consisting of arranging the time, making preparations, and following the sequence with care.

To begin with, set aside a regular time for exercise. If you have a heavy schedule at work or school, this may be difficult, since you're rushed in the morning and exhausted at night, and you have no time in between. However, one solution is simply to get up half an hour earlier in the morning. Look at it this way: If you're already getting up too early, what's an extra half hour? Of course, that time could be cut to fifteen minutes earlier if you could lay out your clothes, set the breakfast table, fill the coffee maker, and gather your books and materials for the next day before you go to bed.

Next, prepare for your exercise session. To begin with, get yourself ready by not eating or drinking anything before exercising. Why risk an upset stomach? Then, dress comfortably in something that allows you to move freely. Since you'll be in your own home, there's no need to invest in a high-fashion dance costume. A loose T shirt and shorts are good. A bathing suit is great in summer, and in winter a set of long underwear is warm and comfortable. If your hair tends to flop in your eyes, pin it back or wear a headband or scarf. Prepare the exercise area, too. Turn off the phone and lock the door to prevent interruptions. Shove the coffee table out of the way so you won't bruise yourself on it or other furniture. Finally, get out the simple materials you'll need to exercise on.

If this is your first attempt at exercising, start slowly. You do not need to do each movement the full number of times at first, but you should try each one. After five or six sessions, you should be able to do each one the full number of times. Try to move in a smooth, rhythmic way; doing so will help prevent injuries and pulled muscles. Pretend you're a dancer and make each move graceful, even if it's just climbing up off the floor. After the last exercise, give yourself five minutes to relax and cool off--you have earned it. Finally, put those sore muscles under a hot shower and get ready for a great day.

Establishing an exercise program isn't difficult, but it can't be achieved by reading about it, talking about it, or watching models exercise on television. To begin with, you're going to have to get up off that couch and do something about it. Otherwise, as my doctor likes to say, "If you don't use it, you'll lose it."

How to Complain

I'm not just a consumer--I'm a victim. If I order a product, it is sure to arrive in the wrong color, size, or quantity. If I hire people to do repairs, they never arrive on the day scheduled. If I owe a bill, the computer is bound to overcharge me. Therefore, in self-defense, I have developed the following consumer's guide to complaining effectively.

The first step is getting organized. I save all sales slips and original boxes. Also, I keep a special file for warranty cards and appliance guarantees. This file does not prevent a product from falling apart the day after the guarantee runs out. One of the problems in our country is the shoddy workmanship that goes into many products. However, these facts give me the ammunition I need to make a complaint. I know the date of the purchase, the correct price (or service charge), where the item was purchased, and an exact description of the product, including model and serial numbers. When I compose my letter of complaint, I find it is not necessary to exaggerate. I just stick to the facts.

The next step is to send the complaint to the person who will get results quickly. My experience has shown that the president of a company is the best person to contact. I call the company to find out the president's name and make sure I note the proper spelling. Then I write directly to that person, and I usually get prompt action. For example, the head of AMF arranged to replace my son's ten-speed "lemon" when it fell apart piece by piece in less than a year. Another time, the president of a Philadelphia department store finally had a twenty-dollar overcharge on my bill corrected after three months of arguing with the computer had brought no results.

If I get no response to a written complaint within ten days, I follow through with a personal telephone call. When I had a new bathtub installed a few years ago, the plumber left a gritty black substance on the bottom of the tub. No amount of scrubbing could remove it. I tried every cleanser on the supermarket shelf, but I still had a dirty tub. The plumber shrugged off my complaints and said to try Fantastik. The manufacturer never answered my letter. Finally, I made a personal phone call to the president of the firm. Within days a well-dressed executive showed up at my door. In a business suit, white shirt, striped tie, and rubber gloves, he cleaned the tub. Before he left, he scolded in an angry voice, "You didn't have to call the president." The point is, I did have to call the president. No one else cared enough to solve the problem.

Therefore, my advice to consumers is to keep accurate records, and when you have to complain, go right to the top. It has always worked for me.

How to Pick the Perfect Class Schedule

As you look at the punch cards or computer printout that lists your courses for next semester, do you experience a terrible sinking feeling in the pit of your stomach? Have you gotten stuck with unwanted courses or a depressing time schedule that cannot be changed? If so, you obviously don't know how to select the perfect schedule. But by following a few simple procedures, you can begin any semester with the right courses at the most convenient times.

First, you must find the right courses. These are the ones that combine the least amount of work with the fewest tests and the most lenient professors. Ask your friends and acquaintances about courses in which they received A's after attending only 25 percent of the classes. Ask around, too, to see which professors have given the same tests for the last fifteen years.

Photocopies of these tests are usually cheap and widely available. Then, pick up a copy of the master schedule and study it carefully. Find the telltale course titles that signal an easy glide through a painless subject. Look for titles like "History of the Animated Cartoon," "Arts and Crafts for Beginners," and "Rock Music of the 1950s."

Next, when you have accumulated lists of easy instructors and subjects, you can begin to block out time periods. The ideal schedule will vary according to your individual needs. If you stay up late in order to watch old movies or work the graveyard shift, you may want a daily schedule that begins no sooner than noon. You should schedule only afternoon courses, too, if you're one of those people who would rather be tortured than forced to leave a warm, cozy bed in the morning. On the other hand, if you are a "lark" who bounds out of bed at dawn, you may want to get your classes out of the way as early as possible. That way you have the rest of the day free. Morning classes are also necessary if you are a soap opera fanatic who can't miss one day's events in Pine Valley or Port Charles.

Finally, you must outsmart the registration process. You want your ideal schedule to pass through official channels untouched. The main way to do this is to register early. Ignore things like registration by first letter of last name or by number of accumulated credits. Desperate stories about dying relatives or heartless employers will get you quickly through a registration line. If a course does happen to be closed because you simply couldn't register at 7:00 A.M., you may still be able to get in. Talk to the professor and convince him or her that a serious, ambitious, hardworking student like yourself would be a shining asset to the class. Be sure to carry a list of backup courses to registration, though, just in case one of your chosen classes switches professors or changes time periods. Be ready to fill in vacant slots with courses that meet your strict requirements.

By following these suggestions, any student can pick the perfect class schedule. College can thus become a nonirritating, almost pleasant activity that disrupts your real life as little as possible. And you never know--you might even learn something in "Creative TV Watching."

■ **Questions**

About Unity

1. Which supporting paragraph in "Successful Exercise" lacks a topic sentence?

---

2. Which sentence in the first supporting paragraph of "How to Complain" should be omitted in the interest of paragraph unity?

About Support

3. After which sentence in the second supporting paragraph in "Successful Exercise" are more specific details needed?

   _____

4. Which paragraph in "How to Complain" uses a single extended example to support its topic sentence?

   _____

5. What are the three key stages in the process of "How to Complain"?

   a. _____

   b. _____

   c. _____

6. What are the three key stages in the process of "Picking the Perfect Class Schedule"?

   a. _____

   b. _____

   c. _____

About Coherence

7. What are the four main transition words in the second supporting paragraph of "Successful Exercise"?

   _____   _____   _____   _____

8. Which topic sentence in "How to Pick the Perfect Class Schedule" functions as a linking sentence between paragraphs?

   _____

About the Introduction and Conclusion

9. Which method of introduction is used in "How to Pick the Perfect Class Schedule"?

   _____

10. Which essay ends with a recommendation?

   _____

WRITING THE ESSAY

■ Writing Assignment 1

Choose one of the ten topics below that you think you can write about in a process paper.

How to do grocery shopping in a minimum of time
How to select a car (new or used), apartment, or home
How to do household cleaning efficiently
How to drive defensively
How to protect a home from burglars
How to gain or lose weight
How to relax
How to study for an important exam
How to play a position (third base, guard, goalie, etc.) in a sport skillfully
How to plan an event (party, wedding, garage sale, etc.)

How to Proceed

a Now freewrite for ten minutes on the topic you have tentatively chosen. Do not worry about spelling, grammar, organization, or other matters of correct form. Just write whatever comes into your head regarding the topic. Keep writing for more than ten minutes if added details about the topic occur to you. This freewriting will give you a base of raw material that you can draw on in the next phase of your work on the essay. After freewriting for ten minutes, you should have a sense of whether there is enough material available for you to write a process essay about the topic. If so, continue as explained below. If not, choose another topic and freewrite about *it* for ten minutes.

b State your thesis in a single clear sentence. In your thesis, you can (1) say it is important that your audience know about this process (''Knowing how to register a complaint can save time and frustration'') or (2) state your opinion of this process (''Growing your own tomatoes is easier than you might think'').

c Make a list of all the steps that you are describing. Here, for example, is the list prepared by the author of ''How to Complain'':

Save sales slips and original boxes
Engrave items with ID number in case of burglary
Write letter of complaint

Make photocopy of letter
Create file of warranties and guarantees
Send complaint letter directly to president
Call company for president's name
Follow through with telephone call if no response
Make thank-you call after action is taken

d   Number your items in time order; strike out items that do not fit in the list; add others you can think of. Thus:

1   Save sales slips and original boxes
~~Engrave items with ID number in case of burglary~~
4   Write letter of complaint
~~Make photocopy of letter~~
2   Create file of warranties and guarantees
5   Send complaint letter directly to president
3   Call company for president's name
6   Follow through with telephone call if no response
~~Make thank-you call after action is taken~~

e   After making the list, decide how the items can be grouped into a minimum of three steps. For example, with "How to Complain," you might divide the process into (1) getting organized, (2) sending the complaint to the president, and (3) following up with further action. Or, with a topic like "How to Grow Tomatoes," you might divide the process into (1) soil preparation, (2) planting, and (3) care.

f   Use your list as a guide to write the first rough draft of your paper. As you write, try to think of additional details that will develop your opening sentence. Do not expect to finish your paper in one draft. You should, in fact, be ready to write a series of lists and drafts as you work toward the goals of unity, support, and coherence.

g   Be sure to use transitions such as *first, next, also, then, after, now, during,* and *finally* so that your paper moves smoothly and clearly from one step in the process to the next.

h   While working on your paper, refer to the checklist on the inside front cover to make sure you can answer *Yes* to the questions about unity, support, and coherence. Also, refer to the checklist when you proofread the next-to-final draft of your paper for sentence-skills mistakes, including spelling.

■ **Writing Assignment 2**

Any one of the topics below can be written as a process paper. Follow the steps suggested for the first essay.

> How to break a bad habit
> How to live with a two-year-old, a teenager, or a parent
> How to make someone like you
> How to make excuses
> How to fall out of love
> How to improve reading skills
> How to do well at a job interview
> How to care for an aging relative
> How to stay young
> How to improve a school or a place of work

■ **Writing Assignment 3**

Everyone is an expert at something. Write a process essay on some skill that you can perform very well. Write from the point of view that "This is how _____ *should* be done." (Remember that a skill can be anything from "starting a fire" to "setting up a new stereo system" to "dealing with unpleasant customers" to "using a personal computer.")

■ **Writing Assignment 4:**
Writing about a Reading Selection

Do *either* of the following.

Option 1:   Read the selection titled "Brett Hauser: Supermarket Box Boy" on pages 377–379. Then write a process essay on how you perform a certain task at a present job (or did at some past job)—how to ring up a charge slip, take inventory, make french fries, load a truck, or do any other task you know how to do. (If you have never had a job, describe how you do a certain household chore.)

You could start by imagining how you would train someone else to perform the task; break it down into a series of clear steps. Then follow steps *d* through *h* under "How to Proceed" on pages 143–144.

Think of your audience for the paper as someone who is going to take over the job for you. Make your essay detailed enough so that it can serve as a brief training guide for that person.

Option 2: Read the selection titled ''How to Make It in College, Now That You're Here'' on pages 424–429. Then write a process essay with the thesis, ''Here are the tips that will help a student succeed in _____'' (name a course in which you are now enrolled or one that you have taken in the past). To get started, think of the advice you would like to have had *before* you took that particular course: What would you have wanted to know about the professor? The assignments? The exams? Policies about attendance, lateness, and so on? Pick three tips that you believe would be most helpful to another student about to enroll in the class, and discuss each one in a separate supporting paragraph. Model your introduction after the one in ''How to Make It in College'' by telling your readers that, on the basis of your own experience, you are going to pass on the secrets for succeeding in this course.

Below are three sample topic sentences for an essay on ''How to Succeed in Communications 101.''

First topic sentence: First of all, a student who wants a good grade in Communications 101 should be prepared at every class meeting for a surprise quiz.

Second topic sentence: In addition, students should speak up during class discussions, for Professor Knox adds ''participation'' into final grades.

Third topic sentence: Most important, students should start early on term papers and turn them in on time.

COMPARISON AND CONTRAST

Comparison and contrast are two thought processes we constantly perform in everyday life. When we *compare* two things, we show how they are similar; when we *contrast* two things, we show how they are different. We may compare or contrast two brand-name products (for example, Sony versus Zenith TV), or two television shows, or two cars, or two teachers, or two jobs, or two friends, or two courses of action we can take within a given situation. The purpose of comparing or contrasting is to understand each of the two things more clearly and, at times, to make judgments about them.

You will be asked in this section to write a paper of comparison or contrast. To help you prepare for this assignment, first read the three essays ahead. Then answer the questions and do the activities that follow the essays.

ESSAYS TO CONSIDER

Second Marriage

Married people live "happily ever after" in fairy tales, but they do so less and less often in real life. I, like many of my friends, got married, divorced, and remarried. I suppose, to some people, I'm a failure. After all, I broke my first solemn promise to "love and cherish until death us do part." But I feel that I'm finally a success. I learned from the mistakes I made in my first marriage. This time around, the ways my husband and I share our free time, make decisions, and deal with problems are very different.

I learned, first of all, not to be a clinging vine. In my first marriage, I felt that every moment we spent apart was wasted. If Ray wanted to go out to a bar with his friends to watch a football game, I felt rejected and talked him into staying home. I wouldn't accept an offer to go to a movie or join an exercise class if it meant that Ray would be home alone. I realize now that we were often on edge or angry with each other just because we spent too much time together. In contrast, my second husband and I spend some of our free time apart and try to have interests of our own. I have started playing racquetball at a health club, and David sometimes takes off to go to the local auto races with his friends. When we are together, we aren't bored with each other; our separate interests make us more interesting people.

I learned not only to be apart sometimes but also to work together when it's time to make decisions. When Ray and I were married, I left all the important decisions to him. He decided how we would spend money, whether we should sell the car or fix it, and where to take a vacation. I know now that I went along with this so that I wouldn't have to take the responsibility when things went wrong. I could always end an argument by saying, "It was your fault!" With my second marriage, I am really trying to be a full partner. We ask each other's opinions on major decisions and try to compromise if we disagree. If we make the wrong choice, we're equally guilty. When we recently rented an apartment, for example, we both had to take the blame for not noticing the drafty windows and the "no pets" clause in our lease.

Maybe the most important thing I've learned is to be a grown-up about facing problems. David and I have made a vow to face our troubles like adults. If we're mad at each other or worried and upset, we say how we feel. Rather than hide behind our own misery, we talk about the problem until we discover how to fix it. Everybody argues or has to deal with the occasional crisis, but Ray and I always reacted like children to these stormy times. I would lock myself in the spare bedroom and pout. Ray would stalk out of the house, slam the door, and race off in the car. Then I would cry and worry till he returned.

I wish that my first marriage hadn't been the place where I learned how to make a relationship work, but at least I did learn. I feel better now about being an independent person, about making decisions, and about facing problems. My second marriage isn't perfect, but it doesn't have the deep flaws that made the first one fall apart.

A Vote for McDonald's

For my birthday this month, my wife has offered to treat me to dinner at the restaurant of my choice. I think she expects me to ask for a meal at the Chalet, the classiest, most expensive restaurant in town. However, I'm going to eat my birthday dinner at McDonald's. When I compare the two restaurants, the advantages of eating at McDonald's are clear.

For one thing, going to the Chalet is more difficult than going to McDonald's. The Chalet has a jacket-and-tie rule, which means I have to dig a sport coat and tie out of the back of my closet, make sure they're semiclean, and try to steam out the wrinkles somehow. The Chalet also requires advance reservations. Since it is downtown, I have to leave an hour early to give myself time to find a parking space within six blocks of the restaurant. The Chalet cancels reservations if a party is more than ten minutes late. Going to McDonald's, on the other hand, is easy. I can feel comfortable wearing jeans or a warm-up suit. I don't have to do any advance planning. I can leave my house whenever I'm ready and pull into a doorside parking space within fifteen minutes.

The Chalet is a dimly lit, formal place. While I'm struggling to see what's on my plate, I worry that I'll knock one of the fragile glass vases off the table. The waiters at the Chalet can be uncomfortably formal, too. As I awkwardly pronounce the French words on the menu, I get the feeling that I don't quite live up to their standards. Even though the food at the Chalet is gourmet, I prefer simpler meals. I don't like unfamiliar food swimming in dead-white sauce or covered with pie pastry. Eating at the Chalet is, to me, less enjoyable than eating at McDonald's. McDonald's is a pleasant place where I feel at ease. It is well lighted, and the bright-colored decor is informal. The employees serve with a smile, and the food is easy to pronounce and identify. I know what I'm going to get when I order a certain type of sandwich.

The most important difference between the Chalet and McDonald's, though, is the price difference. Dinner for two at the Chalet, even one without appetizers or desserts, would easily cost forty dollars. And the forty dollars doesn't include the cost of parking the car and tipping the waiter, which can come to an additional ten dollars. Once, I forgot to bring enough money. At McDonald's, a filling meal for two will cost around six dollars. With the extra forty-four dollars, my wife and I can eat at McDonald's seven more times, or go to the movies five times, or buy play-off tickets to a football game.

So, for my birthday dinner celebration, or any other time, I prefer to eat at McDonald's. It is convenient, friendly, and cheap. And with the money my wife saves by taking me to McDonald's, she can buy me what I really want for my birthday--a new Sears power saw.

Studying: Then and Now

One June day, I staggered into a high school classroom to take my final exam in United States History IV. Bleary-eyed from an all-night study session, I checked my "cheat sheets," which were taped inside the cuffs of my long-sleeved shirt. I had made my usual desperate effort to cram the night before, with the usual dismal results--I had made it only to page seventy-five of a four-hundred-page textbook. My high school study habits, obviously, were a mess. But, in college, I've made an attempt to reform my note-taking, studying, and test-taking skills.

Taking notes is one thing I've learned to do better since high school days. I used to lose interest in what I was doing and begin doodling, drawing Martians, or seeing what my signature would look like if I married the cute guy in the second row. Now, however, I try not to let my mind wander, and I pull my thoughts back into focus when they begin to go fuzzy. In high school, my notes often looked like something written in Arabic. In college, I've learned to use a semiprint writing style that makes my notes understandable. When I would look over my high school notes, I couldn't understand them. There would be a word like "Reconstruction," then a big blank, then the word "important." Weeks later, I had no idea what Reconstruction was or why it was important. I've since learned to write down connecting ideas, even if I have to take the time to do it after class.

Ordinary during-the-term studying is another area where I've made changes. In high school, I let reading assignments go. I told myself that I'd have no trouble catching up on two hundred pages during a fifteen-minute bus ride to school. College courses have taught me to keep pace with the work. Otherwise, I feel as though I'm sinking into a quicksand of unread material. When I finally read the high school assignment, my eyes would run over the words but my brain would be plotting how to get the car for Saturday night. Now, I use several techniques that force me to really concentrate on my reading.

In addition to learning how to cope with daily work, I've also learned to handle study sessions for big tests. My all-night study sessions in high school were experiments in self-torture. Around 2:00 A.M., my mind, like a soaked sponge, simply stopped absorbing things. Now, I space out exam study sessions over several days. That way, the night before can be devoted to an overall review rather than raw memorizing. Most important, though, I've changed my attitude toward tests. In high school, I thought tests were mysterious things with completely unpredictable questions. Now, I ask teachers about the kinds of questions that will be on the exam, and I try to "psych out" which areas or facts teachers are likely to ask about. These practices really work, and for me they've taken much of the fear and mystery out of tests.

Since I've reformed, note-taking and studying are not as tough as they once were. And there's been one benefit that makes the work worthwhile: My college grade sheets look much different from the red-splotched ones of high school days.

■ Questions

About Unity

1. In which supporting paragraph of "A Vote for McDonald's" is the topic sentence in the middle rather than, more appropriately, at the beginning?

2. Which sentence in the third supporting paragraph of "A Vote for Mc-Donald's" should be omitted in the interest of paragraph unity?

_____

About Support

3. After which sentence in the second supporting paragraph of "Studying: Then and Now" are more supporting details needed?

_____

4. In which sentence in the second supporting paragraph of "A Vote for McDonald's" are more supporting details needed?

_____

About Coherence

5. What transition signal is used in "Second Marriage" to indicate emphatic order?

_____

6. What are the transition signals used in the first supporting paragraph of "Second Marriage"?

_____

7. What are the three points of contrast in the first supporting paragraph ("taking notes") of "Studying: Then and Now"?

   a. _____   b. _____

   c. _____

8. Which supporting paragraph in "Second Marriage" fails to follow the pattern of organization set by the other two?

_____

About the Introduction and Conclusion

9. Circle below the method of introduction used in "Studying: Then and Now."

   a. Broad, general statement narrowing to thesis
   b. Idea that is the opposite of the one to be developed
   c. Quotation
   d. Anecdote
   e. Questions

10. Circle the conclusion technique used in "Second Marriage."
     a. Summary
     b. Prediction or recommendation
     c. Question

METHODS OF DEVELOPMENT

There are two methods of development possible in a comparison or contrast essay. Details can be presented in a *one-side-at-a-time* format or in a *point-by-point* format. Each format is illustrated below.

One Side at a Time

Look at the following supporting paragraph from "A Vote for McDonald's":

> For one thing, going to the Chalet is more difficult than going to McDonald's. The Chalet has a jacket-and-tie rule, which means that I have to dig a sport coat and tie out of the back of my closet, make sure they're semiclean, and try to steam out the wrinkles somehow. The Chalet also requires advance reservations. Since it is downtown, I have to leave an hour early to give myself time to find a parking space within six blocks of the restaurant. The Chalet cancels reservations if a party is more than ten minutes late. Going to McDonald's, on the other hand, is easy. I can feel comfortable wearing jeans or a warm-up suit. I don't have to do any advance planning. I can leave my house whenever I'm ready and pull into a doorside parking space within fifteen minutes.

The first half of the paragraph explains fully one side of the contrast; the second half of the paragraph deals entirely with the other side. When you use this method, be sure to follow the same order of points of contrast (or comparison) for each side. An outline of the paragraph shows how the points for each side are developed in a consistent sequence.

Outline (One Side at a Time)

Going to the Chalet is more difficult than going to McDonald's.
1. Chalet
   a. Dress code
   b. Advance reservations
   c. Leave an hour early
   d. Find parking space

2. McDonald's
   a. Casual dress
   b. No reservations
   c. Leave only fifteen minutes ahead of time
   d. Plenty of free parking

Point by Point

Now look at the supporting paragraph below from ''Studying: Then and Now'':

> Taking notes is one thing I've learned to do better since high school days. I used to lose interest in what I was doing and begin doodling, drawing Martians, or seeing what my signature would look like if I married the cute guy in the second row. Now, however, I try not to let my mind wander, and I pull my thoughts back into focus when they begin to go fuzzy. In high school, my notes often looked like something written in Arabic. In college, I've learned to use a semiprint writing style that makes my notes understandable. When I would look over my high school notes, I couldn't understand them. There would be a word like ''Reconstruction,'' then a big blank, then the word ''important.'' Weeks later, I had no idea what Reconstruction was or why it was important. I've since learned to write down connecting ideas, even if I have to take the time to do it after class.

The paragraph contrasts the two methods of note-taking point by point. The outline below illustrates the method.

Outline (Point by Point)

Taking notes is one thing I've learned to do better since high school days.
1. Level of attention in class
   a. High school
   b. College
2. Handwriting
   a. High school
   b. College
3. Completeness of notes
   a. High school
   b. College

When you begin a comparison or contrast paper, you should decide right away whether you are going to use the one-side-at-a-time format or the point-by-point format. An outline is an essential step in writing and planning a clearly organized paper.

Activity 1

Complete the partial outlines given for the supporting paragraphs that follow.

Paragraph a

The most important difference between the Chalet and McDonald's, though, is the price difference. Dinner for two at the Chalet, even one without appetizers or desserts, would easily cost forty dollars. And the forty dollars doesn't include the cost of parking the car and tipping the waiter, which can come to an additional ten dollars. At McDonald's, a filling meal for two will cost around six dollars. With the extra forty-four dollars, my wife and I can eat at McDonald's seven more times, or go to the movies five times, or buy play-off tickets to a football game.

The most important difference between the Chalet and McDonald's is the price difference.

1. Chalet

   a. _____

   b. Additional costs of parking and tipping

2. _____

   a. Six dollars for dinner for two

   b. _____

Complete the following statement: Paragraph *a* uses a _____

_____ method of

development.

Paragraph b

In addition to learning how to cope with daily work, I've also learned to handle study sessions for big tests. My all-night study sessions in high school were experiments in self-torture. Around 2:00 A.M., my mind, like a soaked sponge, simply stopped absorbing things. Now, I space out exam study sessions over several days. That way, the night before can be devoted to an overall review rather than raw memorizing. Most important, though, I've changed my attitude toward tests. In high school, I thought tests were mysterious things with completely unpredictable questions. Now, I ask teachers about the kinds of questions that will be on the exam, and I try to "psych out" which areas or facts teachers are likely to ask about. These practices really work, and for me they've taken much of the fear and mystery out of tests.

In addition to learning how to cope with daily work, I've also learned to handle study sessions for big tests.

1. Planning study time

    a. _____ (all-night study sessions)

    b. College (spread out over several days)

2. _____

    a. High school (tests were mysterious)

    b. _____ (_____)

Complete the following statement: Paragraph *b* uses a _____

_____ method of

development.

Paragraph c

    I learned not only to be apart sometimes but also to work together when it's time to make decisions. When Ray and I were married, I left all the important decisions to him. He decided how we would spend money, whether we should sell the car or fix it, and where to take a vacation. I know now that I went along with this so that I wouldn't have to take the responsibility when things went wrong. I could always end an argument by saying, "It was your fault!" With my second marriage, I am really trying to be a full partner. We ask each other's opinions on major decisions and try to compromise if we disagree. If we make the wrong choice, we're equally guilty. When we recently rented an apartment, for example, we both had to take the blame for not noticing the drafty windows and the "no pets" clause in our lease.

I learned not only to be apart sometimes but also to work together when it's time to make decisions.

1. First marriage
    a. Husband made decisions.
    b. Husband took responsibility and blame.

2. _____

    a. _____

    b. Share responsibility and blame.

Complete the following statement: Paragraph *c* uses a _____

_____ method of

development.

Activity 2

Following is a contrast essay about two sisters. The sentences in each supporting paragraph of the essay are scrambled. For each supporting paragraph, put a number 1 beside the point that all the other scrambled sentences support. Then number the rest of the sentences in a logical order. To do this, you will have to decide whether the sentences should be arranged according to the order of one side at a time or the order of point by point.

Introduction

When my sister and I were growing up, we shared the same bedroom. It wasn't hard to tell which half of the room was mine and which was Kathy's. My side was always as tidy as if a Holiday Inn chambermaid had just left. Kathy's side always looked like the aftermath of an all-night party. Back then, we argued a lot. Kathy said that I was a neatness nut, and I called her a slob. Today, however, we get along just fine, since we have our own homes and don't have to share a room anymore. But Kathy's approach to housekeeping is still much different from mine.

First supporting paragraph

_____ Kathy, on the other hand, believes that a kitchen should look lived-in and not like a hospital operating room.

_____ I treat my kitchen as if a health inspector were waiting to close it down at the least sign of dirt.

_____ I wipe counters with Fantastik while I wait for bread to toast.

_____ She scrambles eggs and leaves the dirty pan on the stove until the nightly cleanup.

_____ She forgets to put the bread away.

_____ When I leave the kitchen, it's usually cleaner than it was before I started to cook.

_____ The kitchen is one room that points up the contrasts between us.

_____ I wrap leftovers in neat packages of aluminum foil or seal them tightly in Tupperware.

_____ Kathy doesn't mind leaving a messy kitchen behind if she has more interesting things to do.

_____ Leftovers go naked into the refrigerator, without covers or foil.

_____ Even as I'm scrambling a couple of eggs, I begin to wash the bowl I used to mix them.

Second supporting paragraph

_____   The clothes in my closet are carefully arranged.

_____   My bedroom is a place of rest, and I can rest only when everything is in order.

_____   A peek into Kathy's bedroom in midmorning might reveal last night's cheese and crackers growing stale on the night table and several magazines hiding under the rumpled bedcovers.

_____   Some clothes are hung haphazardly in the closet, but many more are under the bed, behind the drapes, or on the deck.

_____   When I leave my bedroom in the morning, the bed is made and there are no clothes lying on the floor or over the chairs.

_____   Plastic bags cover out-of-season items, and shoes are lined up on racks.

_____   We still treat our bedrooms differently.

_____   In contrast, Kathy feels that her bedroom is a private place where she can do as she pleases.

Third supporting paragraph

_____   After I brush my hair, I check the sink for stray hairs.

_____   The spot that shows our differences the most, though, is the bathroom.

_____   My bathroom must be sanitized and germ-free.

_____   She cleans her mirror only when she gets tired of the polka-dot effect of hardened toothpaste.

_____   I clean the tub with Ajax before and after taking a bath.

_____   Needless to say, her makeup and toiletries litter every available surface.

_____   Once in a while, she points her hair dryer at the sink to blow away the accumulation of hairs in it.

_____   She cleans the tub, but only after a clearly defined brown ring has formed around it.

_____   I wipe off any spots of toothpaste or soap from the mirror and put all my cosmetics and cleaners in their proper places.

_____   Kathy, however, thinks that Americans worry too much about germs.

Conclusion

> As adults, Kathy and I can joke about the habits that caused us so much trouble as adolescents. We can, at times, even see the other's point of view when it comes to housecleaning. But I'm afraid the patterns are pretty much set. It's too late for this "odd couple" to change.

Complete the following statement: The sentences in each supporting paragraph can be organized using a _____ _____ method of development.

WRITING THE ESSAY

■ Writing Assignment 1

Write an essay of comparison or contrast on one of the topics below:

Two courses	Two singers
Two teachers	Two dates
Two jobs	Two popular magazines
Two bosses	Two games
Two family members	Two vacations
Two friends	Two hobbies
Two pets	Two leisure activities
Two vacations	Two stores
Two sports	Two public figures

How to Proceed

a You must begin by making two decisions: (1) what your topic will be and (2) whether you are going to do a comparison or a contrast. Many times, students choose to do essays centered on the differences between two things. For example, you might write about how a math teacher you have in college differs from one you had in high school. You might discuss important differences between your mother and your father, or between two of your friends. You might contrast a factory job you had packing vegetables with a white-collar job you had as a salesperson in a shoe store.

b After you choose a tentative topic, write a simple thesis statement expressing that topic. Then see what kind of support you can generate for that topic. For instance, if you plan to contrast two restaurants, see if you can think of and jot down three distinct ways they differ. *In other words, prepare a brief outline*. An outline is an excellent prewriting technique to use when doing any essay; it is almost indispensable when planning a comparison or contrast essay. Here is a brief outline prepared by the author of the essay titled "A Vote for McDonald's":

Thesis: The advantages of McDonald's over the Chalet are clear.
1. Going to the restaurants
2. Eating at the restaurants
3. Prices at the restaurants

Keep in mind that this planning stage is probably the most important single phase of work you will do on your paper. Without clear planning, you are not likely to write an effective essay.

c   After you have decided on a topic and the main lines of support, you must decide whether to use a one-side-at-a-time or a point-by-point method of development. Both methods are explained and illustrated in this chapter.

d   Now, freewrite for ten minutes on the topic you have chosen. Do not worry about punctuation, spelling, or other matters relating to correct form. Just get as many details as you can onto the page. You want a base of raw material that you can add to and select from as you now work on the first draft of your paper.

After you do a first draft, try to put it aside for a day or at least several hours. You will then be ready to return with a fresh perspective on the material and build upon what you have already done.

e   As you work on a second draft, be sure that each of your supporting paragraphs has a clear topic sentence.

f   Use transition words like *first, in addition, also, in contrast, another difference, on the other hand, but, however,* and *most important* to link together points in your paper.

g   As you continue working on your paper, refer to the checklist on the inside front cover. Make sure that you can answer *Yes* to the questions about unity, support, and coherence.

h   Finally, use the checklist on the inside front cover to proofread the next-to-final draft of your paper for sentence-skills mistakes, including spelling.

■ Writing Assignment 2

Write a comparison or contrast essay on college versus high school life. Narrow the focus of your paper to a particular aspect of school—teachers, classes, sports, social life, or students' attitudes, for example. *Or,* you may write a paper on dormitory or apartment life versus living at home.

■ Writing Assignment 3

Write an essay that contrasts two attitudes on a controversial subject. The subject might be abortion, marijuana, capital punishment, homosexuality, euthanasia, prostitution, coed prisons, busing, school prayer, nuclear power plants, the social security system, or some other matter on which there are conflicting feelings and opinions. You may want to contrast your views with someone else's or to contrast the way you felt at some point in the past with the way you feel now.

■ Writing Assignment 4

Write an essay that contrasts two characters or two points of view in one or more poems, stories, plays, or novels. The work you choose may be assigned by your instructor, or it may require your instructor's approval. For this assignment, your essay may have two supporting paragraphs, with each paragraph representing one side of the contrast. A student model follows.

Warren and Mary

In "Death of the Hired Man," Robert Frost uses a brief incident--the return of Silas, an aging farmhand--to dramatize the differences between a husband and wife. As Warren and Mary talk about Silas and reveal his story, the reader learns their story, too. By the end of the poem, Warren and Mary emerge as contrasting personalities; one is wary and reserved, while the other is open and giving.

Warren is a kindly man but one whose basic decency is tempered by a sense of practicality and emotional reserve. Warren is upset with Mary for sheltering Silas, who is barely useful and sometimes unreliable: "What use he is there's no depending on." Warren feels that he has already done his duty toward Silas by hiring him the previous summer and that he is under no obligation to care for him now. "Home," says Warren, "is the place where, when you have to go there/They have to take you in." Warren's home is not Silas' home, so Warren does not have a legal or moral duty to keep the shiftless old man. Warren's temperament, in turn, influences his attitude toward Silas' arrival. Warren hints to Mary--through a condescending smile-- that Silas is somehow playing on her emotions or faking his illness. Warren considers Silas' supposed purpose in coming to the farm--to ditch the meadow--nothing but a flimsy excuse for a free meal. The best that Warren can find to say about Silas is that he does have one practical skill: the ability to build a good load of hay.

Mary, in contrast, is distinguished by her giving nature and her concentration on the workings of human emotion. In caring for Silas, Mary sees not his lack of ability or his laziness but the fact that he is "worn out" and needs help. To Mary, home represents not obligation ("They have to take you in") but unconditional love: "I should have called it/Something you somehow haven't to deserve." Mary is observant, not only of outer appearance but also of the inner person; this is why she thinks not that Silas is trying to trick them but that he is a desperate man trying to salvage a little self-respect. She realizes, too, that he will never ditch the meadow, and she knows that Silas' insecurity prompted his arguments with the college boy who helped with the haying. Mary is also perceptive enough to see that Silas could never humble himself before his estranged brother. Mary's attitude toward Silas is more sympathetic than Warren's; whereas Warren wonders why Silas and his brother don't get along, Mary thinks about how Silas "hurt my heart the way he lay/And rolled his old head on that sharp-edged chairback."

In describing Silas, Warren and Mary describe themselves. We see a basically good man, one whose spirit has been toughened by a hard life. Warren, we learn, would have liked to pay Silas a fixed wage but simply couldn't afford to. Life has taught Warren to be practical and to rein in his emotions. In contrast, we see a nurturing woman, alert to human feelings, who could never refuse to care for a dying, lonely man. Warren and Mary are both decent people. This is the reason why, as Mary instinctively feels, Silas chooses their home for his final refuge.

■ Writing Assignment 5:
Writing about a Reading Selection

Read the selection titled "Smash Thy Neighbor" on pages 349–353. Pay special attention to how the author compares and contrasts football and war in paragraphs 5–8 and compares football and the rest of society in paragraph 14. Notice how he makes the comparisons and contrast in order to describe football more fully. Then write an essay in which you use a comparison to more fully describe three aspects of an activity, place, or person. You may use serious or humorous supporting details.

Following are some suggestions for a thesis for this assignment.

Thesis: In a few significant ways,

- going to college is like working at a career.
- the high-school hallways between classes are like a three-ring circus.
- getting divorced is like getting married.
- caring for a pet is like caring for a child.
- meditation is like exercise.
- shopping for Christmas gifts is like playing professional football.
- teachers should be like parents.
- hate is like love.
- raising a family is like caring for a garden.

These are only suggestions; feel free to use any other thesis that makes a comparison in order to fill out a description of an activity, person, or place. (Note that a comparison that points out similarities between things that are otherwise quite different is called an *analogy*.)

In your introduction, you might state your general thesis as well as the three points of comparison. Here, for example, is a possible introduction for an essay on meditation:

> On the surface, meditation may seem to be very different from exercise. A person who meditates is usually very still, while someone who exercises is very active. Yet the two activities are more alike than they might seem. Both require discipline, both bestow physical and mental benefits, and both can be habit-forming.

At the same time as you develop your introduction, you should prepare a general outline for your essay. The outline for the essay started by the introduction above would be as follows:

Thesis: Meditation is like exercise in three ways.
A. Both require discipline.
　　1. Exercise
　　2. Meditation
B. Both have physical and mental rewards.
　　1. Exercise
　　2. Meditation
C. Both can be habit-forming.
　　1. Exercise
　　2. Meditation

(Note that this outline uses the point-by-point method of development. Other topics might, of course, be more suited to the one-side-at-a-time method.)

As you work on your supporting paragraphs, *be sure to outline them first.* Such planning is very helpful in organizing and maintaining control over a comparison or contrast essay. Here, for example, is a sample scratch outline for a paragraph in a point-by-point essay comparing raising children to gardening.

Topic sentence: Just as a garden benefits from both sun and rain, so do children.
A. Benefits of sun and rain to a garden
　　1. Both sun and rain required for life
　　2. Increases growth

B. Benefits of sunny and rainy times to children
   1. Ups and downs natural over a life
   2. Personal growth

Each of your supporting paragraphs should be outlined in this way.

In your conclusion, you might round off the essay by summarizing the three areas of comparison and leaving your readers with a final thought. Do not, however, make the mistake of introducing a completely *new* idea (''Every couple should have children,'' for example) in your conclusion.

DEFINITION

In talking with other people, we at times offer informal definitions to explain just what we mean by a particular term. Suppose, for example, we say to a friend, "Bob is really an inconsiderate person." We might then explain what we mean by "inconsiderate" by saying, "He borrowed my accounting book 'overnight,' but didn't return it for a week. And when I got it back, it was covered with coffee stains." In a written definition, we make clear in a more complete and formal way our own personal understanding of a term. Such a definition typically starts with one meaning of a term. The meaning is then illustrated with a series of details.

You will be asked in this section to write an essay in which you define a term. The three student essays below are all examples of definition essays. Read them and then answer the questions that follow.

ESSAYS TO CONSIDER

Definition of a Baseball Fan

What is a baseball fan? The word fan is an abbreviation of fanatic, meaning "insane." In the case of baseball fans, the term is appropriate. They behave insanely, they are insane about trivia, and they are insanely loyal.

Baseball fans wear their official team T shirts and warm-up jackets to the mall, the supermarket, the classroom, and even--if they can get away with it--to work. Then, whenever the team offers a giveaway item, the fans rush to the ball park to get the roll-up hat or tote bag that is being offered that day.

Baseball fans behave insanely, especially between April and October. In addition, baseball fans cover the walls with items of every kind. When they go to a game, which they do as often as possible, the true baseball fans put on their team colors, grab their pennants, pin on their team buttons, and even bring along hand-lettered bedsheet signs proudly proclaiming "Go Dodgers" or "Braves Are Number One." At the game, these fans form a rooting section, constantly encouraging their favorite players and obediently echoing every cheer flashed on the electronic scoreboard.

Baseball fans, in addition to behaving insanely, are also insanely fascinated by trivia. Every day, they turn to the sports page and study last night's statistics. They simply have to see who has extended his hitting streak and how many strikeouts the winning pitcher recorded. Their bookshelves are crammed with record books, team yearbooks, and baseball almanacs. They delight in remembering such significant facts as who was the last left-handed third baseman to hit into an inning-ending double play in the fifth game of the play-offs. And if you do not show equal interest or enthusiasm, they look at you as if they were doubting your sanity.

Last of all, baseball fans are insanely loyal to the team of their choice. Should the home team lose eight in a row, their fans may begin to call them "bums." They may even suggest, vocally, that the slumping cleanup hitter be sent to the minors or the manager be fired. But these reactions only hide their broken hearts. They still check the sports pages and tune in to get the score. Furthermore, this intense loyalty makes fans dangerous, for anyone who dares to say to a loyal fan that some other team has sharper fielding or a better attitude could be risking permanent physical damage. Incidents of violence on the baseball field have increased in recent years and are a matter of growing concern.

From mid-October through March, baseball fans are like any other human beings. They pay their taxes, take out the garbage, and complain about the high cost of living or the latest home repair. But when April comes, the colors and radios go on, the record books come off the shelves, and the devotion returns. For the true baseball fan, another season of insanity has begun.

Stupidity

Although stupidity is commonly defined as "lack of normal intelligence," stupid behavior is not the behavior of a person lacking intelligence but the behavior of a person not using good judgment or sense. In fact, stupidity comes from a Latin word that means "senseless." Therefore, stupidity can be defined as the behavior of a person of normal intelligence who is acting in a particular situation as if he or she weren't very bright. Stupidity exists on three levels of seriousness.

First is the simple, relatively harmless level. Behavior on this level is often amusing. It is humorous when someone places the food from a fast-food restaurant on the roof of the car while unlocking the door and then drives away with the food still on the roof. We call this absentminded. The person's good sense or intelligence was temporarily absent. On this level, other than passing inconvenience or embarrassment, no one is injured by the stupid behavior.

More dangerous than simple stupidity is the next type--potentially serious stupidity. Practical jokes such as putting sugar in the restaurant salt shakers are on this level. The intent is humorous, but there is a potential for harm. Irresponsible advice given to others is also serious stupidity. An example is the person who plays psychiatrist on the basis of an introductory psychology course or a TV program on psychiatry. The intent may be to help, but if the victims really need psychiatric help, an amateur telling them that they "have no ego" or characterizing them as "neurotic" will only worsen the situation.

Even worse is the third kind of stupidity, which is always harmful. Otherwise kind persons, who would never directly injure another living thing, stupidly dump off a box of six-week-old kittens along a country road. Lacking the heart to have "the poor things put to sleep," they sentence them to almost certain death from parasites, upper respiratory infections, exposure, other animals, or the wheels of a passing vehicle. Yet they are able to tell themselves that "they will find nice homes" or "animals can get along in the wild." Another example of this kind of stupidity is the successful local businessman who tries to have as many office affairs as he can get away with. He risks the loss of his job, his home, his wife and children, and the goodwill of his parents and friends. He fails to see, though, that there is anything wrong with what he is doing. His is the true moral stupidity of a person not willing to think about the results of his actions or to take responsibility for them.

The common defense of the person guilty of stupidity is, "But I didn't think. . . ." This, however, is an inadequate excuse, especially when serious or harmful stupidity is involved. We are all liable when we do not think about the consequences of our actions.

Student Zombies

Schools divide people up into categories. From first grade on up, students are labeled "advanced" or "deprived" or "remedial" or "antisocial." Students pigeonhole their fellow students, too. We've all known the "brain," the "jock," the "dummy," and the "teacher's pet." In most cases, these narrow labels are misleading and inaccurate. But there is one label for a certain type of college student that says it all. That is, of course, "zombie."

Most of us haven't known too many real zombies personally, but we do know how they act. Low-budget horror movies have given us portraits of zombies, the living dead, for years. They stalk around graveyards, their eyes glued open by Hollywood makeup artists, bumping like cheap toy robots into living people. The special effects in horror movies are much better now.

Zombie students in college do just about the same thing. They stalk around campus, eyes glazed, staring off into space. They wander into classrooms, sit down mechanically in a seat, and contemplate the ceiling. Zombie students rarely eat, play sports, or toss Frisbees on campus lawns. Instead, they mysteriously disappear when classes are over and return only when they next feel the urge to drift into a classroom. The urge may not return, however, for weeks.

Where student zombies come from is as weird as the origin of the original zombies of the voodoo cults. According to voodoo legend, zombies are corpses that have come alive again. They have been reanimated by supernatural spells. Student zombies, too, are directed by a strange power. They continue to attend school although they have no apparent motivation to do so. They are completely uninterested in college-related activities like tests, grades, papers, and projects. They seem to be propelled by some inner force that compels them to wander forever through the halls of higher education.

All zombies, unfortunately, have a similar fate. In the movies, they are usually shot, stabbed, or electrocuted, all to no avail. Then the hero or heroine finally realizes that a counterspell is needed. Once the counterspell is cast, with the appropriate props of chicken legs, human hair, and bats' eyeballs, the zombie-corpse can return peacefully to its coffin. Student zombies, if they are to change at all, must undergo a similar traumatic experience. Sometimes the evil spell can be broken by a grade transcript decorated with "F" grades. Sometimes a professor will hold a private, intensive exorcism session. Sometimes, though, the zombies blunder around for years until they are gently persuaded by the college administration to head for another institution that accepts zombies. Then, they enroll in a new college or get a job in the family business.

Every college student knows that it's not necessary to see Night of the Living Dead or Voodoo Island in order to see zombies in action. Forget the campus movie theater or the late, late show. Just sit in a classroom and wait for the students who walk in without books or papers of any kind and sit in the farthest seats in the rear. Day of the Living Dead is showing every day at a college near you.

■ Questions

About Unity

1. Which essay places the topic sentence for its first supporting paragraph within the paragraph rather than, more appropriately, at the beginning?

    _____

2. Which sentence in the first supporting paragraph of "Student Zombies" should be omitted in the interest of paragraph unity?

    _____

3. Which sentence in the third supporting paragraph of "Definition of a Baseball Fan" should be omitted in the interest of unity?

_____

About Support

4. Which supporting paragraph in the essay on stupidity needs more supporting details?

_____

5. Which essay develops its definition through a series of comparisons?

_____

6. Which sentence in the first supporting paragraph of the essay on baseball needs supporting details?

_____

About Coherence

7. Which essay uses emphatic order, saving its most important idea for last?

_____

8. Which two essays use linking sentences between their first and second supporting paragraphs?

_____

9. What are five major transition words that appear in the three supporting paragraphs of "Definition of a Baseball Fan"?

   a. _____   b. _____   c. _____
   d. _____   e. _____

About the Introduction

10. Circle below the kind of introduction used for "Student Zombies."
   a. Broad, general statement narrowing to thesis
   b. Idea that is the opposite of the one to be developed
   c. Quotation
   d. Anecdote
   e. Questions

WRITING THE ESSAY

■   Writing Assignment 1

Shown below are an introduction, a thesis, and supporting points for an essay that defines the word *maturity*. Using separate paper, plan out and write the supporting paragraphs and a conclusion for the essay. Refer to the suggestions on "How to Proceed" that follow.

The Meaning of Maturity

Being a mature student does not mean being an old-timer. Maturity is not measured by the number of years a person has lived. Instead, the yardstick of maturity is marked by the qualities of self-denial, determination, and dependability.

Self-denial is an important quality in the mature student. . . .

Determination is another characteristic of a mature student. . . .

Although self-denial and determination are both vital, probably the most important measure of maturity is dependability. . . .

How to Proceed

a   Prepare examples for each of the three qualities of maturity. For each quality, you should have one extended example that takes up an entire paragraph or two or three shorter examples that together form enough material for a paragraph.

b   To generate these details, ask yourself the following questions:

What could I do, or have I done, that would be an example of self-denial?

What has someone I know ever done that could be described as self-denial?

What kind of behavior on the part of a student could be considered self-denial?

Write down quickly whatever answers occur to you for the questions. Don't worry about writing correct sentences; just concentrate on getting down as many details relating to self-denial as you can think of. Then repeat the questioning and writing process with the qualities of determination and dependability as well.

c   Draw from and add to this material as you work on the drafts of your essay. Also, refer to the checklist on the inside front cover to make sure you can answer *Yes* to the questions about unity, support, and coherence.

d   Write a conclusion for the essay by adding a summarizing sentence or two and a final thought about the subject. See page 53 for an example.

e   Finally, use the checklist on the inside front cover to proofread the next-to-final draft of your paper for sentence-skills mistakes, including spelling.

Writing Assignment 2

Write an essay that defines one of the terms below. Each term refers to a certain kind of person.

Snob	Optimist	Slob
Cheapskate	Pessimist	Tease
Loser	Team player	Practical joker
Good neighbor	Scapegoat	Black sheep of a family
Busybody	Bully	Procrastinator
Complainer	Religious person	Loner
Con artist	Hypocrite	Straight arrow

How to Proceed

a   If you start with a dictionary definition, be sure to choose just one meaning of a term. (A dictionary often provides several different meanings associated with a word.) Also, don't begin your paper with the overused line, "According to Webster, ..."

b Remember that the thesis of a definition essay is actually some version of "What _____ means to me." The thesis presents what *you* think the term actually means.

c You may want to organize the body of your paper around three different parts or qualities of your term. Here are the three-part divisions of the four essays considered in this chapter:

Maturity "is marked by qualities of self-denial, determination, and dependability."

"Stupidity exists on three levels of seriousness."

Baseball fans are fanatics in terms of "their behavior, their fascination with trivia, and their loyalty."

Student zombies usually have the same kind of behavior, origin, and fate.

Each division in a three-part breakdown should be supported by either a series of examples or a single extended example.

d Be sure to outline the essay before you begin to write. As a guide, put your thesis and three supporting points in the spaces below.

Thesis: _____

_____

Support: 1. _____

2. _____

3. _____

e While writing your paper, use as a guide the checklist of the four bases on the inside front cover. Make sure you can answer *Yes* to the questions about unity, support, coherence, and sentence skills.

■ Writing Assignment 3

Write an essay that defines one of the terms below.

Persistence	Nostalgia
Rebellion	Gentleness
Sense of humor	Depression
Escape	Obsession
Laziness	Self-control
Danger	Fear

Curiosity	Arrogance
Common sense	Conscience
Soul	Class
Family	Innocence
Responsibility	Freedom
Insecurity	Violence
Assertiveness	Shyness
Jealousy	Idealism
Practicality	Christianity

As a guide in writing your paper, use the suggestions in "How to Proceed."

■ **Writing Assignment 4:**
Writing about a Reading Selection

Read the selection titled "Shame" on pages 319–322. Then write an essay in which you define a term, as Dick Gregory does in "Shame," through narration. You can use one of the terms listed in Writing Assignment 3 or think up one of your own. In your introduction, fill in a brief background for your readers— when and where the experience happened. Your thesis should express the idea that because of this experience, you (or the person or people you are writing about) learned the meaning of the word _____ (fill in the term you have chosen). Break the narrative at logical points to create three supporting paragraphs. You might first want to look at the examples of narrative essays given on pages 194–197.

Alternatively, you might develop your definition with three experiences that seem to embody the word you have chosen. These could be experiences of your own, ones you know about, or ones you have read about. Develop each in a separate supporting paragraph.

DIVISION AND CLASSIFICATION

When you return home from your weekly trip to the supermarket with five brown bags packed with your purchases, how do you sort them out? You might separate the food items from the nonfood items (like toothpaste, paper towels, and detergent). Or you might divide and classify the items into groups intended for the freezer compartment, the refrigerator, and the kitchen cupboards. You might even put the items into groups like "to be used tonight," "to be used soon," and "to be used last." Sorting supermarket items in such ways is just one small example of how we spend a great deal of our time organizing our environment in one manner or another.

In this section, you will be asked to write an essay in which you divide or classify a subject according to a single principle. To prepare for this assignment, first read the division and classification essays below and then work through the questions and the activity that follow.

ESSAYS TO CONSIDER

Mall People

Having fun can exhaust one's bank account. By the time a person drives to the city and pays the tired-looking parking attendant the hourly fee to park, there is little money left to buy movie tickets, let alone popcorn and soft drinks to snack on. As a result, people have turned from wining, dining, and moviegoing to the nearby free-parking, free-admission shopping malls. Teenagers, couples on dates, and the nuclear family can all be observed having a good time at this alternative recreation spot.

Teenagers are the largest group of mallgoers. The guys saunter by in sneakers, T shirts, and blue jeans, complete with a package of cigarettes sticking out of their pockets. The girls stumble along in high-heeled shoes and daring tank tops, with hairbrushes tucked snugly in the rear pockets of their tight-fitting designer jeans. Traveling in a gang that resembles a wolf pack, the teenagers make the shopping mall their hunting ground. Their raised voices, loud laughter, and occasional shouted obscenities can be heard from as far as half a mall away. They come to "pick up chicks," to "meet guys," and basically just to "hang out."

Couples are now spending their dates at shopping malls. The young lovers are easy to spot because they walk hand in hand, stopping to sneak a quick kiss after every few steps. They first pause at jewelry store windows so they can gaze at diamond engagement rings and gold wedding bands. Then, they wander into furniture departments in the large mall stores. Whispering happily to each other, they imagine how that five-piece living room set or brass headboard would look in their future home. Finally, they drift away, their arms wrapped around each other's waists.

Mom, Dad, little Jenny, and Fred, Jr., visit the mall on Friday and Saturday evenings. Jenny wants to see some of the special mall exhibits geared toward little children. Fred, Jr., wants to head for the places that young boys find appealing. Mom walks around looking at various things until she discovers that Jenny is no longer attached to her hand. She finally finds her in a favorite hiding place. Meanwhile, Dad has arrived at a large store and is admiring the products he would love to buy. Indeed, the mall provides something special for every member of the family.

The teenagers, the couples on dates, and the nuclear family make up the vast majority of mallgoers. These folks need not purchase anything to find pleasure at the mall. They are shopping for inexpensive recreation, and the mall provides it.

Movie Monsters

Dracula rises from the grave--again. Mutant insects, the product of underground nuclear testing, grow to the size of boxcars and attack our nation's cities. Weird-looking aliens from beyond the stars decide to invade our planet. None of these events, if they ever happened, would surprise horror-movie fans. For years, such moviegoers have enjoyed being frightened by every type of monster Hollywood has managed to dream up, whether it be natural, artificial, or extraterrestrial.

One kind of movie monster is a product of nature. These monsters may be exaggerated versions of real creatures, like the single-minded shark in Jaws or the skyscraper-climbing gorilla in King Kong. They may be extinct animals, like the dinosaurs that terrorize cave dwellers and explorers in movies. Actually, cave dwellers and dinosaurs would never have met, for some unexplained event caused the dinosaurs to become extinct before the cave dwellers existed. "Natural" monsters sometimes combine human and animal features. Cat people, werewolves, and vampires fit into this category; so do Bigfoot and the Abominable Snowman. All these monsters seem to frighten us because they represent nature at its most threatening. We may have come a long way since the Stone Age, but we're still scared of what's out there beyond the campfire.

The second type of movie monster is a product of humans. Every giant lobster or house-sized spider that attacks Tokyo or Cleveland is the result of a mad scientist's meddling or a dose of radiation. In these cases, humans interfere with nature somehow, and the results are deadly. Frankenstein's monster, for example, is put together out of spare parts stolen from graveyards. His creator, an insane scientist in love with his own power, uses a healthy jolt of electricity to bring the monster to life. The scientist, along with lots of innocent villagers, dies as a result of his pride. In dozens of other monster movies, creatures grow to enormous proportions after wandering too close to atomic bomb sites. Our real fears about the terrors of technology are given the shape of giant scorpions and cockroaches that devour people.

The third type of movie monster comes from outer space. Since the movies began, odd things have been crawling or sliding down the ramps of spaceships. To modern movie fans, the early space monsters look suspiciously like actors dressed in rubber suits and metal antennas. Now, thanks to special effects, these creatures can horrify the bravest moviegoer. The monster in Alien, for example, invades a spaceship piloted by humans. The monster, which resembles a ten-pound raw clam with arms, clamps onto a crew member's face. Later, it grows into a slimy six-footer with a double jaw and long, toothed tongue. Movies like Alien reflect our fear of the unfamiliar and the unknown. We don't know what's out there in space, and we're afraid it might not be very nice.

Movie monsters, no matter what kind they are, sneak around the edges of our imaginations long after the movies are over. They probably play on fears that were there already. The movies merely give us the monsters that embody those fears.

Selling Beer

The other night, my six-year-old son turned to me and asked for a light beer. My husband and I sat there for a moment, stunned, and then explained to him that beer was only for grown-ups. I suddenly realized how many, and how often, beer ads appear on television. To my little boy, it must seem that every American drinks beer after work, or after playing softball, or while watching a football game. Beer makers have pounded audiences with all kinds of campaigns to sell beer. Each type of ad, however, seems to be targeted toward a different economic level of the TV viewing audience.

The first type of ad appeals to working-class people. There is the "this Bud's for you" approach, which shows the "boys" headed down to the neighborhood tavern after a tough day on the job at the auto plant or the construction site. The Budweiser jingle congratulates them on a job well done and encourages them to reward themselves--with a Bud. Miller beer uses a slightly different approach to appeal to workers. Men are shown completing a tough and unusual job and then relaxing during "Miller time." "Miller time" jobs might be called fantasy blue-collar jobs. Some Miller men, for example, fly helicopters to round up cattle or manage to cap blazing oil well fires.

The second kind of ad aims not at working-class people but at an upper-middle-class audience. The actors in these ads are shown in glamorous or adventurous settings. Some ads show a group of friends in their thirties and forties getting together to play a fancy sport, like tennis or rugby. One Lowenbrau ad, featuring a group of compatible couples at a clambake, is aimed at those rich enough to have a costly beach house.

The third type of ad appeals to people with a weight problem. These are the ads for the light beers, and they use sports celebrities and indirect language to make their points. For example, they never use the phrase "diet beer." Instead, they use phrases like "tastes great, and is less filling." In the macho world of beer commercials, men don't admit that they're dieting--that's too sissy. But if former football coaches and baseball greats can order a Lite without being laughed out of the bar, why can't the ordinary guy?

To a little boy, it may well seem that beer is necessary to every adult's life. After all, we need it to recover from a hard day at work, to celebrate our pleasurable moments, and to get rid of the beer bellies we got by drinking it in the first place. At least, that's what advertisers tell him--and us.

■ Questions

About Unity

1. Which paragraph in "Mall People" lacks a topic sentence?

   Write a topic sentence for the paragraph:

2. Which sentence in the first supporting paragraph of "Movie Monsters" should be omitted in the interest of paragraph unity?

3. Which paragraph in "Selling Beer" does not logically support the thesis statement?

About Support

4. Which supporting paragraph in "Movie Monsters" uses a single extended example?

    _____

5. After which sentence in the third paragraph of "Selling Beer" are more supporting details needed?

    _____

6. Which paragraph in "Mall People" lacks specific details?

    _____

About Coherence

7. What are the transition words used in the second supporting paragraph of "Mall People"?

    a. _____   b. _____   c. _____

8. Which topic sentence in "Selling Beer" functions as a linking sentence between paragraphs?

    _____

About the Introduction and Conclusion

9. Circle the kind of introduction used in "Selling Beer."
    a. Broad, general statement narrowing to thesis
    b. Idea that is the opposite of the one to be developed
    c. Quotation
    d. Anecdote
    e. Questions

10. Which two essays have conclusions that include brief summaries of the essay's supporting points?
    a. "Movie Monsters"
    b. "Mall People"
    c. "Selling Beer"

Activity

This activity will sharpen your sense of the classifying process. In each of the following groups, cross out the one item that has not been classified on the same basis as the other four. Also, indicate in the space provided the single principle of classification used for the four items. Note the examples.

Examples   Shirts

    a. Flannel

    b. Cotton

    c. ~~Tuxedo~~

    d. Denim

    e. Silk

(Unifying principle: *material*)

Sports

    a. Swimming

    b. Sailing

    c. ~~Basketball~~

    d. Water polo

    e. Scuba diving

(Unifying principle: *water sports*)

1. School subjects

    a. Algebra

    b. History

    c. Geometry

    d. Trigonometry

    e. Calculus

(Unifying principle: _____)

2. Movies

    a. *The Sound of Music*

    b. *My Fair Lady*

    c. *Dracula*

    d. *Cabaret*

    e. *The Wizard of Oz*

(Unifying principle: _____)

3. Clothing

    a. Sweat shirt

    b. Shorts

    c. T shirt

    d. Evening gown

    e. Sweat pants

(Unifying principle: _____)

4. Fasteners

    a. Staples

    b. Buttons

    c. Zippers

    d. Snaps

    e. Velcro

(Unifying principle: _____)

5. Sources of information

    a. *Newsweek*

    b. *The New York Times*

    c. *People*

    d. *TV Guide*

    e. *Life*

(Unifying principle: _____)

6. Fibers

    a. Wool

    b. Acrylic

    c. Cotton

    d. Silk

    e. Linen

(Unifying principle: _____)

7. Tapes
    a. Cellophane
    b. Recording
    c. Masking
    d. Duct
    e. Electrical

    (Unifying principle: _____)

8. Fairy-tale characters
    a. Witch
    b. King
    c. Fairy godmother
    d. Wicked queen
    e. Princess

    (Unifying principle: _____)

9. Immigrants
    a. Haitian
    b. Irish
    c. Mexican
    d. Illegal
    e. German

    (Unifying principle: _____)

10. Famous buildings
    a. Lincoln Memorial
    b. Empire State Building
    c. White House
    d. Capitol Building
    e. Washington Monument

    (Unifying principle: _____)

WRITING THE ESSAY

■ Writing Assignment 1

Shown below are an introduction, a thesis, and supporting points for a classification essay on college stress. Using separate paper, plan out and write the supporting paragraphs and a conclusion for the essay. Refer to the suggestions on "How to Proceed" that follow.

College Stress

Jack's heart pounds as he casts panicked looks around the classroom. He doesn't recognize the professor, he doesn't know any of the students, and he can't even figure out what the subject is. In front of him is a test. At the last minute his roommate awakens him. It's only another anxiety dream. The very fact that dreams like Jack's are common suggests that college is a stressful situation for young people. Causes of this stress can be academic, financial, and personal.

Academic stress is common. . . .

> In addition to academic stress, the student often feels financial pressure. . . .

> Along with academic and financial worries, the student faces personal pressures. . . .

How to Proceed

a   To develop some ideas for the essay, freewrite for five minutes apiece on the following:

Academic problems of college students
Financial problems of college students
Personal problems of college students

b   Add to the material you have written by asking yourself these questions:

What are some examples of academic problems that are stressful for students?

What are some examples of financial problems that students must contend with?

What are some examples of personal problems that create stress in students?

Write down quickly whatever answers occur to you for the questions. As with the freewriting, do not worry at this stage about writing correct sentences. Instead, concentrate on getting down as much information as you can think of that supports each of the three points.

c   Now go through all the material you have accumulated. Perhaps some of the details you have written down may help you think of even better details that would fit. If so, write them down. Then make decisions about the exact information that you will use in each supporting paragraph. List the details (1, 2, 3, and so on) in the order in which you will present them.

d   As you work on the drafts of your paper, refer to the checklist on the inside front cover to make sure you can answer *Yes* to the questions about unity, support, and coherence.

e   Write a conclusion for the essay by adding a summarizing sentence or two and a final thought about the subject. See page 53 for an example.

f   Finally, use the checklist on the inside front cover to proofread the next-to-final draft of your paper for sentence-skills mistakes, including spelling.

■ Writing Assignment 2

Write a division and classification essay on one of the following subjects:

Crimes	Jobs
Dates	Shoppers
Teachers	Soap operas
Bosses	Bars
Friends	Clothes
Sports fans	Attitudes toward life
Parties	Eating places
Advertisements	Marriages
Churchgoers	TV watchers
Junk food	College courses

How to Proceed

a   The first step in writing a division and classification essay is to divide your tentative topic into three reasonably complete parts. *Always use a single principle of division when you form your three parts.* For example, if your topic was "Automobile Drivers" and you divided them into slow, moderate, and fast drivers, your single basis for division would be "rate of speed." It would be illogical, then, to have as a fourth type "teenage drivers" (the basis of such a division would be "age") or "female drivers" (the basis of such a division would be "sex"). You probably could classify automobile drivers on the basis of age or sex or another division, for almost any subject can be analyzed in more than one way. What is important, however, is that in any single paper, you choose only one basis for division and stick to it. Be consistent.

In "Movie Monsters," the single basis for dividing monsters into natural, artificial, and extraterrestrial is *origin*. It would have been illogical, then, to have a fourth category dealing with vampires. In "Selling Beer," the intended basis for the types of beer ads was *economic level*. The writer's first group was working-class people; his second group was upper-middle-class people. To be consistent, his third group should have been, perhaps, lower-middle-class people. Instead, the writer confusingly shifted to ads that appeal to people with a weight problem.

b   To avoid such confusion in your own essay, fill in the outline below before starting your paper and make sure you can answer *Yes* to the questions that follow. You should expect to do a fair amount of thinking before coming up with a logical plan for your paper.

Topic: _____
Three-part division of the topic:

1. _____

2. _____

3. _____

Is there a single basis of division for the three parts? _____

Is the division reasonably complete? _____

c   Refer to the checklist of the four bases on the inside front cover while writing the drafts of your paper. Make sure you can answer *Yes* to the questions about unity, support, organization, and sentence skills. Also, use the checklist when you proofread the next-to-final draft of your paper for sentence-skills mistakes, including spelling.

■ Writing Assignment 3:
Writing about a Reading Selection

Read the selection titled "Five Parenting Styles" on pages 417–420. Then write an essay in which you divide and classify a group of people. The group you classify should be *one* of the following:

- Teachers
- Friends
- Coworkers

To begin, you must think of a way—a principle of division—to divide the group you have chosen. If you were considering "coworkers," for example, you could probably imagine several principles of division, such as these:

Ways they treat the boss

Efficiency at work

Punctuality at work

Level of neatness (desks, lockers, work turned in)

Once you have a useful principle of division, you will find that you can easily divide the people you are writing about into groups. If you decided, for instance, to use "ways they treat the boss" as your principle of division, you might write about these three groups:

1. Coworkers who "butter up" the boss
2. Coworkers who get along with the boss
3. Coworkers who dislike the boss

Here are some suggested principles of division for "teachers" and "friends." You should feel free, of course, to come up with your own approach.

Teachers

Teaching methods

Methods of classroom control

Clothing styles

Testing methods

Level of dedication to the job

Friends

Level of loyalty

Where or how you first met them

Length of time you've been friends

Level of emotional closeness

Attitudes toward something (money, college, drugs, and so on)

To complete the essay, follow the suggestions on "How to Proceed" on pages 181–182.

DESCRIPTION

When you describe someone or something, you give a picture in words to your readers. To make the word picture as vivid and real as possible, you must observe and record specific details that appeal to your readers' senses (sight, hearing, taste, smell, and touch). More than any other type of essay, a descriptive paper needs sharp, colorful details. Here is a sentence in which almost none of the senses is used: "In the window was a fan." In contrast, here is a description rich in sense impressions: "The blades of the rusty window fan clattered and whirled as they blew out a stream of warm, soggy air." Sense impressions here include sight (*rusty window fan, whirled*), hearing (*clattered*), and touch (*warm, soggy air*). The vividness and sharpness provided by the sensory details give us a clear picture of the fan and enable us to share in the writer's experience.

In this section, you will be asked to describe sharply a person, place, or thing for the readers through the use of words rich in sensory details. To help you prepare for the assignment, first read the three essays ahead and then answer the questions that follow.

ESSAYS TO CONSIDER

Family Portrait

My mother, who is seventy years old, recently sent me a photograph of herself that I had never seen before. While cleaning out the attic of her Florida home, she came across a studio portrait she had had taken about a year before she married my father. This picture of my mother as a twenty-year-old girl has fascinated me from the moment I began to study it closely.

The young woman in the picture has a face that resembles my own in many ways. Her face is a bit more oval than mine, but the softly waving brown hair around it is identical. The small, straight nose is the same model I was born with. My mother's mouth is closed, yet there is just the slightest hint of a smile on her full lips. I know that if she had smiled, she would have shown the same wide grin and downcurving "smile lines" that appear in my own snapshots. The most haunting features in the photo, however, are my mother's eyes. They are exact duplicates of my own large, dark brown ones. Her brows are plucked into thin lines, which are like two pencil strokes added to highlight those fine, luminous eyes.

I've also carefully studied the clothing and jewelry in the photograph. My mother is wearing a blouse and skirt that, although the photo was taken fifty years ago, could easily be worn today. The blouse is made of heavy eggshell-colored satin and reflects the light in its folds and hollows. It has a turned-down cowl collar and smocking on the shoulders and below the collar. The smocking (tiny rows of gathered material) looks hand-done. The skirt, which covers my mother's calves, is straight and made of light wool or flannel. My mother is wearing silver drop earrings. They are about two inches long and roughly shield-shaped. On her left wrist is a matching bracelet. My mother can't find this bracelet now, despite the fact that we spent hours searching through the attic for it. On the third finger of her left hand is a ring with a large, square-cut stone.

The story behind the picture is as interesting to me as the young woman it captures. Mom, who was earning twenty-five dollars a week as a file clerk, decided to give her boyfriend (my father) a picture of herself. She spent almost two weeks' salary on the skirt and blouse, which she bought at a fancy department store downtown. She borrowed the earrings and bracelet from her older sister, my aunt Dorothy. The ring she wore was a present from another young man she was dating at the time. Mom spent another chunk of her salary to pay the portrait photographer for the hand-tinted print in old-fashioned tones of brown and tan. Just before giving the picture to my father, she scrawled on the lower left-hand corner, "Sincerely, Beatrice."

When I study this picture, I react in many ways. I think about the trouble that Mom went to in order to impress the young man who was to be my father. I laugh when I look at the ring that was probably worn to make my father jealous. I smile at the serious, formal inscription my mother used in this stage of the budding relationship. Sometimes, I am filled with a mixture of pleasure and sadness when I look at this frozen long-ago moment. It is a moment of beauty, of love, and--in a way--of my own past.

My Fantasy Room

Recently, the comic strip "Peanuts" had a story about Lucy's going to camp for two weeks. At Camp Beanbag, Lucy tells Charlie Brown, there is no flag raising or required activity. All the campers do is lie in a room in beanbag chairs and eat junk food. This idea appealed to me, and I began to think. If I could spend two weeks in just one place, what would that place be like? I began to imagine the room of my dreams.

First of all, my fantasy room would be decorated in a way that would make me feel totally at ease. The walls would be painted a tasteful shade of pale green, the color supposed to be the most soothing. Psychologists have conducted studies proving that color can affect a person's mood. Also, a deep plush carpet in an intense blue would cover the floor from wall to wall--the perfect foundation for padding silently around the room. In the entryway, huge closets with sliding doors would contain my wardrobe of size-eight designer originals. The closets I have now are always messy and crowded, stuffed with old shoes and other kinds of junk. Lastly, on the walls, silver frames would hold my memories: pictures of me with my sports star and musician friends, news clippings reporting on my social life, a poster advertising the movie version of my most recent best-selling novel. Everything would be quiet and tasteful, of course.

I'd have a king-sized bed with a headboard full of buttons that would allow me to turn on lights, start music playing, or run hot water for my Jacuzzi bath without getting up. Tall bookcases with enough shelf space for all the souvenirs from my world travels would line an entire wall. Against the opposite wall would be a chrome and glass desk topped with lined pads and a rainbow of felt-tipped pens. They would await the moment when I became inspired enough to begin writing my next best-seller. And for my purebred Persian cat, there would be a lavender satin pillow.

Finally, my fantasy room would have the latest technological advances. The air-conditioning or heating, depending on the season, would function at a whisper. A telephone, operated by a push button from my bed, would put me in touch with the world. Or, if I were feeling antisocial, I could flick on my quadraphonic stereo system and fill the room with music. I could select a movie from my library of videocassette tapes to play on my giant-screen projection TV. Or I could throw a switch, and the satellite dish on my roof would bring me my choice of television programs from all over the world.

It's probably a good idea that my fantasy room exists only in my mind. If it were a real place, I don't think two weeks would be long enough. I might stay in it forever.

The Diner at Midnight

I've been in lots of diners, and they've always seemed to be warm, busy, friendly, happy places. That's why, on a recent Monday night, I stopped in a diner for a cup of coffee. I was returning home after an all-day car trip and needed something to help me make the last forty-five miles. A diner at midnight, however, was not the place I had expected. It was different--and lonely.

My Toyota pulled to a halt in front of the dreary gray aluminum building that looked like an old railroad car. A half-lit neon sign sputtered the message, "Fresh baked goods daily," on the surface of the rain-slick parking lot. Only a half dozen cars and a battered pickup were scattered around the lot. An empty paper coffee cup made a hollow scraping sound as it rolled in small circles on one cement step close to the diner entrance. I pulled hard at the balky glass door, and it banged shut behind me.

The diner was quiet when I entered. As there was no hostess on duty, only the faint odor of stale grease and the dull hum of an empty refrigerated pastry case greeted me. I looked around for a place to sit. The outside walls were lined with empty booths which squatted back to back in their orange vinyl upholstery. On each speckled beige-and-gold table were the usual accessories. The kitchen hid mysteriously behind two swinging metal doors with round windows. I glanced through these windows but could see only a part of the large, apparently deserted cooking area. Facing the kitchen doors was the counter. I approached the length of Formica and slid onto one of the cracked vinyl seats bolted in soldierlike straight lines in front of it.

The people in the diner seemed as lonely as the place itself. Two men in rumpled work shirts sat at the counter, on stools several feet apart, staring wearily into cups of coffee and smoking cigarettes. Their faces sprouted what looked like daylong stubbles of beard. I figured they were probably shift workers who, for some reason, didn't want to go home. Three stools down from the workers, I spotted a thin young man with a mop of black, curly hair. He was dressed in brown Levi cords with a checked western-style shirt unbuttoned at the neck. He wore a blank expression as he picked at a plate of limp french fries. I wondered if he had just returned from a disappointing date. At the one occupied booth was a middle-aged couple. They hadn't gotten any food yet. He was staring off into space, idly tapping his spoon against the table, while she drew aimless parallel lines on her paper napkin with a bent dinner fork. Neither said a word to the other.

Finally, a tired-looking waitress approached me with her thick order pad. I ordered the coffee, but I wanted to drink it fast and get out of there. My car, and the solitary miles ahead of me, would be lonely. But they wouldn't be as lonely as that diner at midnight.

■ **Questions**

About Unity

1. Which supporting paragraph in "My Fantasy Room" lacks a topic sentence?

_____

2. Which two sentences in the first supporting paragraph of "My Fantasy Room" should be omitted in the interest of paragraph unity?

   _____

   _____

3. Which sentence in the second supporting paragraph of "Family Portrait" should be omitted in the interest of paragraph unity?

   _____

About Support

4. How many examples support the topic sentence, "The people in the diner seemed as lonely as the place itself," in "The Diner at Midnight"?
   a. One
   b. Two
   c. Three

5. Label as *sight, touch, hearing,* or *smell* all the sensory details in the following sentences taken from the three essays. The first one is done for you as an example.

   a.   *sight*   *smell*

       "As there was no hostess on duty, only the faint odor of stale grease

                     hearing   *sight*

   and the dull hum of an empty refrigerated pastry case greeted me."

   b. "He was staring off into space, idly tapping his spoon against the table, while she drew aimless parallel lines on her paper napkin with a bent dinner fork."

   c. "Also, a deep plush carpet in an intense blue would cover the floor from wall to wall—the perfect foundation for padding silently around the room."

   d. "The blouse is made of heavy eggshell-colored satin and reflects the light in its folds and hollows."

6. After which sentence in the second supporting paragraph of "The Diner at Midnight" are more details needed?

   _____

About Coherence

7. Which method of organization (time order or emphatic order) does the first supporting paragraph of "Family Portrait" use?

   _____

8. Which sentence in this paragraph indicates the method of organization?

   _____

9. Which of the following topic sentences in "The Diner at Midnight" is a linking sentence?
   a. "My Toyota pulled to a halt in front of the dreary gray aluminum building that looked like an old railroad car."
   b. "The diner was quiet when I entered."
   c. "The people in the diner seemed as lonely as the place itself."

10. In the first supporting paragraph of "My Fantasy Room," what are the major transition words?

   a. _____   b. _____   c. _____

WRITING THE ESSAY

■ Writing Assignment 1

Write an essay about a particular place that you can observe carefully or that you already know well. The place might be one of the following or some other place:

> Pet shop
> Exam room
> Laundromat
> Bar or nightclub
> Video arcade
> Corner store
> Library study area
> Basement or garage
> Hotel or motel lobby
> Your bedroom or the bedroom of someone you know
> Waiting room at a train station or bus terminal
> Winning or losing locker room after an important game
> Antique shop or other small shop

How to Proceed

a Remember that, like all essays, a descriptive paper must have a thesis. Your thesis should state a dominant impression about the place you are describing. State the place you want to describe and the dominant impression you want to make in a short single sentence. The sentence can be refined later. For now, you just want to find and express a workable topic. You might write, for example, a sentence like one of the following:

The study area was noisy.

The exam room was tense.

The pet shop was crowded.

The bar was cozy.

The video arcade was confusing.

The bus terminal was frightening.

The corner store was cheerful.

The antique shop was lonely.

The bedroom was very organized.

The motel lobby was restful.

The winners' locker room was chaotic.

b Now make a list of as many details as you can that support the general impression. For example, the writer of "A Diner at Midnight" made this list:

Tired workers at counter

Rainy parking lot

Empty booths

Quiet

Few cars in lot

Dreary gray building

Lonely young man

Silent middle-aged couple

Out-of-order neon sign

No hostess

Couldn't see anyone in kitchen

Tired-looking waitress

c Organize your paper by using any one or a combination of the following methods:

In terms of *physical order*: that is, move from left to right, or far to near, or in some other consistent order

In terms of *size*: that is, begin with large features or objects and work down to smaller ones

In terms of a *special order* that is appropriate to the subject

For instance, the writer of "The Diner at Midnight" builds his essay around the dominant impression of loneliness. The paper is organized in terms of physical order (from the parking lot to the entrance to the interior); a secondary method of organization is size (large parking lot to smaller diner to still smaller people).

d Use as many senses as possible in describing a scene. Chiefly you will use sight, but to an extent you may be able to use touch, hearing, smell, and perhaps even taste as well. Remember that it is through the richness of your sense impressions that the reader will gain a picture of the scene.

e As you are working on the drafts of your paper, refer to the checklist on the inside front cover. Make sure you can answer *Yes* to the questions about unity, support, and coherence.

■ Writing Assignment 2

Write an essay about a family photograph. You may want to use an order similar to the one in "A Family Portrait," where the first supporting paragraph deals with the subject's face, the second with clothing and jewelry, and the third with the story behind the picture. Another possible order might be (1) the people in the photo (and how they look), (2) the relationships among the people (and what they are doing in the picture), and (3) the story behind the picture (time, place, occasion, relationships, or feelings). Use whatever order seems appropriate for the picture.

■ Writing Assignment 3

Write an essay describing a person. First, decide on a dominant impression you have about the person, and then use only those details which will add to that impression.

Here are some examples of interesting types of people you might want to write about:

Campus character	Teacher
Dentist	Child
Bus driver	Drunk
Close friend	TV or movie personality
Rival	Street person
Enemy	Older person
Clergyman	Employer

■ Writing Assignment 4:
Writing about a Reading Selection

Do *either* of the following.

Option 1:   Read the selection titled "On Being a Mess" on pages 326–328. Then write an essay describing a messy indoor place. You might consider writing about one of the following:

Room in a house or apartment
Cafeteria or restaurant
Teacher's office
Rest room
Basement or attic
Waiting room
Refrigerator
Closet
Shop
Area where you study
Inside of a bus, a subway, a train, or your own car

In your introductory paragraph, you might explain where the place is and why you are familiar with it, if necessary. (For example, you may have spent several hours during the semester conferring with your teacher in his or her office.) Be sure that you state in the thesis that messiness is the dominant impression you have of the place.

Use any order that you feel is appropriate (left to right, near to far, top to bottom, or other) to organize your supporting paragraphs. Use vivid images, as the author of "On Being a Mess" does, to capture your messy place on paper.

Option 2:   Read the selection titled ''A Fable for Tomorrow'' on pages 480–481. Then write an essay describing a neglected outdoor place. You might, for example, describe a street, a park, a downtown area, or even an entire community that is sadly lacking in attention and care.

Use any order that you feel is appropriate to organize your supporting paragraphs. Include plenty of specific details that will give your reader a mental photograph of the place you are describing.

NARRATION

At times we make a statement clear by relating in detail something that has happened to us. In the story we tell, we present the details in the order in which they happened. A person might say, for example, ''I was really embarrassed the day I took my driver's test,'' and then go on to develop that statement with an account of the experience. If the story is sharply detailed, we will be able to see and understand just why the speaker felt that way.

In this section, you'll be asked to tell a story that illustrates some point. The essays ahead all present narrative experiences that support a thesis. Read them and then answer the questions that follow.

ESSAYS TO CONSIDER

My First Professional Performance

I was nineteen, and the invitation to play my guitar and sing at the County Rescue Squad Carnival seemed the ''big break'' aspiring performers dream about. I would be sharing the program with well-known professionals. My spirits were not even dampened by the discovery that I would not be paid. I had no reason to suspect then that my first professional performance was to be the scene of the most embarrassing experience of my life.

I arrived at the carnival grounds early, which proved fortunate. The manager knew that, in addition to the amplifier and speakers, I needed an extra microphone for my guitar and a high stool. However, when I checked the stage, I found the amplifier and speakers but nothing else. I also couldn't find the manager. The drunks who would hassle me later, after I had gotten started, became another problem. Since I couldn't perform without all the equipment, I was ready to call the whole thing off. Only the large potential audience milling around the carnival grounds influenced me to go through with it. One eye on my watch, I drove to the music store, told the owner my story, borrowed the needed equipment, and got back just as the Stone Gravel Rock Band, which preceded me on the program, was finishing its set. The band plays bluegrass music in some local clubs, and the lead singer was recently offered a professional recording contract.

I had some attentive listeners for my first song, but then problems developed. A voice boomed, "Play 'Mister Bojangles.'" A group of noisy drunks, surrounded by empty beer cans, half-eaten hot dogs, and greasy paper plates, were sprawled on picnic tables to one side of the stage. "We want to hear 'Mister Bojangles,'" roared the others, laughing. "Not today," I answered pleasantly, "but if you like 'Bojangles,' you'll like this tune." I quickly slid into my next number. Unfortunately, my comment only encouraged the drunks to act in an even more outrageous manner. As they kept up the disturbance, my audience began drifting away to escape them.

I was falsely cheered by the arrival of a uniformed policeman and several older men in work clothes. "Fans," I thought hopefully. Then I gave a start as a large engine roared very close to me, filling the air with choking diesel fumes. Only then did I realize that my "stage" was really a huge flatbed truck and that the older men in work clothes were in the cab warming up the engine. As I played a song, the policeman approached me. "Hey, lady," he said, "you're going to have to get down from there with all that stuff. They've got to take this rig away now." "I can't do that," I said. "I'm a professional musician in the middle of a performance. Tell him to turn that engine off." (In my confusion, I left the mike open, transmitting this exchange to the entire carnival grounds.) "Sorry, lady, he has to take it now," insisted the policeman. The drunks happily entered into the spirit of the thing, yelling, "Take her away. We don't want her. Yeah, haul her away." To save a small amount of self-respect, I played one more chorus before I began packing up my gear.

Fortunately, in conversations I eventually had with other performers, I heard similar stories of experiences they had when starting out. Then I would tell them about the stage that nearly rolled away with me on it, and we would laugh. Now I see that it's all part of becoming a professional.

Adopting a Handicap

My church recently staged a "Sensitivity Sunday" to make our congregation aware of the problems faced by people with physical handicaps. We were asked to "adopt a handicap" for several hours one Sunday morning. Some members chose to be confined to wheelchairs; others stuffed cotton in their ears, hobbled around on crutches, or wore blindfolds.

Wheelchairs had never seemed like scary objects to me before I had to sit in one. A tight knot grabbed hold in my stomach when I first took a close look at what was to be my only means of getting around for several hours. I was stuck by the irrational thought, "Once I am in this wheelchair, the handicap might become real, and I might never walk again." This thought, as ridiculous as it was, frightened me so much that I needed a large dose of courage just to sit down.

After I overcame my fear of the wheelchair, I had to learn how to cope with it. I wiggled around to find a comfortable position and thought I might even enjoy being pampered and wheeled around. I glanced over my shoulder to see who would be pushing me. It was only then that I realized I would have to navigate the contraption all by myself! My palms reddened and started to sting as I tugged at the heavy metal wheels. I could not seem to keep the chair on an even course or point the wheels in the direction I wanted to go. I kept bumping into doors, pews, and other people. I felt as though everyone was staring at me and commenting on my clumsiness.

When the service started, more problems cropped up to frustrate me even further. Every time the congregation stood up, my view was blocked. I could not see the minister, the choir, or the altar. Also, as the church's aisles were narrow, I seemed to be in the way no matter where I parked myself. For instance, the ushers had to step around me in order to pass the collection plate. This made me feel like a nuisance. Thanks to a new building program, however, our church will soon have the wide aisles and well-spaced pews that will make life easier for the handicapped. Finally, if people stopped to talk to me, I had to strain my neck to look up at them. This made me feel like a little child being talked down to and added to my sense of helplessness.

My few hours as a disabled person left a deep impression on me. Now, I no longer feel resentment at large tax expenditures for ramp-equipped buses, and I wouldn't dream of parking my car in a space marked "Handicapped Only." Although my close encounter with a handicap was short-lived, I can now understand the challenges, both physical and emotional, that wheel-chair-bound people must overcome.

A Night of Violence

According to my history teacher, Adolf Hitler once said that he wanted to sign up "brutal youths" to help him achieve his goals. If Hitler were still alive, he wouldn't have any trouble recruiting the brutal youths he wanted; he could get them right here in the United States. I know, because I was one of them. As a teenager, I ran with a gang. And it took a terrible incident to make me see how violent I had become.

One Thursday night, I was out with my friends. I was still going to school once in a while, but most of my friends weren't. We spent our days on the streets, talking, showing off, sometimes shoplifting a little or shaking people down for a few dollars. My friends and I were close, maybe because life hadn't been very good to any of us. On this night, we were drinking wine and vodka on the corner. For some reason, we all felt tense and restless. One of us came up with the idea of robbing one of the old people who lived in the high rise close by. We would just knock him or her over, grab the money, and party with it.

After about an hour, and after more wine and vodka, we spotted an old man. He came out of the glass door of the building and started up the street. Stuffing our bottles in our jacket pockets, we closed in behind him. Victor, the biggest of us, said, "We want your money, old man. Hand it over." Suddenly, the old man whipped out a homemade wooden club from under his coat and began swinging. The club thudded against the side of Victor's head, making bright-red blood spurt out of his nose. When we saw this, we went crazy. We smashed our bottles over the old man's head. Then Victor ground the jagged edges of a broken bottle into the old man's skull. As we ran, I kept seeing the bottom of that bottle sticking up out of the man's head. It looked like a weird glass crown.

Later, at home, I threw up. I wasn't afraid of getting caught; in fact, we never did get caught. I just knew I had gone over some kind of line. I didn't know if I could step back, now that I had gone so far. But I knew I had to. I had seen plenty of people in my neighborhood turn into the kind who hated their lives, people who didn't care about anything, people who wound up penned in jail or ruled by drugs. I didn't want to become one of them.

That night, I realize now, I decided not to become one of Hitler's "brutal youths." I'm proud of myself for that, even though life didn't get any easier and no one came along to pin a medal on me. I just decided, quietly, to step off the path I was on. I hope my parents and I will get along better now, too. Maybe the old man's pain, in some terrible way, had a purpose.

■ **Questions**

About Unity

1. Which sentence in the third supporting paragraph of ''Adopting a Handicap'' should be omitted in the interest of paragraph unity?

   _____

2. Which sentence in the first supporting paragraph of ''My First Professional Performance'' should be omitted in the interest of paragraph unity?

   _____

3. Which essay lacks a thesis statement?

   _____

About Support

4. Label as *sight*, *touch*, *hearing*, or *smell* all the sensory details in the following sentences taken from the three essays.

    a. "Then I gave a start as a large engine roared very close to me, filling the air with choking diesel fumes."

    b. "The club thudded against the side of Victor's head, making bright-red blood spurt out of his nose."

    c. "My palms reddened and started to sting as I tugged at the heavy metal wheels."

    d. "A group of noisy drunks, surrounded by empty beer cans, half-eaten hot dogs, and greasy paper plates, were sprawled on picnic tables to one side of the stage."

5. In "Adopting a Handicap," how many examples support the topic sentence "When the service started, more problems cropped up to frustrate me even further"?

    _____

6. After which sentence in the second supporting paragraph of "My First Professional Performance" are more specific details needed?

    _____

7. Which supporting paragraphs in "My First Professional Performance" use dialog to help recreate the event?

    _____

About Coherence

8. The first stage of the writer's experience in "Adopting a Handicap" might be called *sitting down in the wheelchair*. What are the other two stages of the experience?

    a. _____

    b. _____

9. In the first supporting paragraph of "My First Professional Performance," which detail is out of chronological (time) order?

    _____

About the Conclusion

10. Which sentence in the conclusion of ''A Night of Violence'' makes the mistake of introducing a completely new idea?

WRITING THE ESSAY

 ### Writing Assignment 1

Write an essay telling about an experience in which a certain emotion was predominant. The emotion might be disappointment, embarrassment, happiness, frustration, or any of the following:

Fear	Anger	Silliness
Pride	Nostalgia	Disgust
Jealousy	Relief	Loss
Sadness	Greed	Sympathy
Terror	Nervousness	Violence
Regret	Hate	Bitterness
Shock	Surprise	Envy
Love	Shyness	Loneliness

The experience should be limited in time. Note that the three essays presented in this chapter all describe experiences that occurred within relatively short periods. One writer described her embarrassing musical debut; another described her frustration in acting as a handicapped person at a morning church service; the third described the terror of a minute's mugging that had lifelong consequences.

How to Proceed

a   Think of an experience or event in your life in which you felt a certain emotion strongly. Then spend at least ten minutes freewriting about that experience. Do not worry at this point about such matters as spelling or grammar or putting things in the right order; instead, just try to get down as many details as you can think of that seem related to the experience.

b   This preliminary writing will help you decide whether your topic is promising enough to continue work on. If it is not, choose another emotion. If it is, do two things:

First, write out your thesis in a single sentence, underlining the emotion you will focus on. For example, "My first day in kindergarten was one of the scariest days of my life."

Second, make up a list of all the details involved in the experience. Then arrange those details in chronological (time) order.

c   Using the list as a guide, prepare a rough draft of your paper. Use time signals such as *first, then, next, after, while, during,* and *finally* to help connect details as you move from the beginning to the middle to the end of your narrative.

d   See if you can divide your story into separate stages (what happened first, what happened next, what finally happened). Put each stage into a separate paragraph. In narratives, it is sometimes difficult to write a topic sentence for each supporting paragraph. You may, then, want to start new paragraphs at points where natural shifts or logical breaks in the story seem to occur.

e   One good way to recreate an event is to include some dialog, as does the writer of "My First Professional Performance." Repeating what you have said or what you have heard someone else say helps make the situation come alive. And, in general, try to provide as many vivid, exact details as you can to help your readers experience the event as it actually happened.

f   As you work on the drafts of your paper, refer to the checklist on the inside front cover to make sure that you can answer *Yes* to the questions about unity, support, and coherence. Also use the checklist to proofread the next-to-final draft of your paper for sentence-skills mistakes, including spelling.

■ Writing Assignment 2

Look over the list of statements below. Think of an experience in your life that supports one of the statements.

■   "Before I got married I had six theories about bringing up children; now I have six children and no theories."—John Wilmot, Earl of Rochester

■   "The chains of habit are too weak to be felt until they are too strong to be broken."—Samuel Johnson

■   "Peter's Law—The unexpected always happens."—Laurence J. Peter

■   "Haste makes waste."—popular saying

■   "Good people are good because they've come to wisdom through failure." —William Saroyan

■   "Lying is an indispensable part of making life tolerable."—Bergen Evans

■   "The key to everything is patience. You get the chicken by hatching the egg—not by smashing it."—Arnold Glasgow

- "A good scare is worth more to a man than good advice."—Ed Howe
- "A fool and his money are soon parted."—popular saying
- "Like its politicians and its wars, society has the teenagers it deserves."—J. B. Priestley
- "It's what you learn after you know it all that counts."—John Wooden
- "Wise sayings often fall on barren ground; but a kind word is never thrown away."—Sir Arthur Helps
- "What a tangled web we weave/When first we practice to deceive."—Walter Scott
- "All marriages are happy. It's the living together afterward that causes all the trouble."—Raymond Hull
- "We lie loudest when we lie to ourselves."—Eric Hoffer
- "The worst country to be poor in is America."—Arnold Toynbee
- "Criticism—a big bite out of someone's back."—Elia Kazan
- "Work is what you do so that sometime you won't have to do it anymore."—Alfred Polgar
- "You grow up the day you have your first real laugh—at yourself."—Ethel Barrymore
- "Hoping and praying are easier but do not produce as good results as hard work."—Andy Rooney
- "A little learning is a dangerous thing."—Alexander Pope
- "Nothing is so good as it seems beforehand."—George Eliot
- "Give a pig a finger, and he'll take the whole hand."—folk saying

Now write a narrative essay using as a thesis one of the above statements. Refer to the suggestions in "How to Proceed" on pages 199–200 in doing your paper. Remember that the point of your story is to *support* your thesis. Feel free to carefully select from and even add to your experience so that your story truly supports the thesis of your paper.

■ Writing Assignment 3:
Writing about a Reading Selection

Read the selection titled "Why Do Bad Things Happen to Good People?" on pages 467–470. Then write a narrative essay on a time when a bad thing happened to you, your family, a friend, or someone you know.

You might consider writing about:

An accident
A death
Being the victim of a crime
Sickness
Being fired
A fire

Or you might write about any other incident of a very serious or tragic nature.

In your introduction, provide a few sentences of background information to prepare your readers for the narrative. Your thesis may simply state that this particular event was shocking, terrible, or heartbreaking. Or, as Kushner does, you may want to state that the incident seemed incomprehensible to the people who knew of it.

Organize the essay by dividing your narrative into two or three logical time phases, and cover each one in a separate supporting paragraph. You will find it helpful to look at the sample narrative essays on pages 194–197 to see how other writers have created logical breaks in the stories of their experiences.

ARGUMENTATION AND PERSUASION

Most of us know someone who enjoys a good argument. Such a person usually challenges any sweeping statement we might make. "Why do you say that?" he or she will ask. "Give your reasons." Our questioner then listens carefully as we state our case, waiting to see if we really do have solid evidence to support our point of view. Such a questioner may make us feel uncomfortable, but we may also feel grateful to him or her for helping us clarify our opinions.

Your ability to advance sound and compelling arguments is an important skill in everyday life. You can use persuasion to make a point in a class discussion, persuade a friend to lend you money, and talk an employer into giving you a day off from work. Learning about persuasion based on clear, logical reasoning can also help you see through the sometimes faulty arguments in advertisements, newspaper articles, political speeches, and the other persuasive appeals you see and hear every day.

In this section, you will be asked to argue a position and defend it with a series of solid reasons. You are in a general way doing the same thing—making a point and then supporting it—with all the essays in the book. The difference here is that, in a more direct and formal manner, you will advance a point about which you feel strongly and seek to persuade your readers to agree with you.

ESSAYS TO CONSIDER

Teens and Jobs

"The pressure for a teenager to work is great, and not just because of the economic plight in the world today. Much of it is peer pressure to have a little bit of freedom and independence, and to have their own spending money. The concern we have is when the part-time work becomes the primary focus," says Roxanne Bradshaw, educator and officer of the National Education Association. Many people argue that working can be a valuable experience for the young. However, working more than about fifteen hours a week is harmful to adolescents because it reduces their involvement with school, encourages a materialistic and expensive lifestyle, and increases the chance of having problems with drugs and alcohol.

Schoolwork and the benefits of extracurricular activities tend to go by the wayside when adolescents work long hours. As more and more teens have filled the numerous part-time jobs offered by fast-food restaurants and mall stores, teachers have faced increasing difficulties. They must both keep the attention of tired pupils and give homework to students who simply don't have time to do it. In addition, educators have noticed less involvement in the extracurricular events many consider healthy influences of young people. School bands and athletic teams are losing players to work, and sports events are poorly attended by working students. Those teenagers who try to do it all--homework, extracurricular activities, and work--may find themselves exhausted and prone to illness. A recent newspaper story, for example, described a girl in Pennsylvania who came down with mononucleosis as a result of aiming for good grades, playing on two school athletic teams, and working thirty hours a week.

Another drawback of too much work is that it may promote materialism and an unrealistic lifestyle. Some parents say that work teaches adolescents the value of a dollar. Undoubtedly, it can, and it's true that some teenagers work to help out with the family budget or save for college. However, surveys have shown that the majority of working teens use their earnings to buy luxuries--stereos, tape decks, clothing, even cars. These young people, some of whom earn three hundred dollars and more a month, don't worry about spending wisely--they can just about have it all. In many cases, experts point out, they are becoming accustomed to a lifestyle they won't be able to afford several years down the road, when they'll no longer have parents to pay for car insurance, food and lodging, and so on. At that point, they'll be hard pressed to pay for necessities as well as luxuries.

Finally, teenagers who work a lot are more likely than others to get involved with alcohol and drugs. Teens who put in long hours may seek a quick release from stress, just like the adults who need to drink a couple of martinis after a hard day at work. Stress is probably greater in our society today than it has been at any time in the past. Also, teens who have money are more likely, for various obvious reasons, to get involved with drugs.

Teenagers can enjoy the benefits of work while avoiding its drawbacks simply by limiting their work hours during the school year. As is probably often the case in life, a moderate approach is one that will prove to be the most healthy and rewarding.

A Vote against Computers

I was excited when my English composition instructor announced that computers would be a major part of our writing course. "Half of the classes will be held in the computer lab," she said, "and all required work will be done on the computer." I was thrilled while touring the new computer lab to see all the magical-looking machines with their glowing green screens. The machines hummed as if they were alive. I thought to myself excitedly, "We're living in the middle of the computer revolution, and here's my chance to get on board." But three months later, I've had some second thoughts. I now believe that computers are a bad idea in the writing classroom. The computer does not help me plan a paper, it requires too much time and trouble to use, and it has changed my instructor from a teacher to a technician.

To begin with, the computer does not help me go about writing a paper. When I start an essay, I like to use a yellow pad and scribble out my ideas. I may write a couple of sentences, scratch them out, and then write a few more. I may make a couple of rough outlines, and then cross out parts of them, and then combine those leftover parts to make a third outline. I may go back to some idea I rejected at first and write another idea in the margin. I may circle something from one part of the page and join it with something on another part. At any one time, I want to see everything I'm doing in front of me. With a computer, I can't do that. If I delete something, I can't look back at it later. If I write too much, I have to scroll back and forth, since not everything can fit on the screen at once. There's no room in the margin for questions. And I can't circle things on the computer screen and connect them the way I can on a sheet of paper. I want a chance to see and change everything at once when planning a paper, and a computer does not let me do that.

Next, the mechanics involved in using a computer are complicated and time-consuming. Before I can get down to some honest-to-goodness writing, I have to show the computer lab technician my student ID card and sign out the appropriate software. Then I have to find an open terminal, turn on my computer and monitor, insert the proper disks, create or find a file, and set the required format. When I'm finished writing, I have to make sure that my work is properly saved, that there's paper in the printer, and that the printer is on-line. And at any point, when I have mechanical problems or questions about the computer, I have to wait five or ten minutes or more for the teacher or a student technician to come to help me. Worst of all, I'm not a good typist. I spend half of my time hunting and pecking for the proper letters on the keyboard. If I had wanted to get a lot of typing practice, I would have taken a typing course, but this is supposed to be a writing course.

Finally, when we meet in the computer lab, the teacher spends most of the class walking around and helping students log on and off the computer, handing out and collecting software, and trying to locate and retrieve lost documents. I sat here the other day watching the class trying to write on computers, and my impression was that 75 percent of what the teacher did involved computers rather than writing. I've had other writing courses, before computers, where the teacher spent a lot of time going over students' work on a one-on-one basis or in a class discussion. It was in this workshop setting that I believe my writing improved the most. Now, my professor has much less time to devote to individual help and feedback. She's too busy being a computer troubleshooter.

In conclusion, it may be wise to take another look at the use of the computer in college writing courses. At first glance the computer offers excitement and a world of promise, but I think there's a serious question about whether it actually improves students' writing.

Once Over Lightly: Local TV News

Are local television newscasts a reliable source of news? Do they provide in-depth coverage and analysis of important local issues? Unfortunately, all too often they do not. In their battle for high ratings, local television news shows provide more entertainment than news. News personalities are emphasized at the expense of stories; visual appeal has more priority than actual news; and stories and reports are too brief and shallow.

Local TV newscasters are as much the subject of the news as are the stories they present. Nowhere is this more obvious than in weather reports. Weatherpersons spend valuable news time by joking, drawing cartoons, chatting about weather fronts as "good guys" and "bad guys," and dispensing weather trivia such as statistics about relative humidity and record highs and lows for the date. Reporters, too, draw attention to themselves. Rather than just getting the story, we are shown the reporters jumping into or getting out of helicopters to get the story. When reporters interview crime victims or the residents of poor neighborhoods, the camera angle typically includes them and their reaction as well as their subjects. When they report on a storm, they stand outside in the storm, their styled hair blowing, so we can admire how they "brave the elements." Then there are the anchorpersons, who are chosen as much for their looks as for their skills. They too dilute the news by putting their personalities on center stage.

Often the selection of stories and the way they are presented is based on visual impact rather than news value. If a story is not accompanied by an interesting film clip, it is unlikely to be shown on the local news. The result is an overemphasis on fires and car crashes and little attention to such important issues as the local employment situation. As much as possible, every story is presented with a reporter standing "live" in front of something. If city hall has passed a resolution, for instance, then the reporter will be shown standing live in front of city hall. Very often, cars are zooming by or neighborhood kids are waving at the camera or passersby are recognizing suddenly that they are being filmed. Most people are natural hams, and they love to discover that they are on stage. Such background happenings are so distracting that viewers may not even listen to what the reporter is saying. And even if a story is not live, the visuals that accompany a story are often distracting. A recent story on falling oil prices, for example, was accompanied by footage of a working oil well that drew away attention from the important economic information in the report.

Finally, the desire of the local stations to entertain viewers is demonstrated in short news stories and shallow treatment. On the average, about half a minute is devoted to a story. Clearly, stories that take less than half a minute are superficial. Even the longest stories, which can take up several minutes, are not accompanied by meaningful analysis. Instead, the camera jumps from one location to another and the newscaster simplifies and trivializes the issues. For instance, one recent "in-depth" story about the homeless consisted of a glamorous reporter talking to a homeless person and asking him what should be done about the problem. The poor man was in no condition to respond intelligently. The story then cut to an interview with a city bureaucrat who mechanically rambled on about the need for more government funding. There were also shots of homeless people sleeping in doorways and on top of heating vents, and there were interviews with people on the street, all of whom said something should be done about the terrible problem of the homeless. There was, in all of this, no real exploration of the issue and no proposed solutions. It was also apparent that the homeless were just the issue-for-the-week. After the week's coverage was over, the topic was not mentioned again.

Because of the emphasis on newscasters' personalities and on the visual impact of stories and the short time span for stories, local news shows provide little more than diversion. What viewers need instead is news that has real significance. Rather than being amused and entertained, we need to deal with complex issues and learn uncomfortable truths that will help us become more responsible consumers and citizens.

■ Questions

About Unity

1. Which sentence in the third supporting paragraph of "Teens and Jobs" should be omitted in the interest of paragraph unity?

   _____

2. Which supporting paragraph in "A Vote against Computers" lacks a topic sentence?

   _____

   Write a topic sentence for the paragraph: _____

   _____

About Support

3. Which paragraph in "Teens and Jobs" develops its point by citing and then refuting an opposing point of view?

    _____

4. After which sentence in the third supporting paragraph of "Teens and Jobs" are specific details needed?

    _____

5. After which sentence in the first supporting paragraph of "Once Over Lightly: Local TV News" is support needed?

    _____

6. Which supporting paragraph of which essay uses the longest single supporting example?

    _____

About Coherence

7. What three transition words are used to introduce the three supporting paragraphs in "A Vote against Computers"?

    a. _____   b. _____   c. _____

8. What are the two main transition words in the first supporting paragraph of "Once Over Lightly: Local TV News"?

    a. _____   b. _____

About the Introduction and Conclusion

9. From the choices below, select the method of introduction used in "Teens and Jobs" _____, "A Vote against Computers" _____, and "Once Over Lightly: Local TV News" _____.

    a. Broad, general statement narrowing to thesis
    b. Idea that is the opposite of the one to be developed
    c. Quotation
    d. Anecdote
    e. Questions

10. Which essay has a conclusion that briefly summarizes the essay's supporting points?

    _____

Activity

In scratch-outline form on separate paper, provide brief supporting reasons for at least five of the fifteen statements below. Note the example. Make sure that you have three *separate* and *distinct* reasons for each statement.

Example   Recycling of newspapers, cans, and bottles should be mandatory.
  a.   Towns make money on sales of recycled items rather than pay for dumping.
  b.   Natural resources are protected.
  c.   Respect for the environment is encouraged.

1.   Couples should be required to live together for six months before marriage.
2.   Many Americans are more concerned with buying things than with trying to be decent human beings.
3.   High schools should distribute birth control devices and information to students.
4.   All teachers should be graded by their students, and the grades should be posted.
5.   TV commercials are often particularly insulting to women.
6.   Professional boxing should be outlawed.
7.   Attendance at college classes should be optional.
8.   When technology makes it possible, our government should have the right to control the weather.
9.   People should begin planning for retirement when they are young.
10.   Cigarette companies should not be allowed to advertise.
11.   Television does more harm than good.
12.   Killing animals for food is wrong.
13.   School does not prepare you for life.
14.   Governments should not pay ransom for terrorist kidnappings.
15.   All companies should be required to have day-care centers.

WRITING THE ESSAY

■ Writing Assignment 1

Decide, perhaps through discussion with your instructor or classmates, which of the outlines prepared in the preceding activity would be the most promising to develop into an essay. Make sure that your supporting reasons are logical ones that actually back up your thesis statement. Ask yourself in each case, "Does this reason truly support my thesis idea?"

How to Proceed

a   On separate paper, make a list of details that might go under each of the supporting points. Provide more details than you can possibly use. Here, for example, are the details generated by the writer of "Teens and Jobs" when she was working on her first supporting paragraph:

School problems:

Less time for sports and other activities
Lower attendance at games
Students leave right after school
Students sleep in class and skip homework
Teachers are angry and frustrated
More time buying things like clothing and compact disks
More stress for students and less concentration
Some students try to do it all and get sick
Students miss school to go to work
Some drop out of school

b   Decide which reasons and details you will use to develop each of your supporting paragraphs. Also, number the items in the order in which you will present them. Here is how the writer of "Teens and Jobs" made decisions on what to develop:

2   School problems
~~Less time for sports and other activities~~
~~Lower attendance at games~~
~~Students leave right after school~~
1   Students sleep in class and skip homework
~~Teachers are angry and frustrated~~
~~More time buying things like clothing and compact disks~~
~~More stress for students and less concentration~~
3   Some students try to do it all and get sick
~~Students miss school to go to work~~
~~Some drop out of school~~

c   As you are working on the drafts of your paper, refer to the checklist on the inside front cover. Make sure that you can answer *Yes* to the questions about unity, support, and coherence.

d   You may also want to refer to pages 49–52 for suggestions on writing an effective introduction and conclusion to your essay.

e   Finally, use the checklist on the inside front cover when you are proofreading the next-to-final draft of your paper for sentence-skills mistakes, including spelling.

■ Writing Assignment 2

Write a paper in which you argue *for* or *against* any *one* of the three comments below. Support and defend your argument by drawing upon your reasoning ability and general experience.

Option 1

In some ways, television has proved to be one of the worst inventions of recent times. All too often, television is harmful because of the shows it broadcasts and the way it is used in the home.

Option 2

College athletes devote a lot of time and energy to teams that sometimes make a great deal of money for their schools. Often athletes stress a sport at the expense of their education. And their efforts rarely give these young men and women experiences and skills that are useful after college. It is only fair, therefore, that college athletes be paid for their work.

Option 3

Many of society's worst problems with drugs result from the fact that they are illegal. During Prohibition, America discovered that making popular substances unlawful causes more problems than it solves. Like alcohol, drugs should be legal in this country.

How to Proceed

a   Take several minutes to think about the comments. Which one in particular are you for or against—and *why?*

b   On a sheet of paper, make up a brief outline of support for *your* position on one of the comments. Preparing the outline will give you a chance to think further about your position. And the outline will show whether you have enough support for your position. (If you don't, choose another position, and prepare another outline.)

   This initial thinking and outlining that you do is the key to preparing a solid paper. Your goal should be to decide on a position for which you can provide the most convincing evidence.

The writer of the model essay on computers was originally asked to take a position for or against the use of computers in the classroom. After a good deal of thinking, he came up with the following brief outline:

I am against the use of computers.
1. Don't help me plan a paper.
2. Are complicated to use.
3. Take up teacher's time.

While he had not yet written his first draft, he had already done the most important work on the paper.

c   Next, decide how you will develop each of your three supporting points. Make up brief outlines of the three points. Here, for example, is what the author of the computer essay did:

1. Don't help me plan a paper:
   Like to scribble.
   Use margins.
   Circle details on different parts of paper.
   See whole thing at once.
2. Are complicated to use:
   Sign out software.
   Get machine started.
   Wait for help.
   Type slowly.
3. Take up teacher's time:
   Helps students use computers.
   Has less time for writing feedback.

Such preliminary work is vital; to do a good paper, you must *think and plan and prewrite*. In addition to preparing brief outlines, you may also find that other prewriting techniques are useful. You may, variously, want to freewrite, brainstorm, and make up lists—all of which are described on pages 95–98 of this book.

d   Decide in what order you want to present your paragraphs. Often, emphatic order (in which you end with the most important reason) is an effective way to organize an argument, for the final reason is the one your reader is most likely to remember.

e   Provide as many convincing details as possible. For example, in the computer essay, the writer includes such supportive details as the following:

"If I write too much [on the computer], I have to scroll back and forth, since not everything can fit on the screen at once."

"I spend half of my time hunting and pecking for the proper letters on the keyboard."

"I sat here the other day watching the class trying to write on computers, and my impression was that 75 percent of what the teacher did involved computers rather than writing."

f As you write, imagine that your audience is a jury that will ultimately believe or disbelieve your argument. Have you presented a convincing case? Do you need more details? If *you* were on the jury, would you be favorably impressed with this argument?

g As you are working on the drafts of your paper, keep the four bases of unity, support, coherence, and sentence skills in mind.

h Finally, proofread the next-to-final draft of your paper for sentence-skills mistakes, including spelling.

■ Writing Assignment 3

Write a paper in which you argue *for* or *against* any *one* of the three comments below. Support and defend your argument by drawing upon your reasoning ability and general experience.

Option 1

While it is now well known that smoking is very unhealthy, it would be very difficult in our society to make it illegal. But that does not mean smoking should be encouraged. On the contrary, cigarette advertising should be banned.

Option 2

By the time many students reach high school, they have learned the basics in most subjects. Some still have much to gain from the education that high schools offer, but others might be better off spending the next four years in other ways. For their benefit, high school attendance should be voluntary, not compulsory.

Option 3

It is sad but true that some of the most miserable days in many people's lives are their last days. It is also true there is no way to avoid dying. But establishing centers where people can choose to end their lives in peace can eliminate the long suffering that many fatal illnesses cause. The government should take an active role in creating such centers.

Remember that the best way to get started is *to think, plan, and prewrite*. Which comment do you feel most strongly for or against? What are three solid reasons you can give to support your position? After you work out a satisfactory scratch outline, go on to follow the rest of the steps described in Writing Assignment 2.

■ Writing Assignment 4

Write a paper in which you argue *for* or *against* any *one* of the three comments below. Support and defend your argument by drawing upon your reasoning ability and general experience.

Option 1

Giving students grades does more harm than good. Schools should replace grades with evaluations, which would benefit both students and parents.

Option 2

Because our jails are overcrowded and expensive, the fewer people sentenced to jail the better. Of course, it is necessary to put violent criminals in jail in order to protect others. Society, however, would benefit if nonviolent criminals received punishments other than jail sentences.

Option 3

Physical punishment is often a successful way of disciplining children. After all, no child wants to experience pain. But adults who frequently spank and hit are also teaching the lesson that violence is a good method of accomplishing a goal. Nonviolent methods are a more effective way of training children.

■ Writing Assignment 5

Write a paper in which you argue *for* or *against* any *one* of the three comments below. Support and defend your argument by drawing upon your reasoning ability and general experience.

Option 1

Junk food is available in school cafeterias and school vending machines, and the cafeteria menus do not encourage the best of eating habits. But good education should include good examples as well as class work. Schools should practice what they preach about a healthy diet and stop providing junk food.

Option 2

The sale of handguns to private citizens should be banned throughout America. It is true that the Constitution guarantees the right to bear arms, but that does not necessarily mean any type of arms. Some weapons, including handguns, are simply too dangerous to be legal.

Option 3

Many of today's young people are mainly concerned with prestigious careers, making money, and owning things. It seems we no longer teach the benefits of spending time and money to help the community, the country, and the world. Our country can strengthen these human values and improve the world by requiring young people to spend a year working in some type of community service.

■ Writing Assignment 6

Write a paper in which you use research findings to help support one of the statements on page 209. Research the topic you have chosen in one or both of the following ways:

- Look up the topic in the subject section of your library card catalog. Possible subject headings for some of the statements on page 209 include *Birth control, Marriage contracts, Day-care centers, Advertising, Weather, Retirement, Smoking,* and *Terrorism.* Select the books listed under a heading that seem likely to give you relevant information about your topic. Then find the books in the library stacks.
- Look up the topic in recent issues of *Readers' Guide to Periodical Literature.* Try some of the same headings suggested above. Select the articles listed under a heading that appear most likely to provide information on your topic. Then see if you can find some of these articles in the periodicals section of your library.

Reading material on your topic will help you think about that topic. See if you can organize your paper in the form of three reasons that support the topic.

Put these reasons into a scratch outline, and use it as a guide in writing your paragraph. Here is an example:

Prayer should not be allowed in the public schools.
a. Children who are not religious will feel excluded.
b. Children may still pray silently whenever they please.
c. Not all schools and teachers will keep prayer nondenominational.

Note that statistical information, the results of studies, and the advice of experts may all help develop the supporting reasons for your thesis. Do not hesitate to cite such information in a limited way; it helps make your argument more objective and compelling.

■ **Writing Assignment 7:**
Writing about a Reading Selection

Read the selection titled "College Lectures" on pages 440–443. Notice how the author gives reasons *against* lectures and *for* interactive classes. Then write an essay in which you try to persuade your readers that a particular classroom activity, method, or policy is good or bad by presenting reasons for or against it. You may wish, for instance, to argue for or against one of the following:

Weekly quizzes

Grades

Evaluations instead of grades

Class discussions

Mandatory attendance

Choose a subject for which you can find three strong reasons pro or con. Each of your reasons or points will form a topic sentence for one supporting paragraph. Following, for example, is a brief outline for an essay persuading readers of the benefits of weekly quizzes. Each of the three reasons is a topic sentence for one supporting paragraph.

Thesis: Weekly quizzes can be a useful part of students' education.
1. They help motivate students to keep up with class work.
2. They give students frequent feedback on their work.
3. They give teachers frequent insight into students' progress.

Develop your supporting paragraphs by explaining each topic sentence, using examples to illustrate your points.

PART FOUR

HANDBOOK
OF SENTENCE
SKILLS

SUBJECTS
AND VERBS

The basic building blocks of English sentences are subjects and verbs. Understanding them is an important first step toward mastering a number of sentence skills.

Every sentence has a subject and a verb. Who or what the sentence speaks about is called the *subject;* what the sentence says about the subject is called the *verb.* In the following sentences, the subject is underlined once and the verb twice:

The boy cried.

That fish smells.

Many people applied for the job.

The show is a documentary.

A SIMPLE WAY TO FIND A SUBJECT

To find a subject, ask *who* or *what* the sentence is about. As shown below, your answer is the subject.

Who is the first sentence about? The boy

What is the second sentence about? That fish

Who is the third sentence about? Many people

What is the fourth sentence about? The show

A SIMPLE WAY TO FIND A VERB

To find a verb, ask what the sentence *says about* the subject. As shown below, your answer is the verb.

What does the first sentence *say about* the boy? He cried.

What does the second sentence *say about* the fish? It smells.

What does the third sentence *say about* the people? They applied.

What does the fourth sentence *say about* the show? It is a documentary.

A second way to find the verb is to put *I, you, he, she, it,* or *they* in front of the word you think is a verb. If the result makes sense, you have a verb. For example, you could put *he* in front of *cried* in the first sentence above, with the result, *he cried,* making sense. Therefore you know that *cried* is a verb. You could use the same test with the other three verbs as well.

Finally, it helps to remember that most verbs show action. In the sentences already considered, the three action verbs are *cried, smells,* and *applied.* Certain other verbs, known as *linking verbs,* do not show action. They do, however, give information about the subject. In "The show is a documentary," the linking verb *is* tells us that the show is a documentary. Other common linking verbs include *am, are, was, were, feel, appear, look, become,* and *seem.*

Activity

In each of the following sentences, draw one line under the subject and two lines under the verb.

1. The ripening tomatoes glistened on the sunny windowsill.
2. Biofeedback reduces the pain of my headaches.
3. Elena nervously twisted a strand of hair around her fingers.
4. My brother made our stereo cabinet from inexpensive particle board.
5. A jackrabbit bounds up to fifteen feet in one leap.

MORE ABOUT SUBJECTS AND VERBS

1   A sentence may have more than one verb, more than one subject, or several subjects and verbs.

   The engine coughed and sputtered.
   Broken glass and empty cans littered the parking lot.
   Joyce, Brenda, and Robert met after class and headed downtown.

2   The subject of a sentence never appears within a prepositional phrase. A *prepositional phrase* is simply a group of words that begins with a preposition. Following is a list of common prepositions:

about	before	by	inside	over
above	behind	during	into	through
across	below	except	of	to
among	beneath	for	off	toward
around	beside	from	on	under
at	between	in	onto	with

Cross out prepositional phrases when looking for the subject of a sentence.

   The weathered old house perched unsteadily on its rotted foundation.
   The label on that mayonnaise jar can be easily removed with hot water.
   The color picture on our TV set turns black and white during a storm.
   The murky waters of the polluted lake spilled over the dam.
   The amber lights on its sides outlined the tractor-trailer in the hazy dusk.

3   Many verbs consist of more than one word. Here, for example, are some of the many forms of the verb *work*:

work	worked	should work
works	were working	will be working
does work	have worked	can work
is working	had worked	could be working
are working	had been working	must have worked

Notes

a   Words like *not, just, never, only,* and *always* are not part of the verb although they may appear within the verb.

Rebecca has just finished filling out her tax form.

The intersection has not always been this dangerous.

b   No verb preceded by *to* is ever the verb of a sentence.

At night, my son likes to read under the covers.

Evelyn decided to separate from her husband.

c   No *-ing* word by itself is ever the verb of a sentence. (It may be part of the verb, but it must have a helping verb in front of it.)

They going on a trip this weekend.   (not a sentence, because the verb is not complete)

They are going on a trip this weekend.   (a sentence)

Activity

Draw a single line under subjects and a double line under verbs. Crossing out prepositional phrases may help you to find the subjects.

1. The top of our refrigerator is covered with dusty pots and pans.
2. A new muffler and tailpipe were just installed in my car.
3. The people in the all-night coffee shop seemed weary and lost.
4. Every plant in the dim room bent toward the small window.
5. A glaring headline about the conviction of a local congressman attracted my attention.

■ Final Activity

Draw a single line under subjects and a double line under verbs. Crossing out prepositional phrases may help you to find the subjects.

1. With one graceful motion, the shortstop fielded the grounder and threw to first base.
2. Forty-seven czars are buried within the walls of Moscow's Kremlin.
3. Before class, Barbara and Aaron rushed to the coffee machine in the hall.
4. I punched and prodded my feather pillow before settling down to sleep.
5. Matt has been exercising twice a day to keep his weight down.
6. Cattle branding was practiced by ancient Egyptians over four thousand years ago.
7. Lilacs and honeysuckle perfume our yard on summer nights.
8. The mail carrier abruptly halted her Jeep and backed up toward the mailbox.
9. During the American Revolution, some brides rejected white wedding gowns and wore red as a symbol of rebellion.
10. The little girl's frantic family called a psychic to help locate the child.

SENTENCE FRAGMENTS

Every sentence must have a subject and a verb and must express a complete thought. A word group that lacks a subject or a verb or that does not express a complete thought is a *fragment*. The four most common types of fragments that people write are explained on the following pages.

DEPENDENT-WORD FRAGMENTS

Some word groups that begin with a dependent word are fragments. Here is a list of common dependent words:

after	if, even if	when
although	in order that	where
as	since	whether
because	that, so that	which
before	unless	while
until	who	whose

Whenever you start a sentence with one of these words, you must be careful that a fragment does not result. The word group beginning with the dependent word *After* in the example below is a fragment.

> After I cashed my paycheck. I treated myself to dinner.

A *dependent statement*—one starting with a dependent word like *After*—cannot stand alone. It depends on another statement to complete the thought. *After I cashed my paycheck* is a dependent statement. It leaves us hanging. We expect in the same sentence to find out *what happened after* the writer cashed the check. When a writer does not follow through and complete a thought, a fragment results.

In most cases you can correct a dependent-word fragment by attaching it to the sentence that comes after it or the sentence that comes before it:

> After I cashed my paycheck, I treated myself to dinner.

Remember, then, that a *dependent statement by itself is a fragment.* It must be attached to a statement that makes sense standing alone.

Activity

Underline the dependent-word fragment in each selection. Then correct the fragment by attaching it to the sentence that comes before or the sentence that comes after it. Put a comma after the dependent-word group if it starts the sentence.

1. Whenever I spray deodorant. My cat arches her back. She thinks she is hearing a hissing enemy.

   _____

   _____

2. I bought a calendar watch. Which is running fast. Last week had eight days.

   _____

   _____

3. If Kim takes too long saying good-bye to her boyfriend. Her father will start flicking the porch light.

   _____

   _____

-ING OR TO FRAGMENTS

When an -ing word appears at or near the start of a word group, a fragment may result. A fragment may also result when to appears at or near the start of a word group.

The word group beginning with trying in the example below is a fragment:

Ellen walked all over the neighborhood yesterday. Trying to find her dog Bo. Several people claimed they had seen him only hours before.

The word group beginning with to in the example below is also a fragment:

At the Chinese restaurant, Tim used chopsticks. To impress his date. He spent one hour eating a small bowl of rice.

An -ing or to fragment can often be corrected by attaching the fragment to the sentence that comes before or after it:

Ellen walked all over the neighborhood yesterday, trying to find her dog Bo.
At the Chinese restaurant, Tim used chopsticks to impress his date.

In some cases, you may want to add a subject to the fragment and change the -ing verb part, as in the following example. (The fragment begins with Not.)

We sat back to watch the movie. Not expecting anything special. The movie then kept us on the edge of our seats for the next two hours.
We sat back to watch the movie. We did not expect anything special. (The subject we has been added and the verb changed to did not expect.)

Activity

Underline the -ing or to fragment in each selection. Then correct the fragment by using one of the two methods of correction described on the preceding page.

1. Flora scratched her mosquito bites. Trying to stop the itching. Instead, they began to bleed.

_____

_____

2. I put a box of baking soda in the freezer. To get rid of the musty smell. However, my ice cubes still taste like old socks.

    _____

    _____

3. Staring at the clock on the far wall. I nervously began my speech. I was afraid to look at any of the people in the room.

    _____

    _____

ADDED-DETAIL FRAGMENTS

Added-detail fragments lack a subject and verb; they often begin with *also, especially, except, for example, including,* or *such as.*

The word group beginning with *Such as* in the following example is a fragment:

> Before a race, I eat starchy food. Such as bread and spaghetti. The carbohydrates provide quick energy.

An added-detail fragment can often be corrected by attaching it to the preceding sentence:

> Before a race, I eat starchy food such as bread and spaghetti.

Adding a subject and verb is sometimes necessary to correct an added-detail fragment. In the following example, the word group beginning with *Also* is a fragment:

> Bob is taking a night course in auto mechanics. Also, one in plumbing. He wants to save money on household repairs.

In order to correct the fragment, you must add a subject and verb:

> Bob is taking a night course in auto mechanics. Also, he is taking one in plumbing.

Activity

Underline the added-detail fragment in each selection. Then correct the fragment by using one of the methods of correction shown on the preceding page.

1. I wonder now why I had to learn certain subjects. Such as geometry. No one has ever asked me about the hypotenuse of a triangle.

   _____

   _____

2. Schools are beginning to use advanced technology. For instance, computers and word processors. Tomorrow's students will be "computer-literate."

   _____

   _____

3. My mother likes watching daytime TV shows. Especially old movies and soap operas. She says that daytime TV is less violent.

   _____

   _____

MISSING-SUBJECT FRAGMENTS

Missing-subject fragments are word groups in which the subject is missing.

The word group beginning with *But* in the following example is a missing-subject fragment:

Alice loved getting her wedding presents. But hated writing the thank-you notes.

You can correct a missing-subject fragment by either (1) attaching the fragment to the preceding sentence or (2) adding a subject to the fragment.

Alice loved getting her wedding presents but hated writing the thank-you notes. (The fragment has been attached to the sentence.)

Alice loved getting her wedding presents. But she hated writing the thank-you notes. (The subject *she* has been added.)

Activity

Underline the missing-subject fragment in each selection. Then correct the fragment by using one of the methods of correction described above.

1. Every other day, Karen runs two miles. Then does fifty sit-ups. As a result, she has more energy.

   _____

   _____

2. To be a defensive driver, you must assume the worst. Every other driver on the road is incompetent. And is out there trying to kill you.

   _____

   _____

3. My brother has orange soda and potato chips for breakfast. Then eats more junk food, like root beer and cookies, for lunch.

   _____

   _____

■ Final Activity 1

Each word group in the student paragraph below is numbered. In the spaces provided on the next page, write C if a word group is a complete sentence; write F if it is a fragment. You will find eight fragments in the paragraph.

[1]I'm starting to think that there is no safe place left. [2]To ride a bicycle. [3]When I try to ride on the highway, in order to go to school. [4]I feel like a rabbit being pursued by predators. [5]Drivers whip past me at high speeds. [6]And try to see how close they can get to my bike without actually killing me. [7]When they pull onto the shoulder of the road or make a right turn. [8]Drivers completely ignore my vehicle. [9]On city streets, I feel more like a cockroach than a rabbit. [10]Drivers in the city despise bicycles. [11]Regardless of an approaching bike rider. [12]Street-side car doors will unexpectedly open. [13]Frustrated drivers who are stuck in traffic will make nasty comments. [14]Or shout out obscene propositions. [15]Even pedestrians in the city show their disregard for me. [16]While jaywalking across the street. [17]The pedestrian will treat me, a law-abiding bicyclist, to a withering look of disdain. [18]Pedestrians may even cross my path deliberately. [19]As if to prove their higher position in the pecking order of the city streets. [20]Today, bicycling can be hazardous to the rider's health.

1. _____	11. _____
2. _____	12. _____
3. _____	13. _____
4. _____	14. _____
5. _____	15. _____
6. _____	16. _____
7. _____	17. _____
8. _____	18. _____
9. _____	19. _____
10. _____	20. _____

■ Final Activity 2

Underline the two fragments in each selection that follows. Then make whatever changes are needed to turn the fragments into sentences.

Example   Sharon was going to charge her new suit. But then decided to pay cash instead. She remembered her New Year's resolution. To cut down on her use of credit cards.

1. We both began to tire. As we passed the halfway mark in the race. But whenever I heard Jim's footsteps behind me. I pumped my legs a little faster.

2. I have a few phobias. Such as fear of heights and fear of dogs. My ultimate nightmare is to be trapped in a hot-air balloon. With three German shepherds.

3. Dom passed the computer school's aptitude test. Which qualifies him for nine months of training. Dom kidded that anyone could be accepted. If he had four thousand dollars.

4. Punching all the buttons on his radio in sequence. Phil kept looking for a good song. He was in the mood to cruise down the highway. And sing at the top of his voice.

5. I noticed two cartons of cigarettes. Sticking up out of my neighbor's trash bag. I realized he had made up his mind. To give up smoking for the fifth time this year.

RUN-ONS

A run-on is two complete thoughts that are run together with no adequate sign given to mark the break between them. Some run-ons have no punctuation at all to mark the break between the thoughts:

> Tim told everyone in the room to be quiet his favorite show was on.
> My blow dryer shorted out I showed up for work with Harpo Marx hair.

Most run-ons, however, occur as *comma splices:* the writer places a comma between two complete thoughts. But the comma alone is *not enough* to join two complete thoughts:

> Tim told everyone in the room to be quiet, his favorite show was on.
> My blow dryer shorted out, I showed up for work with Harpo Marx hair.

Note: People often write run-on sentences when the second complete thought begins with one of the following words: *I, you, he, she, it, we, they, there, this, that, now, then, next.*

METHODS OF CORRECTING A RUN-ON

Here are four common methods of correcting a run-on.

1   Use a period and a capital letter to mark the break between the thoughts:

Tim told everyone in the room to be quiet. His favorite show was on.

My blow dryer shorted out. I showed up for work with Harpo Marx hair.

2   Use a comma plus a joining word (*and, but, for, or, nor, so, yet*) to connect the two complete thoughts:

Tim told everyone in the room to be quiet, for his favorite show was on.

My blow dryer shorted out, and I showed up for work with Harpo Marx hair.

3   Use a semicolon to connect the two complete thoughts:

Tim told everyone in the room to be quiet; his favorite show was on.

My blow dryer shorted out; I showed up for work with Harpo Marx hair.

Note: A semicolon is sometimes used with an adverbial conjunction and a comma to join two complete thoughts:

Tim believes in being prepared for emergencies; *therefore,* he stockpiles canned goods in his basement.

I tried to cash my paycheck; *however,* I had forgotten to bring identification.

Other common adverbial conjunctions are *nevertheless, furthermore, on the other hand, instead, meanwhile, otherwise, in addition, also, moreover, thus, as a result,* and *consequently.*

4   Use a dependent word such as *after, because, since, when,* or *although* to connect the thoughts:

Tim told everyone in the room to be quiet because his favorite show was on.

When my blow dryer shorted out, I showed up for work with Groucho Marx hair.

Other common dependent words are *as, before, until, if, unless, that, who, which,* and *while.* More information is provided about the use of dependent words in the section on subordination on page 291.

Activity

In the space provided, write R-O beside run-on sentences. Write C beside sentences that are correctly punctuated. Some of the run-ons have no punctuation between the two complete thoughts; others have only a comma.

1. He glanced in the dusty bakery window, a rat was crawling over a cake.

2. Several cities in the United States sponsor odd food festivals Vineland, New Jersey, celebrates spring with a dandelion-eating spree.

3. Chuck bent over and lifted the heavy tray he heard an ominous crack in his back.

4. I felt sorry for the muzzled dog, he was trying to yawn.

5. The boys dared each other to enter the abandoned building then they heard a strange rustling noise coming from the murky interior.

6. Mice scurry along close walls, for they use their sensitive whiskers as feelers.

7. Kathy applied for a small bank loan she wanted to establish a credit history.

8. We stocked our backpacks with high-calorie candy bars, we also brought bags of dried apricots and peaches.

9. I waited impatiently for the clanking train to clear the intersection, but rusty boxcars continued to roll slowly along the rails.

10. Don was afraid to get in the supermarket express lane he had one item too many in his cart.

■ Final Activity 1

Correct each run-on with either (1) a period and a capital letter, (2) a comma and a logical joining word, (3) a semicolon, or (4) a dependent word.

but

Example Jim was exhausted, ∧he wanted to finish painting the garage before it rained.

1. I hopped crazily around the living room, my feet had fallen asleep.

2. The magazine had lain in the damp mailbox for two days its pages were blurry and swollen.

3. Dotty painted stars on her fingernails, then she drew little butterflies on her toenails.

4. Arnie reconditions used running shoes he slices off the old soles and glues on new ones.

5. Joan slipped off her high heels, she plunged her swollen feet into a bath of baking soda and hot water.

6. Suitcases circled on the conveyor belt at the airline baggage claim area loose oranges from a broken carton tumbled along with them.

7. Irene peeled off the tight wool knee socks she massaged the vertical red ridges imprinted on her skin.

8. My sister is a cleanliness fanatic, she washes the peels of bananas and oranges.

9. Hypnosis has nothing to do with the occult it is merely a state of deep relaxation.

10. The cost of living is higher than ever many young adults are being forced to stay at home and share expenses with their parents.

Final Activity 2

Follow the directions for the preceding activity.

1. The children stared at the artichokes on their plates they did not know how to eat the strange vegetable.

2. I changed that light bulb just last week now it's blown again.

3. The "no-frills" supermarket does not sell perishables like milk or meat customers must bring their own bags or boxes to pack their bargains.

4. Elaine woke up at 3 A.M. to the smell of sizzling bacon her husband was having another insomnia attack.

5. Jamie curled up under the covers she tried to get warm by grasping her icy feet with her chilly hands.

6. My dog was panting from the heat I decided to wet him down with the garden hose.

7. The bristles of the paintbrushes were very stiff soaking them in turpentine made them soft again.

8. We knew there had been a power failure all the clocks in the building were forty-seven minutes slow.

9. Jackie smeared cream cheese on the bagel half then she popped it into her mouth.

10. Cockroaches adapt to any environment they have even been found living inside nuclear reactors.

IRREGULAR VERBS

Regular verbs form the past tense and the past participle (the form of the verb used with *have, has,* or *had*) simply by adding *-d* or *-ed* to the present. For example, the past tense of the regular verb *enjoy* is *enjoyed;* the past participle is *have, has,* or *had enjoyed.* However, other verbs have irregular forms in their past tense and past participle. For example, the past tense of the irregular verb *grow* is *grew;* the past participle is *have, has,* or *had grown.*

LIST OF IRREGULAR VERBS

Almost everyone has some degree of trouble with irregular verbs. When you are unsure about the form of a verb, you can check this list of irregular verbs. Or you can check your dictionary, which gives the principal parts of irregular verbs.

Present	*Past*	*Past Participle*
arise	arose	arisen
awake	awoke *or* awaked	awoken *or* awaked
be (am, are, is)	was (were)	been
become	became	become
begin	began	begun
bend	bent	bent
bite	bit	bitten
blow	blew	blown

Present	*Past*	*Past Participle*
break	broke	broken
bring	brought	brought
build	built	built
burst	burst	burst
buy	bought	bought
catch	caught	caught
choose	chose	chosen
come	came	come
cost	cost	cost
cut	cut	cut
do (does)	did	done
draw	drew	drawn
drink	drank	drunk
drive	drove	driven
eat	ate	eaten
fall	fell	fallen
feed	fed	fed
feel	felt	felt
fight	fought	fought
find	found	found
fly	flew	flown
freeze	froze	frozen
get	got	got *or* gotten
give	gave	given
go (goes)	went	gone
grow	grew	grown
have (has)	had	had
hear	heard	heard
hide	hid	hidden
hold	held	held
hurt	hurt	hurt
keep	kept	kept
know	knew	known
lay	laid	laid
lead	led	led
leave	left	left
lend	lent	lent
let	let	let
lie	lay	lain
light	lit	lit

Present	Past	Past Participle
lose	lost	lost
make	made	made
meet	met	met
pay	paid	paid
ride	rode	ridden
ring	rang	rung
run	ran	run
say	said	said
see	saw	seen
sell	sold	sold
send	sent	sent
shake	shook	shaken
shrink	shrank	shrunk
shut	shut	shut
sing	sang	sung
sit	sat	sat
sleep	slept	slept
speak	spoke	spoken
spend	spent	spent
stand	stood	stood
steal	stole	stolen
stick	stuck	stuck
sting	stung	stung
swear	swore	sworn
swim	swam	swum
take	took	taken
teach	taught	taught
tear	tore	torn
tell	told	told
think	thought	thought
wake	woke *or* waked	woken *or* waked
wear	wore	worn
win	won	won
write	wrote	written

Activity

Cross out the incorrect verb form in each of the following sentences. Then write the correct form of the verb in the space provided.

flown   ***Example***   After it had ~~flew~~ into the picture window, the dazed bird huddled on the ground.

_____ 1. As graduation neared, Michelle worried about the practicality of the major she'd chose.

_____ 2. Before we could find seats, the theater darkened and the opening credits begun to roll.

_____ 3. To be polite, I drunk the slightly sour wine that my grandfather poured from his carefully hoarded supply.

_____ 4. With a thunderous crack, the telephone pole breaked in half from the impact of the speeding car.

_____ 5. The inexperienced nurse shrunk from touching the patient's raw, burned skin.

_____ 6. After a day on the noisy construction site, Sam's ears rung for hours with a steady hum.

_____ 7. Sheila had forgot to write her social security number on the test form, so the computer rejected her answer sheet.

_____ 8. If I had went to work ten minutes earlier, I would have avoided being caught in the gigantic traffic snarl.

_____ 9. After the bicycle hit a patch of soft sand, the rider was throwed into the thorny bushes by the roadside.

_____ 10. Prehistoric people blowed paint over their outstretched hands to stencil their handprints on cave walls.

THREE COMMON IRREGULAR VERBS:
DIALECT AND STANDARD FORMS

The following charts compare the community dialect and the standard English forms of the common irregular verbs *be, have,* and *do.*

BE

Community Dialect		Standard English	
(Do not use in your writing)		(Use for clear communication)	
Present tense			
I be (*or* is)	we be	I am	we are
you be	you be	you are	you are
he, she, it be	they be	he, she, it is	they are
Past tense			
I were	we was	I was	we were
you was	you was	you were	you were
he, she, it were	they was	he, she, it was	they were

HAVE

Community Dialect		Standard English	
(Do not use in your writing)		(Use for clear communication)	
Present tense			
I has	we has	I have	we have
you has	you has	you have	you have
he, she, it have	they has	he, she, it has	they have
Past tense			
I has	we has	I had	we had
you has	you has	you had	you had
he, she, it have	they has	he, she, it had	they had

DO

<table>
<tr><td colspan="2" align="center">**Community Dialect**
(Do not use in your writing)</td><td colspan="2" align="center">**Standard English**
(Use for clear communication)</td></tr>
<tr><td colspan="4" align="center">*Present tense*</td></tr>
<tr><td>I does</td><td>we do</td><td>I do</td><td>we do</td></tr>
<tr><td>you does</td><td>you does</td><td>you do</td><td>you do</td></tr>
<tr><td>he, she, it do</td><td>they does</td><td>he, she, it does</td><td>they do</td></tr>
<tr><td colspan="4" align="center">*Past tense*</td></tr>
<tr><td>I done</td><td>we done</td><td>I did</td><td>we did</td></tr>
<tr><td>you done</td><td>you done</td><td>you did</td><td>you did</td></tr>
<tr><td>he, she, it done</td><td>they done</td><td>he, she, it did</td><td>they did</td></tr>
</table>

Note: Many people have trouble with one negative form of *do*. They will say, for example, "He don't agree" instead of "He doesn't agree," or they will say "The door don't work" instead of "The door doesn't work." Be careful to avoid the common mistake of using *don't* instead of *doesn't*.

Activity

Cross out the nonstandard verb form in each sentence. Then write the standard form of *be, have,* or *do* in the space provided.

_____ 1. My cat, Tugger, be the toughest animal I know.

_____ 2. He have survived many close calls.

_____ 3. Three years ago, he were caught inside a car's engine.

_____ 4. He have one ear torn off and lost the sight in one eye.

_____ 5. We was surprised that he lived through the accident.

_____ 6. Within weeks, though, he were back to normal.

_____ 7. Then, last year, we was worried that we would lose Tugger.

_____ 8. Lumps that was growing on his back turned out to be cancer.

_____ 9. But the vet done an operation that saved Tugger's life.

_____ 10. By now, we know that Tugger really do have nine lives.

■ Final Activity

Underline the correct verb in the parentheses.

1. Single parents have (become, became) one of the fastest-growing segments of the American population.
2. The thieves would have (stole, stolen) my stereo, but I had had it engraved with a special identification number.
3. At the Chinese restaurant, Dave (choose, chose) his food by the number.
4. He had (tore, torn) his girl friend's picture into little pieces and tossed them out the window.
5. As I (has, have) asthma, I carry an inhaler to use when I lose my breath.
6. The health inspectors (come, came) into the kitchen as the cook picked up a hamburger off the floor.
7. The grizzly bear, with the dart dangling from its side, (began, begun) to feel the effects of the powerful tranquilizer.
8. Those cans of spray enamel (is, are) so old that the paint comes out in blobs.
9. Bill thought he had (laid, lain) the tiles correctly until they started peeling off the floor.
10. Nancy (stuck, sticked) notes on the refrigerator with fruit-shaped magnets.

SUBJECT-VERB AGREEMENT

A verb must agree with its subject in number. A singular subject (one person or thing) takes a singular verb. A plural subject (more than one person or thing) takes a plural verb. Mistakes in subject-verb agreement are sometimes made in each of the four situations explained below.

1 WORDS BETWEEN THE SUBJECT AND THE VERB

Words that come between the subject and the verb do not change subject-verb agreement. In the sentence

The crinkly <u>lines</u> around Joan's eyes <u>give</u> her a friendly look.

the subject (*lines*) is plural, and so the verb (*give*) is plural. The words *around Joan's eyes* that come between the subject and the verb do not affect subject-verb agreement.

To find the subject of certain sentences, you should cross out prepositional phrases.

The lumpy <u>salt</u> ~~in the shakers~~ <u>needs</u> to be changed.
An old <u>television</u> ~~with a round screen~~ <u>has sat</u> ~~in our basement for years~~.

2   VERB BEFORE THE SUBJECT

A verb agrees with its subject even when the verb comes *before* the subject. Words that may precede the subject include *there, here,* and (in questions) *who, which, what,* and *where.* Here are some examples of verbs before subjects:

There <u>are</u> wild <u>dogs</u> in our neighborhood.
In the distance <u>was</u> a <u>billow</u> of black smoke.

3   COMPOUND SUBJECTS

Compound subjects joined by *and* generally take a plural verb:

A patchwork <u>quilt</u> and a sleeping <u>bag</u> <u>cover</u> my bed in the winter.
<u>Clark</u> and <u>Lois</u> <u>are</u> a contented couple.

When subjects are joined by *either . . . or, neither . . . nor,* or *not only . . . but also,* the verb agrees with the subject closer to the verb:

Neither the government negotiator nor the union <u>leaders</u> <u>want</u> a strike.

The nearer subject, *leaders,* is plural, and so the verb is plural.

4   INDEFINITE PRONOUNS

Indefinite pronouns always take singular verbs. Indefinite pronouns include *one, anyone, everyone, someone, nobody, anybody, everybody, somebody, nothing, anything, everything, something, each, either,* and *neither.*

<u>Neither</u> of those hairstyles <u>suits</u> the shape of your face.
<u>Everyone</u> <u>enters</u> the college kite-flying contest in the spring.

Note: *Both* always takes a plural verb.

Activity 1

Write the correct form of the verb in the space provided.

(mope, mopes) 1. Behind the bars of the cage _____ a sad, flea-bitten lion.

(was, were) 2. Each of their children _____ given a name picked at random from a page of the Bible.

(make, makes) 3. A metal grab bar bolted onto the tile _____ it easier for elderly people to get in and out of the bathtub.

(was, were) 4. Several packages and a supermarket circular _____ lying on the porch mat.

(work, works) 5. Anyone who _____ with fiberglass insulation should wear heavy gloves and protective goggles.

(want, wants) 6. Some members of the parents' association _____ to ban certain books from the school library.

(cover, covers) 7. Spidery cracks and a layer of dust _____ the ivory keys on the old piano.

(force, forces) 8. The rising costs of necessities like food and shelter _____ many elderly people to live in poverty.

(give, gives) 9. Something in certain kinds of cheese _____ me a headache.

(is, are) 10. There _____ dozens of frenzied shoppers waiting for the store to open.

Activity 2

Underline the correct verb in parentheses.

1. The use of metal chains and studded tires (damage, damages) roadways by chipping away at the paved surface.
2. Next to the cash register (was, were) a can for donations to the animal protection society.
3. In exchange for a reduced rent, Karla and James (clean, cleans) the dentist's office beneath their second-floor apartment.
4. The human being is the only animal that (communicate, communicates)— through the ability to write—with future generations.
5. Some wheelchair-bound patients, in an interesting experiment, (is, are) using trained monkeys as helpers.

6. Anyone who (try, tries) out for the women's rowing team must pass a rigorous swimming test.

7. A man in his thirties often (begin, begins) to think about making a contribution to the world and not just about himself.

8. Neither of the textbooks (contain, contains) the answer to question 5 of the "open-book" exam.

9. One of the hospital's delivery rooms (is, are) furnished with bright carpets and curtains to resemble a room at home.

10. Envelopes, file folders, and plastic sandwich bags filled with store coupons (is, are) jammed into Karen's kitchen drawers.

ADDITIONAL INFORMATION ABOUT VERBS

The purpose of this special section is to provide additional information about verbs. Some people will find the grammar terms here a helpful reminder of earlier school learning about verbs. For them, the terms will increase their understanding of how verbs function in English. Other people may welcome more detailed information about terms used elsewhere in the text. In either case, remember that the most common mistakes that people make when writing verbs have been treated in earlier sections of the book.

VERB TENSE

Verbs tell us the time of an action. The time that a verb shows is usually called *tense*. The most common tenses are the simple present, past, and future. In addition, there are nine other tenses that enable us to express more specific ideas about time than we could with the simple tenses alone. Shown below are the twelve verb tenses and examples of each tense. Read them over to increase your sense of the many different ways of expressing time in English.

Tenses	*Examples*
Present	I *work*.
	Tony *works*.
Past	Ellen *worked* on her car.
Future	You *will work* on a new project next week.

247

Tenses	*Examples*
Present perfect	He *has worked* on his term paper for a month. They *have worked* out a compromise.
Past perfect	The nurse *had worked* two straight shifts.
Future perfect	Next Monday, I *will have worked* here exactly two years.
Present progressive	I *am working* on my speech for the debate. You *are working* too hard. The tape recorder *is* not *working* properly.
Past progressive	He *was working* in the basement. The contestants *were working* on their talent routines.
Future progressive	My son *will be working* in our family business this summer.
Present perfect progressive	Sarah *has been working* late this week.
Past perfect progressive	Until recently, I *had been working* nights.
Future perfect progressive	My mother *will have been working* as a nurse for forty-five years by the time she retires.

Activity

On separate paper, write twelve sentences using the twelve verb tenses.

CONSISTENT VERB TENSE

Do not shift verb tenses unnecessarily. If you begin writing a paper in the present tense, do not shift suddenly to the past. If you begin in the past, do not shift without reason to the present. Notice the inconsistent verb tenses in the following selection:

Jean *punched* down the risen yeast dough in the bowl. Then she *dumps* it onto the floured work table and *kneaded* it into a smooth, shiny ball.

The verbs must be consistently in the present tense:

Jean *punches* down the risen yeast dough in the bowl. Then she *dumps* it onto the floured work table and *kneads* it into a smooth, shiny ball.

Or the verbs must be consistently in the past tense:

> Jean *punched* down the risen yeast dough in the bowl. Then she *dumped* it onto the floured work table and *kneaded* it into a smooth, shiny ball.

Activity

Make the verbs in each sentence consistent with the *first* verb used. Cross out the incorrect verb and write the correct form in the space at the right.

ran   **Example**   Aunt Helen tried to kiss her little nephew, but he r̸u̸n̸s̸ out of the room.

_____   1. An aggressive news photographer knocked a reporter to the ground as the movie stars arrive for the Oscar awards.

_____   2. As we leafed through the old high school yearbook, we laughed at our outdated clothes and hairstyles.

_____   3. "My husband is so dumb," said Martha, "that when he went to Las Vegas he tries to play the stamp machines."

_____   4. In a zero-gravity atmosphere, water breaks up into droplets and floated around in space.

_____   5. Elliot lights the oven pilot and then stands back as the blue gas flames flared up.

HELPING VERBS

There are three common verbs that can either stand alone or combine with (and "help") other verbs. Here are the verbs and their forms:

> be (being, been, am, are, is, was, were)
> have (has, having, had)
> do (does, did)

Examples of the verbs:

Used Alone	*Used as Helping Verbs*
I *was* angry.	I *was growing* angry.
Sue *has* the key.	Sue *has forgotten* the key.
He *did* well in the test.	He *did fail* the previous test.

There are nine helping verbs (traditionally known as *modals,* or *modal auxiliaries*) that are always used in combination with other verbs. Here are the nine verbs and sentence examples of each:

can	I *can see* the rainbow.
could	I *could* not *find* a seat.
may	The game *may be postponed.*
might	Cindy *might resent* your advice.
shall	I *shall see* you tomorrow.
should	He *should get* his car serviced.
will	Tony *will want* to see you.
would	They *would* not *understand.*
must	You *must visit* us again.

Note from the examples that these verbs have only one form. They do not, for instance, add an *-s* when used with *he, she, it,* or any one person or thing.

Activity

On separate paper, write nine sentences using the nine helping verbs.

ACTIVE AND PASSIVE VERBS

When the subject of a sentence performs the action of a verb, the verb is in the *active voice.* When the subject of a sentence receives the action of a verb, the verb is in the *passive voice.*

The passive form of a verb consists of a form of the verb *be* plus the past participle of the main verb. Look at these active and passive forms:

Active	*Passive*
Jan sewed the kitchen curtains. (The subject, *Jan,* is the doer of the action.)	The kitchen curtains were sewn by Jan. (The subject, *curtains,* does not act. Instead, something happens to them.)
The repairman fixed the air conditioner. (The subject, *repairman,* is the doer of the action.)	The air conditioner was fixed by the repairman. (The subject, *air conditioner,* does not act. Instead, something happens to it.)

In general, active verbs are more effective than passive ones. Active verbs give your writing a simpler and more vigorous style. At times, however, the passive form of verbs is appropriate when the performer of the action is unknown or is less important than the receiver of the action. For example:

The tests were graded yesterday.
(The performer of the action is unknown.)

Alan was very hurt by your thoughtless remark.
(The receiver of the action, Alan, is being emphasized.)

Activity

Change the sentences on the following page from the passive to the active voice. Note that you may have to add a subject in some cases.

Examples   The dog was found by a police officer.

A police officer found the dog.

The baseball game was called off.

The officials called off the baseball game.
(Here a subject had to be added.)

1. Most of our furniture was damaged by the fire.

    _____

2. Marsha's new dress was singed by a careless smoker.

    _____

3. The problem was solved by the quiet student in the back of the room.

    _____

4. The supermarket shelves were restocked after the truckers' strike.

    _____

5. The children were mesmerized by the magician's sleight of hand.

    _____

MISPLACED
AND DANGLING
MODIFIERS

MISPLACED MODIFIERS

Misplaced modifiers are words that, because of awkward placement, do not describe the words the writer intended them to describe. Misplaced modifiers often confuse the meaning of a sentence. To avoid them, place words as close as possible to what they describe.

Misplaced Words

George couldn't drive to work in his small sports car *with a broken leg.*

(The sports car had a broken leg?)

The toaster was sold to us by a charming salesman *with a money-back guarantee.*

(The salesman had a money-back guarantee?)

He *nearly* brushed his teeth for twenty minutes every night.

(He came close to brushing his teeth but in fact did not brush them at all?)

Correctly Placed Words

With a broken leg, George couldn't drive to work in his small sports car.
(The words describing George are now placed next to the word *George.*)

The toaster with a money-back guarantee was sold to us by a charming salesman.
(The words describing the toaster are now placed next to it.)

He brushed his teeth for nearly twenty minutes every night.
(The meaning—that he brushed his teeth for a long time—is now clear.)

DANGLING MODIFIERS

A modifier that opens a sentence must be followed immediately by the word it is meant to describe. Otherwise, the modifier is said to be *dangling,* and the sentence takes on an unintended meaning. Here are some sentences with dangling modifiers. Read the explanations of why they are dangling and look carefully at the ways they are corrected.

Dangling	*Correct*
Shaving in front of a steamy mirror, the razor nicked Ed's chin. (*Who* was shaving in front of the mirror? The answer is not *razor* but *Ed*. The subject *Ed* must be added.)	Shaving in front of the steamy mirror, Ed nicked his chin with the razor. *Or:* When Ed was shaving in front of the steamy mirror, he nicked his chin with the razor.
While turning over the bacon, hot grease splashed my arm. (*Who* is turning over the bacon? The answer is not *hot grease,* as it unintentionally seems to be, but *I*. The subject *I* must be added.)	While I was turning over the bacon, hot grease splashed my arm. *Or:* While turning over the bacon, I was splashed on the arm by hot grease.
Taking the exam, the room was so stuffy that Paula almost fainted. (*Who* took the exam? The answer is not *room* but *Paula*. The subject *Paula* must be added.)	Taking the exam, Paula found the room so stuffy that she almost fainted. *Or:* When Paula took the exam, the room was so stuffy that she almost fainted.
To impress the interviewer, punctuality is essential. (*Who* is to impress the interviewer? The answer is not *punctuality* but *you*. The subject *you* must be added.)	To impress the interviewer, you must be punctual. *Or:* For you to impress the interviewer, punctuality is essential.

Activity

Underline the misplaced or dangling modifier in each sentence. Then rewrite the sentence, placing related words together or adding a logical subject, to make the meaning clear.

1. Kicked carelessly under the bed, Marion finally found her sneakers.

   _____

   _____

2. Working at the copying machine, the morning dragged on.

   _____

   _____

3. The latest James Bond movie has almost opened in 1,200 theaters across the country.

   _____

   _____

4. Tired and exasperated, the fight we had was inevitable.

   _____

   _____

5. The newscaster spoke softly into a microphone wearing a bulletproof vest.

   _____

   _____

6. The tenants left town in a dilapidated old car owing two months' rent.

   _____

   _____

7. Sitting at a sidewalk café, all sorts of interesting people passed by.

   _____

   _____

8. Packed tightly in a tiny can, Fran had difficulty removing the anchovies.

   _____

   _____

9. The woman picked up a heavy frying pan with arthritis.

   _____

   _____

10. I discovered an unusual plant in the greenhouse that oozed a milky juice.

    _____

    _____

FAULTY PARALLELISM

Words in a pair or a series should have a parallel structure. By balancing the items in a pair or a series so that they have the same kind of structure, you will make the sentence clearer and easier to read. Notice how the parallel sentences that follow read more smoothly than the nonparallel ones.

Nonparallel (Not Balanced)	*Parallel (Balanced)*
My job includes checking the inventory, initialing the orders, and to call the suppliers.	My job includes checking the inventory, initialing the orders, and calling the suppliers. (A balanced series of *-ing* words: *checking, initialing, calling*)
The game-show contestant was told to be cheerful, charming, and with enthusiasm.	The game show contestant was told to be cheerful, charming, and enthusiastic. (A balanced series of descriptive words: *cheerful, charming,* and *enthusiastic*)
Lola likes to ride her moped, to do needlepoint, and playing games on her personal computer.	Lola likes to ride her moped, to do needlepoint, and to play games on her personal computer. (A balanced series of *to* verbs: *to ride, to do, to play*)
We painted the trim in the living room; the wallpaper was put up by a professional.	We painted the trim in the living room; a professional put up the wallpaper. (Balanced verbs and word order: *We painted*; *a professional put up*)

Balanced sentences are not a skill you need worry about when writing first drafts. But when you rewrite, you should try to put matching words and ideas into matching structures. Such parallelism will improve your writing style.

Activity

Draw a line under the unbalanced part of each sentence. Then rewrite the unbalanced part so that it matches the other item or items in the sentence. The first one is done for you as an example.

1. Curling overgrown vines, <u>porch furniture that was rotted</u>, and sagging steps were my first impressions of the neglected house.   *rotting porch furniture*

2. In many ways, starting college at forty is more difficult than to start at eighteen.

   _____

3. The little girl came home from school with a tear-streaked face, a black eye, and her shirt was torn.

   _____

4. Studying a little every day is more effective than to cram.

   _____

5. At the body shop, the car was sanded down to the bare metal, painted with primer, and red enamel was sprayed on.

   _____

6. There are only two ways to the top floor: climb the stairs or taking the elevator.

   _____

7. While waiting for the exam to start, small groups of nervous students glanced over their notes, drank coffee, and were whispering to each other.

   _____

8. In order to become a dancer, Lena is taking lessons, working in amateur shows, and auditioned for professional companies.

   _____

9. The homeless woman shuffled along the street, bent over to pick something up, and was putting it in her shopping bag.

   _____

10. A teamsters' strike now would mean interruptions in food deliveries, a slowdown in the economy, and losing wages for workers.

    _____

PRONOUN AGREEMENT, REFERENCE, AND POINT OF VIEW

Pronouns are words that take the place of nouns (persons, places, or things). In fact, the word *pronoun* means "for a noun." Pronouns are shortcuts that keep you from unnecessarily repeating words in writing. Here are some examples of pronouns:

> Eddie left *his* camera on the bus. (*His* is a pronoun that takes the place of *Eddie's*.)
>
> Sandy drank the coffee even though *it* was cold. (*It* replaces *coffee*.)
>
> As I turned the newspaper's damp pages, *they* disintegrated in my hands. (*They* is a pronoun that takes the place of *pages*.)

This section presents rules that will help you avoid three common mistakes people make with pronouns. The rules are:

1   A pronoun must agree in number with the word or words it replaces.
2   A pronoun must refer clearly to the word it replaces.
3   Pronouns should not shift unnecessarily in point of view.

PRONOUN AGREEMENT

A pronoun must agree in number with the word or words it replaces. If the word a pronoun refers to is singular, the pronoun must be singular; if that word is plural, the pronoun must be plural. (Note that the word a pronoun refers to is known as the *antecedent*.)

Marie showed me her antique wedding band.
Students enrolled in the art class must provide their own supplies.

In the first example, the pronoun *her* refers to the singular word *Marie;* in the second example, the pronoun *their* refers to the plural word *Students.*

Indefinite Pronouns

The following words, known as *indefinite pronouns*, are always singular.

one	nobody	each
anyone	anybody	either
everyone	everybody	neither
someone	somebody	

Somebody left her pocketbook on the back of a chair.
Everyone in the club must pay his dues next week.

In each example, the pronoun is singular because it refers to one of the indefinite pronouns.

Note: In the last example, if everyone in the club was a woman, the pronoun would be *her*. If the club was a mixed group of men and women, the pronoun form would be *his or her*. Some writers follow the traditional practice of using *his* to refer to both men and women. Some use *his or her* to avoid an implied sexual bias. To avoid using *his* or the somewhat awkward *his or her,* a sentence can often be rewritten in the plural:

Club members must pay their dues next week.

PRONOUN REFERENCE

A sentence may be confusing and unclear if a pronoun appears to refer to more than one word or if the pronoun does not refer to any specific word. Look at this sentence:

Miriam was annoyed when they failed her car for a faulty turn signal.

Who failed her car? There is no specific word that *they* refers to. Be clear:

Miriam was annoyed when the inspectors failed her car for a faulty turn signal.

Here are sentences with other kinds of faulty pronoun references. Read the explanations of why they are faulty and look carefully at the ways they are corrected.

Faulty	*Clear*
Peter told Alan that his wife was unhappy. (Whose wife is unhappy, Peter's or Alan's? Be clear.)	Peter told Alan, ''My wife is unhappy.''
Sue is really a shy person, but she keeps it hidden. (There is no specific word that *it* refers to. It would not make sense to say, ''Sue keeps shy hidden.'')	Sue is really a shy person, but she keeps her shyness hidden.
Marsha attributed her success to her husband's support, which was generous. (Does *which* mean that Marsha's action was generous, or that her husband's support was generous?)	Generously, Marsha attributed her success to her husband's support.

PRONOUN POINT OF VIEW

Pronouns should not shift their point of view unnecessarily. When writing a paper, be consistent in your use of first-person or third-person pronouns.

For instance, if you start writing in the first person, *I*, do not jump suddenly to the second person, *you*. Or if you are writing in the third person, *they*, do not shift unexpectedly to *you*. Look at the examples that follow.

Inconsistent	*Consistent*
One of the fringe benefits of my job is that *you* can use a company credit card for gasoline.	One of the fringe benefits of my job is that *I* can use a company credit card for gasoline.
(The most common mistake people make is to let a *you* slip into their writing after they start with another pronoun.)	
In this course, a person can be in class for weeks before the professor calls on *you*.	In this course, a person can be in class for weeks before the professor calls on *him*.
(Again, the *you* is a shift in point of view.)	(See also the note on *his or her* references on page 258.)

Activity

Underline the correct word in the parentheses.

1. Each of these computers has (its, their) drawbacks.
2. During the border crisis, each country refused to change (its, their) aggressive stand.
3. Darlene tried to take notes during class, but she didn't really understand (it, the lecture).
4. At the city council meeting, we asked (them, the members) to provide better police protection for our neighborhood.
5. If people don't like what the government is doing, (you, they) should let Congress know.
6. Neither of those girls appreciates (her, their) parents' sacrifices.
7. There wasn't much to do on Friday nights after (they, the owners) closed the only movie theater in town.
8. Rita never buys a dress with horizontal stripes because she knows they make (you, her) look fat.
9. No one enjoys admitting (his or her, their) mistakes.
10. If anyone from the women's club calls when I'm out, tell (her, them) that I'll be back in about an hour.

CAPITAL LETTERS

MAIN USES OF CAPITAL LETTERS

Capital letters are used with:

1 The first word in a sentence or direct quotation.

The corner grocery was robbed last night.
The alien said, ''Take me to your leader.''

2 Names of persons and the word *I*.

Last night, I saw a hilarious silent movie starring Stan Laurel and Oliver Hardy.

3 Names of particular places.

Although Bill dropped out of Port Charles High School, he eventually earned his degree and got a job with Atlas Realty Company.

But: Use small letters if the specific name of a place is not given.

Although Bill dropped out of high school, he eventually earned his degree and got a job with a real estate company.

4   Names of days of the week, months, and holidays.

On the last Friday afternoon in May, the day before Memorial Day, my boss is having a barbecue for all the employees.

But: Use small letters for the seasons—summer, fall, winter, spring.

Most people feel more energetic in the spring and fall.

5   Names of commercial products.

My little sister knows all the words to the jingles for Oscar Mayer hot dogs, Diet Pepsi, Meow Mix cat food, and McDonald's hamburgers.

But: Use small letters for the type of product (hot dogs, cat food, hamburgers, and so on).

6   Titles of books, magazines, newspapers, articles, stories, poems, films, television shows, songs, papers that you write, and the like.

We read the book *Hiroshima,* by John Hersey, for our history class.
In the doctor's waiting room, I watched *All My Children,* read an article in *Reader's Digest,* and leafed through the *Miami Herald.*

7   Names of companies, associations, unions, clubs, religious and political groups, and other organizations:

Joe Naples is a Roman Catholic, but his wife is a Methodist.
The Hilldale Square Dancers' Club has won many competitions.
Brian, a member of Bricklayers Local 431 and the Knights of Columbus, works for Ace Construction.

OTHER USES OF CAPITAL LETTERS

Capital letters are also used with:

1   Names that show family relationships.

All his life, Father has been addicted to gadgets.
I browsed through Grandmother's collection of old photographs.

But: Do not capitalize words like *mother, father, grandmother, grandfather, uncle, aunt,* and so on when they are preceded by a possessive word (*my, your, his, her, our, their*).

All his life, my father has been addicted to gadgets.
I browsed through my grandmother's collection of old photographs.

2 Titles of persons when used with their names.

I contributed to Congressman McGrath's campaign fund.
Is Dr. Gregory on vacation?

But: Use small letters when titles appear by themselves, without specific names.

I contributed to my congressman's campaign fund.
Is the doctor on vacation?

3 Specific school courses.

The college offers evening sections of Introductory Psychology I, Abnormal Psychology, Psychology and Statistics, and Educational Psychology.

But: Use small letters for general subject areas.

The college offers evening sections of many psychology courses.

4 Languages and geographic locations.

My grandfather's Polish accent makes his English difficult to understand.
He grew up in the Midwest but moved to the South to look for a better job.

But: Use small letters in directions.

Head west for five blocks and then turn south on State Street.

5 Historical periods and events.

During the Middle Ages, the Black Death killed over one-quarter of Europe's population.

6 Races and nationalities.

The census questionnaire asked if the head of our household was Caucasian, Negro, Oriental, or Native American.

Denise's beautiful features are the result of her Chinese and Mexican parentage.

7 Opening and closing of a letter.

Dear Sir:	Sincerely yours,
Dear Ms. Henderson:	Truly yours,

Note: Capitalize only the first word in a closing.

Activity

Add the capitals needed in each of the following sentences.

Example In an injured tone, Mary demanded, "why wasn't uncle you invited to the party?"

1. At a restaurant on Broad street called Joe's italian palace, the chefs use pasta machines to make fresh noodles right in the dining room.
2. After having her baby, joan received a card from one of her friends that read, "congratulations; we all knew you had it in you."
3. A nature trail for the blind in cape cod, massachusetts, has signs written in braille which encourage visitors to smell and touch the plants.
4. Fidel Castro, the cuban leader, once tried out for the washington senators, a professional baseball team.
5. Every november, I make another vow that I will not gain weight between thanksgiving and new year's day.
6. Celebrities earn big money for endorsing items like polaroid cameras, trident gum, and sanka coffee.
7. During world war II, many americans were afraid that the japanese would invade california.

8. When uncle harvey got the bill from his doctor, he called the american medical association to complain.

9. This spring, the boy scouts and the jaycees are planning to clean up madison park.

10. I was halfway to the wash & dry laundromat on elm street when I realized that my box of tide was still home on the kitchen counter.

APOSTROPHE

The two main uses of the apostrophe are:

1 To show the omission of one or more letters in a contraction

2 To show ownership or possession

Each use is explained on the pages that follow.

APOSTROPHE IN CONTRACTIONS

A contraction is formed when two words are combined to make one word. An apostrophe is used to show where letters are omitted in forming the contraction. Here are two contractions:

> have + not = haven't (the *o* in *not* has been omitted)
> I + will = I'll (the *wi* in *will* has been omitted)

The following are some other common contractions:

I + am = I'm	it + is = it's
I + have = I've	it + has = it's
I + had = I'd	is + not = isn't
who + is = who's	could + not = couldn't
do + not = don't	I + would = I'd
did + not = didn't	they + are = they're

Note: *Will* + *not* has an unusual contraction: *won't.*

266

APOSTROPHE TO SHOW
OWNERSHIP OR POSSESSION

To show ownership or possession, we can use such words as *belongs to, possessed by, owned by,* or (most commonly) *of*.

> the umbrella that *belongs to* Mark
>
> the tape recorder *owned by* the school
>
> the gentleness *of* my father

But the apostrophe plus *s* (if the word does not end in *s*) is often the quickest and easiest way to show possession. Thus we can say:

> Mark's umbrella
>
> the school's tape recorder
>
> my father's gentleness

Notes

1   When you want to make a word plural, just add an *s* at the end of the word. Do *not* add an apostrophe. For example, the plural of the word *movie* is *movies*, not *movie's* or *movies'*. Look at this sentence:

> Tim coveted his roommate's collection of cassette tapes and video disks.

The words *tapes* and *disks* are simple plurals, meaning "more than one tape," "more than one disk." The plural is shown by adding *s* only. On the other hand, the *'s* after *roommate* shows possession—that the roommate owns the tapes and disks.

2   If a word ends in *-s*, show possession by adding only an apostrophe. Most plurals end in *-s*, and so you should show possession simply by adding the apostrophe.

> the Thompsons' porch
>
> James' cowboy boots
>
> the players' victory
>
> her parents' motor home
>
> Ray Charles' last album
>
> the soldiers' hats

Activity

In each sentence underline the two words that need apostrophes. Then write the words correctly in the spaces provided.

———————— 1. Although I hadnt met him before, Donalds voice sounded familiar to me.
————————

———————— 2. A shaky rope ladder led from the barns wooden floor to the haylofts dusty shadows.
————————

———————— 3. The paperback books glaring purple and orange cover was designed to attract the hurrying customers eye.
————————

———————— 4. Phils essay was due in a matter of hours, but he suffered a writers block that emptied his brain.
————————

———————— 5. As he waited in his boss office, Charlies nervous fingers shredded a Styrofoam coffee cup into a pile of jagged flakes.
————————

———————— 6. Jacks son stepped cautiously along the top of the farmyards splintery wooden fence.
————————

———————— 7. Members of the parents association constructed a maze made of old tires for the childrens playground.
————————

———————— 8. At his doctors request, Greg pulled up his shirt and revealed the zipper-like scars from last years operation.
————————

———————— 9. The suns rays beat down until the streets blacktop surface softened with the heat.
————————

———————— 10. The rivers swirling floodwaters lapped against the Thompsons porch.
————————

QUOTATION MARKS

The two main uses of quotation marks are:

1   To set off the exact words of a speaker or writer
2   To set off the titles of short works

Each use is explained on the pages that follow.

TO SET OFF THE WORDS
OF A SPEAKER OR WRITER

Use quotation marks to show the exact words of a speaker or writer.

"I feel as though I've been here before," Angie murmured to her husband.
(Quotation marks set off the exact words that Angie spoke to her husband.)

Ben Franklin once wrote, "To lengthen thy life, lessen thy meals."
(Quotation marks set off the exact words that Ben Franklin wrote.)

"Did you know," said the nutrition expert, "that it's healthier to be ten pounds overweight?"
(Two pairs of quotation marks are used to enclose the nutrition expert's exact words.)

The biology professor said, ''Ants are a lot like human beings. They farm their own food and raise smaller insects as livestock. And, like humans, ants send armies to war.''
(Note that the end quotation marks do not come until the end of the biology professor's speech. Place quotation marks before the first quoted word and after the last quoted word. As long as no interruption occurs in the speech, do not use quotation marks for each new sentence.)

Notes

1   In the four examples above, notice that a comma sets off the quoted part from the rest of the sentence. Also observe that commas and periods at the end of a quotation always go *inside* quotation marks.

2   An *indirect* quotation is a rewording of someone else's comments, rather than a word-for-word direct quotation. The word *that* often signals an indirect quotation, as shown in the example below:

Direct Quotation

The nurse said, ''Some babies can't tolerate cows' milk.''
(The nurse's exact spoken words are given, so quotation marks are used.)

Indirect Quotation

The nurse said that some babies cannot tolerate cows' milk.
(We learn the nurse's words indirectly, so no quotation marks are used.)

TO SET OFF THE TITLES OF SHORT WORKS

Titles of short works are usually set off by quotation marks, while titles of long works are underlined. Use quotation marks to set off the titles of short works such as articles in books, newspapers, or magazines; chapters in a book; short stories; poems; and songs. But you should underline the titles of books, newspapers, magazines, plays, movies, record albums, and television shows.

Note: In printed works, italic type—slanted type that looks *like this*—is used instead of underlining.

Quotation Marks

the essay ''On Self-Respect''

the article ''The Problem of Acid Rain''

Underlines

in the book Slouching towards Bethlehem

in the newspaper The New York Times

Quotation Marks	*Underlines*
the article "Living with Inflation"	in the magazine Newsweek
the chapter "Chinese Religion"	in the book Paths of Faith
the story "Hands"	in the book Winesburg, Ohio
the poem "When I Have Fears"	in the book Complete Poems of John Keats
the song "Billie Jean"	in the album Thriller
	the television show Frontline
	the movie High Noon

Activity

Insert quotation marks where needed in the sentences that follow.

1. The psychology class read a short story called Silent Snow, Secret Snow about a young boy who creates his own fantasy world.

2. When asked for advice on how to live a long life, the old man said, Don't look back; something may be gaining on you.

3. I'm against grade school students' using pocket calculators, said Fred. I spent three years learning long division, and so should they.

4. One updated version of an old saying goes, Absence makes the heart grow fonder—of somebody else.

5. When I gagged while taking a foul-tasting medicine, my wife said, Put an ice cube on your tongue first, and then you won't taste it.

6. I looked twice at the newspaper headline that read, Man in River Had Drinking Problem.

7. Gene reported to his business class on an article in *Money* magazine entitled Cashing in on the Energy Boom.

8. When a guest at the wedding was asked what he was giving the couple, he replied, About six months.

9. Theodore Roosevelt, a pioneer in conservation, once said, When I hear of the destruction of a species, I feel as if all the works of some great writer had perished.

10. Did you know, the counselor said to my husband and me, that it now costs $85,000 to raise a child to the age of eighteen?

COMMA

SIX MAIN USES OF THE COMMA

Commas are used mainly as follows:

1. To separate items in a series
2. To set off introductory material
3. On both sides of words that interrupt the flow of thought in a sentence
4. Between two complete thoughts connected by *and, but, for, or, nor, so, yet*
5. To set off a direct quotation from the rest of a sentence
6. For certain everyday material

You may find it helpful to remember that the comma often marks a slight pause or break in a sentence. Read aloud the sentence examples given for each rule, and listen for the minor pauses or breaks that are signaled by commas.

Between Items in a Series

Use commas to separate items in a series.

The street vendor sold watches, necklaces, and earrings.
The pitcher adjusted his cap, pawed the ground, and peered over his shoulder.
The exercise instructor told us to inhale, exhale, and relax.
Joe peered into the hot, still-smoking engine.

Notes

1   The final comma in a series is optional, but often it is used.
2   A comma is used between two descriptive words in a series only if *and* inserted between the words sounds natural. You could say:

Joe peered into the hot *and* still-smoking engine.

But notice in the following sentence that the descriptive words do not sound natural when *and* is inserted between them. In such cases, no comma is used.

Tony wore a pale green tuxedo. (A pale *and* green tuxedo does not sound right, so no comma is used.)

Activity

Place commas between items in a series.

1. The old kitchen cabinets were littered with dead insects crumbs and dust balls.
2. The children splashed through the warm deep swirling rainwater that flooded the street.
3. Rudy stretched out on the swaying hammock popped open a frosty can of soda and balanced it carefully on his stomach.

After Introductory Material

Use a comma to set off introductory material.

Just in time, Sherry slid a plastic tray under the overwatered philodendron.
Muttering under his breath, Ken reviewed the list of definitions he had memorized.
Although he had been first in the checkout line, Dave let an elderly woman go ahead of him.

Note: If the introductory material is brief, the comma is sometimes omitted.

Activity

Place commas after introductory material.

1. As Patty struggled with the stuck window gusts of cold rain blew in her face.
2. In a wolf pack the dominant male holds his tail higher than the other pack members.
3. Setting down a glass of murky water the waitress tossed Dennis a greasy menu and asked if he'd care to order.

Around Interrupters

Use a comma on both sides of words or phrases that interrupt the flow of thought in a sentence.

The vinyl car seat, sticky from the heat, clung to my skin.

Marty's personal computer, which his wife got him as a birthday gift, occupies all of his spare time.

The hallway, dingy and dark, was illuminated by a bare bulb hanging from a wire.

By reading a sentence aloud, you can usually ''hear'' words that interrupt the flow of thought. In cases where you are not sure if certain words are interrupters, remove them from the sentence. If it still makes sense without the words, you know that the words are interrupters and that the information they give is nonessential. *Such nonessential or extra information is set off with commas.*

In the following sentence,

Sue Dodd, who goes to aerobics class with me, was in a serious car accident.

the words *who goes to aerobics class with me* are extra information not needed to identify the subject of the sentence, *Sue Dodd*. Commas go around such nonessential information. On the other hand, in the sentence

The woman who goes to aerobics class with me was in a serious accident.

the words *who goes to aerobics class with me* supply essential information—information needed for us to identify the woman being spoken of. If the words were removed from the sentence, we would no longer know who was in the accident.

Activity

Use commas to set off interrupting words.

1. A slight breeze muggy with heat ruffled the bedroom curtains.
2. Lenny's wallet which he keeps in his front pants pocket was linked to his belt with a metal chain.
3. The defrosting chickens loosely wrapped in plastic film left a pool of drippings on the counter.

Between Two Complete Thoughts

Use a comma between two complete thoughts connected by *and, but, for, or, nor, so, yet.*

Sam closed all the windows in the house before bedtime, but the predicted thunderstorms never arrived.

I like wearing comfortable clothing, so I buy oversized shirts and sweaters in the men's department.

Peggy doesn't envy the skinny models in magazines, for she is happy with her own well-rounded body.

Notes

1 The comma is optional when the complete thoughts are short ones.

The ferris wheel started and Bob closed his eyes.

Irene left the lecture hall for her head was pounding.

I made a wrong turn so I doubled back.

2 Be careful not to use a comma in sentences having one subject and a double verb. The comma is used only in sentences made up of two complete thoughts (two subjects and two verbs). In the sentence

The doctor stared over his bifocals and lectured me about smoking.

there is only one subject (*doctor*) and a double verb (*stared* and *lectured*). No comma is needed.

Likewise, the sentence

Frank switched the fluorescent tube on and off and then tapped it with his fingers.

has only one subject (*Frank*) and a double verb (*switched* and *tapped*); therefore, no comma is needed.

Activity

Use a comma to set off two complete thoughts.

1. The TV show was interrupted for a special news bulletin and I poked my head out of the kitchen to hear the announcement.
2. The tuna sandwich in my lunch bag was crushed but the jelly doughnuts remained intact.
3. The puppy must have been beaten by its former owner for it cringed whenever someone tried to pet it.

With Direct Quotations

Use a comma to set off a direct quotation from the rest of a sentence.

The carnival barker cried, "Step right up and win a prize!"
"Now is the time to yield to temptation," my horoscope read.
"I'm sorry," said the restaurant hostess. "You'll have to wait."
"For my first writing assignment," said Scott, "I have to turn in a five-hundred-word description of a stone."

Activity

Use commas to set off direct quotations from the rest of the sentence.

1. "A grapefruit" said the comedian "is a lemon that had a chance and took advantage of it."
2. The zookeeper explained to the visitors "We can't tell the sex of a giant gorilla for almost ten years after its birth."
3. "In order to measure your lung capacity" the coach announced "you're going to try to blow up a plastic bag with one breath."

With Everyday Material

Use a comma with certain everyday material.

Persons Spoken to

If you're the last to leave, Paul, please switch off the lights.
Fred, I think we're on the wrong road.
Did you see the play-off game, Lisa?

Dates

June 30, 1987, is the day I make the last payment on my car.

Addresses

I buy discount children's clothing from Isaacs Baby Wear Factory, Box 900, Chicago, Illinois 60614.

Note: No comma is used to mark off the zip code.

Openings and Closings of Letters

Dear Santa,	Sincerely yours,
Dear Larry,	Truly yours,

Note: In formal letters, a colon is used after the opening:

Dear Sir: *or*   Dear Madam:

Numbers

The insurance agent sold me a $50,000 term life insurance policy.

Activity

Place commas where needed.

1. Would you mind George if we borrowed your picnic cooler this weekend?
2. On August 23 1963 over 2000000 blacks and whites marched for civil rights in Washington D.C.
3. The coupon refund address is 2120 Industrial Highway Minneapolis Minnesota 55455.

■ Final Activity 1

Insert commas where needed. In the space provided under each sentence, summarize briefly the rule that explains the comma or commas used.

1. "Kleenex tissues" said the history professor "were first used as gas mask filters in World War I."

    _____

2. Dee ordered a sundae with three scoops of rocky road ice cream miniature marshmallows and raspberry sauce.

    _____

3. While waiting to enter the movie theater we studied the faces of the people just leaving to see if they had liked the show.

    _____

4. I had left my wallet on the store counter but the clerk called me at home to say it was safe.

    _____

5. The demonstrators protesting nuclear arms carried signs reading "Humans have never invented a weapon they haven't used."

    _____

6. Large cactus plants which now sell for very high prices are being stolen from national parks and protected desert areas.

    _____

7. On March 3 1962 Wilt Chamberlain scored one hundred points in a game against the New York Knicks.

    _____

8. Tom watched nervously as the dentist assembled drills mirrors clamps picks and cylinders of cotton on a tray next to the reclining chair.

    _____

9. The talk show guest a former child star said that one director threatened to shoot her dog if she didn't cry on cue.

   _____

10. Cats and dogs like most animals love the taste of salt and will lick humans' hands to get it.

    _____

■ Final Activity 2

Insert commas where needed. Mark the one sentence that is correct with a C.

1. Before leaving for the gym Ellen added extra socks and a tube of shampoo to the gear in her duffel bag.
2. Samuel Johnson observed long ago ''People in general do not willingly read if they can have anything else to amuse them.''
3. Clogged with soggy birds' nests the chimney had allowed dangerous gases to accumulate in our house.
4. Bill took a time-exposure photo of the busy highway and the cars' taillights appeared in the developed print as winding red ribbons.
5. The graduating students sweltering in their hot black gowns fanned their faces with commencement programs.
6. Puffing a cigarette twitching his lips and adjusting his hat Bogie sized up the situation.
7. On May 31 1889 a great flood in Johnstown Pennsylvania killed 2200 people.
8. ''When I was little'' said Ernie ''my brother told me it was illegal to kill praying mantises. I still don't know if that's true or not.''
9. A huge side of beef its red flesh marbled with streaks of creamy fat hung from a razor-sharp steel hook.
10. The nurse who was taking a blood sample taped Jake's arm to make a large vein stand out.

OTHER PUNCTUATION MARKS

COLON

Use the colon at the end of a complete statement to introduce a list, a long quotation, or an explanation.

1   A list:

The store will close at noon on the following dates: November 26, December 24, and December 31.

2   A long quotation:

The scientist Stephen Jay Gould wrote: "I am, somehow, less interested in the weight and convolutions of Einstein's brain than in the near certainty that people of equal talent have lived and died in cotton fields and sweatshops."

3   An explanation:

Here's a temporary solution to a dripping faucet: tie a string to it and let the drops slide down the string to the sink.

SEMICOLON

The main use of the semicolon is to mark the break between two complete thoughts, as explained on page 232. Another use is to mark off items in a series when the items themselves contain commas. Here are some examples:

Sharon's children are named Melantha, which means ''black flower''; Yonina, which means ''dove''; and Cynthia, which means ''moon goddess.''

My favorite albums are *Rubber Soul,* by the Beatles; *Songs in the Key of Life,* by Stevie Wonder; and *Bridge over Troubled Water,* by Simon and Garfunkel.

DASH

A dash signals a degree of pause longer than a comma but not as complete as a period. Use a dash to set off words for dramatic effect:

I was so exhausted that I fell asleep within seconds—standing up.

He had many good qualities—sincerity, honesty, and thoughtfulness—yet he had few friends.

The pardon from the governor finally arrived—too late.

Notes

1 The dash is formed on the typewriter by striking the hyphen twice (--). In handwriting, the dash is as long as two letters would be.
2 Be careful not to overuse dashes.

PARENTHESES

Parentheses are used to set off extra or incidental information from the rest of a sentence:

In 1913, the tax on an annual income of four thousand dollars (a comfortable salary at that time) was one penny.

A small mirror (a double-faced one) is useful to a camper for flashing signals or starting fires.

Note: Do not use parentheses too often in your writing.

HYPHEN

1   Use a hyphen with two or more words that act as a single unit describing a noun.

The light-footed burglar silently slipped open the sliding glass door.

While being interviewed on the late-night talk show, the quarterback announced his intention to retire.

With a needle, Rich punctured the fluid-filled blister on his toe.

2   Use a hyphen to divide a word at the end of a line of writing or typing. When you need to divide a word at the end of a line, divide it between syllables. Use your dictionary to be sure of correct syllable divisions.

Mark's first year at college was a time filled with new pressures and re-sponsibilities.

Notes

a   Do not divide words of one syllable.

b   Do not divide a word if you can avoid doing so.

At the appropriate spot, place the punctuation mark shown in the margin.

;

1. A bad case of flu, a burglary, the death of an uncle it was not what you would call a pleasant week.

( )

2. My grandfather who will be ninety in May says that hard work and a glass of wine every day are the secrets of a long life.

-

3. Mark Twain once wrote "The difference between the right word and the nearly right word is the difference between lightning and the lightning bug."

:

4. The passengers in the glass bottomed boat stared at the colorful fish in the water below.

( )

5. Ellen's birthday December 27 falls so close to Christmas that she gets only one set of presents.

___

6. The police officer had spotted our broken headlight consequently, he stopped us at the next corner.

—　　7. I feel I have two chances of winning the lottery slim and none.

-　　8. Well stocked shelves and friendly service are what Mrs. Dale demands of her staff.

;　　9. Some people need absolute quiet in order to study they can't concentrate with the soft sounds of a radio, air conditioner, or television in the background.

:　10. There are three work habits my boss hates taking long coffee breaks, making personal phone calls, and missing staff meetings.

WORDINESS

Wordiness—using more words than necessary to express a meaning—is often a sign of lazy or careless writing. Your readers may resent the extra time needed to understand your writing if it is indirect and overlong. Here are examples of wordy sentences:

> In this paper, I am planning to describe the hobby that I enjoy of collecting old comic books.
>
> In Dan's opinion, he thinks that cable television will change and alter our lives in the future.

Omitting needless words improves the sentences:

> I enjoy collecting old comic books.
>
> Dan thinks that cable television will change our lives.

Activity

Rewrite the following sentences, omitting needless words.

1. In conclusion, I would like to end my paper by summarizing each of the major points covered within my report.

    _____

    _____

2. Controlling the quality and level of the television shows that children watch is a continuing challenge to parents that they must meet on a daily basis.

    _____

    _____

3. In general, I am the sort of person who tends to be shy, especially in large crowds or with strangers I don't know well.

    _____

    _____

4. Someone who is analyzing magazine advertising can find hidden messages that, once uncovered, are seen to be clever and persuasive.

    _____

    _____

5. My greatest mistake that I made last week was to hurt my brother's feelings and then not to have the nerve to apologize and say how sorry I was.

    _____

    _____

EFFECTIVE WORD CHOICE

Choose your words carefully when you write. Always take the time to think about your word choices rather than simply use the first word that comes to mind. You want to develop the habit of selecting words that are appropriate and exact for your purposes. One way you can show your sensitivity to language is by avoiding slang, clichés, and pretentious words.

SLANG

We often use *slang* expressions when we talk because they are so vivid and colorful. However, slang is usually out of place in formal writing. Here are some examples of slang expressions:

Someone *ripped off* Ken's new sneakers from his locker.

After the game, we *stuffed our faces* at the diner.

I finally told my parents to *get off my case*.

The movie really *grossed me out*.

Slang expressions have a number of drawbacks. They go out of date quickly, they become tiresome if used excessively in writing, and they may communicate clearly to some readers but not to others. Also, the use of slang can be an evasion of the specific details that are often needed to make one's meaning clear in writing. For example, in "The movie really grossed me out," the writer has not provided the specific details about the movie necessary for us to understand the statement clearly. Was it the acting, the special effects, or violent scenes in the movie that the writer found so disgusting? In general, then, you should avoid the use of slang in your writing. If you are in doubt about whether an expression is slang, it may help to check a recently published hardbound dictionary.

CLICHÉS

A *cliché* is an expression that has been worn out through constant use. Some typical clichés are:

piece of my mind	at a loss for words
it dawned on me	it goes without saying
taking a big chance	word to the wise
work like a dog	break the ice
needle in a haystack	tired but happy
drop in the bucket	hour of need
last but not least	ladder of success
sigh of relief	

Clichés are common in speech but make your writing seem tired and stale. Also, they are often an evasion of the specific details that you must work to provide in your writing. You should, then, avoid clichés and try to express your meaning in fresh, original ways.

PRETENTIOUS WORDS

Some people feel they can improve their writing by using fancy *pretentious words* rather than more simple and natural words. They use artificial and stilted language that more often obscures their meaning than communicates it clearly. Here are some unnatural-sounding sentences:

It was a splendid opportunity to get some slumber.

We relished the delicious repast.

The officer apprehended the intoxicated operator of the vehicle.

This establishment sells women's apparel and children's garments.

The same thoughts can be expressed more clearly and effectively by using plain, natural language, as follows:

It was a good chance to get some sleep.

We enjoyed the delicious meal.

The officer arrested the car's drunken driver.

This store sells women's and children's clothes.

Activity

Certain words are italicized in the following sentences. In the space provided, identify the words as slang (S), clichés (C), or pretentious words (PW). Then replace the words with more effective diction.

_____ 1. Losing weight is *easier said than done,* especially for someone who likes sweets.

_____

_____ 2. After dinner we washed the *culinary utensils* and wrapped up the *excess* food.

_____

_____ 3. Bruce is so stubborn that talking to him is like *talking to a brick wall.*

_____

_____ 4. Michelle spent the summer *watching the tube* and *catching rays.*

_____

_____ 5. The fans, *all fired up* after the game, *peeled out* of the parking lots and honked their horns.

_____

_____ 6. The stew I made contained *everything but the kitchen sink.*

_____

_____ 7. That *guy* isn't really a criminal; he's just gotten a *bum rap.*

_____

_____ 8. My new *stereophonic component system* is so complex that playing records is a *formidable undertaking.*

_____

_____ 9. During the movie, I laughed *so hard I thought I'd die.*

_____

_____ 10. I *perused* several *periodicals* while I waited for the doctor.

_____

SENTENCE VARIETY

One part of effective writing is to vary the kind of sentences that you write. If every sentence follows the same pattern, writing may become monotonous to read. This section of the book explains four ways you can create variety and interest in your writing style. It will also describe coordination and subordination—two important techniques for achieving different kinds of emphasis in writing.

The following are three methods you can use to make simple sentences more complex and sophisticated:

1   Add a second complete thought (coordination) or a dependent thought (subordination).
2   Begin with a special opening word or phrase.
3   Place adjectives or verbs in a series.

Each method will be discussed in turn.

COORDINATION AND SUBORDINATION

Coordination

When you add a second complete thought to a simple sentence, the result is a compound (or double) sentence. The two complete statements in a compound sentence are usually connected by a comma plus a joining or coordinating word (*and, but, for, or, nor, so, yet*).

A compound sentence is used when you want to give equal weight to two closely related ideas. The technique of showing that ideas have equal importance is called *coordination*. Following are some compound sentences. In each case, the sentence contains two ideas that the writer regards as equal in importance.

Frank worked on the engine for three hours, but the car still wouldn't start.

Bananas were on sale this week, so I bought a bunch for the children's lunches.

We laced up our roller skates, and then we moved cautiously onto the rink.

Subordination

When you add a dependent thought to a simple sentence, the result is a complex sentence. A dependent thought begins with words such as *after, because, since, unless, when,* and *although*. (A list of dependent words is on page 224.)

A complex sentence is used when you want to emphasize one idea over another in a sentence. Look at the following complex sentence:

Although the exam room was very quiet, I still couldn't concentrate.

The idea that the writer wishes to emphasize here—*I still couldn't concentrate*—is expressed as a complete thought. The less important idea—*Although the exam room was very quiet*—is subordinated to the complete thought. The technique of giving one idea less emphasis than another is called *subordination*.

Following are other examples of complex sentences. In each case, the part starting with the dependent word is the less emphasized part of the sentence.

Even though I was tired, I stayed up to watch the horror movie.

Before I take a bath, I check for spiders in the tub.

When Ivy feels nervous, she pulls on her earlobe.

Activity

On separate paper, use coordination or subordination to combine each group of simple sentences below and on the following page into one or more longer sentences. Omit repeated words. Since different combinations are possible, you might want to jot down several combinations in each case. Then read them aloud to find the combination that sounds best.

Keep in mind that very often the relationship among ideas in a sentence will be clearer when subordinating rather than coordinating words are used.

Example ■   Lew arrived at the supermarket.
        ■   Lew had a painful thought.
        ■   He had clipped all the coupons from the paper.
        ■   He had forgotten to bring them.

    When Lew arrived at the supermarket, he had a painful thought. He had clipped all the coupons from the paper, but he had forgotten to bring them.

Comma Hints

a   Use a comma at the end of a word group that starts with a subordinating word (as in "When Lew arrived at the supermarket, . . .").

b   Use a comma between independent word groups connected by *and, but, for, or, nor, so, yet* (as in "He had clipped all the coupons from the paper, but . . .").

1. ■   Dan had repaired his broken watchband with a paper clip.
   ■   The clip snapped.
   ■   The watch slid off his wrist.
2. ■   The therapist watched.
   ■   Julie tried to stand on her weakened legs.
   ■   They crumpled under her.
3. ■   There were spaces on the street.
   ■   Richie pulled into an expensive parking garage.
   ■   He had just bought a new car.
   ■   He was afraid it would get dented.
4. ■   A sudden cold front hit the area.
   ■   The temperature dropped thirty degrees in less than an hour.
   ■   My teeth began to chatter.
   ■   I was not wearing a warm jacket.

5. ■   The verdict was announced.
   ■   The spectators broke into applause.
   ■   The defendant looked stunned.
   ■   Then he let out a whoop of joy.

SPECIAL OPENING WORD OR PHRASE

Among the special openers that can be used to start sentences are *-ed* words, *-ing* words, *-ly* words, *to* word groups, and prepositional phrases. Here are examples of all five kinds of openers:

-ed word	Concerned about his son's fever, Paul called a doctor.
-ing word	Humming softly, the woman browsed through the rack of dresses.
-ly word	Hesitantly, Sue approached the instructor's desk.
to word group	To protect her hair, Eva uses the lowest setting on her blow dryer.
Prepositional phrase	During the exam, drops of water fell from the ceiling.

Activity

Combine each pair of simple sentences into one sentence by using the opener shown at the left and omitting repeated words. Use a comma to set off the opener from the rest of the sentence.

Example   -ing *word*   ■   The pelican scooped small fish into its baggy bill.
   ■   It dipped into the waves.

Dipping into the waves, the pelican scooped small fish into its baggy bill.

-ed *word*   1. ■   The night sky glittered.
   ■   It was studded with thousands of stars.

_____

_____

-ing *word*   2. ■   She wondered how to break the news to the children.
   ■   She sat in the cold living room.

_____

_____

-ly word   3. ■ Shirley signed the repair contract.

                ■ She was reluctant.

_____

_____

to *word*   4. ■ Alan volunteered to work overtime.

group   ■ He wanted to improve his chances of promotion.

_____

_____

prepositional 5. ■ The accused murderer grinned at the witnesses.

phrase   ■ He did this during the trial.

_____

_____

ADJECTIVES OR VERBS IN A SERIES

Various parts of a sentence may be placed in a series. Among these parts are adjectives (descriptive words) and verbs. Here are examples of both in a series:

    Adjectives   I gently applied a *sticky new* Band-Aid to the *deep, ragged* cut on my finger.

        Verbs   The trunk *bounced* off a guardrail, *sideswiped* a tree, and *plunged* down the embankment.

Activity

Combine the simple sentences into one sentence by using adjectives or verbs in a series and by omitting repeated words. In most cases, use a comma between the adjectives or verbs in a series.

Example ■ Jesse spun the basketball on one finger.

          ■ He rolled it along his arms.

          ■ He dribbled it between his legs.

Jesse spun the basketball on one finger, rolled it along his arms, and dribbled it between his legs.

1. ▪ The baby toddled across the rug.
   ▪ He picked up a button.
   ▪ He put the button in his mouth.

   _____

   _____

2. ▪ Water dribbled out of the tap.
   ▪ The water was brown.
   ▪ The water was foul-tasting.
   ▪ The tap was rusty.
   ▪ The tap was metal.

   _____

   _____

3. ▪ In the dressing room, Pat tried on the swimsuit.
   ▪ She looked in the full-length mirror.
   ▪ She screamed.

   _____

   _____

4. ▪ Art approached the wasps' nests hanging under the eaves.
   ▪ The nests were large.
   ▪ The nests were papery.
   ▪ The eaves were old.
   ▪ The eaves were wooden.

   _____

   _____

5. ▪ Reeds bordered the pond.
   ▪ The reeds were slim.
   ▪ The reeds were brown.
   ▪ The pond was green.
   ▪ The pond was stagnant.

   _____

   _____

MANUSCRIPT FORM

GUIDELINES FOR MANUSCRIPT PREPARATION

When you hand in a paper that is due for any one of your courses, probably the first thing you will be judged on is its format. It is important, then, that you do certain things to make your papers look attractive, neat, and easy to read. Here are guidelines to follow in preparing a paper for an instructor.

1   Use full-sized theme or typewriter paper, 8½ by 11 inches.

2   Keep wide margins (1 to 1½ inches) all around the paper. In particular, do not crowd the right-hand or bottom margins. The white space makes your paper more readable; also, the instructor has room for comments.

3   If you write by hand:

   a   Use a blue or black pen (*not* a pencil).

   b   Be careful not to overlap letters or to make decorative loops on letters. On narrow-ruled paper, write on every other line.

   c   Make all your letters distinct. Pay special attention to *a, e, i, o,* and *u*— five letters that people sometimes write illegibly.

   d   Keep your capital letters clearly distinct from small letters. You may even want to print all capital letters.

4   Center the title of your paper on the first line of page 1. Do not put quotation marks around the title or underline the title. Capitalize all the major words in a title, including the first word. Small connecting words within a title, such as *and, of, for, the, in,* and *to,* are not capitalized.

5   Skip a line between the title and the first line of your text. Indent the first line of each paragraph about five spaces (half an inch) from the left-hand margin.

6   Make commas, periods, and other punctuation marks firm and clear. Leave a slight space after each period. When typing, many people leave a double space after a period.

7   If you break a word at the end of a line, break only between syllables (see page 282). Do not break words of one syllable.

8   Put your name, date, and course number where your instructor asks for them.

Activity

Identify the mistakes in format in the following lines from a student theme. Explain the mistakes in the spaces provided. One mistake is described for you as an example.

	"being alone"
	There seem to be two kinds of people in the world — the
	ones who enjoy being alone and the ones who can't bear it.
	Unfortunately, I belong to the second group. Whenever
	I'm cooped up with only myself for company, I'll do pra-
	ctically anything for human contact. For example, if I have

1. *Hyphenate only between syllables.* _____

2. _____

3. _____

4. _____

5. _____

6. _____

EDITING
TESTS

PROOFREADING FOR
SENTENCE-SKILLS MISTAKES

The five editing tests in this section will give you practice in proofreading for sentence-skills mistakes. People often find it hard to proofread a paper carefully. They have put so much work into their writing, or so little, that it's almost painful for them to look at the paper one more time. You may simply have to *force* yourself to proofread. Remember that eliminating sentence-skills mistakes will improve an average paper and help ensure a strong grade on a good paper. Further, as you get into the habit of ''proofing'' your papers, you will get into the habit of using the sentence skills consistently. They are a basic part of clear and effective writing.

In the first three tests, the spots where errors occur have been underlined; your job is to identify each error. In the last two tests, you must locate as well as identify the errors.

■ **Editing Test 1**

Identify the sentence-skills mistakes at the underlined spots in the selection that follows. From the box below, choose the letter that describes each mistake and write it in the space provided. The same mistake may appear more than once. In one case, there is no mistake.

a. run-on	d. missing quotation marks
b. mistake in subject-verb agreement	e. wordiness
	f. slang
c. faulty parallelism	g. no mistake

<u>It is this writer's opinion that</u> smokers should quit smoking for the sake of those
1

who are around them. Perhaps the most helpless group that suffers from being near

smokers <u>are</u> unborn <u>babies, one</u> study suggests that the risk of having an undersized
2   3

baby is doubled if pregnant women <u>is</u> exposed to cigarette smoke for about two hours a
4

day. Pregnant women both should refrain from smoking and <u>to avoid</u> smoke-filled rooms.
5

Spouses of smokers are also <u>in big trouble</u>. They are more likely than spouses of
6

nonsmokers to die of heart disease and <u>the development of</u> fatal cancers. Office workers
7

are a final group that can be harmed by a smoke-filled environment. The U.S. Surgeon

general has <u>said "Workers</u> who smoke are a health risk to their <u>coworkers. While</u>
8   9

<u>it is undoubtedly true that</u> one can argue that smokers have the right to hurt themselves,
10

they do not have the right to hurt others. Smokers should abandon their deadly habit

for the health of others at home and at work.

1. _____   3. _____   5. _____   7. _____   9. _____

2. _____   4. _____   6. _____   8. _____   10. _____

■ **Editing Test 2**

Identify the sentence-skills mistakes at the underlined spots in the selection that follows. From the box below, choose the letter that describes each mistake and write it in the space provided. The same mistake may appear more than once. In one case, there is no mistake.

a. sentence fragment	f. dangling modifier
b. run-on	g. homonym mistake
c. mistake in subject-verb agreement	h. missing apostrophe
	i. cliché
d. missing comma	j. no mistake
e. missing capital letter	

Cars can destroy your ego. First of <u>all the</u> kind of car you drive can make you feel
₁
like a second-class citizen. <u>If you can't afford a new, expensive car, and are forced to</u>
₂
<u>drive an old clunker.</u> You'll be the object of pitying stares and nasty sneers. Drivers of

newer-model cars just <u>doesn't</u> appreciate it when a '68 <u>buick</u> with terminal body rust
₃   ₄
lurches into the next parking slot. You may even find that drivers go out of <u>their</u> way
₅
not to park near you. Breakdowns, too, can damage your self-respect. You may be an

assistant bank manager or a job <u>foreman, you'll</u> still feel <u>like two cents</u> when <u>your</u> sitting
₆   ₇   ₈
on the side of the road. As the other cars whiz past, you'll stare helplessly at your <u>cars</u>
₉
open hood or steaming radiator. In cases like this, you may even be turned into that

lowest of creatures, the pedestrian. <u>Shuffling humbly along the highway to the nearest</u>
₁₀
<u>pay phone</u>, your car has delivered another staggering blow to your self-esteem.

1. _____   3. _____   5. _____   7. _____   9. _____

2. _____   4. _____   6. _____   8. _____   10. _____

Editing Test 3

Identify the sentence-skills mistakes at the underlined spots in the selection that follows. From the box below, choose the letter that describes each mistake and write it in the space provided. The same mistake may appear more than once. In one case, there is no mistake.

a. sentence fragment	e. dangling modifier
b. run-on	f. missing comma
c. mistake in subject- verb agreement	g. wordiness
	h. slang
d. misplaced modifier	i. no mistake

America will never be a drug-free <u>society but</u> we could eliminate many of our drug-
₁

related problems by legalizing drugs. Drugs would then be sold by companies <u>and not</u>
₂

<u>by criminals</u>. The drug trade would take place like any other <u>business freeing</u> the
₃

police and courts to devote their time to other problems. Lawful drugs would be sold at

a fair <u>price, no</u> one would need to steal in order to buy them. <u>By legalizing drugs,</u>
₄   ₅

organized crime would lose one of its major sources of revenue. <u>It goes without saying</u>
₆

<u>that</u> we would, instead, create important tax revenues for the government. Finally, if

drugs <u>was</u> sold through legal outlets, we could reduce the drug problem among our
₇

young people. It would be illegal to sell drugs to people under a certain age. <u>Just as is</u>

<u>the case now with alcohol</u>. And because the profits on drugs would no longer <u>be out of</u>
₈   ₉

<u>sight</u>, there would be little incentive for drug pushers to sell to young people.

Decriminalizing drugs, in short, could be a solution. <u>To many of the problems that result</u>
₁₀

<u>from the illegal drug trade</u>.

1. _____   3. _____   5. _____   7. _____   9. _____

2. _____   4. _____   6. _____   8. _____   10. _____

■ **Editing Test 4**

See if you can locate and correct the ten sentence-skills mistakes in the following passage. The mistakes are listed in the box below. As you locate mistakes, place checks in the spaces provided.

---

2 sentence fragments _____
_____
1 run-on _____
1 mistake in subject-verb
agreement _____

1 nonparallel structure _____

2 apostrophe mistakes _____
_____

3 missing commas _____
_____ _____

Most products have little or nothing to do with sex but a person would never know that by looking at ads'. A television ad for a headache remedy, for example shows the product being useful because it ends a womans throbbing head pain just in time for sex. Now she will not say "Not tonight, Honey." Another ad features a detergent that helps a single woman meet a man in a laundry room. When it comes to products that do relate to sex appeal advertisers often present more obvious sexuality. A recent magazine ad for women's clothing, for instance, make no reference to the quality of or how comfortable are the company's clothes. Instead, the ad features a picture of a woman wearing a low-cut sleeveless T shirt and a very short skirt. Her eyes are partially covered by semi-wild hair. And stare seductively at the reader. A recent television ad for perfume goes even further. In this ad, a boy not older than twelve reaches out to a beautiful woman. Sexily dressed in a dark room filled with sensuous music. With such ads, it is no wonder that young people seem preoccupied with sex.

■ Editing Test 5

See if you can locate and correct the ten sentence-skills mistakes in the following passage. The mistakes are listed in the box below. As you locate mistakes, place checks in the spaces provided.

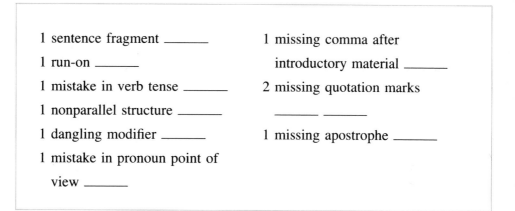

1 sentence fragment _____   1 missing comma after

1 run-on _____   introductory material _____

1 mistake in verb tense _____   2 missing quotation marks

1 nonparallel structure _____   _____ _____

1 dangling modifier _____   1 missing apostrophe _____

1 mistake in pronoun point of

   view _____

The greatest of my everyday fears is technology. Beginning when I couldn't master bike riding and extending to the present day. Fear kept me from learning to operate a jigsaw, start an outboard motor, or even using a simple tape recorder. I almost didn't learn to drive a car. At age sixteen, Dad lifted the hood of our Chevy and said, All right, you're going to start learning to drive. Now, this is the distributor. . . When my eyes glazed over he shouted, ''Well, I'm not going to bother if youre not interested!'' Fortunately, the friend who later taught me to drive skipped what goes on under the hood. My most recent frustration is the 35 mm camera, I would love to take professional-quality pictures. But all the numbers and dials and meters confuse me. As a result, my unused camera is hidden away on a shelf in my closet. Just last week, my sister gives me a beautiful digital watch for my birthday. I may have to put it on the shelf with the camera—the alarm keeps going off, and you can't figure out how to stop it.

PART FIVE

READINGS
FOR WRITING

INTRODUCTION
TO THE
READINGS

The reading selections in this part of the book will help you find topics for writing. Each selection deals in some way with interesting, often thought-provoking concerns or experiences of contemporary life. One selection, for example, describes the new kinds of stress that students face in college; another reminds us of the benefits that can come from expressing appreciation to others; a third touches on the agonizing problem of why good people sometimes suffer so much ill fortune. The varied subjects should inspire lively class discussions as well as serious individual thought. The selections should also provide a continuing source of high-interest material for a wide range of writing assignments.

The selections serve another purpose as well. They will help develop reading skills with direct benefits to you as a writer. Through close reading, you will learn how to recognize the thesis in a selection and to identify and evaluate the supporting material that develops the thesis. In your writing, you will aim to achieve the same essential structure: an overall thesis followed by detailed and valid support for that thesis. Close reading will also help you explore a selection and its possibilities thoroughly. The more you understand about what is said in a piece, the more ideas and feelings you may have about writing on an assigned topic or a related topic of your own. A third benefit of close reading is becoming more aware of authors' stylistic devices—for example, their introductions and conclusions, their ways of presenting and developing a point, their use of transitions, their choice of language to achieve a particular tone. Recognizing these devices in other people's writing will help you enlarge your own range of ideas and writing techniques.

THE FORMAT OF EACH SELECTION

Each selection begins with a short overview that gives helpful background information and stimulates interest in the piece. A selection is then followed by two sets of questions.

■   First, there are ten reading comprehension questions to help you measure your understanding of the material. These questions involve several important reading skills: recognizing a subject or topic, determining the thesis or main idea, identifying key supporting points, making inferences, and understanding vocabulary in context. Answering the questions will enable you and your instructor to check quickly your basic understanding of a selection. More significantly, as you move from one selection to the next, you will sharpen your reading skills as well as strengthen your thinking skills—two key factors in making you a better writer.

■   Following the comprehension questions are several discussion questions. In addition to dealing with issues of content, these questions focus on matters of structure, style, and tone as well.

Finally, several writing assignments accompany each selection. The assignments range from personal narratives to expository and persuasive essays about issues in the world at large. Many assignments provide detailed guidelines on how to proceed, including suggestions for prewriting and appropriate methods of development. When writing your essay responses to the readings, you will have opportunities to apply all the methods of development presented in Part Three of this book.

HOW TO READ WELL: FOUR GENERAL STEPS

Skillful reading is an important part of becoming a skillful writer. Following is a series of four steps that will make you a better reader—both of the selections here and in your reading at large.

1   Concentrate As You Read

To improve your concentration, follow these tips. First, read in a place where you can be quiet and alone. Don't choose a spot where there is a TV or stereo on or where friends or family are talking nearby. Next, sit in an upright position when you read. If your body is in a completely relaxed position, sprawled across a bed or nestled in an easy chair, your mind is also going to be completely relaxed. The light muscular tension that comes from sitting in an upright chair promotes concentration and keeps your mind ready to work. Finally, consider using your index finger (or a pen) as a pacer while you read. Lightly underline each line of print with your index finger as you read down a page. Hold your hand slightly above the page and move your finger at a speed that is a little too fast for comfort. This pacing with your index finger, like sitting upright on a chair, creates a slight physical tension that will keep your body and mind focused and alert.

2   Skim Material before You Read It

In skimming, you spend about two minutes rapidly surveying a selection, looking for important points and skipping secondary material. Follow this sequence when skimming:

- Begin by reading the overview that precedes the selection.
- Then study the title of the selection for a few moments. A good title is the shortest possible summary of a selection; it often tells you in several words just what a selection is about. For example, the title "Shame" suggests that you're going to read about a deeply embarrassing condition or incident in a person's life.
- Next, form a basic question (or questions) out of the title. For instance, for the selection titled "Shame," you might ask, "What exactly is the shame?" "What caused the shame?" "What is the result of the shame?" Forming questions out of the title is often a key to locating a writer's thesis, your next concern in skimming.
- Read the first and last couple of paragraphs in the selection. Very often a writer's thesis, *if* it is directly stated, will appear in one of these places and will relate to the title. For instance, in "Why Are Students Turned Off?" the author says in his second paragraph that ". . . many students are turned off because they have little power and responsibility for their own education."
- Finally, look quickly at the rest of the selection for other clues to important points. Are there any subheads you can relate in some way to the title? Are there any words the author has decided to emphasize by setting them off in *italic* or **boldface** type? Are there any major lists of items signaled by words such as *first, second, also, another,* and so on?

3   Read the Selection Straight Through with a Pen in Hand

Don't slow down or turn back; just aim to understand as much as you can the first time through. Place a check or star beside answers to basic questions you formed from the title, and beside other ideas that seem important. Number as 1, 2, 3 . . . lists of important points. Circle words you don't understand. Put question marks in the margin next to passages that are unclear and that you will want to reread.

4   Work with the Material

Go back and reread passages that were not clear the first time through. Look up words that block your understanding of ideas and write their meanings in the margin. Also, reread carefully the areas you identified as most important; doing so will enlarge your understanding of the material. Now that you have a sense of the whole, prepare a short outline of the selection by answering the following questions on a sheet of paper:

- What is the thesis?
- What key points support the thesis?
- What seem to be other important ideas in the selection?

By working with the material in this way, you will increase significantly your understanding of a selection. Effective reading, just like effective writing, does not happen all at once. Rather, it must be worked on. Often you begin with a general impression of what something means, and then, by working at it, you move to a deeper level of understanding of the material.

HOW TO ANSWER THE COMPREHENSION QUESTIONS: SPECIFIC HINTS

Several important reading skills are involved in the ten reading-comprehension questions that follow each selection. The skills are:

- Summarizing the selection in a title
- Determining the main idea
- Recognizing key supporting details
- Making inferences
- Understanding vocabulary in context

The following hints will help you apply each of these reading skills:

- **Subject or title.** Remember that the title should accurately describe the *entire* selection. It should be neither too broad nor too narrow for the material in the selection. It should answer the question ''What is this about?'' as specifically as possible. Note that you may at times find it easier to do the title question *after* the main-idea question.

- **Main idea.** Choose the statement that you think best expresses the main idea or thesis of the entire selection. Remember that the title will often help you focus on the main idea. Then ask yourself the question, ''Does most of the material in the selection support this statement?'' If you can answer *Yes* to this question, you have found the thesis.

- **Key details.** If you were asked to give a two-minute summary of a selection, the major details are the ones you would include in that summary. To determine the key details, ask yourself the question, ''What are the major supporting points for the thesis?''

- **Inferences.** Answer these questions by drawing upon the evidence presented in the selection and your own common sense. Ask yourself, ''What reasonable judgments can I make on the basis of the information in the selection?''

- **Vocabulary in context.** To decide on the meaning of an unfamiliar word, consider its context. Ask yourself, ''Are there any clues in the sentence that suggest what this word means?''

On pages 486–487 is a chart on which you can keep track of your performance as you answer the ten questions for each selection. The chart will help you identify reading skills you may need to strengthen.

LOOKING INWARD

Thank You

Alex Haley

Alex Haley, the author of *Roots*, served in the Coast Guard during World War II. On an especially lonely day at sea—Thanksgiving—he began to give serious thought to a holiday that has become, for most of us, a day of overeating and watching endless games of football. Haley decided to celebrate the true meaning of Thanksgiving, not by remembering the Pilgrims and their turkey dinner, but by writing three very special letters.

It was 1943, during World War II, and I was a young U.S. coastguardsman, serial number 212-548, a number we never seem to forget. My ship, the USS *Murzim*, had been under way for several days. Most of her holds contained thousands of cartons of canned or dried foods. The other holds were loaded with five-hundred-pound bombs packed delicately in padded racks. Our destination was a big base on the Island of Tulagi in the South Pacific. 1

I was one of the *Murzim*'s several cooks and, quite the same as for folk ashore, this Thanksgiving morning had seen us busily preparing a traditional dinner featuring roast turkey. 2

Well, as any cook knows, it's a lot of hard work to cook and serve a big meal, and clean up and put everything away. But finally, around sundown, with our whole galley crew just bushed, we finished at last and were free to go flop into our bunks in the fo'c'sle.   3

But I decided first to go out on the *Murzim*'s afterdeck for a breath of open air. I made my way out there, breathing in great, deep draughts while walking slowly about, still wearing my white cook's hat and the long apron, my feet sensing the big ship's vibrations from the deep-set, turbine diesels and my ears hearing that slightly hissing sound the sea makes in resisting the skin of a ship.   4

I got to thinking about Thanksgiving. In reflex, my thoughts registered the historic imagery of the Pilgrims, Indians, wild turkeys, pumpkins, corn on the cob and the rest.   5

Yet my mind seemed to be questing for something else—some way that I could personally apply to the waning Thanksgiving. It must have taken me a half hour to sense that maybe some key to an answer could result from reversing the word "Thanksgiving"—at least that suggested a verbal direction, "Giving thanks."   6

Giving thanks—as in praying, thanking God, I thought. Yes, of course. Certainly.   7

Yet my mind continued nagging me. Fine. But something else.   8

After awhile, like a dawn's brightening, a further answer did come—that there were *people* to thank, people who had done so much for me that I could never possibly repay them. The embarrassing truth was I'd always just accepted what they'd done, taken all of it for granted. Not one time had I ever bothered to express to any of them so much as a simple, sincere "Thank you."   9

At least seven people had been particularly and indelibly helpful to me. I realized, with a gulp, that about half of them had since died—so they were forever beyond any possible expression of gratitude from me. The more I thought about it, the more ashamed I became. Then I pictured the three who were still alive and, within minutes, I was down in the fo'c'sle.   10

Sitting at a mess table with writing paper and memories of things each had done, I tried composing genuine statements of heartfelt appreciation and gratitude to my dad, Simon A. Haley, a professor at the old AMNC (Agricultural Mechanical Normal College) in Pine Bluff, Ark., now a branch of the University of Arkansas; to my grandma, Cynthia Palmer, back in our little hometown of Henning, Tenn.; and to the Rev. Lonual Nelson, my grammar school principal, retired and living in Ripley, six miles north of Henning.   11

I couldn't even be certain if they would recall some of their acts of years past, acts that I vividly remembered and saw now as having given me vital training, or inspiration, or directions, if not all of these desirables rolled into one.   12

The texts of my letters began something like, "Here, this Thanksgiving at sea, I find my thoughts upon how much you have done for me, but I have never stopped and said to you how much I feel the need to thank you—" And briefly I recalled for each of them specific acts performed in my behalf.   13

For instance, something uppermost about my father was how he had impressed 14 upon me from boyhood to love books and reading. In fact, this graduated into a family habit of after-dinner quizzes at the table about books read most recently and new words learned. My love of books never diminished and later led me toward writing books myself. So many times I have felt a sadness when exposed to modern children so immersed in the electronic media that they have little to no awareness of the wondrous world to be discovered in books.

I reminded the Reverend Nelson how each morning he would open our little 15 country town's grammar school with a prayer over his assembled students. I told him that whatever positive things I had done since had been influenced at least in part by his morning school prayers.

In the letter to my grandmother, I reminded her of a dozen ways she used to 16 teach me how to tell the truth, to be thrifty, to share, and to be forgiving and considerate of others. (My reminders included how she'd make me pull switches from a peach tree for my needed lesson.) I thanked her for the years of eating her good cooking, the equal of which I had not found since. (By now, though, I've reflected that those peerless dishes are most gloriously flavored with a pinch of nostalgia.) Finally, I thanked her simply for having sprinkled my life with stardust.

Before I slept, my three letters went into our ship's office mail sack. They got 17 mailed when we reached Tulagi Island.

We unloaded cargo, reloaded with something else, then again we put to sea 18 in the routine familiar to us, and as the days became weeks, my little personal experience receded. Sometimes, when we were at sea, a mail ship would rendezvous and bring us mail from home, which, of course, we accorded topmost priority.

Every time the ship's loudspeaker rasped, "Attention! Mail call!" two-hundred- 19 odd shipmates came pounding up on deck and clustered about the raised hatch atop which two yeomen, standing by those precious bulging gray sacks, were alternately pulling out fistfuls of letters and barking successive names of sailors who were, in turn, hollering "Here! Here!" amid the jostling.

One "mail call" brought me responses from Grandma, Dad and the Reverend 20 Nelson—and my reading of their letters left me not only astounded, but more humbled than before.

Rather than saying they would forgive that I hadn't previously thanked them, 21 instead, for Pete's sake, they were thanking *me*—for having remembered, for having considered they had done anything so exceptional.

Always the college professor, my dad had carefully avoided anything he 22 considered too sentimental, so I knew how moved he was to write me that, after having helped educate many young people, he now felt that his best results included his own son.

The Reverend Nelson wrote that his decades as a "simple, old-fashioned 23 principal" had ended with grammar schools undergoing such swift changes that he had retired in self-doubt. "I heard more of what I had done wrong than what I did right," he said, adding that my letter had brought him welcome reassurance that his career had been appreciated.

A glance at Grandma's familiar handwriting brought back in a flash memories **24** of standing alongside her white wicker rocking chair, watching her "settin' down" some letter to relatives. Frequently touching her pencil's tip to pursed lips, character by character, each between a short, soft grunt, Grandma would slowly accomplish one word, then the next, so that a finished page would consume hours. I wept over the page representing my Grandma's recent hours invested in expressing her loving gratefulness to *me*—whom she used to diaper!

Much later, retired from the Coast Guard and trying to make a living as a **25** writer, I never forgot how those three "thank you" letters gave me an insight into something nigh mystical in human beings, most of whom go about yearning in secret for more of their fellows to express appreciation for their efforts.

I discovered in time that, even in the business world, probably no two words **26** are more valued than "thank you," especially among people at stores, airlines, utilities and others that directly serve the public.

Late one night, I was one of a half-dozen passengers who straggled weary and **27** grumbling off a plane that had been forced to land at the huge Dallas/Fort Worth Airport. Suddenly, a buoyant, cheerful, red-jacketed airline man waved us away from the regular waiting room seats, saying, "You sure look bushed. I know a big empty office where you can stretch out while you wait." And we surely did. When the weather improved enough for us to leave, "Gene Erickson" was in my notebook and, back home, I wrote the president of that airline describing his sensitivity and his courtesy. And I received a thank you!

I travel a good deal on lecture tours and I urge students especially to tell their **28** parents, grandparents, and other living elders simply "thank you" for all they have done to make possible the lives they now enjoy. Many students have told me they found themselves moved by the response. It is not really surprising, if one only reflects how it must feel to be thanked after you have given for years.

Now, approaching Thanksgiving of 1982, I have asked myself what will I wish **29** for all who are reading this, for our nation, indeed for our whole world—since, quoting a good and wise friend of mine, "In the end we are mightily and merely people, each with similar needs." First, I wish for us, of course, the simple common sense to achieve world peace, that being paramount for the very survival of our kind.

And there is something else I wish—so strongly that I have had this line printed **30** across the bottom of all my stationery: *"Find the good—and praise it."*

■ **Reading Comprehension Questions**

1. Which of the following would be a good alternative title for this selection?
   a. The Importance of Showing Gratitude
   b. The Three Most Important People in My Life
   c. A Lonely Time
   d. Why Letters Are Important

2. Which sentence best expresses the main idea of the selection?
   a. The author took the people he loved for granted.
   b. The author felt grateful to arrive home safely from the war.
   c. The author's father, grandmother, and grammar school principal were delighted to receive letters of thanks.
   d. Writing letters of thanks to the important people in his life taught the author the value of showing appreciation.

3. During World War II, the author served
   a. on a transport ship.
   b. in the Navy.
   c. on an Army base.
   d. on an aircraft carrier.

4. The author encourages his lecture audiences to
   a. make Thanksgiving a special day.
   b. write to company presidents.
   c. thank their elders.
   d. work for world peace.

5. *True or false?* _____ The author's father taught him to love books and reading.

6. The author implies that
   a. children should watch less television.
   b. he disliked his job as a cook aboard ship.
   c. some people do not enjoy being thanked.
   d. his grandmother had never written a letter before.

7. The author implies that
   a. his father was not openly emotional.
   b. the Reverend Lonual Nelson's teaching methods were ineffective.
   c. he never achieved success as a professional writer.
   d. Thanksgiving should be a day of prayer.

8. The author assumed that the people he wrote to
   a. would have expected thanks much sooner.
   b. would not reply.
   c. would have forgotten the incidents he referred to.
   d. would brag about his letters.

9. The word *indelibly* in "seven people had been particularly and indelibly helpful to me" (paragraph 10) means
   a. partially.
   b. temporarily.
   c. unforgettably.
   d. unhappily.

10. The word *immersed* in "modern children so immersed in the electronic media" (paragraph 14) means
    a. ignorant.
    b. absorbed.
    c. frightened.
    d. misled.

■ **Discussion Questions**

About Content

1. In your opinion, which of the three people Haley wrote to was most influential in his decision to become a writer? Why do you think so?
2. Haley quotes a friend who says, "In the end we are mightily and merely people, each with similar needs." What are two needs Haley says we all share?
3. Alex Haley was far from home when he decided to thank the important people in his life. What might have prevented him from thanking people if he had remained home?

About Structure

4. The technique Haley uses to develop most of his essay is
   a. comparison.
   b. narration.
   c. reasons.
5. How many times does the author use the key word *thank* (or *thanks*) in paragraphs 6 through 9? _____

About Style and Tone

6. When Haley tells us about the letter he wrote to his grandmother, he adds, "By now, though, I've reflected that those peerless dishes are most gloriously flavored with a pinch of nostalgia." What is he implying about her cooking?
7. Does Haley simply want to tell us about a lesson he has learned, or is he trying to persuade us to do something? How can you tell?

■ **Writing Assignments**

Assignment 1

There's an old Chinese proverb that goes: "Give me a fish, and I will eat for a day. Teach me to fish, and I will eat for a lifetime." Think of someone in your life who taught you something important that you have used (or benefited from) ever since. Write a thank-you letter to this person, telling him or her exactly how you have gained or what you have learned as a result. The person might be a parent, a family friend, a favorite teacher, an employer, another family member, a coach, or a favorite sports hero or movie star.

Organize your letter in the form of a five-paragraph essay. In your introduction, you might mention how you know this person or why you were prompted to write the letter. In your thesis, state that this person has been especially important to you because you learned something important from him or her—and tell what that "something" is. In each of your supporting paragraphs, show one way in which this knowledge or skill has made a difference in your life.

Alternatively, write about three different people, each of whom has taught you something important.

Assignment 2

Pretend that it is Thanksgiving, and one of the members of your family, who is not in a very good mood, says, "I don't have anything to be thankful for this year." Persuade this person that there are some things to be thankful for. Think of at least three and develop each with specific details. Here are some areas you could consider:

Jobs or job opportunities

Educational opportunities

Loved ones

A recent success or triumph in the family

Something beautiful

A recovery from an accident or illness

A prayer that was answered or seemed to be

Being together

Sharing a meaningful experience

Learning a valuable lesson

Assignment 3

At the end of his essay, Alex Haley says we should "Find the good—and praise it." Can you think of three kinds of people who do important work yet receive little praise? Such people might include:

Teachers
Nurses
Garbage collectors
Police officers
Fathers or mothers
School maintenance workers
People who keep essential services going

Write an essay about three of these groups, giving specific reasons why each deserves to be praised for good work. Alternatively, write an essay about one of these groups, discussing three specific areas in which it deserves praise.

Shame

Dick Gregory

In this selection, Dick Gregory—the comedian and social critic—narrates a painful experience from his boyhood. Although the incident shows graphically what it can be like to grow up black and poor, the essay also deals with universal emotions: shame, embarrassment, and the burning desire to hold onto one's self-respect.

I never learned hate at home, or shame. I had to go to school for that. I was about 1
seven years old when I got my first big lesson. I was in love with a little girl named Helene Tucker, a light-complected little girl with pigtails and nice manners. She was always clean and she was smart in school. I think I went to school then mostly to look at her. I brushed my hair and even got me a little old handkerchief. It was a lady's handkerchief, but I didn't want Helene to see me wipe my nose on my hand. The pipes were frozen again, there was no water in the house, but I washed my socks and shirt every night. I'd get a pot, and go over to Mister Ben's grocery

store, and stick my pot down into his soda machine. Scoop out some chopped ice. By evening the ice melted to water for washing. I got sick a lot that winter because the fire would go out at night before the clothes were dry. In the morning I'd put them on, wet or dry, because they were the only clothes I had.

Everybody's got a Helene Tucker, a symbol of everything you want. I loved her 2 for her goodness, her cleanness, her popularity. She'd walk down my street and my brothers and sisters would yell, "Here comes Helene," and I'd rub my tennis sneakers on the back of my pants and wish my hair wasn't so nappy and the white folks' shirt fit me better. I'd run out on the street. If I knew my place and didn't come too close, she'd wink at me and say hello. That was a good feeling. Sometimes I'd follow her all the way home, and shovel the snow off her walk and try to make friends with her Momma and her aunts. I'd drop money on her stoop late at night on my way back from shining shoes in the taverns. And she had a Daddy, and he had a good job. He was a paper hanger.

I guess I would have gotten over Helene by summertime, but something 3 happened in that classroom that made her face hang in front of me for the next twenty-two years. When I played the drums in high school it was for Helene and when I broke track records in college it was for Helene and when I started standing behind microphones and heard applause I wished Helene could hear it, too. It wasn't until I was twenty-nine years old and married and making money that I finally got her out of my system. Helene was sitting in that classroom when I learned to be ashamed of myself.

It was on a Thursday. I was sitting in the back of the room, in a seat with a 4 chalk circle drawn around it. The idiot's seat, the troublemaker's seat.

The teacher thought I was stupid. Couldn't spell, couldn't read, couldn't do 5 arithmetic. Just stupid. Teachers were never interested in finding out that you couldn't concentrate because you were so hungry, because you hadn't had any breakfast. All you could think about was noontime, would it ever come? Maybe you could sneak into the cloakroom and steal a bite of some kid's lunch out of a coat pocket. A bite of something. Paste. You can't really make a meal of paste, or put it on bread for a sandwich, but sometimes I'd scoop a few spoonfuls out of the big paste jar in the back of the room. Pregnant people get strange tastes. I was pregnant with poverty. Pregnant with dirt and pregnant with smells that made people turn away, pregnant with cold and pregnant with shoes that were never bought for me, pregnant with five other people in my bed and no Daddy in the next room, and pregnant with hunger. Paste doesn't taste too bad when you're hungry.

The teacher thought I was a troublemaker. All she saw from the front of the 6 room was a little black boy who squirmed in his idiot's seat and made noises and poked the kids around him. I guess she couldn't see a kid who made noises because he wanted someone to know he was there.

It was on a Thursday, the day before the Negro payday. The eagle always flew   **7**
on Friday. The teacher was asking each student how much his father would give
to the Community Chest. On Friday night, each kid would get the money from his
father, and on Monday he would bring it to the school. I decided I was going to
buy a Daddy right then. I had money in my pocket from shining shoes and selling
papers, and whatever Helene Tucker pledged for her Daddy I was going to top it.
And I'd hand the money right in. I wasn't going to wait until Monday to buy me a
Daddy.

I was shaking, scared to death. The teacher opened her book and started calling   **8**
out names alphabetically.

"Helene Tucker?"   **9**

"My Daddy said he'd give two dollars and fifty cents."   **10**

"That's very nice, Helene. Very, very nice indeed."   **11**

That made me feel pretty good. It wouldn't take too much to top that. I had   **12**
almost three dollars in dimes and quarters in my pocket. I stuck my hand in my
pocket and held onto the money, waiting for her to call my name. But the teacher
closed her book after she called everybody else in the class.

I stood up and raised my hand.   **13**

"What is it now?"   **14**

"You forgot me?"   **15**

She turned toward the blackboard. "I don't have time to be playing with you,   **16**
Richard."

"My Daddy said he'd . . ."   **17**

"Sit down, Richard, you're disturbing the class."   **18**

"My Daddy said he'd give . . . fifteen dollars."   **19**

She turned around and looked mad. "We are collecting this money for you and   **20**
your kind, Richard Gregory. If your Daddy can give fifteen dollars you have no
business being on relief."

"I got it right now, I got it right now, my Daddy gave it to me to turn in today,   **21**
my Daddy said . . ."

"And furthermore," she said, looking right at me, her nostrils getting big and   **22**
her lips getting thin and her eyes opening wide, "we know you don't have a
Daddy."

Helene Tucker turned around, her eyes full of tears. She felt sorry for me. Then   **23**
I couldn't see her too well because I was crying, too.

"Sit down, Richard."   **24**

And I always thought the teacher kind of liked me. She always picked me to   **25**
wash the blackboard on Friday, after school. That was a big thrill, it made me feel
important. If I didn't wash it, come Monday the school might not function right.

"Where are you going, Richard!"   **26**

I walked out of school that day, and for a long time I didn't go back very often.   **27**
There was shame there.

Now there was shame everywhere. It seemed like the whole world had been 28
inside that classroom, everyone had heard what the teacher had said, everyone
had turned around and felt sorry for me. There was shame in going to the Worthy
Boys Annual Christmas Dinner for you and your kind, because everybody knew
what a worthy boy was. Why couldn't they just call it the Boys Annual Dinner,
why'd they have to give it a name? There was shame in wearing the brown and
orange and white plaid mackinaw the welfare gave to three thousand boys. Why'd
it have to be the same for everybody so when you walked down the street the
people could see you were on relief? It was a nice warm mackinaw and it had a
hood, and my Momma beat me and called me a little rat when she found out I
stuffed it in the bottom of a pail full of garbage way over on Cottage Street. There
was shame in running over to Mister Ben's at the end of the day and asking for his
rotten peaches, there was shame in asking Mrs. Simmons for a spoonful of sugar,
there was shame in running out to meet the relief truck. I hated that truck, full of
food for you and your kind. I ran into the house and hid when it came. And then
I started to sneak through alleys, to take the long way home so the people going
into White's Eat Shop wouldn't see me. Yeah, the whole world heard the teacher
that day, we all know you don't have a Daddy.

It lasted for a while, this kind of numbness. I spent a lot of time feeling sorry 29
for myself. And then one day I met this wino in a restaurant. I'd been out hustling
all day, shining shoes, selling newspapers, and I had googobs of money in my
pocket. Bought me a bowl of chili for fifteen cents, and a cheeseburger for fifteen
cents, and a Pepsi for five cents, and a piece of chocolate cake for ten cents. That
was a good meal. I was eating when this old wino came in. I love winos because
they never hurt anyone but themselves.

The old wino sat down at the counter and ordered twenty-six cents worth of 30
food. He ate it like he really enjoyed it. When the owner, Mister Williams, asked
him to pay the check, the old wino didn't lie or go through his pocket like he
suddenly found a hole.

He just said: "Don't have no money." 31

The owner yelled: "Why in hell you come in here and eat my food if you don't 32
have no money? That food cost me money."

Mister Williams jumped over the counter and knocked the wino off his stool 33
and beat him over the head with a pop bottle. Then he stepped back and watched
the wino bleed. Then he kicked him. And he kicked him again.

I looked at the wino with blood all over his face and I went over. "Leave him 34
alone, Mister Williams. I'll pay the twenty-six cents."

The wino got up, slowly, pulling himself up to the stool, then up to the counter, 35
holding on for a minute until his legs stopped shaking so bad. He looked at me
with pure hate. "Keep your twenty-six cents. You don't have to pay, not now. I
just finished paying for it."

He started to walk out, and as he passed me, he reached down and touched 36
my shoulder. "Thanks, sonny, but it's too late now. Why didn't you pay it before?"

I was pretty sick about that. I waited too long to help another man. 37

■ Reading Comprehension Questions

1. Which of the following would be a good alternative title for this selection?
   a. Helene Tucker
   b. The Pain of Being Poor
   c. Losing a Father
   d. Mr. Williams and the Wino

2. Which sentence best expresses the main idea of the selection?
   a. Richard felt that being poor was humiliating.
   b. Richard liked Helene Tucker very much.
   c. Richard had to work hard as a child.
   d. The wino refused Richard's money.

3. The teacher disliked Richard because
   a. he was dirty.
   b. he liked Helene.
   c. he was a troublemaker.
   d. he ate paste.

4. *True or false?* _____ Helene Tucker felt sorry for Richard when the teacher embarrassed him.

5. Richard's problems in school were due to his being
   a. hungry.
   b. distracted by Helene.
   c. lonely.
   d. unable to read.

6. The author implies that
   a. Richard was not intelligent.
   b. Richard was proud.
   c. Richard had many friends.
   d. Richard and Helene became friends.

7. The author implies that
   a. Mr. Williams felt sorry for the wino.
   b. Richard's teacher was insensitive.
   c. Richard liked people to feel sorry for him.
   d. Richard's father was dead.

8. The author implies that
   a. the mackinaws were poorly made.
   b. Helene was a sensitive girl.
   c. Helene disliked Richard.
   d. the wino was ashamed of his poverty.

9. The word *pregnant* in "pregnant with poverty" (paragraph 5) means
    a. full of.
    b. empty of.
    c. sick.
    d. satisfied.

10. The word *hustling* in "I'd been out hustling all day" (paragraph 29) means
    a. learning.
    b. stealing.
    c. making friends.
    d. working hard.

■ **Discussion Questions**

About Content

1. How could Dick Gregory's teacher have handled the Community Chest incident without making him feel ashamed?
2. What are some of the lessons Gregory learns from the incident involving the wino at the restaurant?
3. Where in "Shame" do we find evidence that Dick Gregory finally does escape from poverty?

About Structure

4. Since Dick Gregory is actually writing about his embarrassing incident in school, why does he devote his first three paragraphs to his feelings about Helene Tucker?
5. What is the connection between the incident involving the wino at the restaurant and the rest of the essay?

About Style and Tone

6. In the paragraph beginning, "Now there was shame everywhere," Gregory uses a device called *repetition* when he begins several sentences with the words "There was shame . . ." What is the effect of this repetition?
7. Why does Gregory use dialog when he narrates the incidents in the classroom and in the restaurant?

■ **Writing Assignments**

Assignment 1

Dick Gregory tells us in ''Shame'' that he was ashamed of his poverty and of being on welfare—to the point that he threw away the warm hooded mackinaw he had been given simply because it was obvious proof that he and his family were on relief. Do you think Gregory was justified in feeling so ashamed of his situation? How about other people who are on welfare? Should they feel ashamed? Choose either of the following thesis statements and develop it in an essay of several paragraphs:

- People on welfare should feel ashamed of themselves.
- People on welfare should not feel ashamed of themselves.

Then develop your thesis by thinking of several reasons to support the statement you have chosen.

You might think along the following lines:

Availability of jobs

Education or lack of education

Number of young children at home requiring care

Illness, physical disability

Psychological factors—depression, work habits, expectations, mental illness

Assignment 2

At some time in your life, you probably had an experience like Dick Gregory's in ''Shame''—something that happened in a classroom, a group of friends or peers, or a family situation that proved to be both embarrassing and educational. At the time, the experience hurt you very much, but you learned from it. Write a narrative essay in which you retell this experience. Try to include vivid details and plenty of conversation so that the incident will come to life.

Assignment 3

Write an essay about three basic things that people must have in order to feel self-respect. In your thesis statement, name these three necessities and state that a person must possess them in order to feel self-respect. Here are some ideas to consider:

A certain number of material possessions

A job

A loving family or a special person

A clear conscience

A feeling of belonging

Freedom from addictions

In your supporting paragraphs, discuss the factors you have chosen, showing specifically why each is so important. In order to avoid falling into the trap of writing generalities, you may want to give examples of people who lack these necessities and show how such people lose self-respect. Your examples may be drawn from personal experience, or they may be hypothetical examples of the type explained on page 92.

On Being a Mess

Elizabeth Ames

 Do you have any messy habits that are out of control? Does your home, apartment, or bedroom bear an uncomfortable resemblance to the local landfill? If so, you will probably identify with the author of the following essay. On the other hand, if you are compulsively neat, Elizabeth Ames may be able to explain to you why some people just can't get out from under "The Mess."

I am one of those people who simply cannot clean up. To me, the prospect of an   1
orderly living space is as remote—and problematic—as trying to climb Mount Kilimanjaro.

There's a definite syndrome of sloppiness. Many people, I've noticed, go about   2
being sloppy in much the same way. I'm not sure what to call us. Messaholics? Mess-addicts? Whatever we are, the one thing we are *not* is slobs. Slobs wallow in their mess. Messy people (for want of a better label) groan over it. We're continually apologizing to the tune of, "My apartment is such a pigsty. My house is such a mess." We are always embarrassed.

When my place is at its worst, I frequently invite another Messy Person over.   3
We'll engage in an odd one-upmanship that is both competition and consolation. "I'm sorry, the place is terrible." "You should see *mine*. It's ten times worse." "Oh, no, it isn't." "Yes, it is." Etc.

Messy People want to clean up, but we can't. Not that we don't try. We do,   4
and probably more strenuously than most Neat People. I have scoured and dusted
my tiny apartment on more sunny Saturdays than I can count. I have slogged
through three-day marathons (attacking the kitchen, the living room, the bedroom
and bathroom in turn). Yet somehow the apartment will not come to order. Soon
after I've thrown in the sponge, I'm again tripping on the same sneakers and piles
of underwear.

Omnivorous. We can never quite conquer the Mess. Rout it from the living   5
room, and it withdraws to the bedroom. From there it may retreat under the bed or
into dresser drawers. A protean monster, it forever changes form to evade us.

To complicate matters, it is also omnivorous. It eats my keys (usually before I   6
go out). It eats my shoes. And worst of all, it eats my bills. That can have sticky
consequences because who, after all, misses bills? Occasionally, it takes the threat
of legal action for me to discover that the Mess devoured my bills before I had a
chance to pay them.

Often the Mess seems to rule our lives. I have declined dozens of casual   7
engagements because "I have to get rid of that Mess." Then there are the potential
visitors I've had to meet in restaurants "because there is a giant Mess in my
apartment."

Other times, the only way to subdue the Mess is to invite people to dinner. But   8
even when I've labored over my apartment all afternoon—even when I think I have
it licked—the Mess rears its ugly head.

"What about the newspapers on the floor?" a well-meaning friend will chide.   9
"What about those files and legal pads on the dining-room table?"

"But I haven't *finished* those newspapers and I *work* on the dining room table."   10
My friends shake their heads sadly. I am surely a lost cause.

And that's on a good day. On bad days, the Mess takes over completely. There   11
is no space at all on that dining-room table, or anywhere else for that matter.
Everything I own is lost under the rubble. On tiptoe, I pick my way around the
books and assorted papers, trying not to step on anything important.

On bad days I frequently cannot decide what to wear, partly because half my   12
wardrobe—the clothes I wore last week—is heaped on the bedroom desk.

As for the kitchen, it can be downright scary. I dread opening the dark   13
refrigerator, certain that some forgotten tomatoes have metamorphosed into new
forms of life. Who knows what lurks in the sink? The dishes there form towers that
lean precariously. They usually manage to fall over between 2 and 3 A.M.

I'm convinced that on one bad day I will enter my apartment and suddenly   14
panic—thinking I've been robbed when I haven't. After all, how could a normal
person wreak such havoc? I must be living with some invisible maniac, or a crazed
gorilla.

Perhaps that is why so many Messy People feel "exposed" when a stranger   15
glimpses their Mess. Beneath our attempts at denial, we have seen the enemy and
he is certainly no crazed gorilla . . .

Reality, however, is not always easy to face. Thus we have devised several   16
ingenious myths to justify our Mess—and ourselves. They are:

The Clean Mess. This myth is our primary protection against the gruesome   17
label, "slob." Slobs, of course, live in filth. Messy People live amid a profusion of
sterile objects. "What's wrong," we ask, "with some basically clean clothes lying
around? At least they're not fungus."

The Intellectual Mess. According to this one, we are too busy pondering the   18
state of the universe to bother with such earthly realities as unmade beds. We are
creative nonconformists whose order is disorder. People with Intellectual Messes
look down their noses at unimaginative organized souls. There's no challenge, they
insist, in finding a dictionary *right away*. How routine. How dull.

It's My Mother's Fault. Behind nearly every Messy Person is a Meticulous   19
Mother. We love to recount our childhood torments at her hands and bemoan its
effects: "She ordered me to do the bathroom so many times! I now have convulsions
at the sight of window cleaner . . . So much talk about eating off her floors warped
my subconscious. I'm acting out delusions of being an animal." And so on.

It's My Apartment's Fault. People who rely on this complain, "There's no   20
place left to put anything. My closets are full. What would I do with those things
I'm saving for the Salvation Army? What would I do with my stuffed giraffe, Snookie?
And those old broiler pans belonged to my grandfather!"

Such are the myths of Mess. Myths, because there are plenty of neat folks with   21
brains, badgering mothers and small apartments. Being a mess is no blessing. The
only way out is to probe your true motives, discard the excuses and accept
responsibility. For me, that was a gut-wrenching process. It was so powerful, in
fact, that I didn't wash dishes for two weeks.

■ **Reading Comprehension Questions**

1. Which of the following would be a good alternative title for this selection?
   a. Slobs
   b. The Myths of Messiness
   c. Problems of Working at Home
   d. Messy People
2. Which sentence best expresses the main idea of the selection?
   a. Being a mess has certain advantages.
   b. Being messy creates problems, but messy people can't help themselves.
   c. Messy people don't like strangers to see their messiness.
   d. Messy people fool themselves with myths.
3. *True or false?* _____ The author's apartment has been robbed several
   times.

4. One thing messy people are not is
   a. competitive.
   b. embarrassed.
   c. disorganized.
   d. content.

5. Which of the following is *not* one of the myths that messy people use to justify their messes?
   a. The Clean Mess
   b. It's My Mother's Fault
   c. The Children's Mess
   d. The Intellectual Mess

6. The author implies that
   a. messy people are basically lazy.
   b. messy people are not proud of their bad habits.
   c. neat people are snobs.
   d. small apartments are messier than large homes.

7. The author implies that
   a. she has reformed her messy habits.
   b. friends will overlook her messiness.
   c. she will never change.
   d. her mother caused her messy habits.

8. The author implies that
   a. messy people need myths because they are ashamed of themselves.
   b. she doesn't mind being called a slob.
   c. messy people live in sterile conditions.
   d. she keeps her work separate from the household mess.

9. The word *protean* in "a protean monster, it forever changes form to evade us" (paragraph 5) means
   a. horrible.
   b. healthful.
   c. avoidable.
   d. changeable.

10. The word *omnivorous* in "the Mess . . . is also omnivorous" (paragraph 6) means
    a. helpful.
    b. enjoyable.
    c. all-consuming.
    d. easily defeated.

■ **Discussion Questions**

About Content

1. Elizabeth Ames offers several excuses for being messy. What are they? Are any of them *good* excuses?

2. Ames insists that she is not a slob, only a messy person. What does she say is the difference between a slob and a messy person? Do you agree that she is not a slob?

3. The author states in the final paragraph that she decided to "accept responsibility" for her messiness. What happened? Do you think that Ames should stay the way she is, or do you think she should try to change?

About Structure

4. What change-of-direction signal is used in paragraph 4? _____

5. To what does the pronoun *it* refer in the first four sentences of paragraph 6? _____

About Style and Tone

6. Why do you think the author always capitalizes the word *mess*?

7. Point out one place in the selection where the author uses exaggeration to make her point.

■ **Writing Assignments**

Assignment 1

Imagine that you are an efficiency expert, and Elizabeth Ames has come to you for help in overcoming her messiness. After you interview her and learn all the details that are in her essay, what suggestions would you make to her for how to be a neater person? What should she do first, second, and third? What routine should she follow to prevent the mess from coming back?

Write a report of several paragraphs in which you explain to Ames the process whereby she can overcome her messy habits and be a neater person.

Start with an introductory paragraph in which you identify the problem she has and make the point that she can cure it if she follows a few simple steps (thesis statement).

Then, in the paragraphs that follow, describe each step in detail, giving specific examples of what she should do to achieve her goal. Refer to some of the same problems she mentions in her essay, and show her how she could clean them up and keep them cleaned up.

In your conclusion, summarize your recommendations, and then encourage Ames by telling her just how much better her life will be once she gets rid of the messes in it.

Assignment 2

In her essay, Elizabeth Ames is careful to distinguish between being a mess (which she says she is) and being a slob (which she insists she is not). Write your own essay, using as your title "On Being a Slob." What are the character traits of a slob? What kinds of things do slobs do? What would a slob's apartment or house or workplace look like? (One clue Ames gives is the statement, "Slobs wallow in their mess." How—and in what ways—would a slob "wallow"?) Pick out at least three ways in which a slob can be identified and develop each of these ways in a separate paragraph of your essay.

Assignment 3

Think of a word that you could use to characterize yourself. (Ames calls herself a "messy person.") Then write an essay titled "On Being _____."
You might, for example, characterize yourself in one of the following ways:

Neat	A compulsive saver
Gullible	Talkative
Too generous	A gambler
An eternal optimist	A dreamer
Suspicious	Helpless
Lucky	Unlucky
Skeptical	A loner

Each of the topic sentences for your supporting paragraphs should make a point about an effect this quality has had on your life. Then you should support the point with specific details. Here, for example, are the thesis statement and topic sentence for an essay titled "On Being a Compulsive Shopper":

Thesis: Being a compulsive shopper has caused me many problems.

Topic sentence 1: First, I buy all kinds of things I don't need.

Topic sentence 2: In addition, I can waste hours just drifting around in stores.

Topic sentence 3: Most important, I overspend rather than comparison-shop for the best price.

The Ambivalence of Abortion

Linda Bird Francke

Abortion is an issue almost everyone has strong opinions about. It is both a national question debated by the Supreme Court and a very personal problem confronted by millions of women in the privacy of their own hearts. In the following essay, Linda Bird Francke narrates the story of her decision to have an abortion. As you will see, it was ultimately a very lonely decision—despite the support of her husband. Is the writer for abortion, against abortion, or neither? That is something you, as a reader, will have to decide.

1   We were sitting in a bar on Lexington Avenue when I told my husband I was pregnant. It is not a memory I like to dwell on. Instead of the champagne and hope which had heralded the impending births of the first, second and third child, the news of this one was greeted with shocked silence and Scotch. "Jesus," my husband kept saying to himself, stirring the ice cubes around and around. "Oh, Jesus."

2   Oh, how we tried to rationalize it that night as the starting time for the movie came and went. My husband talked about his plans for a career change in the next year, to stem the staleness that fourteen years with the same investment-banking firm had brought him. A new baby would preclude that option.

3   The timing wasn't right for me either. Having juggled pregnancies and child care with what free-lance jobs I could fit in between feedings, I had just taken on a full-time job. A new baby would put me right back in the nursery just when our youngest child was finally school age. It was time for *us*, we tried to rationalize. There just wasn't room in our lives now for another baby. We both agreed. And agreed. And agreed.

4   How very considerate they are at the Women's Services, known formally as the Center for Reproductive and Sexual Health. Yes, indeed, I could have an abortion that very Saturday morning and be out in time to drive to the country that afternoon. Bring a first morning urine specimen, a sanitary belt and napkins, a money order or $125 cash—and a friend.

5   My friend turned out to be my husband, standing awkwardly and ill at ease as men always do in places that are exclusively for women, as I checked in at 9 A.M. Other men hovered around just as anxiously, knowing they had to be there, wishing they weren't. No one spoke to each other. When I would be cycled out of there four hours later, the same men would be slumped in their same seats, locked downcast in their cells of embarrassment.

The Saturday morning women's group was more disspirited than the men in   6
the waiting room. There were around fifteen of us, a mixture of races, ages and
backgrounds. Three didn't speak English at all and a fourth, a pregnant Puerto Rican
girl around eighteen, translated for them.

There were six black women and a hodgepodge of whites, among them a   7
T-shirted teenager who kept leaving the room to throw up and a puzzled middle-
aged woman from Queens with three grown children.

"What form of birth control were you using?" the volunteer asked each one of   8
us. The answer was inevitably "none." She then went on to describe the various
forms of birth control available at the clinic, and offered them to each of us.

The youngest Puerto Rican girl was asked through the interpreter which she'd   9
like to use: the loop, diaphragm, or pill. She shook her head "no" three times.
"You don't want to come back here again, do you?" the volunteer pressed. The
girl's head was so low her chin rested on her breastbone. "*Sí,*" she whispered.

We had been there two hours by that time, filling out endless forms, giving   10
blood and urine, receiving lectures. But unlike any other group of women I've been
in, we didn't talk. Our common denominator, the one which usually floods across
language and economic barriers into familiarity, today was one of shame. We were
losing life that day, not giving it.

The group kept getting cut back to smaller, more workable units, and finally I   11
was put in a small waiting room with just two other women. We changed into
paper bathrobes and paper slippers, and we rustled whenever we moved. One of
the women in my room was shivering and an aide brought her a blanket.

"What's the matter?" the aide asked her. "I'm scared," the woman said. "How   12
much will it hurt?" The aide smiled. "Oh, nothing worse than a couple of bad
cramps," she said. "This afternoon you'll be dancing a jig."

I began to panic. Suddenly the rhetoric, the abortion marches I'd walked in,   13
the telegrams sent to Albany to counteract the Friends of the Fetus, the Zero
Population Growth buttons I'd worn, peeled away, and I was all alone with my
microscopic baby. There were just the two of us there, and soon, because it was
more convenient for me and my husband, there would be one again.

How could it be that I, who am so neurotic about life that I step over bugs   14
rather than on them, who spend hours planting flowers and vegetables in the spring
even though we rent out the house and never see them, who make sure the children
are vaccinated and inoculated and filled with vitamin C, could so arbitrarily decide
that this life shouldn't be?

"It's not a life," my husband had argued, more to convince himself than me.   15
"It's a bunch of cells smaller than my fingernail."

But any woman who has had children knows that certain feeling in her taut,   16
swollen breasts, and the slight but constant ache in her uterus that signals the arrival
of a life. Though I would march myself into blisters for a woman's right to exercise
the option of motherhood, I discovered there in the waiting room that I was not
the modern woman I thought I was.

When my name was called, my body felt so heavy the nurse had to help me 17 into the examining room. I waited for my husband to burst through the door and yell "Stop," but of course he didn't. I concentrated on three black spots in the acoustic ceiling until they grew in size to the shape of saucers, while the doctor swabbed my insides with antiseptic.

"You're going to feel a burning sensation now," he said, injecting Novocain 18 into the neck of the womb. The pain was swift and severe, and I twisted to get away from him. He was hurting my baby, I reasoned, and the black saucers quivered in the air. "Stop," I cried. "Please stop." He shook his head, busy with his equipment. "It's too late to stop now," he said. "It'll just take a few more seconds."

What good sports we women are. And how obedient. Physically the pain 19 passed even before the hum of the machine signaled that the vacuuming of my uterus was completed, my baby sucked up like ashes after a cocktail party. Ten minutes start to finish. And I was back on the arm of the nurse.

There were twelve beds in the recovery room. Each one had a gaily flowered 20 draw sheet and a soft green or blue thermal blanket. It was all very feminine. Lying on these beds for an hour or more were the shocked victims of their sex, their full wombs now stripped clean, their futures less encumbered.

It was very quiet in that room. The only voice was that of the nurse, locating 21 the new women who had just come in so she could monitor their blood pressure, and checking out the recovered women who were free to leave.

Juice was being passed about, and I found myself sipping a Dixie cup of 22 Hawaiian Punch. An older woman with tightly curled bleached hair was just getting up from the next bed. "That was no goddamn snap," she said, resting before putting on her miniskirt and high white boots. Other women came and went, some walking out as dazed as they had entered, others with a bounce that signaled they were going right back to Bloomingdale's.

Finally then, it was time for me to leave. I checked out, making an appointment 23 to return in two weeks for an IUD insertion. My husband was slumped in the waiting room, clutching a single yellow rose wrapped in a wet paper towel and stuffed into a Baggie.

We didn't talk the whole way home, but just held hands very tightly. At home 24 there were more yellow roses and a tray in bed for me and the children's curiosity to divert.

It had certainly been a successful operation. I didn't bleed at all for two days 25 just as they had predicted, and then I bled only moderately for another four days. Within a week my breasts had subsided and the tenderness vanished, and my body felt mine again instead of the eggshell it becomes when it's protecting someone else.

My husband and I are back to planning our summer vacation and his career 26 switch.

And it certainly does make more sense not to be having a baby right now—we 27 say that to each other all the time. But I have this ghost now. A very little ghost that only appears when I'm seeing something beautiful, like the full moon on the ocean last weekend. And the baby waves at me. And I wave at the baby. "Of course, we have room," I cry to the ghost. "Of course, we do."

■ Reading Comprehension Questions

1. Which of the following would be a good alternative title for this selection?
   a. Abortion: A Difficult Decision
   b. The Process of Abortion
   c. Safe Abortions
   d. The Wrong Decision

2. Which sentence best expresses the main idea of the selection?
   a. Abortion clinics today are clean, safe, and friendly.
   b. The author realized that her decision to have an abortion was a selfish one.
   c. Deciding to have an abortion was a painful and unforgettable decision for the author.
   d. Husbands should support wives if they decide to have an abortion.

3. The patients at the clinic are
   a. mostly black.
   b. teenagers.
   c. a mixture of races and ages.
   d. welfare clients.

4. *True or false?* _____ The abortion clinic was a cold, unfriendly place.

5. Before having her own abortion, the author
   a. had been opposed to abortion.
   b. had never considered the issue.
   c. had been unable to make up her mind about the issue.
   d. had been actively in favor of abortion.

6. The author implies that
   a. her career is more important than having another child.
   b. her husband felt worse about the abortion than she did.
   c. women can tolerate pain better than men can.
   d. she will now join an antiabortion group.

7. The author implies that
   a. career considerations should not enter into a decision to have an abortion.
   b. birth control is unreliable.
   c. she still does not feel completely comfortable with her decision.
   d. the young Puerto Rican girl is irresponsible.

8. *True or false?* _____ The author implies that the men and women at the clinic felt ashamed to be there.

9. The word *preclude* in "A new baby would preclude that option" (paragraph 2) means
   a. include.
   b. prevent.
   c. delay.
   d. force.

10. The word *arbitrarily* in "could so arbitrarily decide that this life shouldn't be" (paragraph 14) means
   a. reluctantly.
   b. unhappily.
   c. thoughtfully.
   d. lightly.

■ **Discussion Questions**

About Content

1. What reasons does Linda Bird Francke give for her decision to have an abortion? Which are her reasons, and which are her husband's reasons?
2. In what ways are the people at Women's Services considerate to the author? In what ways are they *not* considerate?
3. Why do you think the men are ill at ease and embarrassed?

About Structure

4. What method of introduction does the author use?
   a. Broad to narrow
   b. Anecdote
   c. Questions
5. The author begins and ends her essay with the idea of ambivalence: conflicting feelings or thoughts existing at the same time. How is the ambivalence reflected at the end?

About Style and Tone

6. Why does the author repeat the word *agreed* so often at the end of the third paragraph?
7. A *simile* is a figure of speech in which a writer compares one thing to another, very different thing, using the word *like* or *as* to bring out a surprising relationship between the two. In paragraph 19, the author uses a simile when she writes that her baby was "sucked up like ashes after a cocktail party." Why do you think she uses this simile? What is she saying here about her unborn child and her feelings about the abortion?

■ Writing Assignments

Assignment 1

Imagine that a friend has come to you and told you that she is pregnant. Your friend doesn't know what to do. Write an essay about the three most important questions your friend should ask herself in order to arrive at the best decision. In each supporting paragraph, state what the question is and describe why the answer is so important in the decision-making process. Possible questions are:

What are my future goals?

How does the baby's father feel?

How will I support myself and the baby?

What is best for me?

What is best for the baby?

What is the morally right thing to do?

What does my religion teach?

Whom will I hurt by having or not having the baby?

What are the alternatives to abortion?

In your conclusion, you could mention the decision that you hope your friend will come to.

Assignment 2

Think of a difficult decision you are in the process of making now (or one you will soon have to make). Write an essay in which you examine your conflicting feelings. Organize the essay into two supporting paragraphs, covering (1) the arguments in favor of one side, and (2) the arguments for the other side. In your conclusion, you might mention the decision you are leaning toward. Here are a sample thesis, topic sentences, and brief outline for an essay on this topic:

Thesis: Making a decision about whether to continue going to college or get a full-time job has been difficult for me.

Topic sentence 1: Continuing in school might be the best course of action.
   a. Degree means better future earning power
   b. Convenient—my parents available now to baby-sit for my children
   c. Enjoyment of learning

Topic sentence 2: However, getting a full-time job seems urgent now.
   a. Need money to move to larger apartment
   b. Local job opportunity might not be available later
   c. Would have more money for everyday things

Assignment 3

Write a narrative essay on an action you took that you gave considerable thought to but later regretted. The action may be an important one that lends itself to a serious tone (such as filing for divorce, punishing a child, quitting a job, or getting married). Or the action may be one that could be written about in a light, humorous tone (such as getting a haircut, going skiing, wearing a certain outfit, or going out on a particular date).

Salvation

Langston Hughes

In the following selection from his autobiography, Langston Hughes describes the time he was brought to church to be ''saved.'' During the service, he is confronted with a situation common to all of us: should he go along with the group, even though his inner self tells him not to? You'll see how he resolved his conflict and how his decision had lasting effects on his life.

I was saved from sin when I was going on thirteen. But not really saved. It happened like this. There was a big revival at my Auntie Reed's church. Every night for weeks there had been much preaching, singing, praying, and shouting, and some very hardened sinners had been brought to Christ, and the membership of the church had grown by leaps and bounds. Then just before the revival ended, they held a special meeting for children, ''to bring the young lambs to the fold.'' My aunt spoke of it for days ahead. That night I was escorted to the front row and placed on the mourners' bench with all the other young sinners, who had not yet been brought to Jesus. 1

My aunt told me that when you were saved you saw a light, and something happened to you inside! And Jesus came into your life! And God was with you from then on! She said you could see and hear and feel Jesus in your soul. I believed her. I had heard a great many old people say the same thing and it seemed to me they ought to know. So I sat there calmly in the hot, crowded church, waiting for Jesus to come to me. 2

The preacher preached a wonderful rhythmical sermon, all moans and shouts and lonely cries and dire pictures of hell, and then he sang a song about the ninety and nine safe in the fold, but one little lamb was left out in the cold. Then he said: ''Won't you come? Won't you come to Jesus? Young lambs, won't you come?'' And he held out his arms to all us young sinners there on the mourners' bench. 3

And the little girls cried. And some of them jumped up and went to Jesus right away. But most of us just sat there.

A great many old people came and knelt around us and prayed, old women   4
with jet-black faces and braided hair, old men with work-gnarled hands. And the church sang a song about the lower lights are burning, some poor sinners to be saved. And the whole building rocked with prayer and song.

Still I kept waiting to see Jesus.   5

Finally all the young people had gone to the altar and were saved, but one boy   6
and me. He was a rounder's son named Westley. Westley and I were surrounded by sisters and deacons praying. It was very hot in the church, and getting late now. Finally Westley said to me in a whisper: "God damn! I'm tired o' sitting here. Let's get up and be saved." So he got up and was saved.

Then I was left all alone on the mourners' bench. My aunt came and knelt at   7
my knees and cried, while prayers and songs swirled all around me in the little church. The whole congregation prayed for me alone, in a mighty wail of moans and voices. And I kept waiting serenely for Jesus, waiting, waiting—but he didn't come. I wanted to see him, but nothing happened to me. Nothing! I wanted something to happen to me, but nothing happened.

I heard the songs and the minister saying: "Why don't you come? My dear   8
child, why don't you come to Jesus? Jesus is waiting for you. He wants you. Why don't you come? Sister Reed, what is this child's name?"

"Langston," my aunt sobbed.   9

"Langston, why don't you come? Why don't you come and be saved? Oh,   10
Lamb of God! Why don't you come?"

Now it was really getting late. I began to be ashamed of myself, holding   11
everything up so long. I began to wonder what God thought about Westley, who certainly hadn't seen Jesus either, but who was now sitting proudly on the platform, swinging his knickerbockered legs and grinning down at me, surrounded by deacons and old women on their knees praying. God had not struck Westley dead for taking his name in vain or for lying in the temple. So I decided that maybe to save further trouble, I'd better lie, too, and say that Jesus had come, and get up and be saved.

So I got up.   12

Suddenly the whole room broke into a sea of shouting, as they saw me rise.   13
Waves of rejoicing swept through the place. Women leaped in the air. My aunt threw her arms around me. The minister took me by the hand and led me to the platform.

When things quieted down, in a hushed silence, punctuated by a few ecstatic   14
"Amens," all the new young lambs were blessed in the name of God. Then joyous singing filled the room.

That night, for the last time in my life but one—for I was a big boy twelve years   15
old—I cried. I cried, in bed alone, and couldn't stop. I buried my head under the quilts, but my aunt heard me. She woke up and told my uncle I was crying because the Holy Ghost had come into my life, and because I had seen Jesus. But I was really crying because I couldn't bear to tell her that I had lied, that I had deceived everybody in the church, that I hadn't seen Jesus, and that now I didn't believe there was a Jesus any more, since he didn't come to help me.

■ **Reading Comprehension Questions**

1. Which of the following would be a good alternative title for this selection?
   a. How a Revival Meeting Works
   b. The Day I Lied in Church
   c. The Importance of Religion
   d. How Jesus Came into My Life

2. Which sentence best expresses the main idea of the selection?
   a. Anyone who wants to be saved can be.
   b. Some people do not believe in God.
   c. Some people cannot be helped.
   d. Some people give in to outside pressure.

3. Hughes was taken to church by his
   a. mother.
   b. father.
   c. aunt.
   d. brother.

4. The author stands up to be saved because
   a. he feels pressured.
   b. Westley motions to him.
   c. his aunt tells him to.
   d. the minister convinces him.

5. *True or false?* _____ Westley gets up because he sees Jesus.

6. *True or false?* _____ We can assume that Westley was pretending to be "saved."

7. We can assume that Auntie Reed
   a. would have felt very upset if Hughes had not gotten up to be "saved."
   b. didn't care if Hughes were saved or not.
   c. knew that Hughes had not really been saved.
   d. liked Westley more than she liked Hughes.

8. We can conclude that Hughes cried that night because
   a. he had not liked being left alone on the bench.
   b. the sermon frightened him.
   c. the Holy Ghost had visited him.
   d. he felt he had been dishonest.

9. The word *dire* in "all moans and shouts . . . and dire pictures" (paragraph 3) means
   a. dreadful.
   b. appealing.
   c. lively.
   d. unrealistic.

10. The word *ecstatic* in "punctuated by a few ecstatic 'Amens' " (paragraph
    14) means
    a. loud.
    b. delighted.
    c. confusing.
    d. threatening.

■ **Discussion Questions**

About Content

1. Hughes is under pressure from several sources to stand up and be saved.
   How does his aunt put him under pressure?
2. How does the minister put him under pressure? The congregation? Westley?
3. Why does Hughes say, at the end, that he "didn't believe there was a Jesus
   any more"? How does this help you understand his statement in the first
   paragraph that he was "saved. . . . But not really saved"?

About Structure

4. The author uses transition words to move his narrative smoothly from one
   stage to the next. List three that are used to begin paragraphs:

   _____   _____   _____

About Style and Tone

5. Hughes uses vivid imagery to make his experience live for his readers. For
   example, he uses language that appeals to our sight ("old women with jet-
   black faces and braided hair") and to our sense of hearing ("the whole
   building rocked with prayer and song"). Pick out another sight image and
   another hearing image and write them below:

   _____

   _____

6. The dialog in this selection, too, makes the experience vivid and real. List
   three speakers whose actual words we hear in the selection:

   _____   _____   _____

7. *Irony* is the use of language to suggest the opposite of what is stated. Explain
   the irony in the word "Salvation" that the author has used as the title of his
   experience.

■ Writing Assignments

Assignment 1

Although Langston Hughes lies in the selection, it is clear that he is a good person. Write an essay in the form of a letter to Hughes in which you reassure him that he has several good qualities. In your introduction, explain that you know that he lied in church, but you still feel he is basically a good person. Then back up this statement in the next few paragraphs. Each of these paragraphs can focus on one good quality that Hughes possesses. Give examples from "Salvation" to back up these qualities. Finally, end with a brief conclusion in which you again reassure Hughes.

Assignment 2

In this selection, Hughes, in effect, loses his innocence. He learns something about the adult world that he finds very disillusioning. Write a narrative essay about a time you learned a truth about adult life that disappointed you. For example, you might have learned:

Your idol wasn't all he or she appeared to be.

Parents aren't perfect.

People lie.

People wear masks.

You can get away with a lie. *Or:* Sometimes it's best to lie.

You may find it helpful to read first the three narrative essays on pages 194–197.

Assignment 3

If you had been in Hughes' place, what would you have done? Reread "Salvation." Then write a five-paragraph essay in which you give three reasons to support *either* of these thesis statements:

- If I had been in the church, I would have come up to be saved.
- If I had been in the church, I would not have come up to be saved.

To get started, brainstorm your answers to the following questions. As you think about or jot down your answers, you will probably decide (if you have not already done so) which thesis you will best be able to develop.

How would your parents or relatives feel if you did (didn't)?

How would your friends react?

How important to you are other people's reactions?

Is appearing to be religious important to you? How important is religion in your life?

Is it ever all right to lie? Under what conditions?

Success Means Never Feeling Tired

Mortimer Adler

Do you ever feel tired without knowing why? According to Mortimer Adler, the reason could be your failure to approach problems in the right way. Putting off solving a problem can be more exhausting than tackling it head on. In this article, Adler, a world-famous philosopher with twenty-eight books to his credit, shares the secret of his success.

Failure is probably the most fatiguing experience a person ever has. There is nothing more enervating than not succeeding—being blocked, not moving ahead. It is a vicious circle. Failure breeds fatigue, and the fatigue makes it harder to get to work, which compounds the failure. 1

We experience this tiredness in two main ways: as start-up fatigue and performance fatigue. In the former case, we keep putting off a task that we are under some compulsion to discharge. Either because it is too tedious or because it is too difficult, we shirk it. And the longer we postpone it, the more tired we feel. 2

Such start-up fatigue is very real, even if not actually physical, not something in our muscles and bones. The remedy is obvious, though perhaps not easy to apply: an exertion of willpower. The moment I find myself turning away from a job, or putting it under a pile of other things I have to do, I clear my desk of everything else and attack the objectionable item first. To prevent start-up fatigue, always tackle the most difficult job first. 3

Years ago, when editing *Great Books of the Western World,* I undertook to write 102 essays, one on each of the great ideas discussed by the authors of those books. The writing took me 2½ years, working at it—among my other tasks—seven days a week. I would never have finished if I had allowed myself to write first about the ideas I found easiest to expound. Applying my own rule, I determined to write the essays in strict alphabetical order, from ANGEL to WORLD, never letting myself skip a tough idea. And I always started the day's work with the difficult task of essay-writing. Experience proved, once again, that the rule works. **4**

Performance fatigue is more difficult to handle. Here we are not reluctant to get started, but we cannot seem to do the job right. Its difficulties appear insurmountable and, however hard we work, we fail again and again. That mounting experience of failure carries with it an ever-increasing burden of mental fatigue. In such a situation, I work as hard as I can—then let the unconscious take over. **5**

When I was planning the fifteenth edition of *Encyclopaedia Britannica,* I had to create a topical table of contents for its alphabetically arranged articles. Nothing like this had ever been done before, and day after day I kept coming up with solutions that fell short. My fatigue became almost overpowering. **6**

One day, mentally exhausted, I put down on paper all the reasons why this problem could *not* be solved. I tried to convince myself that what appeared insoluble really *was* insoluble, that the trouble was with the problem, not me. Having gained some relief, I sat back in an easy chair and went to sleep. **7**

An hour or so later, I woke up suddenly with the solution clearly in mind. In the weeks that followed, the correctness of the solution summoned up by my unconscious mind was confirmed at every step. Though I worked every bit as hard as before, if not harder, my work was not attended by any weariness or fatigue. Success was now as exhilarating as failure had been depressing. I was experiencing the joy of what psychologists today call *flow.* Life offers few pleasures more invigorating than the successful exercise of our faculties. It unleashes energies for additional work. **8**

Sometimes the snare is not in the problem itself, but in the social situation—or so it appears. Other people somehow seem to prevent us from succeeding. But, as Shakespeare wrote, "The fault, dear Brutus, is not in our stars but in ourselves." Why blame other people and shrug off our own responsibility for misunderstandings? Doing a job successfully means doing whatever is necessary—and that *includes* winning the cooperation of others. **9**

More often, the snare that blocks us is purely personal. Subject to human distractions, we let personal problems weigh on us, producing a fatigue-failure that blocks our productivity in every sphere. **10**

A friend of mine went into a decline over a family problem that she had let slide. Her daughter had secretly married a man she thought her father would disapprove of. The daughter told her mother but made her promise to keep silent. Worrying about the problem, and carrying a burden of guilt over the secrecy, exhausted the mother. Her fatigue spilled over into her job and turned her usual successes there into failures. She was saved from serious depression only when other people intervened and told the father—who didn't display any of the anticipated **11** negative reaction. It seems incredible that a person can allow his or her life to get snarled up in this fashion, but this is how problems can fester if they aren't solved as they come along.

So, our first step should be to use inexplicable fatigue that has no physical base   **12** as a radar—an early-warning system—and trace the fatigue to its source; to find the defeat we are papering over and not admitting. Then we must diagnose the cause of this failure. In rare cases, it may be that the task really is too difficult for us, that we are in over our head. If so, we can acknowledge the fact and bow out. Or the block may simply be in refusing to confront the problem. In most cases, it can be solved by patient attention to the task at hand—with all the skill and resolution we can muster. That, plus the inspired help of the unconscious.

I have already given an example of one way of achieving a breakthrough. First,   **13** put down all the reasons why the problem is insoluble. Try to box yourself in, like Houdini, so no escape appears possible. Only then, like Houdini, can you break out. Having tied yourself up in knots, stop thinking consciously about the problem for a while. Let your unconscious work on untying the knots. Nine times out of ten, it will come up with a solution.

The worst mistake we can make is to regard mental fatigue as if it were physical   **14** fatigue. We can recuperate from the latter by giving our bodies a chance to rest. But mental fatigue that results from failure cannot be removed by giving in to it and taking a rest. That just makes matters worse. Whatever the specific stumbling block is, it must be cleared up, and fast, before the fatigue of failure swamps us.

Human beings, I believe, *must* try to succeed. This necessity is built into our   **15** biological background. Without trying to define success, it's enough to say that it is related to continuous peak performance, to doing tasks and solving problems as they come along. It is experiencing the exuberance, the joy, the "flow" that goes with the unimpeded exercise of one's human capabilities.

Success, then, means never feeling tired.   **16**

■ Reading Comprehension Questions

1. Which of the following would be a good alternative title for this selection?
    a.   Feeling Tired
    b.   Fighting the Fatigue of Failure
    c.   Performance Fatigue
    d.   Fighting Fatigue

2. Which sentence best expresses the main idea of the selection?
    a.   Failure leads to fatigue.
    b.   The mental fatigue of failure should be recognized and then overcome in various ways.
    c.   A growing experience of failure brings a growing burden of mental fatigue.
    d.   When we let personal problems get out of hand, mental fatigue can block productivity.

3. Start-up fatigue is
    a. always physical.
    b. preventable.
    c. never overcome.
    d. caused by physical fatigue.

4. Overcoming performance fatigue requires
    a. doing the most difficult job first.
    b. doing the job right the first time.
    c. using the unconscious mind and working hard.
    d. increasing sleep time.

5. *True or false?* _____ Mental fatigue should be treated very much like physical fatigue.

6. The author implies that hard work
    a. always results in mental fatigue.
    b. results only in physical fatigue.
    c. always cures mental fatigue.
    d. can lead to great joy.

7. Adler implies that
    a. intelligent people don't experience the fatigue of failure.
    b. our minds can solve problems even when we're asleep.
    c. worrying about personal problems is useful.
    d. he never has mental fatigue.

8. The author implies that to fight mental fatigue, we should
    a. solve problems as they come along.
    b. put aside all our problems.
    c. avoid social situations at work.
    d. recognize that others are to blame.

9. The word *shirk* in "because [a task] is too tedious or too difficult, we shirk it" (paragraph 2) means
    a. avoid.
    b. welcome.
    c. picture.
    d. reduce.

10. The word *expound* in "to write first about the ideas I found easiest to expound" (paragraph 4) means
    a. forget.
    b. install.
    c. express.
    d. reduce.

■ Discussion Questions

About Content

1. What are the differences between ''start-up fatigue'' and ''performance fatigue''? How does Adler feel that each should be dealt with? What experiences have you had with either type of fatigue?

2. Why does Adler state, ''The worst mistake we can make is to regard mental fatigue as if it were physical fatigue'' (paragraph 14)?

3. What do you think Adler means when he writes that our need to succeed ''is built into our biological background'' (paragraph 15)?

About Structure

4. What is the main method of development used in paragraphs 6–8?
   a. definition.
   b. classification.
   c. narration.

5. Adler discusses two main ways we experience the fatigue of failure. List them here:

   _____

   _____

6. Adler describes two types of situations in which we fail to solve our problems. List them here:

   _____

   _____

About Style and Tone

7. For what audience do you think Adler wrote this article?
   a. Doctors
   b. The general public
   c. Homemakers
   d. Psychologists

8. The author supports his points with
   a. statistics.
   b. direct quotations.
   c. personal experiences.
   d. research.

■ **Writing Assignments**

Assignment 1

Adler writes: "Problems can fester if they aren't solved as they come along." Think of a time when you had a problem that began to "fester" because it dragged on too long. How did you feel having the problem on your mind? How did you finally solve the problem? Write a narrative about your experience with mental fatigue, the steps you finally took, and the eventual outcome. One possible central point for this narrative is: "When I experienced mental fatigue because of _____ (the problem), I finally solved the problem by following a series of steps." Following are a few suggestions for the type of problem you may wish to write about.

> A difficult choice
>
> A seemingly impossible assignment at work or school
>
> A communication problem with a family member
>
> A difficulty with a relationship

Here is an example of an outline for this assignment:

> Thesis: A conflict with my mother caused me much mental fatigue until I faced and solved the problem.
> a. I told my boyfriend I'd spend Thanksgiving with his family, but my mother insisted I be home for Thanksgiving.
> b. I ignored the problem, and the resulting mental fatigue interfered with everything I did.
> c. I finally faced the problem and found a compromise that satisfied me and everyone else involved.

Assignment 2

Alternatively, think of a problem you are facing now that is troubling you. Apply Adler's strategy of putting down all the reasons why the problem *cannot* be solved. List and explain these reasons in one or several paragraphs. Your central point this time might be: "My current problem of _____ seems impossible for several reasons." Then you may wish to put the problem out of your mind and let your unconscious go to work. If a workable solution results, write an extra paragraph explaining how you solved your problem.

Assignment 3

What is your own formula for success? Think of one, two, or three "ground rules" you follow in order to make sure that you finish a project or succeed at something you want very much to do. Then write about this rule or these rules in one or several paragraphs. Support each rule with specific examples, as specific as Adler's 102 essays, so that your reader can see what you mean and how your rules would work.

Smash Thy Neighbor

John McMurtry

We think of football as one of those all-American things, like baseball or apple pie. Children are encouraged to play football from fifth grade through college. Hundreds of hours of network TV are devoted to football coverage. And *Monday Night Football* is almost a patriotic ritual. In this selection, however, a former football player says that football games are cruel contests that injure players and bring out the worst in fans.

A few months ago my neck got a hard crick in it. I couldn't turn my head; to look 1
left or right I had to turn my whole body. But I'd had cricks in my neck since I
started playing grade-school football and hockey, so I just ignored it. Then I began
to notice that when I reached for any sort of large book (which I do pretty often as
a philosophy teacher at the University of Guelph), I had trouble lifting it with one
hand. I was losing the strength in my left arm, and I had such a steady pain in my
back that I often had to stretch out on the floor to relieve the pressure.

Several weeks after my problems with book-lifting, I mentioned to my brother, 2
an orthopedic surgeon, that I'd lost the power in my arm since my neck began to
hurt. Twenty-four hours later I was in a Toronto hospital, not sure whether I might
end up with a wasted upper limb. Apparently the steady pounding I had received
playing college and professional football in the late fifties and early sixties had
driven my head into my backbone so that the disks had crumpled together at the
neck—"acute herniation"—and had cut the nerves to my left arm like a pinched
telephone wire (without nerve stimulation, of course, the muscles atrophy, leaving
the arm crippled). So I spent my Christmas holidays in the hospital in heavy traction,
and much of the next three months with my neck in a brace. Today most of the
pain has gone, and I've recovered most of the strength in my arm. But from time
to time I still have to don the brace, and surgery remains a possibility.

Not much of this will surprise anyone who knows football. It is a sport in which   3
body wreckage is one of the leading conventions. A few days after I went into the
hospital for that crick in my neck, another brother, an outstanding football player
in college, was undergoing spinal surgery in the same hospital two floors above
me. In his case it was a lower, more massive herniation, which every now and
again buckled him so that he was unable to lift himself off his back for days. By
the time he entered the hospital for surgery he had already spent several months in
bed. The operation was successful, but, as in all such cases, it will take him a year
to recover fully.

These aren't isolated experiences. Just about anybody who has ever played   4
football for any length of time, in high school, college, or one of the professional
leagues, has suffered for it later.

Indeed, it is arguable that body shattering is the very *point* of football, as killing   5
and maiming are of war. (In the United States, for example, the game results in
fifteen to twenty deaths a year and about fifty thousand major operations on knees
alone.) To grasp some of the more conspicuous similarities between football and
war, it is instructive to listen to the imperatives most frequently issued to the players
by their coaches, teammates, and fans. "Hurt 'em!" "Level 'em!" "Kill 'em!" "Take
'em apart!" Or watch for the plays that are most enthusiastically applauded by the
fans, where someone is "smeared," "knocked silly," "creamed," "nailed," "broken
in two," or even "crucified." (One of my coaches when I played corner linebacker
with the Calgary Stampeders in 1961 elaborated, often very inventively, on this
language of destruction: admonishing us to "unjoin" the opponent, "make 'im
remember you," and "stomp 'im like a bug.") Just as in hockey, where a fight will
bring fans to their feet more often than a skillful play, so in football the mouth
waters most of all for the really crippling block or tackle. For the kill. Thus the
good teams are "hungry," the best players are "mean," and "casualties" are as
much a part of the game as they are of a war.

The family resemblance between football and war is, indeed, striking. Their   6
languages are similar: "field general," "long bomb," "blitz," "take a shot," "front
line," "pursuit," "good hit," "the draft," and so on. Their principles and practices
are alike: mass hysteria, the art of intimidation, absolute command and total
obedience, territorial aggression, censorship, inflated insignia and propaganda,
blackboard maneuvers and strategies, drills, uniforms, formations, marching bands,
and training camps. And the virtues they celebrate are almost identical: hyper-
aggressiveness, coolness under fire, and suicidal bravery.

One difference between war and football, though, is that there is little or no   7
protest against football. Perhaps the most extraordinary thing about the game is that
the systematic infliction of injuries excites in people not concern, as would be the
case if they were sustained at, say, a rock festival, but a collective rejoicing and
euphoria. Players and fans alike revel in the spectacle of a combatant felled into
semiconsciousness, "blindsided," "clotheslined," or "decapitated." I can remember, in fact, being chided by a coach in pro ball for not "getting my hat" injuriously
into a player who was lying helpless on the ground.

After every game, of course, the papers are full of reports on the day's injuries, **8** a sort of post-battle "body count," and the respective teams go to work with doctors and trainers, tape, whirlpool baths, cortisone, and morphine to patch and deaden the wounds before the next game. Then the whole drama is reenacted—injured athletes held together by adhesive, braces, and drugs—and the days following it are filled with even more feverish activity to put on the show yet again at the end of the week. (I remember being so taped up in college that I earned the nickname "Mummy.") The team that survives this merry-go-round spectacle of skilled masochism with the fewest incapacitating injuries usually wins. It is a sort of victory by ordeal: "We hurt them more than they hurt us."

My own initiation into this brutal circus was typical. I loved the game from the **9** moment I could run with a ball. Played shoeless on a green, open field with no one keeping score and in a spirit of reckless abandon and laughter, it's a very different sport. Almost no one gets hurt, and it's rugged, open, and exciting (it still is for me). But, like everything else, it starts to be regulated and institutionalized by adult authorities. And the fun is over.

So it was as I began the long march through organized football. Now there **10** were a coach and elders to make it clear by their behavior that beating other people was the only thing to celebrate and that trying to shake someone up every play was the only thing to be really proud of. Now there were severe rule enforcers, audiences, formally recorded victors and losers, and heavy equipment to permit crippling bodily moves and collisions (according to one survey, more than 80 percent of all football injuries occur to fully equipped players). And now there was the official "given" that the only way to keep playing was to wear suffocating armor, to play to defeat, to follow orders silently, and to renounce spontaneity in favor of joyless drill. The game has been, in short, ruined. But because I loved to play, and play skillfully, I stayed. And progressively and inexorably, as I moved through high school, college, and pro leagues, my body was dismantled. Piece by piece.

I started off with torn ligaments in my knee at thirteen. Then, as the organization **11** and the competition increased, the injuries came faster and harder. Broken nose (three times), broken jaw (fractured in the first half and dismissed as a "bad wisdom tooth," so I played with it for the rest of the game), ripped knee ligaments again. Torn ligaments in one ankle and a fracture in the other (which I remember feeling relieved about because it meant I could honorably stop drill-blocking a 270-pound defensive end). Repeated rib fractures and cartilage tears (usually carried, again, through the remainder of the game). More dislocations of the left shoulder than I can remember (the last one I played with because, as the Calgary Stampeders' doctor said, it "couldn't be damaged any more"). Occasional broken or dislocated fingers and toes. Chronically hurt lower back (I still can't lift with it or change a tire without worrying about folding). Separated right shoulder (as with many other injuries, like badly bruised hips and legs, needled with morphine for the games). And so on. The last pro game I played—against the Winnipeg Blue Bombers in the Western finals in 1961—I had a recently dislocated left shoulder, a more recently wrenched right shoulder, and a chronic pain center in one leg. I was so tied up with soreness that I couldn't drive to the airport. But it never occurred to me that I should miss a play as a corner linebacker.

By the end of my football career, I had learned that physical injury—giving it   12
and taking it—is the real currency of the sport. And that in the final analysis, the
"winner" is the man who can hit to kill even if only half his limbs are working. In
brief, a warrior game with a warrior ethos into which (like almost everyone I played
with) my original boyish enthusiasm had been relentlessly conditioned.

In thinking back on how all this happened, though, I can pick out no villains.   13
As with the social system as a whole, the game has a life of its own. Everyone
grows up inside it, accepts it, and fulfills its dictates as obediently as Helots. Far
from questioning the principles of the activity, most men simply concentrate on
executing these principles more aggressively than anybody else. The result is a
group of people who, as the leagues become of a higher and higher class, are
progressively insensitive to the possibility that things could be otherwise. Thus, in
football, anyone who might question the wisdom or enjoyment of putting on heavy
equipment on a hot day and running full speed at someone else with the intention
of knocking him senseless would be regarded as not really a devoted athlete and
probably "chicken." The choice is made straightforward. Either you, too, do your
very utmost to smash efficiently and be smashed, or you admit incompetence or
cowardice and quit. Since neither of these admissions is very pleasant, people
generally keep any doubts they have to themselves, and carry on.

Of course, it would be a mistake to suppose that there is more blind acceptance   14
of brutal practices in organized football than elsewhere. On the contrary, a recent
Harvard study argues that football's characteristics of "impersonal acceptance of
inflicted injury," an overriding "organization goal," the "ability to turn oneself on
and off," and being, above all, "out to win" are prized by ambitious executives in
many large corporations. Clearly, football is no sicker than the rest of our society.
Even its organized destruction of physical well-being is not anomalous. A very large
part of our wealth, work, and time is, after all, spent in systematically destroying
and harming human life; manufacturing, selling, and using weapons that tear
opponents to pieces; making ever bigger and faster predator-named cars with which
to kill and injure one another by the million every year; and devoting our very lives
to outgunning one another for power in an ever-more-destructive rat race. Yet all
these practices are accepted without question by most people, even zealously
defended and honored. Competitive, organized injuring is integral to our way of
life, and football is one of the more intelligible mirrors of the whole process: a sort
of colorful morality play showing us how exciting and rewarding it is to Smash Thy
Neighbor.

Now, it is fashionable to rationalize our collaboration in all this by arguing that,   15
well, men *like* to fight and injure their fellows, and such games as football should
be encouraged to discharge this original-sin urge into less harmful channels than,
say, war. Public-show football, this line goes, plays the same sort of cathartic role
as Aristotle said stage tragedy does: without real blood (or not much), it releases
players and audience from unhealthy feelings stored up inside them.

As an ex-player in this seasonal coast-to-coast drama, I see little to recommend   16
such a view. What organized football did to me was make me *suppress* my natural
urges and reexpress them in alienating, vicious form. Spontaneous desires for free

bodily exuberance and fraternization with competitors were shamed and forced under ("If it ain't hurtin', it ain't helpin' "), and in their place were demanded armored, mechanical moves and cool hatred of all opposition. Endless authoritarian drill and dressing-room harangues (ever wonder why competing teams can't prepare for a game in the same dressing room?) were the kinds of mechanisms employed to reconstruct joyful energies into mean and alien shapes. I am quite certain that everyone else around me was being similarly forced into this heavily equipped military precision and angry antagonism, because there was always a mutinous attitude about full-dress practices, and everybody (the pros included) had to concentrate incredibly hard for days to whip himself into just one hour's hostility a week against another club. The players never speak of these things, of course, because everyone is anxious to appear tough.

The claim that men like seriously to battle one another to some sort of finish is **17** a myth. It endures only because it wears one of the oldest and most propagandized of masks—the romantic combatant. I sometimes wonder whether the violence all around us doesn't depend for its survival on the existence and preservation of this tough-guy disguise.

As for the effect of organized football on the spectator, the fans are not so **18** much released from supposed feelings of violent aggression by watching their athletic heroes perform it as they are encouraged in the view that people-smashing is an admirable mode of self-expression. The most savage attackers, after all, are, by general agreement, the most efficient and worthy players of all (the biggest applause I ever received as a football player occurred when I ran over people or slammed them so hard that they couldn't get up). . . . Watching well-advertised strong men knock other people around, make them hurt, is in the end like other tastes. It does not weaken with feeding and variation in form. It grows.

I got out of football in 1962. In a preseason intersquad game, I ripped the **19** cartilage in my ribs on the hardest block I'd ever thrown. I had trouble breathing, and I had to shuffle-walk with my torso on a tilt. The doctor in the local hospital said three weeks rest; the coach said scrimmage in two days. Three days later I was back home reading philosophy.

■ **Reading Comprehension Questions**

1. Which of the following would be a good alternative title for this selection?
   a. The Violence of Football
   b. Football in the United States
   c. A Man Who Played Football
   d. Football and Corporate Competition

2. Which sentence best expresses the main idea of the selection?
   a. Playing football has caused the author much physical pain.
   b. Most football coaches try to make the game less violent.
   c. Football's popularity is a reflection of some negative aspects of society.
   d. Violence is a central part of organized football both for the teams and for the fans.

3. The author says that organized football is like
    a.   all other sports.
    b.   philosophy.
    c.   war.
    d.   football played without coaches and rules.

4. For the author, football was ruined by
    a.   people who play without equipment.
    b.   the regulation of adult authorities.
    c.   people who dislike football's violence.
    d.   ambitious executives.

5. According to the author, watching football makes people
    a.   believe that ''smash thy neighbor'' is good.
    b.   realize that football is too violent.
    c.   feel a great release from their own violent feelings.
    d.   escape from the anxieties of their jobs.

6. The author implies that
    a.   society is much less brutally competitive than football.
    b.   football players never have doubts about the brutality of the game.
    c.   the brutal values of football exist in other parts of society.
    d.   many people question the violence in football.

7. The author imples that fans
    a.   get rid of unhealthy feelings when watching football.
    b.   encourage the violence in football.
    c.   are unaware of the violence in football.
    d.   discourage the really savage attacks in football.

8. In the last paragraph of the selection, the author implies that
    a.   his injuries were mild.
    b.   the doctor exaggerated the extent of his injuries.
    c.   the coach thought that his injuries were mild.
    d.   the coach cared more about winning than about his players' injuries.

9. The word *atrophy* in ''without nerve stimulation, of course, the muscles atrophy, leaving the arm crippled'' (paragraph 2) means
    a.   get stronger.
    b.   flex.
    c.   weaken.
    d.   are unaffected.

10. The word *imperatives* in "It is instructive to listen to the imperatives most frequently issued to the players. . . . 'Hurt 'em!' 'Level 'em!' 'Kill 'em!' '' (paragraph 5) means
    a. insults.
    b. commands.
    c. compliments.
    d. questions.

■ **Discussion Questions**

About Content

1. According to McMurtry, what qualities of our society does football reflect?
2. The author makes an analogy between war and football. In what ways are the two activities alike?
3. Do you agree that the violence of football encourages people's taste for "people-smashing as an admirable mode of self-expression" (paragraph 18)?

About Structure

4. What method of introduction does the author use?
    a. Anecdote
    b. An opposite
    c. Quotation
5. What method of development is used in paragraphs 5 and 6?
    a. Reasons
    b. Comparison
    c. Examples

About Style and Tone

6. Why does the author call his essay "Smash Thy Neighbor"? To answer, think about how the title may be a play on the words in a familiar biblical command.
7. McMurtry uses terms such as *body wreckage, body shattering,* and *skilled masochism* to describe organized football. What effect does he hope this language will have on the reader? Find three other phrases the author uses to describe football (beginning with paragraph 9), and write them here:

_____

_____

_____

■ Writing Assignments

Assignment 1

Imagine that you are a professional football coach (or, if you prefer, the head coach of your school's football team.) You have just read "Smash Thy Neighbor" in a national magazine, and you feel angered and hurt by McMurtry's opinion of football. How would you answer his accusations about the sport? Write a letter to the editor of the magazine in which you give three reasons why John McMurtry is wrong about football and its effects on people. You might want to get started with this thesis statement:

I feel John McMurtry is wrong about football for several reasons.

Then continue your letter, describing each reason in detail in its own paragraph.

Alternatively, write a letter in which you detail three reasons for agreeing with McMurtry.

Assignment 2

Write a narrative essay about a bad experience you had with sports. Among the topics you might write about are:

An injury
Not being chosen for a team
Missing an important point or goal
Being pressured by a parent or coach
Being the clumsiest person in gym class
Being embarrassed while trying to learn a sport

You could begin the essay with a sentence or two about your experience with sports in general—whether sports have been an area of pain or pleasure for you. Your thesis should name the particular experience you will write about and tell your readers that this experience was bad (or embarrassing, or humiliating, or disillusioning, or any other word that seems appropriate).

Then organize your supporting paragraphs by dividing your experience into two or three time phases. You may want to review the chapter on the narrative essay (pages 194–202) first.

Assignment 3

Write an essay about a sport you feel is a good one. In each of your supporting paragraphs, give one reason why this sport is good for either players or spectators.

A Hanging

George Orwell

You are about to attend an execution. In this essay, George Orwell (author of *1984*) recalls a hanging he witnessed when he was an English police officer stationed in Burma. Orwell's sensitivity and vividly descriptive writing will make you see and feel what it is like to take the seemingly endless walk from cell to gallows. You will share the guards' uneasiness and the prisoner's terror. And, after you finish the selection, you may also share Orwell's views on capital punishment.

1 It was in Burma, a sodden morning of the rains. A sickly light, like yellow tinfoil, was slanting over the high walls into the jail yard. We were waiting outside the condemned cells, a row of sheds fronted with double bars, like small animal cages. Each cell measured about ten feet by ten and was quite bare within except for a plank bed and a pot of drinking water. In some of them brown silent men were squatting at the inner bars, with their blankets draped round them. These were the condemned men, due to be hanged within the next week or two.

2 One prisoner had been brought out of his cell. He was a Hindu, a puny wisp of a man, with a shaven head and vague liquid eyes. He had a thick, sprouting moustache, absurdly too big for his body, rather like the moustache of a comic man on the films. Six tall Indian warders were guarding him and getting him ready for the gallows. Two of them stood by with rifles with fixed bayonets, while the others handcuffed him, passed a chain through his handcuffs and fixed it to their belts, and lashed his arms tight to his sides. They crowded very close about him, with their hands always on him in a careful, caressing grip, as though all the while feeling him to make sure he was there. It was like men handling a fish which is still alive and may jump back into the water. But he stood quite unresisting, yielding his arms limply to the ropes, as though he hardly noticed what was happening.

3 Eight o'clock struck and a bugle call, desolately thin in the wet air, floated from the distant barracks. The superintendent of the jail, who was standing apart from the rest of us, moodily prodding the gravel with his stick, raised his head at the sound. He was an army doctor, with a grey toothbrush moustache and a gruff voice. "For God's sake hurry up, Francis," he said irritably. "The man ought to have been dead by this time. Aren't you ready yet?"

4 Francis, the head jailer, a fat Dravidian in a white drill suit and gold spectacles, waved his black hand. "Yes sir, yes sir," he bubbled. "All iss satisfactorily prepared. The hangman iss waiting. We shall proceed."

5 "Well, quick march, then. The prisoners can't get their breakfast till this job's over."

We set out for the gallows. Two warders marched on either side of the prisoner, with their files at the slope; two others marched close against him, gripping him by arm and shoulder, as though at once pushing and supporting him. The rest of us, magistrates and the like, followed behind. Suddenly, when we had gone ten yards, the procession stopped short without any order or warning. A dreadful thing had happened—a dog, come goodness knows whence, had appeared in the yard. It came bounding among us with a loud volley of barks, and leapt round us wagging its whole body, wild with glee at finding so many human beings together. It was a large woolly dog, half Airedale, half pariah. For a moment it pranced round us, and then, before anyone could stop it, it had made a dash for the prisoner, and jumping up tried to lick his face. Everyone stood aghast, too taken aback even to grab at the dog. 6

"Who let that bloody brute in here?" said the superintendent angrily. "Catch it, someone!" 7

A warder, detached from the escort, charged clumsily after the dog, but it danced and gambolled just out of his reach, taking everything as part of the game. A young Eurasian jailer picked up a handful of gravel and tried to stone the dog away, but it dodged the stones and came after us again. Its yaps echoed from the jail walls. The prisoner, in the grasp of the two warders, looked on incuriously, as though this was another formality of the hanging. It was several minutes before someone managed to catch the dog. Then we put my handkerchief through its collar and moved off once more, with the dog still straining and whimpering. 8

It was about forty yards to the gallows. I watched the bare brown back of the prisoner marching in front of me. He walked clumsily with his bound arms, but quite steadily, with that bobbing gait of the Indian who never straightens his knees. At each step his muscles slid neatly into place, the lock of hair on his scalp danced up and down, his feet printed themselves on the wet gravel. And once, in spite of the men who gripped him by each shoulder, he stepped slightly aside to avoid a puddle on the path. 9

It is curious, but till that moment I had never realised what it means to destroy a healthy, conscious man. When I saw the prisoner step aside to avoid the puddle, I saw the mystery, the unspeakable wrongness, of cutting a life short when it is in full tide. This man was not dying; he was alive just as we were alive. All the organs of his body were working—bowels digesting food, skin renewing itself, nails growing, tissues forming—all toiling away in solemn foolery. His nails would still be growing when he stood on the drop, when he was falling through the air with a tenth of a second to live. His eyes saw the yellow gravel and the grey walls, and his brain still remembered, foresaw, reasoned—reasoned even about puddles. He and we were a party of men walking together, seeing, hearing, feeling, understanding the same world; and in two minutes, with a sudden snap, one of us would be gone—one mind less, one world less. 10

The gallows stood in a small yard, separate from the main grounds of the prison, and overgrown with tall prickly weeds. It was a brick erection like three sides of a shed, with planking on top, and above that two beams and a crossbar with the rope dangling. The hangman, a grey-haired convict in the white uniform 11 of the prison, was waiting beside his machine. He greeted us with a servile crouch as we entered. At a word from Francis the two warders, gripping the prisoner more closely than ever, half led, half pushed him to the gallows and helped him clumsily up the ladder. Then the hangman climbed up and fixed the rope round the prisoner's neck.

12 We stood waiting, five yards away. The warders had formed in a rough circle round the gallows. And then, when the noose was fixed, the prisoner began crying out to his god. It was a high, reiterated cry of "Ram! Ram! Ram! Ram!" not urgent and fearful like a prayer or a cry for help, but steady, rhythmical, almost like the tolling of a bell. The dog answered the sound with a whine. The hangman, still standing on the gallows, produced a small cotton bag like a flour bag and drew it down over the prisoner's face. But the sound, muffled by the cloth, still persisted, over and over again: "Ram! Ram! Ram! Ram! Ram!"

13 The hangman climbed down and stood ready, holding the lever. Minutes seemed to pass. The steady, muffled crying from the prisoner went on and on, "Ram! Ram! Ram!" never faltering for an instant. The superintendent, his head on his chest, was slowly poking the ground with his stick; perhaps he was counting the cries, allowing the prisoner a fixed number—fifty, perhaps, or a hundred. Everyone had changed colour. The Indians had gone grey like bad coffee, and one or two of the bayonets were wavering. We looked at the lashed, hooded man on the drop, and listened to his cries—each cry another second of life; the same thought was in all our minds: oh, kill him quickly, get it over, stop that abominable noise!

14 Suddenly the superintendent made up his mind. Throwing up his head he made a swift motion with his stick. "Chalo!" he shouted almost fiercely.

15 There was a clanking noise, and then dead silence. The prisoner had vanished, and the rope was twisting on itself. I let go of the dog, and it galloped immediately to the back of the gallows; but when it got there it stopped short, barked, and then retreated into a corner of the yard, where it stood among the weeds, looking timorously out at us. We went round the gallows to inspect the prisoner's body. He was dangling with his toes pointed straight downwards, very slowly revolving, as dead as a stone.

16 The superintendent reached out with his stick and poked the bare body; it oscillated, slightly. "*He's* all right," said the superintendent. He backed out from under the gallows, and blew out a deep breath. The moody look had gone out of his face quite suddenly. He glanced at his wristwatch. "Eight minutes past eight. Well, that's all for this morning, thank God."

17 The warders unfixed bayonets and marched away. The dog, sobered and conscious of having misbehaved itself, slipped after them. We walked out of the gallows yard, past the condemned cells with their waiting prisoners, into the big central yard of the prison. The convicts, under the command of warders armed with lathis, were already receiving their breakfast. They squatted in long rows, each man holding a tin pannikin, while two warders with buckets marched round ladling out rice; it seemed quite a homely, jolly scene, after the hanging. An enormous relief had come upon us now that the job was done. One felt an impulse to sing, to break into a run, to snigger. All at once everyone began chattering gaily.

The Eurasian boy walking beside me nodded towards the way we had come, 18 with a knowing smile: "Do you know, sir, our friend (he meant the dead man), when he heard his appeal had been dismissed, he pissed on the floor of his cell. From fright.—Kindly take one of my cigarettes, sir. Do you not admire my new silver case, sir? From the boxwallah, two rupees eight annas. Classy European style."

Several people laughed—at what, nobody seemed certain. 19

Francis was walking by the superintendent, talking garrulously: "Well, sir, all 20 hass passed off with the utmost satisfactoriness. It wass all finished—flick! like that. It iss not always so—oah, no! I have known cases where the doctor wass obliged to go beneath the gallows and pull the prisoner's legs to ensure decease. Most disagreeable!"

"Wriggling about, eh? That's bad," said the superintendent. 21

"Ach, sir, it iss worse when they become refractory! One man, I recall, clung 22 to the bars of hiss cage when we went to take him out. You will scarcely credit, sir, that it took six warders to dislodge him, three pulling at each leg. We reasoned with him. 'My dear fellow,' we said, 'think of all the pain and trouble you are causing to us!' But no, he would not listen! Ach, he wass very troublesome!"

I found that I was laughing quite loudly. Everyone was laughing. Even the 23 superintendent grinned in a tolerant way. "You'd better all come out and have a drink," he said quite genially. "I've got a bottle of whisky in the car. We could do with it."

We went through the big double gates of the prison, into the road. "Pulling at 24 his legs!" exclaimed a Burmese magistrate suddenly, and burst into a loud chuckling. We all began laughing again. At that moment Francis's anecdote seemed extraordinarily funny. We all had a drink together, native and European alike, quite amicably. The dead man was a hundred yards away.

■ Reading Comprehension Questions

1. Which of the following would be a good alternative title for this selection?
   a. A Burmese Prisoner
   b. Capital Punishment
   c. Eyewitness to an Execution
   d. What It Means to Take a Life

2. Which sentence best expresses the main idea of the selection?
   a. Capital punishment is unpleasant to carry out, but it is necessary in some cases.
   b. Executions in Burma were done in an inefficient and amateurish way.
   c. Taking another person's life, no matter what the reason, is morally wrong.
   d. No one cared about the Burmese prisoner who was hanged.

3. Just before he was executed, the prisoner
   a.   protested his innocence.
   b.   cried out to his god.
   c.   tried to escape from the gallows.
   d.   said a quiet prayer.

4. *True or false?* _____ The prisoner had been convicted of murder.

5. After the execution, the author and the other authorities
   a.   felt relief.
   b.   became very depressed.
   c.   realized they had done something wrong.
   d.   couldn't speak for a long while.

6. The author implies that
   a.   the dog who interrupted the march to the gallows belonged to the prisoner.
   b.   no one has the right to take another person's life.
   c.   the authorities knew the prisoner was innocent.
   d.   other methods of execution are more humane than hanging.

7. The author implies that
   a.   the prisoner would have escaped if he had not been so heavily guarded.
   b.   the prisoner did not die immediately.
   c.   the hangman had volunteered for the job.
   d.   the superintendent of the jail was nervous and upset about the hanging.

8. The author implies that
   a.   the people who witnessed the hanging later laughed and joked to cover up the uneasiness they felt.
   b.   the native people and the Europeans felt differently about the hanging.
   c.   he had become friends with the prisoner before the execution.
   d.   Burmese officials were corrupt.

9. The word *reiterated* in "the high, reiterated cry of 'Ram! Ram!'" (paragraph 12) means
   a.   reluctant.
   b.   lonely.
   c.   repeated.
   d.   useless.

10. The word *amicably* in "we all had a drink together, . . . quite amicably" (paragraph 24) means
   a.   with hostility.
   b.   unnecessarily.
   c.   quietly.
   d.   in a friendly way.

■ Discussion Questions

About Content

1. How does the prisoner act as he is led out to be hanged? On the basis of his actions, what state of mind do you feel he is in?

2. Why does everyone stand ''aghast'' when the stray dog licks the prisoner's face? Why is this incident important? (To answer, you might consider what qualities the dog represents or symbolizes.)

3. The author has a moment of understanding when the prisoner steps ''slightly aside to avoid a puddle on the path.'' What realization does the author come to? How is this realization related to the small incident of avoiding a puddle?

About Structure

4. The best statement of the author's thesis is in paragraph 10. Find it and write it in the space provided:

   _____

   _____

About Style and Tone

5. Why do you think Orwell ends the narrative with the statement, ''The dead man was a hundred yards away''?

6. Orwell uses several *similes* (comparisons using the words *like* or *as*) to add vividness to the narrative. He says, for example, that the guards handled the prisoner ''like men handling a fish which is still alive and may jump back into the water.'' Find two more similes and write them here:

   _____

   _____

7. In part, Orwell uses dialog to tell his story; we hear the actual voices of the superintendent, Francis, the prisoners, and others. Find and underline all the lines spoken by the superintendent. Discuss how the words the superintendent speaks (and the tone of voice he speaks them in) reflect the emotional changes the superintendent goes through.

■ Writing Assignments

Assignment 1

Use examples and details from ''A Hanging'' to support the following thesis statement:

> In ''A Hanging,'' George Orwell constantly contrasts death with life in order to show us how wrong it is to kill another human being.

You might organize your supporting paragraphs by showing how death is contrasted with life (1) on the way to the gallows; (2) at the gallows; (3) after the hanging.

To get started, reread the selection closely, noting words and incidents that seem to be closely related to either death or life. For example, in paragraph 2, Orwell describes the prisoner as ''quite unresisting, yielding his arms limply to the ropes.'' It is as if the prisoner is already dead. In contrast, the guards are filled with life and action: they handcuff the prisoner, lash his arms, and keep a ''careful, caressing grip'' on him. At many other points in the story, this strong contrast between death and life is described.

Use a point-by-point method of contrast in developing your essay. You may want to look first at the example of this method on page 153.

Assignment 2

Find out (1) if capital punishment is legal in your state, and (2) which method of execution is used. (You could find this information by calling your city or county library.) Then imagine that a statewide vote will soon be taken to find out if voters want to change this law. Decide if you would (or would not) change the law. Give reasons for your decision. For example, if your state does have capital punishment, and you would vote not to change the law, you might give the following reasons:

> Thesis: Our state law allows a jury to vote for ''death by lethal injection'' for convicted criminals, and I would not vote to change this law.

> Topic sentences:
> a. First of all, the death penalty saves thousands of tax dollars that would be spent to keep criminals in prison for life.
> b. In addition, the punishment acts as a deterrent to other criminals.
> c. Most important, death is an appropriate punishment for someone who commits a terrible crime.

In order to avoid writing in vague, general terms, you may want to use specific examples of cases or crimes currently being discussed in the news. You may also need facts and statistics you can find by consulting the card catalog in your college library under the subject heading *Capital Punishment* and by skimming the appropriate books.

Assignment 3

Read the selection ''Can Society Banish Cruelty?'' on pages 473–476. Then, on the basis of the knowledge you have gained by reading both selections, write an essay with *either* of the thesis statements below:

■ Executions today are as brutal as those described in ''A Hanging'' and ''Can Society Banish Cruelty?''

■ Executions today are humane compared with those described in ''A Hanging'' and ''Can Society Banish Cruelty?''

You may want to write about each of the following areas in your supporting paragraphs:

Methods of execution and atmosphere in which executions are conducted

Kinds of people who are executed

Fairness of the trials and judges

OBSERVING OTHERS

An Adventure in the City

Steve Lopez

A big city is an impersonal place where you can feel alone in a crowd of all sorts of people. City people, it seems, just don't have enough in common to take time to help each other. Or do they? This article by Steve Lopez, a columnist for the newspaper *The Philadelphia Inquirer,* suggests that the differences between people are less important than their attitudes.

This is a story of life in the city, where a simple outing can turn into an adventure. 1

Harris Cohen has this thing with his kids. On their birthdays, they are king. 2
They can celebrate however they chose, and he picks up the tab.

For his seventeenth birthday, Mike Cohen chose Peking duck, sushi, something 3
from his favorite Chinese bakery and a neon sign for his bedroom. Which is a little
easier than a sailboat and a BMW.

He and his dad—the family lives in Overbrook Hills—were headed to their 4
favorite restaurant in Philadelphia's Chinatown when Harris saw a new place in the
900 block of Race Street. *Friendly Peking Duck Inn.*

"I'm a sucker for friendly," Harris Cohen says. "I like a place where you get 5
service with a smile."

He had no idea. 6

The owners and their staff visited the Cohens' table and welcomed them. The 7
Cohens said that they were celebrating Mike's birthday and that they were going to
the Chinese bakery afterward. The staff was curious about Mike's rowing for the
Lower Merion High School crew team.

Raised in Vietnam. Kevin, Robert, Victor, Sam and Scott then told the Cohens 8 about themselves. Kevin Vuong, one of three owners, is Chinese but was raised in Vietnam. He paid $2,500 to flee on a boat.

Vuong, 27, worked in other restaurants, saving up for the day when he could 9 buy his own. He told the Cohens he wanted a "new generation" restaurant in which customers would feel as comfortable as if they were in their own home. With that, he invited them into the kitchen.

"I was taken aback by how friendly they were," Harris Cohen says. 10

When the two-hour lunch had ended, Vuong told the Cohens to remember 11 something: "If you ever need anything, you've got a friend in Chinatown."

Father and son were feeling pretty good as they left. The sushi place was closed, 12 but they made it to the neon store and the bakery. Then they went back to where they had parked. And that's where the story takes a turn.

From three stories above, a construction crew shouted down to the Cohens 13 that their car had just been towed. The no-parking period had recently changed from 4 P.M. to 3 P.M., and the Cohens didn't realize it.

Given the choice of having your car towed in Philadelphia or sticking your 14 finger in a light socket, those who have done both would probably go for the zap. But the Cohens found a friendly policeman who explained the procedure and told them to pay the towing fee at 334 North Broad Street.

Need Cash. After their crosstown walk, Cohen pulled out his credit card. No 15 good. He went for the checkbook. No checks accepted. The fee was $40 and he had $35. No deal. There was no easy way out of the jam. But the birthday boy had a thought.

"You know," Mike told his dad, "I think those guys at the restaurant were 16 being sincere when they talked about being our friends."

It was worth a try. Harris Cohen placed the call. 17

"No problem," Kevin Vuong said. "I'll send Scott right over." 18

The Cohens were a bit stunned. As they waited, another towing victim overheard 19 their predicament and gave them $5, no strings attached. He was a total stranger.

After paying, Harris Cohen realized his car wasn't there, but sixteen blocks 20 away at the impoundment lot. That's when Scott arrived in the Friendly Peking Duck hospitality wagon, carrying cold cash.

Harris said they didn't need money, but could use a ride to their car. Scott 21 gave them both. The money was for gas or spare change, in case of another emergency.

At the impoundment lot, one police officer was apologetic. He told the Cohens 22 it was a shame to see people get a bad impression of the city because of parking hassles.

Three weeks later, the Cohens are still talking about their adventure. 23

Changing View. "I think it's changed Mike in that he views people and himself 24 as a citizen of the world rather than just a local, and views people generally as just fellow people," Harris Cohen said. "Forget about how they talk, what they look like, what business they're in."

Two days after the birthday lunch, the family went back to the Friendly Peking   25
Duck Inn. Mike brought a card he had made himself, and Harris and his wife,
Renee, brought a gift.

After a feast, the staff disappeared. They returned carrying a birthday cake, with   26
candles, from Mike's favorite Chinese bakery. The staff sang "Happy Birthday."

"They refused to accept any money for the meal," Harris said.   27

Kevin Vuong, whose family didn't make it out of Vietnam, told the Cohens that   28
good friends were more important to him than money.

■ Reading Comprehension Questions

1. Which of the following would be a good alternative title for this selection?
   a. Vietnamese Americans
   b. Service with a Smile
   c. Help in Unexpected Places
   d. Parking Problems

2. Which sentence best expresses the central point of the selection?
   a. Kids should celebrate their birthdays in whatever way they choose.
   b. An act of friendship can change the way we view the world.
   c. Parking problems leave people with a bad impression of a city.
   d. Owning a restaurant is a good way to make friends.

3. Harris Cohen wanted to try the new restaurant because
   a. he knew Kevin Vuong.
   b. his son wanted to try Chinese food.
   c. it was near his home.
   d. he was attracted by its name.

4. *True or false?* _____ The Cohens were not at all surprised that Kevin
   Vuong was willing to help them.

5. Kevin Vuong
   a. escaped with his family from Vietnam.
   b. wants customers to feel at home in his restaurant.
   c. would not take the Cohens' gift.
   d. is the only owner of the restaurant.

6. *True or false?* _____ We can conclude that it is common for people to be
   so helpful in Philadelphia.

7. From Kevin Vuong's story, we can assume that
   a. his business will never make much money.
   b. his family did not want to escape from Vietnam.
   c. hardships can influence people's values.
   d. he was friendly just to get more customers.

8. We can assume that
    a. the Cohens will never go back to the restaurant.
    b. the Cohens told their story to the author.
    c. Mike Cohen has had many equally memorable birthdays.
    d. the Cohens will never park their car in Philadelphia again.

9. The word *predicament* in "another towing victim overheard their predicament and gave them $5" (paragraph 19) means
    a. good news.
    b. adventure.
    c. difficult situation.
    d. investigation.

10. The word *impoundment* in "his car wasn't there, but . . . at the impoundment lot" (paragraph 20) means
    a. confinement.
    b. cheap.
    c. abandoned.
    d. insecure.

■ **Discussion Questions**

About Content

1. At first, the thesis of this article seems to be clearly presented in the first paragraph: "A simple outing in the city can turn into an adventure." After reading the article, however, we realize there is much more to the Cohens' experiences than having "an adventure." What might be a good way to state this article's thesis?

2. Mike, his father said, seems to have changed as a result of their adventure (paragraph 24). Why do you think their experience could have significantly affected Mike?

3. The story in this article centers on the Cohens and the owners and staff of the Friendly Peking Duck Inn. Why, then, did the author decide to include the reactions of the other towing victim and the police officer (paragraphs 19 and 22)?

4. Had you ever received help from a friendly stranger? Have you ever given help to a stranger? What were the circumstances?

About Structure

5. The author uses transition words that show *time* to move his narrative smoothly along. List three time signals:

_____   _____   _____

About Style and Tone

6. How is the author's point of view revealed in the following excerpts?

> "For his 17th birthday, Mike Cohen chose Peking duck . . . and a neon sign for his bedroom. Which is a little easier than a sailboat and a BMW." (paragraph 3)

> " 'I'm a sucker for friendly,' Harris Cohen says. 'I like a place where you get service with a smile.'
> He had no idea." (paragraphs 5 and 6)

"That's when Scott arrived in the Friendly Peking Duck hospitality wagon, carrying cold cash." (paragraph 20)

7. The author concludes his article with a
   a. summary.
   b. prediction.
   c. significant detail.
   d. final thought.

■ Writing Assignments

Assignment 1

Write a narrative about a time a stranger helped you or someone you know, or a time you helped a stranger. Like Lopez, begin your story by giving an account of how the situation came about. Then give the details of the problem involved and how help was given. If there is an interesting follow-up to the event, include that as well. Use time signals (*first of all, then, next, after,* and so on) to help your reader follow the events of your story. And don't forget to include some colorful details and dialogue so that your reader can see and hear what happened. (Glance through Lopez's article to see how details and dialog can spice up a story.)

Assignment 2

A story like "An Adventure in the City" probably appeals to readers not only because it describes the kinds of events many approve of but because such events are not as common as readers would like. Why do you think help and friendship like that given to the Cohens is not more common? Write an essay on three factors in people's lives that keep them from reaching out to each other more. Following are some factors that may affect how much we do or do not reach out to others. You may use these or any others to develop in your three supporting paragraphs. As you develop those paragraphs, use specific details and examples to clarify your points.

Being busy

Fear of strangers

Reluctance to part with money

Fear of looking foolish

People's reluctance to ask for help

Assignment 3

Which appeals to you more, big-city, small-town or suburban life? Write an essay on the advantages or disadvantages of life in one of those three places.

In preparation for this essay, jot down several characteristics of the type of lifestyles you know best. Then select three advantages or disadvantages of the big city, the small town, or the suburb. Remember to include your thesis in the first paragraph of this essay. As you develop the body of your essay, include examples for your main points.

Following are a few possible thesis sentences for this assignment.

Crowds, noise, and high expenses make life in the big city difficult.

A big city is an ideal place to live because it is easier to find work there, it has many and varied cultural resources, and it is a good place to meet all kinds of people.

A small town is a wonderful place to live because it is a friendly, safe, and inexpensive place to bring up a family.

The suburbs offer good schools and a clean and wholesome environment for children while being close enough to the city to enjoy some of its advantages.

A Kite

James Herndon

In the following selection from James Herndon's book *How to Survive in Your Native Land*, you'll meet a truly unforgettable student named Piston. Piston outrages the administration, baffles teachers, and angers his fellow students. But Piston's most rebellious act is building a monster and unleashing it on the entire school. You'll see in this selection how Piston's creation lives only for a moment but has a profound impact on all who experience it.

I might as well begin with Piston. Piston was, as a matter of description, a redheaded 1 medium-sized chubby eighth grader; his definitive characteristic was, however, stubbornness. Without going into a lot of detail, it became clear right away that what Piston didn't want to do, Piston didn't do; what Piston did want to do, Piston did.

It really wasn't much of a problem. Piston wanted mainly to paint, draw 2 monsters, scratch designs on mimeograph blanks and print them up, write an occasional horror story—some kids referred to him as The Ghoul—and when he didn't want to do any of those, he wanted to roam the halls and on occasion (we heard) investigate the girls' bathrooms.

We had minor confrontations. Once I wanted everyone to sit down and listen 3 to what I had to say—something about the way they had been acting in the halls. I was letting them come and go freely and it was up to them (I planned to point out) not to raise hell so that I had to hear about it from other teachers. Sitting down was the issue—I was determined everyone was going to do it first, then I'd talk. Piston remained standing. I reordered. He paid no attention. I pointed out that I was talking to him. He indicated he heard me. I inquired then why in hell didn't he sit down. He said he didn't want to. I said I did want him to. He said that didn't matter to him. I said do it anyway. He said why? I said because I said so. He said he wouldn't. I said Look I want you to sit down and listen to what I'm going to say. He said he *was* listening. I'll listen but I won't sit down.

Well, that's the way it goes sometimes in schools. You as teacher become 4 obsessed with an issue—I was the injured party, conferring, as usual, unheard-of freedoms, and here they were as usual taking advantage. It ain't pleasant coming in the teachers' room for coffee and having to hear somebody say that so-and-so and so-and-so from *your* class were out in the halls *without a pass* and *making faces* and *giving the finger* to kids in *my* class during the most *important* part of *my* lesson about *Egypt*—and you ought to be allowed your tendentious speech, and most everyone will allow it, sit down for it, but occasionally someone wises you up by refusing to submit where it isn't necessary. But anyway, it's not the present point, which is really only Piston's stubbornness. Another kid told me that when Piston's father got mad at him and punished him, as Piston thought, unjustly (one cannot imagine Piston considering any punishment just), Piston got up in the middle of the night, went into the garage and revenged himself on his father's car. Once he took out and threw away two spark plugs. Another time he managed to remove all the door handles. You get a nice picture of Piston sitting quiet all evening long brooding about not being allowed to watch some favorite science-fiction program because he'd brought home a note about unsatisfactory this-or-that at school, sitting there unresponding and impassive, and then his father getting up in the morning to go to work, perhaps in a hurry or not feeling well, trying to start the car or looking at the locked doors and rolled up windows and the places where the door handles had been pried off. How did any of us get into this? we ought to be asking ourselves.

It was probably Frank Ramirez who brought up the idea of making kites. Frank 5 was a teacher, not a kid; we were working together. All the kids were making them suddenly; they scrounged the schoolrooms and maddened the shop teachers looking for suitable lengths of wood. Frank brought in fancy paper. The kites were wonderful.

Naturally we plunged down to the lower field to fly them. They flew well, or badly, or not at all, crashed and were broken, sailed away, got caught in overhead wires, the kids ran and yelled and cried and accused one another. It went on for several days and of course we heard a lot about classes overlooking the lower field being interrupted in the most important parts of the lessons about Egypt, for after all those kids wanted to know why they couldn't be flying kites instead of having Egypt, and Frank and I were cocky enough to state aloud that indeed we also wondered why they couldn't be flying kites too, after all who was stopping them? Piston, up in Room 45, was preparing our comeuppance.

Piston had been making a kite for several days. He continued making it while 6 others were flying theirs. It had only one definitive characteristic too; it was huge. The cross-pieces were 1 × 2 boards. The covering was heavy butcher paper, made heavier by three coats of poster paint in monstrous designs. The cord was clothesline rope. It was twenty feet long. Piston was finished with his kite about the time when everyone else had finished with the whole business of making and flying kites and had settled down in the room anticipating a couple of weeks of doing nothing, resting up for some future adventure. Piston produced his finished product, which was universally acclaimed a masterpiece. It was. Pictorially monstrous as usual, its *size,* its heavy *boards,* its *rope,* aroused a certain amount of real awe. Piston was really something else, we could see that. None of us had had such a concept.

But when Piston announced he was prepared to fly it, we all hooted, relieved. 7 It was easier to have Piston-the-nut back again than to put up with Piston-the-genius-artist. No one had thought of it as something to fly—only as something to look at and admire. In any case, it clearly would not fly. It was too big, too heavy, too awkward, unbalanced, there wasn't enough wind, you couldn't run with it— we had lots of reasons. Stubborn Piston hauled it down to the field past amazed windows of classbound kids ignoring Egypt once again to goggle and exclaim. Down on the grass we all gathered around the inert monster. If nothing else, Frank and I thought, Piston had prepared a real scene, something memorable—David being drawn through the streets of Florence.

The kite flew. Piston had prepared no great scene. Instead he had (I think) 8 commanded the monster kite to fly. So it flew. Of course it flew. Two of the biggest and strongest boys were persuaded to run with the kite; Piston ran with the rope. Everyone participated in what was believed to be a charade. We would act as if we thought the kite would fly. It would be in itself a gas. They ran; he pulled. The kite lumbered into the air, where it stayed aloft menacingly for perhaps four or five minutes. Then it dove, or rather just fell like a stone (like an avalanche!), with a crash. When it crashed, everyone was seized with a madness and rushed to the kite, jumped on it, stomped it, tore it . . . all except Frank and I, and we wanted to. (Great difficulties at that very moment were angrily reported to us later by teachers of Egypt classes.)

The kite was saved, though. Piston repaired and repapered it, repainted it. 9 Frank and I hung it in the room and admired it, and forgot it. But next week, Lou, the principal, approached us at lunchtime with great excitement. What about Piston? he wanted to know, and what about that Kite? Whose idea . . . ? and so on. His concern was not Egypt, but the fact that Piston and others had taken it out to the playground during lunch and flown it again. So? So! screamed Lou, the goddamn thing was a menace! It weighed a hundred pounds. It fell down and damn near killed thirty or forty seventh grade girls, and their mothers were calling him up and was this Piston crazy or were we, or what? And he wanted it made clear that flying that kite was out! O-U-T, out! He had enough troubles with our goddamn class running around all over the place and other teachers griping and smoking in the bathrooms and parents complaining they weren't learning nothing and he'd always supported us but he couldn't have that giant kite. Couldn't have it! We soothed him, agreeing to tell Piston in no uncertain terms and so on. We walked outside with Lou, who had calmed down and had begun admiring the kite in retrospect, realizing that there was no way such a creation could fly (*aerodynamically speaking,* he said), and yet it did fly and this Piston or whatever his name was must be a pretty exceptional kid, and we were agreeing and realizing what a great guy Lou was for a principal even if, we reminded him, he had goofed up our schedule for this marvelous class we'd planned which had resulted in that extraordinary kite and other grand exploits, along with, we admitted, a certain amount of difficulty for him, Lou, and how well he'd handled it and supported us and . . . when Lou suddenly screamed Aarrghhh! and fell back. I thought he'd been stung by a bee—we'd had a lot of bees that year, which also interrupted Egypt quite a bit, flying in the classroom where kids could scream with fake or real fear or try to kill them by throwing objects, often Egypt books, at them, exempt from retribution by the claim that they were just trying to save some *allergic kid* from *death*—but then he screamed There it is again! and pointed up, and there was The Monster from Outer Space, seventy-five feet up, plunging and wheeling and lurching through the thin air, a ton of boards and heavy paper and ghouls and toothy vampires leering down at an amazed lunchtime populace of little seventh grade girls, all with mothers and phones. Jesus Christ, look out! yelled Lou, and rushed for the playground, just as the giant came hurtling down like a dead flying mountain. It crashed; seventh grade girls scattered. (Their mothers reached for the phones.) Kids rushed from every direction and hurled themselves at the kite. They stomped it and tore it and killed it in wildest glee. They lynched it and murdered it and executed it and mercy-killed it and put it out of its misery, and when it was over and Lou had everyone pulled off the scattered corpse of the kite and sitting down on benches and shut up there was nothing left of it but bits and pieces of painted butcher paper and 1 × 2 boards and clothesline rope.

■ Reading Comprehension Questions

1. Which of the following would be a good alternative title for this selection?
   a. Piston and His Monster Kite
   b. Chaos in the Classroom
   c. Different Types of Teachers
   d. Stubbornness in Students

2. Which sentence best expresses the main idea of the selection?
   a. Piston's kite was the biggest one made in the class.
   b. The author and the ''Egypt'' teachers had different teaching methods.
   c. Piston's falling kites threatened children's lives.
   d. Piston represented a threat to established school practices.

3. *True or false?* _____ At one point, the author himself wanted to destroy Piston's kite.

4. When people saw the kite Piston had made, they
   a. felt a little awed by it.
   b. thought it had a chance of flying.
   c. were frightened by it.
   d. were proud of Piston.

5. According to the author, Piston's main characteristic was
   a. originality.
   b. disobedience.
   c. stubbornness.
   d. intelligence.

6. We can conclude that the other children attacked Piston's kite because
   a. the kite was ugly.
   b. their teachers wanted them to.
   c. Piston's behavior confused and angered them.
   d. they wanted to disturb the ''Egypt'' teachers.

7. From the selection we can conclude that
   a. the author was not an effective teacher.
   b. the author believes that education should involve more than ''Egypt'' classes.
   c. most students preferred ''Egypt'' classes to making kites.
   d. the author would rather have taught ''Egypt'' classes.

8. From the selection we can conclude that
   a. the students in the ''Egypt'' classes were getting a better education.
   b. the principal would have liked to fire the author and his friend Frank Ramirez.
   c. the other teachers began to adopt the author's methods.
   d. the other teachers disapproved of the author's methods.

9. The word *definitive* in ''It had only one definitive characteristic'' (paragraph 6) means
   a. hidden.
   b. puzzling.
   c. ridiculous.
   d. essential.

10. The word *retribution* in "exempt from retribution" (paragraph 9) means
   a. confusion.
   b. enjoyment.
   c. punishment.
   d. repetition.

■ Discussion Questions

About Content

1. In what ways is Piston stubborn? Give examples from the reading selection.
2. Why did the students want to wreck the kite? What might the kite represent?
3. What seems to be Herndon's attitude toward Piston?

About Structure

4. What is the synonym for *kite* used in paragraph 7?
5. In paragraph 3, what do the pronouns *they* and *them* refer to?

About Style and Tone

6. Why does Herndon refer to lessons about Egypt so often? Since it would be highly unlikely that all the other classes in Herndon's school were studying Egypt, Herndon is probably using Egypt as a symbol (something that stands for something else). What might Egypt stand for?
7. The kite is obviously a symbol as well. What is the kite a symbol of? In what ways does the kite reflect Piston's personality?

■ Writing Assignments

Assignment 1

Write an essay in which you present three reasons to support *either* of the following thesis statements:

- Piston would be an asset to any school.
- Piston would be a detriment to any school.

If you choose the first statement, think of several ways in which Piston would be good for a school. Here are possible topic sentences for such an essay. (You might use some of them or think of your own.)

Piston, first of all, would make teachers question some of their more meaningless rules and regulations.

In addition, Piston might inspire students with his originality and ambition.

Finally, Piston would teach other students to respect people who are "different."

You should support each of your reasons why Piston would be an asset to a school with examples drawn from "A Kite" as well as with ideas based on your own understanding of Piston's personality.

If you choose the second statement, think of reasons why Piston would be a bad student for a school to have. Again, here are possible topic sentences for this kind of essay:

For one thing, Piston would disrupt all his classes and prevent other students from learning.

Also, Piston might encourage other students to misbehave.

Worst of all, Piston might endanger people's lives.

As before, support your reasons with details and examples from "A Kite" and ideas based on your own understanding of Piston.

Assignment 2

James Herndon obviously considered Piston one of the most unforgettable characters he had ever met. Whom do you know, or whom have you known at some time in your life, who is equally unforgettable—or just as much of a "character" as Piston? In an introductory paragraph, describe exactly who the person is and how long you have known the person. Also, express in your thesis exactly what qualities make the person so vivid for you. If Herndon had had a thesis statement, he might have said, "One of my eighth-grade students is the most stubborn, vengeful, and daring person I have ever known." Then support your reasons by giving us specific examples of the character's words and actions. Provide the details needed for us to see for ourselves why that person is so colorful and special.

Assignment 3

Piston was an unusual person, but so was his teacher. Why was Herndon an unusual kind of schoolteacher? Think of several reasons and develop each in a separate paragraph. Alternatively, compare or contrast Herndon with some teacher you know.

Brett Hauser:
Supermarket Box Boy

Studs Terkel

For his book *Working,* Studs Terkel interviewed dozens of people about their jobs—what they did, what they liked about their jobs, what made them unhappy about their work. In this selection, a teenage box boy at a supermarket (a person who packs the groceries and often carries them out to the customer's car) talks about his job. You may never have been a box boy, but you will understand some of his complaints about his work: the impersonal atmosphere, the concern with trivial details, and the office politics.

He is seventeen. He had worked as a box boy at a supermarket in a middle-class 1
suburb on the outskirts of Los Angeles. "People come to the counter and you put things in their bags for them. And carry things to their cars. It was a grind."

You have to be terribly subservient to people: "Ma'am, can I take your bag?" 2
"Can I do this?" It was at a time when the grape strikers were passing out leaflets. They were very respectful people. People'd come into the check stand, they'd say, "I just bought grapes for the first time because of those idiots outside." I had to put their grapes in the bag and thank them for coming and take them outside to the car. Being subservient made me very resentful.

It's one of a chain of supermarkets. They're huge complexes with bakeries in 3
them and canned music over those loudspeakers—Muzak. So people would relax while they shopped. They played selections from *Hair.* They'd play "Guantanamera," the Cuban Revolution song. They had *Soul on Ice,* the Cleaver book, on sale. They had everything dressed up and very nice. People wouldn't pay any attention to the music. They'd go shopping and hit their kids and talk about those idiots passing out anti-grape petitions.

Everything looks fresh and nice. You're not aware that in the back room it 4
stinks and there's crates all over the place and the walls are messed up. There's graffiti and people are swearing and yelling at each other. You walk through the door, the music starts playing, and everything is pretty. You talk in hushed tones and are very respectful.

You wear a badge with your name on it. I once met someone I knew years 5
ago. I remembered his name and said, "Mr. Castle, how are you?" We talked about this and that. As he left, he said, "It was nice talking to you, Brett." I felt great, he remembered me. Then I looked down at my name plate. Oh shit. He didn't remember me at all, he just read the name plate. I wish I put "Irving" down on my name plate. If he'd have said, "Oh yes, Irving, how could I forget you . . . ?" I'd have been ready for him. There's nothing personal here.

You have to be very respectful to everyone—the customers, to the manager, to the checkers. There's a sign on the cash register that says: Smile at the customer. Say hello to the customer. It's assumed if you're a box boy, you're really there 'cause you want to be a manager some day. So you learn all the little things you have absolutely no interest in learning. **6**

The big thing there is to be an assistant manager and eventually manager. The male checkers had dreams of being manager, too. It was like an internship. They enjoyed watching how the milk was packed. Each manager had his own domain. There was the ice cream manager, the grocery manager, the dairy case manager. . . . They had a sign in the back: Be good to your job and your job will be good to you. So you take an overriding concern on how the ice cream is packed. You just die if something falls off a shelf. I saw so much crap there I just couldn't take. There was a black boy, an Oriental box boy, and a kid who had a Texas drawl. They needed the job to subsist. I guess I had the luxury to hate it and quit. **7**

When I first started there, the manager said, "Cut your hair. Come in a white shirt, black shoes, a tie. Be here on time." You get there, but he isn't there. I just didn't know what to do. The checker turns around and says, "You new? What's your name?" "Brett." "I'm Peggy." And that's all they say and they keep throwing this down to you. They'll say, "Don't put it in that, put it in there." But they wouldn't help you. **8**

You had to keep your apron clean. You couldn't lean back on the railings. You couldn't talk to the checkers. You couldn't accept tips. Okay, I'm outside and I put it in the car. For a lot of people, the natural reaction is to take a quarter and give it to me. I'd say, "I'm sorry, I can't." They'd get offended. When you give someone a tip, you're sort of suave. You take a quarter and you put it in their palm and you expect them to say, "Oh, thanks a lot." When you say, "I'm sorry, I can't," they feel a little put down. They say, "No one will know." And they put it in your pocket. You say, "I really can't." It gets to a point where you have to do physical violence to a person to avoid being tipped. It was not consistent with the store's philosophy of being cordial. Accepting tips was a cordial thing and made the customer feel good. I just couldn't understand the incongruity. One lady actually put it in my pocket, got in the car, and drove away. I would have had to throw the quarter at her or eaten it or something. **9**

When it got slow, the checkers would talk about funny things that happened. About Us and Them. Us being the people who worked there, Them being the stupid fools who didn't know where anything was—just came through and messed everything up and shopped. We serve them but we don't like them. We know where everything is. We know what time the market closes and they don't. We know what you do with coupons and they don't. There was a camaraderie of sorts. It wasn't healthy, though. It was a put-down of the others. **10**

There was this one checker who was absolutely vicious. He took great delight in making every little problem into a major crisis from which he had to emerge victorious. A customer would give him a coupon. He'd say, "You were supposed to give me that at the beginning." She'd say, "Oh, I'm sorry." He'd say, "Now I gotta open the cash register and go through the whole thing. Madam, I don't watch out for every customer. I can't manage your life." A put-down. **11**

It never bothered me when I would put something in the bag wrong. In the general scheme of things, in the large questions of the universe, putting a can of dog food in the bag wrong is not of great consequence. For them it was. **12**

There were a few checkers who were nice. There was one that was incredibly sad. She could be unpleasant at times, but she talked to everybody. She was one of the few people who genuinely wanted to talk to people. She was saying how she wanted to go to school and take courses so she could get teaching credit. Someone asked her, "Why don't you?" She said, "I have to work here. My hours are wrong. I'd have to get my hours changed." They said, "Why don't you?" She's worked there for years. She had seniority. She said, "Jim won't let me." Jim was the manager. He didn't give a damn. She wanted to go to school, to teach, but she can't because every day she's got to go back to the supermarket and load groceries. Yet she wasn't bitter. If she died a checker and never enriched her life, that was okay, because those were her hours. **13**

She was extreme in her unpleasantness and her consideration. Once I dropped some grape juice and she was squawking like a bird. I came back and mopped it up. She kept saying to me, "Don't worry about it. It happens to all of us." She'd say to the customers, "If I had a dime for all the grape juice I dropped . . ." **14**

Jim's the boss. A fish-type handshake. He was balding and in his forties. A lot of managers are these young, clean-shaven, neatly cropped people in their twenties. So Jim would say things like "groovy." You were supposed to get a ten-minute break every two hours. I lived for that break. You'd go outside, take your shoes off, and be human again. You had to request it. And when you took it, they'd make you feel guilty. **15**

You'd go up and say "Jim, can I have a break?" He'd say, "A break? You want a break? Make it a quick one, nine and a half minutes." Ha ha ha. One time I asked the assistant manager, Henry. He was even older than Jim. "Do you think I can have a break?" He'd say, "You got a break when you were hired." Ha ha ha. Even when they joked it was a put-down. **16**

The guys who load the shelves are a step above the box boys. It's like upperclassmen at an officer candidate's school. They would make sure that you conformed to all the prescribed rules, because they were once box boys. They know what you're going through, your anxieties. But instead of making it easier for you, they'd make it harder. It's like a military institution. **17**

I kept getting box boys who came up to me, "Has Jim talked to you about your hair? He's going to because it's getting too long. You better get it cut or grease it back or something." They took delight in it. They'd come to me before Jim had told me. Everybody was out putting everybody down. . . . **18**

■ **Reading Comprehension Questions**

   1. Which of the following would be a good alternative title for this selection?
      a.   The Value of Hard Work
      b.   Why I Quit My Job
      c.   The Trouble with Bosses
      d.   Getting Along with Customers

2. Which sentence best expresses the main idea of the selection?
   a. Brett Hauser hated his job.
   b. Supermarket workers have to be nice to everybody.
   c. Working as a box boy is a dead-end job.
   d. Brett Hauser's boss was unfair to his employees.

3. One complaint Brett had about his job was that
   a. he had to get a haircut.
   b. he had to wear a uniform.
   c. he was not allowed breaks.
   d. he was not promoted to assistant manager.

4. One supermarket checker liked to put down customers by
   a. refusing to accept tips from them.
   b. criticizing them for giving him coupons at the end of the order.
   c. calling them stupid.
   d. taking a break whenever a customer appeared.

5. When Brett talks of *Us* and *Them*, *Them* refers to
   a. customers.
   b. bosses.
   c. grape strikers.
   d. checkers.

6. We can assume that Brett did not like
   a. being nice to people he did not respect.
   b. carrying heavy bags to people's cars.
   c. listening to music all day long.
   d. customers who forgot to give him a tip.

7. What seems to have bothered Brett the most about his job was
   a. the hours.
   b. the routine.
   c. the pay.
   d. the people.

8. *True or false?* _____ We can assume that Brett needed a job very badly.

9. The word *subservient* in "You have to be terribly subservient to people"
   (paragraph 2) means
   a. sneaky.
   b. submissive.
   c. firm.
   d. pushy.

10. The word *incongruity* in ''I just couldn't understand the incongruity''
    (paragraph 9) means
    a. contrast.
    b. attitude.
    c. anger.
    d. saving.

■ Discussion Questions

About Content

1. Which does Brett dislike more, the job itself or the people he must deal
    with? How can you tell?
2. Do you think Brett was justified in quitting his job? Why or why not?
3. What qualities does Brett dislike in the checker who wants to be a teacher
    but says she can't go to school? Is Brett also afraid of being trapped?

About Structure

4. As Brett Hauser describes his job, he jumps around from topic to topic, with
    little attention to transitions or other methods of organization—as most
    people do when they talk. (The interview was originally tape-recorded.) If
    Brett were to write up his interview as an organized essay, what are three
    areas he might divide it into and discuss one at a time?
5. In the fifth sentence of paragraph 9, the pronoun *it* has no reference word.
    To what does this pronoun refer?

About Style and Tone

6. Brett uses some slang words and phrases. List three:

    _____   _____   _____

7. Brett also has a good vocabulary of more difficult standard English words,
    such as *subservient* and *domain*. List three other words that show that Brett
    has an extensive vocabulary:

    _____   _____   _____

■ Writing Assignments

Assignment 1

Perhaps, at some point in your life, you have held a job about which you had strong feelings (positive ones or negative ones). Or maybe you know someone who is presently holding a job and loves it—or, like Brett, hates it. Write a description of this job, focusing on at least three different aspects of it. Have *either* of these thesis statements in your introduction:

- ■ I really enjoyed working as a _____.
- ■ When I worked as a _____, I couldn't wait for quitting time.

Then describe the job. As in Studs Terkel's selection, use vivid details that make very clear your (or your friend's) attitude toward the job.

Alternatively, if you have never worked at a job about which you have strong feelings, rewrite ''Brett Hauser'' as a well-organized five-hundred-word essay. Include an introduction, three supporting paragraphs for your thesis that ''Working as a supermarket box boy is the worst job I have ever had,'' and a conclusion. Feel free to invent added details you might need to round out your supporting paragraphs.

Assignment 2

Compare or contrast Brett's job with a summer or part-time job you have had. (If you have never worked outside the home, compare or contrast Brett's job with that of being a homemaker—or a full-time student.) Here are some of the areas on which you might want to focus:

Hours

Pay

Working conditions

Coworkers

Customers

Bosses—how they treated employees

Chances for advancement

In your conclusion, decide which job, yours or Brett's, is better—and why.

Assignment 3

Studs Terkel gathered his information by interviewing different kinds of workers. Interview a person you know about his or her job. Use the material to write an essay about that person's job.

You could organize the essay into paragraphs dealing with the following:

What the person does on the job
Reasons why the person likes the job
Reasons why the person dislikes the job

Or you might decide to write about three of the following (in separate paragraphs):

Things the person likes or dislikes about the duties of the job
Things the person likes or dislikes about the employer
Things the person likes or dislikes about the coworkers
Things the person likes or dislikes about the working conditions

Defense Mechanisms

Ronald B. Adler and Neil Towne

The ancient Greeks understood defense mechanisms. In the Greek fable of the fox and the grapes, a fox who cannot reach the topmost grapes on a vine tells himself that they were probably sour anyway. As you will see in the following textbook selection, the fox was using a defense mechanism—rationalization— to protect his self-image. As you read, you will probably be able to identify defense mechanisms that both you and people you know use.

How do we manage self-deception? In the following pages you'll read about some of the methods we use. They are generally referred to as defense mechanisms. Just as the two methods of protecting yourself from physical attack are to flee or to fight, the mechanisms for psychological defense involve either avoidance or counterattack. The fact that these defense mechanisms operate unconsciously and have as their goal the avoidance of, or escape from, threat and anxiety makes them difficult to recognize in ourselves. And when we fail to realize that we're distorting the reality that makes up our lives, communication with others suffers.   1

Rationalization Reader for Students	
Situation	**What to Say**
When the course is the lecture type:	We never get a chance to say anything.
When the course is the discussion type:	The professor just sits there. We don't know how to teach the course.
When all aspects of the course are covered in class:	All he does is follow the text.
When you're responsible for covering part of the course outside class:	He never covers half the things we're tested on.
When you're given objective tests:	They don't allow for any individuality for us.
When you're given essay tests:	They're too vague. We never know what's expected.
When the instructor gives no tests:	It isn't fair! He can't tell how much we really know.
When you have a lot of quizzes instead of a midterm and final:	We need major exams. Quizzes don't cover enough to really tell anything.
When you have only two exams for the whole course:	Too much rides on each one. You can just have a bad day.

Defense mechanisms are not always undesirable. There are times when 2 protecting a private self is desirable, particularly when such disclosure would be treated cruelly by others. Also, confronting too many unpleasant truths or perceptions of one's self too quickly can be unmanageable, and thus these mechanisms serve as protective gear for handling the process of self-discovery at a safe rate. However, your own experience will show that, most often, acting in the following defensive ways can damage your relationships with others. We therefore believe that acquainting you with some of the most common defense mechanisms—with the hope of reducing them in your life—is a valuable step in helping you become a better communicator.

Rationalization. One of the most common ways of avoiding a threat to our 3 self-concept is to *rationalize,* that is, to think up a logical but untrue explanation that protects the unrealistic picture we hold of ourselves.

Have you ever justified cheating in school by saying the information you were **4** tested on wasn't important anyway or that everybody cheats a little? Were those your real reasons, or just excuses? Have you ever shrugged off hurting someone's feelings by saying she'll soon forget what you've done? In cases like these it's often tempting to explain behavior you feel guilty about by justifying it in terms that fit your self-concept. . . .

Reaction Formation. People who use reaction formation avoid facing an **5** unpleasant truth by acting exactly opposite from the way they truly feel. The common expression that describes this behavior is "whistling in the dark."

For example, you may have known somebody who acts like the life of the **6** party, always laughing and making jokes, but who you suspect is trying to fool everybody—including himself—into missing the fact that he is sad and lonely. Another example of reaction formation involves the person who goes overboard to be open-minded, insisting, "I'm not prejudiced! Why, some of my best friends are ——!" It's easy to suspect that someone who makes such a fuss about being tolerant may be unwilling to admit that just the opposite is true. . . .

Projection. In projection you avoid an unpleasant part of yourself by disowning **7** that part and attributing it to others. For instance, on the days when as instructors we aren't as prepared for class as we might be, it's tempting to claim that the hour hasn't gone well because the students didn't do *their* homework. Similarly, you may have found yourself accusing others of being dishonest, lazy, or inconsiderate when in fact such descriptions fit your behavior quite well. In all of these cases we project an unpleasant trait of our own onto another, and in so doing we avoid facing it in ourselves. It doesn't matter whether the accusation you make about others is true or not: In projection the important point is that you are escaping from having to face the truth about yourself.

The mechanism of projection explains the common experience of taking an **8** instant dislike to someone you've just met and realizing later that the traits you found so distasteful in that person are precisely those you dislike in yourself. By criticizing the new acquaintance you can put the undesirable characteristic "out there," and not have to admit it belongs to you.

A surefire test to determine whether you are using projection to fool yourself is **9** to take every attack you make on others and substitute "I" for the words you use to identify the other person. For example, "She talks too much" becomes "I talk too much," or "They're being unfair" is instead "I'm being unfair." When you try this simple experiment and your accusation of another seems to be true of you, you are projecting. . . .

Fantasy. When a person's desires or ambitions are frustrated, he often resorts **10** to a fantasy world to satisfy them. We often daydream ourselves out of our "real" world into one that is more satisfying. A good example of this is the young career woman who finds herself bored with her dull life as a typist. To insulate herself from this unbearable existence she escapes into the excitement of her own fantasies.

She becomes the leading lady in the romance magazine stories, the television dramas, and the movies she frequents. No matter how exciting and glamorous these fantasies are, they're not connected to the problem of her reality and therefore can't help her make changes to improve her life.

There is much to be said for the short daydream that lifts the boredom of an unpleasant task, or the fantasies that can be creative tools to help us think up new solutions to problems. But as with all defense mechanisms, the danger of fantasizing is that it keeps us from dealing squarely with what's bothering us by providing a temporary escape which doesn't really solve the problem.   11

Repression. Sometimes rather than facing up to an unpleasant situation and trying to deal with it, we protect ourselves by denying its existence. Quite simply, we "forget" what would otherwise be painful. Take a couple, for example, who can't seem to agree about how to handle their finances. One partner thinks that money is meant to be spent, while the other believes that it's important to save for the future. Rather than working to solve this important problem, the husband and wife pretend nothing is wrong. This charade may work for a while, but as time goes by, each partner will probably begin to feel more and more uncomfortable and will likely begin to build up resentments about the way the other one uses their common money. Eventually these resentments are almost sure to leak into other areas of the marriage.   12

In the same way, we've seen families with serious problems—an alcoholic parent, a teenager into drugs, a conflict between members—try to pretend that everything is perfectly all right, as if acting that way will make it so. Of course, it's unlikely that they'll solve these problems without admitting that they exist. . . .   13

Emotional Insulation and Apathy. Often, rather than face an unpleasant situation, people will avoid hurt by not getting involved or pretending they don't care. Probably the most common example of *emotional insulation* is the person who develops a strong attachment to someone only to have the relationship break up. The pain is so great that the sufferer refuses to become involved like this again. At other times people who are hurt in this way defend their feeling of self-worth by becoming *apathetic,* by saying they don't care about whoever hurt them.   14

The sad thing about emotional insulation and apathy is that they prevent the person who uses them from doing anything about dealing with the cause of the defensiveness. As long as I say I don't care about dating when I really do, I can't go out with anyone because this would be inconsistent with my artificial self-concept. As long as I don't admit that I care about you, our relationship has little chance of growing.   15

Displacement. This occurs when we vent aggressive or hostile feelings against people or objects that are seen as less dangerous than the person or persons who caused the feelings originally. The child who is reminded that she has to clean up her room before she can play may get rid of some of her hostility by slamming the door to her bedroom or beating up a younger brother or sister. She knows it might   16 cause her more pain if she expressed this hostility against her parents. In the same way, displacement occurs when, for example, a workman gets angry at the boss but doesn't want to risk getting fired and so takes out his frustration by yelling at his family. . . .

Verbal Aggression. Sometimes, when we can get away with it, the easiest   17
way to avoid facing criticism is to drown it out. Verbal aggression illustrates the old saying "The best defense is a good offense." Counterattacking somebody who threatens our self-concept tends to relieve tension and helps the defensive person feel better because his fireworks probably cover up whatever it was in the original remark that threatened him.

A good example of verbal aggression is the "so are you" defensive maneuver.   18
When a person says something we feel is too critical, we counterattack by telling her all her faults. Our remarks may be true, but they don't answer her criticism and only wind up making her more defensive.

Temper tantrums, hitting below the belt, and bringing up past grievances are   19
some other types of verbal aggression.

Now that you've had a look at several ways people defend an unrealistic self-   20
concept, we hope you'll be able to detect the role defense mechanisms play in your life. We want to repeat that these mechanisms aren't usually destructive unless they're practiced to the point where an individual's view of reality becomes distorted. . . . Our hope is that you can look at *yourself* with a little more knowledge of how you operate when you detect a threat to your self-concept.

Finally, you'll find defensive mechanisms don't usually appear as simple, clear-   21
cut behaviors. We usually use them in combination because it's only natural to protect one's self in as many ways as possible.

■ Reading Comprehension Questions

1. Which of the following would be a good alternative title for this selection?
   a. Undesirable Behaviors
   b. Facing the Truth
   c. Ways We Avoid Reality
   d. How We Communicate

2. Which sentence best expresses the main idea of the selection?
   a. Defense mechanisms are dangerous when carried to an extreme.
   b. A good communicator never uses defense mechanisms.
   c. People use various defense mechanisms to protect their self-image.
   d. Rationalization and projection are the most dangerous kinds of defense mechanisms.

3. Bringing up past grievances and throwing temper tantrums are examples of
   a. repression.
   b. rationalization.
   c. emotional insulation.
   d. verbal aggression.

4. *True or false?* _____ Taking a dislike to someone because he or she has some negative traits you see in yourself is an example of reaction formation.

5. Using defense mechanisms can be healthy when
   a. you are defending your private self from the cruelty of others.
   b. you are looking for an escape from your problems.
   c. you are trying to forget about a parent's alcoholism.
   d. you are trying to get over a broken relationship.

6. The authors imply that
   a. repression is a way to solve some marital problems.
   b. apathetic people have lost their self-worth.
   c. students using rationalization will criticize a class no matter how it is conducted.
   d. people who are outgoing and sociable at parties are really covering up the fact that they are sad and lonely.

7. We can conclude that a woman who argues with her husband and then releases her anger by driving recklessly is using
   a. displacement.
   b. apathy.
   c. projection.
   d. fantasy.

8. The authors imply that
   a. teachers use projection more than any other defense mechanism.
   b. a good communicator deals with reality.
   c. defense mechanisms are more helpful than harmful.
   d. some people never need to use defense mechanisms.

9. The word *charade* in "the husband and wife pretend nothing is wrong. . . . This charade" (paragraph 12) means
   a. problem.
   b. game.
   c. solution.
   d. discussion.

10. The word *vent* in "when we vent aggressive or hostile feelings" (paragraph 16) means
    a. repress.
    b. protect.
    c. let out.
    d. list.

■ **Discussion Questions**

About Content

1. In what two instances, according to Adler and Towne, is the use of defense mechanisms desirable? When do defense mechanisms become psychologically destructive?
2. What do you think is probably the most common defense mechanism that people use in everyday life? Give examples.
3. The authors say that we often use defense mechanisms in combination. Give an example of a situation in which a person would be using two defense mechanisms.
4. What are the benefits, if any, of fantasizing? What are the drawbacks?

About Structure

5. What is the method of development used for most paragraphs in the selection?
6. Paragraph 2 contains three types of transition signals: an addition signal, change-of-direction signal, and conclusion signal. What are they?

    _____   _____   _____

About Style and Tone

7. One of the ways the authors of this selection achieve a friendly, helpful tone is by speaking directly to the reader. For example, in paragraph 4, the authors ask the reader questions: "Have you ever justified cheating in school . . . ? Were those your real reasons . . . ? Have you ever shrugged off hurting someone's feelings . . . ?" Find two other places in the selection where the authors use the "you" point of view to speak directly to their audience. Write the numbers of those paragraphs here: _____   _____

■ **Writing Assignments**

Assignment 1

You may have recognized your own behavior in several of these descriptions of defense mechanisms. Write an essay about the three defense mechanisms you use most often. In your thesis, state that you rely on three kinds of defense mechanisms in everyday life. Then, in each of your supporting paragraphs, give examples (or an extended example) of times you found yourself using that particular defense mechanism.

Assignment 2

Write an essay about three defense mechanisms you see someone else using. (The person should be someone you know well, such as a family member, friend, or coworker.) As in Assignment 1, use examples to develop your supporting paragraphs.

Assignment 3

Write an essay proving that some students often use rationalization, fantasy, and repression (*or* regression) to cope with school. Develop your supporting paragraphs with hypothetical examples of fictional students (see page 92 for an explanation of hypothetical examples). In each supporting paragraph, describe how your fictional student uses one of the defense mechanisms to cope with academic, social, or personal problems.

The First Step to the Cemetery

Kenneth Bernard

People don't retire, according to Kenneth Bernard—they buy a ticket to second-class citizenship. In the following essay, Bernard makes several controversial points about how we treat the elderly. To most Americans, says Bernard, old people are excess baggage best shipped away to those concentration camps called nursing homes and senior citizen centers.

The prevailing vision of the good life in America has for some time included early 1 retirement. Numerous voices speak in its behalf, from insurance companies to unions to government agencies. Quit while you're ahead, still healthy and young enough to enjoy a generous spread of the sunset years. Not only should you enjoy the fruit of your labors in this most bountiful of countries, say the many voices, but you should also give the young folk their chance to move up by exiting gracefully. There are, you are told, numerous benefits—tax, medical, recreational, psychological. It is not only foolish to overlook the opportunity; it is downright un-American.

So why not do it? Why not? Because it will probably be the worst decision you have ever made. Here's why.

To begin, it is an immediate, and usually irrevocable, step into second-class ² citizenship. Once retired, you are one with blacks, Hispanics, the handicapped, homosexuals, jailbirds, the insane, the retarded, children and women: America's Third World hordes. America doesn't like old people, and retired people are old people, whether they are forty-five, fifty-five, or sixty-five. Old people clutter up the landscape. Their families don't want them. Their communities don't want them. They are a nightmare vision of everyone's future. They are of interest mainly to doctors and hospitals, real-estate brokers and travel agents—but not as people, rather as bodies from whom some final payments can still be exacted.

Colonies. In America you are primarily valued not for your good deeds or ³ your good character. You are valued for the money you command. The more money you have, the better you are treated by everyone from your local cop to your congressman. If you doubt this, go to any store or social agency. Go, for example, to any urban clinic and see what it is like to be old, sick and poor. There is a living hell. You get neither kindness nor respect nor service. To voluntarily take a step toward that condition you have to be either blind or mad. For as your ability to command money decreases, so too does your stature as a human being. To doctors, you are less important than the forms they must process to get money for their services. To landlords, you are a barrier to higher rents. Small wonder that retirees band together in colonies, in clubs, homes and hospitals. They want to belong, and they can do so only with their own kind. Everywhere else, their money will be taken, but they will be shut out.

What are these colonies like? To be sure, just as there are decent people who ⁴ respect old people, so too there are homes, hospitals and communities that are genuinely humanitarian, that perform genuine functions. But how many? Our public knowledge of old-age homes is that they are less clean and only slightly less efficient than slaughterhouses, dismal halfway houses to the grave: turnover is profit.

In some societies where people live to be very old, it is observable that they, ⁵ whatever their age, have useful, needed work to perform. In America, activities for old people are manufactured. People get degrees in how to occupy old people with busy-work. But this has nothing to do with life; it is all meaningless filler. These people are out of it. Although everyone knows it, everyone lies about it and society conspires to keep them there. It is a not so genteel form of genocide. The old people know it, too; and, knowing it (and often being very gracious), they cooperate: they begin to die in spirit and then bodily. And no amount of shuffleboard, creative writing, canasta or sight-seeing can hide the unpleasant truth. Society's message is: spend money, but stay out of the way, and make no demands.

Old people are besieged by indifference, loneliness and uselessness. They are ⁶ also physically assaulted by toughs and criminals. They are, understandably, fearful. Often they are imprisoned in their own homes. Yes, the perpetrators are few in number, but the assaults could not take place without a climate of sentiment, a cast of mind, that allowed for them. Our society fears the natural extinction of life so much that it behaves grotesquely. After all, with luck we will all grow old someday. Thus the mistreatment of the old is a form of self-mutilation. Nevertheless, the cruelty persists.

Faced with such barbarism, why join the legions of the doomed and damned? 7
All your life you maintain a certain schedule. You break that routine once or twice
a year. You go on this way thirty or forty years. Your heart, your bowels, your mind
keep time with it. And then you stop. You leave your pleasures, your sorrows, your
family, everything. You might as well run full speed into a brick wall. No body or
mind was meant to stop like that. Things have to go wrong—your heart, your
bowels, your mind. It is the first giant step to the cemetery. Why take it? What's
the percentage? Why, indeed, do it younger and younger when people are living
to be older and older? Would you invest money with the same logic? Does it make
any sense? Perhaps it would if there were alternatives (for example, working less)
but there aren't any alternatives for most of us. It's out, totally out, out all the way,
and don't try to get back in.

Don't Quit. In our society, life is useful work and continuing income. Even 8
what seems like a large retirement income is to be regarded with deep suspicion
in this day of inflation. Life and respect are work and money. It shouldn't be so,
but it is.

There is something suicidal in retirement, just as there is something suicidal in 9
society's callousness toward the old. So forget the young. You worked to get what
you have. Keep it; enjoy it. They are young and strong; let them struggle. It isn't
your problem, you shouldn't take the rap. Don't leave your job one minute before
you have to—even if you hate it—unless you can't get out of bed. You have
something to give. It isn't true that to be old is to be incompetent. Fight. Don't quit.
Elect your own to legislative office. Band together: the old-age party, the life party.
Don't let them convince you that the "golden years" await you. It's a lie. No one
should go down without a struggle. Kick. Scream. Be heard all the way to
Washington. You have nothing to lose but your dignity and your life.

■ Reading Comprehension Questions

1. Which of the following would be a good alternative title for this selection?
   a. America's Values
   b. Don't Retire
   c. The Problems of the Old
   d. Old People's Homes

2. Which sentence best expresses the main idea of the selection?
   a. Retirement is a serious and deadly mistake.
   b. Older people should become more politically active.
   c. A regular work schedule is essential for good health.
   d. In America, money equals power.

3. The author urges people
   a. to refuse to retire.
   b. to retire in a caring community.
   c. to retire only if wealthy.
   d. not to retire before age sixty-five.

4. *True or false?* _____ The author concedes that some homes and hospitals for old people are decent places.

5. The author believes that people in America are valued primarily for their
    a. age.
    b. profession.
    c. good deeds.
    d. money.

6. The author implies that
    a. doctors are cheating the Medicare system.
    b. travel and hobbies can make retirement easier.
    c. America's minorities are treated disrespectfully.
    d. old people exaggerate the crime problem.

7. The author implies that
    a. retirement inevitably means a reduction in income.
    b. landlords believe old people are unreliable tenants.
    c. money cannot buy respect.
    d. being old means being incompetent.

8. The author implies that
    a. our treatment of the old is based on our fears of death.
    b. old people should give up their jobs to the young.
    c. you should retire only if you hate your job.
    d. the government is deliberately lying about the benefits of retirement.

9. The word *perpetrators* in ''the perpetrators are few in number, but the assaults . . .'' (paragraph 6) means
    a. elderly people.
    b. police officers.
    c. con artists.
    d. doers or performers.

10. The word *callousness* in ''society's callousness toward the old'' (paragraph 9) means
    a. attitude.
    b. insensitivity.
    c. selfishness.
    d. inability.

■ **Discussion Questions**

About Content

1. Bernard says that our society ''fears the natural extinction of life so much that it behaves grotesquely.'' What does he mean? Can you think of some examples of how our society does this?

2. In paragraph 3, the author writes, "In America, you are primarily valued not for your good deeds or for your good character. You are valued for the money you command." Do you agree with this statement? Why or why not?

3. Do you think that Bernard has overstated the evils of retirement? Do you know any retired people who are enjoying their retirement? How do they spend their time?

About Structure

4. What method of introduction does Bernard use?
   a. Anecdote
   b. Questions
   c. Beginning with an opposite

5. What conclusion technique does the author use?
   a. Summary
   b. Recommendation
   c. Quotation

About Style and Tone

6. Kenneth Bernard uses some "loaded" words in his essay: words that bring out strong emotional responses in readers. Two examples of these are *jailbirds* (paragraph 2) and *slaughterhouses* (paragraph 4). Find four other examples and write them here:

   _____   _____

   _____   _____

   Why do you think the author uses these words instead of others that would be less upsetting?

7. In his essay, Bernard uses a number of *rhetorical questions*—that is, questions that an author does not actually expect readers to answer. In some cases, a writer may want readers to think about the answers to the questions, or may plan to answer the questions in the essay. Count the number of rhetorical questions used in this selection and put the number here: _____

■ **Writing Assignments**

Assignment 1

Kenneth Bernard gives some compelling reasons why people should not retire early. However, there is another point of view. Can you think of any reason why people *should* retire early? Make a list of these reasons. Then choose the best three and develop them into a five-paragraph essay. Your thesis could be that early retirement is a good idea for several reasons.

As an alternative, write an essay on what you feel are three reasons why people should *not* retire early.

Assignment 2

In paragraph 2 of ''The First Step to the Cemetery,'' Bernard suggests that retired people are treated just like ''blacks, Hispanics, the handicapped, homosexuals, jailbirds, the insane, the retarded, children and women.'' What do retired people have in common with any of these other minority groups in our society? Pick out *one* of the groups Bernard lists here and compare or contrast retired people with them. Here are some topics you could discuss:

Stereotyped notions
Job opportunities
Freedom of movement
Economic level
Jokes told about them
Prejudices against them
Ways that people behave in their presence

Choose any three of these or other topics. Then write a comparison or contrast essay using one of the two methods of development (one side at a time or point by point) explained on pages 152–153.

Assignment 3

Bernard says that Americans are valued only if they have money. Is this true? Can you think of examples of times people are treated better, get better service, or get out of trouble more easily because they have money? Write an essay with the thesis idea that people with money are treated better in our society. In each of your supporting paragraphs, cover one area of life in which well-off people are treated better than others.

Why Are Students Turned Off?

Casey Banas

A teacher pretends to be a student and sits in on several classes. What does she find in the typical class? Boredom. Routine. Apathy. Manipulation. Discouragement. If this depressing list sounds familiar, you will be interested in the following analysis of why classes often seem to be more about killing time than about learning.

1   Ellen Glanz lied to her teacher about why she hadn't done her homework; but, of course, many students have lied to their teachers. The difference is that Ellen Glanz was a twenty-eight-year-old high school social studies teacher who was a student for six months to improve her teaching by gaining a fresh perspective of her school.

2   She found many classes boring, students doing as little as necessary to pass tests and get good grades, students using ruses to avoid assignments, and students manipulating teachers to do the work for them. She concluded that many students are turned off because they have little power and responsibility for their own education.

3   Ellen Glanz found herself doing the same things as the students. There was the day when Glanz wanted to join her husband in helping friends celebrate the purchase of a house, but she had homework for a math class. For the first time, she knew how teenagers feel when they think something is more important than homework.

4   She found a way out and confided: "I considered my options: Confess openly to the teacher, copy someone else's sheet, or make up an excuse." Glanz chose the third option—the one most widely used—and told the teacher that the pages needed to complete the assignment had been ripped from the book. The teacher accepted the story, never checking the book. In class, nobody else did the homework; and student after student mumbled responses when called upon.

5   "Finally," Glanz said, "the teacher, thinking that the assignment must have been difficult, went over each question at the board while students copied the problems at their seats. The teacher had 'covered' the material and the students had listened to the explanation. But had anything been learned? I don't think so."

6   Glanz found this kind of thing common. "In many classes," she said, "people simply didn't do the work assignment, but copied from someone else or manipulated the teacher into doing the work for them."

"The system encourages incredible passivity," Glanz said. "In most classes   7
one sits and listens. A teacher, whose role is activity, simply cannot understand
the passivity of the student's role," she said. "When I taught," Glanz recalled, "my
mind was going constantly—figuring out how to best present an idea, thinking about
whom to call on, whom to draw out, whom to shut up; how to get students
involved, how to make my point clearer, how to respond; when to be funny, when
serious. As a student, I experienced little of this. Everything was done to me."

Class methods promote the feeling that students have little control over or   8
responsibility for their own education because the agenda is the teacher's, Glanz
said. The teacher is convinced the subject matter is worth knowing, but the student
may not agree. Many students, Glanz said, are not convinced they need to know
what teachers teach; but they believe good grades are needed to get into college.

Students, obsessed with getting good grades to help qualify for the college of   9
their choice, believe the primary responsibility for their achievement rests with the
teacher, Glanz said. "It was his responsibility to teach well rather than their
responsibility to learn carefully."

Teachers were regarded by students, Glanz said, not as "people," but as "role-   10
players" who dispensed information needed to pass a test. "I often heard students
describing teachers as drips, bores, and numerous varieties of idiots," she said.
"Yet I knew that many of the same people had travelled the world over, conducted
fascinating experiments or learned three languages, or were accomplished musicians, artists, or athletes."

But the sad reality, Glanz said, is the failure of teachers to recognize their   11
tremendous communications gap with students. Some students, she explained,
believe that effort has little value. Some have heard reports of unemployment among
college graduates and others, and after seeing political corruption they conclude
that honesty takes a back seat to getting ahead any way one can, she said. "I
sometimes estimated that half to two-thirds of a class cheated on a given test,"
Glanz said. "Worse, I've encountered students who feel no remorse about cheating
but are annoyed that a teacher has confronted them on their actions."

Glanz has since returned to teaching at Lincoln-Sudbury. Before her stint as a   12
student, she would worry that perhaps she was demanding too much. "Now I know
I should have demanded more," she said. Before, she was quick to accept the
excuses of students who came to class unprepared. Now she says, "You are
responsible for learning it." But a crackdown is only a small part of the solution.

The larger issue, Glanz said, is that educators must recognize that teachers and   13
students, though physically in the same school, are in separate worlds and have
an on-going power struggle. "A first step toward ending this battle is to convince
students that what we attempt to teach them is genuinely worth knowing," Glanz
said. "We must be sure, ourselves, that what we are teaching is worth knowing."
No longer, she emphasized, do students assume that "teacher knows best."

■ Reading Comprehension Questions

1. Which of the following would be a good alternative title for the selection?
   a. How to Get Good Grades
   b. Why Students Dislike School
   c. Cheating in Our School Systems
   d. Students Who Manipulate Teachers

2. Which sentence best expresses the main idea of the selection?
   a. Ellen Glanz is a burned-out teacher.
   b. Ellen Glanz lied to her math teacher.
   c. Students need good grades to get into college.
   d. Teachers and students feel differently about schooling.

3. How much of a class, according to the author's estimate, would often cheat on a test?
   a. One-quarter or less
   b. One-half or less
   c. One-half to two-thirds
   d. Almost everyone

4. *True or false?* _____ As a result of her experience, Glanz now accepts more of her students' excuses.

5. Glanz found that the school system encourages an inevitable amount of
   a. false expectations.
   b. passivity.
   c. temporary learning.
   d. hostility.

6. The author implies that
   a. few students cheat on tests.
   b. most students enjoy schoolwork.
   c. classroom teaching methods should be changed.
   d. Glanz had a lazy math teacher.

7. The author implies that
   a. Glanz should not have become a student again.
   b. Glanz is a better teacher than she was before.
   c. Glanz later told her math teacher that she lied.
   d. social studies is an unimportant subject.

8. The author implies that
   a. most students who cheat on tests are caught by their teachers.
   b. most teachers demand too little of their students.
   c. students who get good grades in high school do so in college.
   d. students never question what teachers say.

9. The word *agenda* in "the agenda is the teacher's" (paragraph 8) means
   a. program.
   b. boredom.
   c. happiness.
   d. book.

10. The word *ruses* in "students using ruses to avoid assignments" (paragraph 2) means
    a. questions.
    b. sicknesses.
    c. parents.
    d. tricks.

■ Discussion Questions

About Content

1. Are you surprised that a twenty-eight-year-old high school teacher would become as "turned off" as a high school student? Why or why not?

2. Glanz feels that nothing is learned when a teacher goes over an assignment that nobody has done—in effect doing the students' homework for them. Do you agree with her? If so, what do you feel should be done about the problem?

3. Glanz feels that students have little power and responsibility where their own education is concerned. What examples of this situation does she give? Can you think of others?

About Structure

4. What method of introduction is used in paragraph 1?
   a. Brief anecdote
   b. Quotation
   c. Questions

5. The last paragraph uses a combination of conclusion techniques. What are they?
   a. Recommendation and quotation
   b. Prediction and anecdote
   c. Questions and summary

About Style and Tone

6. The author of this article focuses on Ellen Glanz. Glanz wants to persuade us of the importance of her observations. But what is the *author's* purpose in writing this selection?
   a. To report Ellen Glanz's story
   b. To agree with Ellen Glanz
   c. To disagree with Ellen Glanz

7. Parallel structure can create a smooth, readable style (see page 255). For example, note the series of *-ing* verbs in the following sentence from paragraph 2: ". . . students *doing* as little as necessary to pass tests and get good grades, students *using* ruses to avoid assignments, and students *manipulating* teachers to do the work for them." Find two other places where parallelism is used in this selection and write the sentences in the spaces below.

_____

_____

_____

_____

■ Writing Assignments

Assignment 1

Play the role of student observer in one of your college classes. Then write an essay with *either* of the following theses:

■ In my _____ class, students are turned off.

■ In my _____ class, students are active and interested.

In each supporting paragraph, state and detail one reason why the atmosphere in that particular class is either boring or interesting. You might want to consider areas such as

The teacher: presentation, tone of voice, level of interest and enthusiasm, teaching aids used, ability to handle questions, sense of humor, and so on

The students: level of enthusiasm, participation in class, attitude (as shown by body language and other actions), and so on

Other factors: condition of classroom, length of class period, noise level in classroom, and so on

Assignment 2

Glanz says that students like to describe their teachers as ''drips, bores, and numerous varieties of idiots.'' Write a description of one of your teachers (high school or college) who either *does* or *does not* fit that description. Show, in your essay, that your teacher was as weak, boring, and idiotic as Glanz says—or just the opposite (dynamic, creative, and bright). In either case, your focus should be on providing specific details that *enable your readers to see for themselves* that your thesis is a valid one.

Assignment 3

How does the classroom situation Ellen Glanz describes compare with a classroom situation with which you are familiar—either one from the high school you attended or one from the school in which you are presently enrolled? Select one class you were or are a part of, and write an essay in which you compare or contrast your class with the ones Ellen Glanz describes. Here are some areas you might wish to include in your essay:

How interesting the class was

How many of the students did their assignments

What the instructor's teaching methods were

How much was actually learned

How active the teacher was

How passive the students were

What the students thought of the teacher

Choose any three of the above or other areas. Then decide whether you are going to use a *one-side-at-a-time* or a *point-by-point* method of development (see pages 152–153).

The Thin Grey Line

Marya Mannes

  The "thin grey line" Marya Mannes discusses is the one separating honesty and dishonesty, lawfulness and unlawfulness. You—like most other people— probably cross over the line quite often. You may feel that you are a pretty honest person, but . . . Have you ever cheated on a test? Filled in false information on your tax return? "Borrowed" office supplies? Kept quiet when a mistake on a check was in your favor? If you have, Mannes is talking to you.

1   "Aw, they all do it," growled the cabdriver. He was talking about cops who took payoffs for winking at double parking, but his cynicism could as well have been directed at any of a dozen other instances of corruption, big-time and small-time. Moreover, the disgust in his voice was overlaid by an unspoken "So what?": the implication that since this was the way things were, there was nothing anybody could do.

2   Like millions of his fellow Americans, the cabdriver was probably a decent human being who had never stolen anything, broken any law or willfully injured another; somewhere, a knowledge of what was probably right had kept him from committing what was clearly wrong. But that knowledge had not kept a thin grey line that separates the two conditions from being daily greyer and thinner—to the point that it was hardly noticeable.

3   On the one side of this line are They: the bribers, the cheaters, the chiselers, the swindlers, the extortioners. On the other side are We—both partners and victims. They and We are now so perilously close that the only mark distinguishing us is that They get caught and We don't.

4   The same citizen who voices outrage at police corruption will slip the traffic cop on his block a handsome Christmas present in the belief that his car, nestled under a "No Parking" sign, will not be ticketed. The son of that nice woman next door has a habit of stealing cash from her purse because his allowance is smaller than his buddies'. Your son's friend admitted cheating at exams because "everybody does it."

5   Bit by bit, the resistance to and immunity against wrong that a healthy social body builds up by law and ethics and the dictation of conscience have broken down. And instead of the fighting indignation of a people outraged by those who prey on them, we have the admission of impotence: "They all do it."

Now, failure to uphold the law is no less corrupt than violation of the law. And 6 the continuing shame of this country now is the growing number of Americans who fail to uphold and assist enforcement of the law, simply—and ignominiously—out of fear. Fear of "involvement," fear of reprisal, fear of "trouble." A man is beaten by hoodlums in plain daylight and in view of bystanders. These people not only fail to help the victim, but, like the hoodlums, flee before the police can question them. A city official knows of a colleague's bribe but does not report it. A pedestrian watches a car hit a woman but leaves the scene, to avoid giving testimony. It happens every day. And if the police get cynical at this irresponsibility, they are hardly to blame. Morale is a matter of giving support and having faith in one another; where both are lacking, "law" has become a worthless word.

How did we get this way? What started this blurring of what was once a thick 7 black line between the lawful and the lawless? What makes a "regular guy," a decent fellow, accept a bribe? What makes a nice kid from a middle-class family take money for doing something he must know is not only illegal but wrong?

When you look into the background of an erring "kid" you will often find a 8 comfortable home and a mother who will tell you, with tears in her eyes, that she "gave him everything." She probably did, to his everlasting damage. Fearing her son's disapproval, the indulgent mother denies him nothing except responsibility. Instead of growing up, he grows to believe that the world owes him everything.

The nice kid's father crosses the thin grey line himself in a dozen ways, day in 9 and day out. He pads his expenses on his income-tax returns as a matter of course. As a landlord, he pays the local inspectors of the city housing authority to overlook violations in the houses he rents. When his son flunked his driving test, he gave him ten dollars to slip the inspector on his second test. "They all do it," he said.

The nice kid is brought up with boys and girls who have no heroes except 10 people not much older than themselves who have made the Big Time, usually in show business or in sports. Publicity and money are the halos of their stars, who range from pop singers who can't sing to ballplayers who can't read: from teen-age starlets who can't act to television performers who can't think. They may be excited by the exploits of spacemen, but the work's too tough and dangerous.

The nice kids have no heroes because they don't believe in heroes. Heroes are 11 suckers and squares. To be a hero you have to stand out, to excel, to take risks, and above all, not only choose between right and wrong, but defend the right and fight the wrong. This means responsibility—and who needs it?

Today, no one has to take any responsibility. The psychiatrists, the sociologists, 12 the novelists, the playwrights have gone a long way to help promote irresponsibility. Nobody really is to blame for what he does. It's Society. It's Environment. It's a Broken Home. It's an Underprivileged Area. But it's hardly ever You.

Now we find a truckload of excuses to absolve the individual from responsibility 13 for his actions. A fellow commits a crime because he's basically insecure, because he hated his stepmother at nine, or because his sister needs an operation. A policeman loots a store because his salary is too low. A city official accepts a payoff because it's offered to him. Members of minority groups, racial or otherwise, commit crimes because they can't get a job, or are unacceptable to the people living around them. The words "right" and "wrong" are foreign to these people.

But honesty is the best policy. Says who? Anyone willing to get laughed at. But 14
the laugh is no laughing matter. It concerns the health and future of a nation. It
involves the two-dollar illegal bettor as well as the corporation price-fixer, the
college-examination cheater and the payroll-padding Congressman, the expense-
account chiseler, the seller of pornography and his schoolboy reader, the bribed
judge and the stealing delinquent. All these people may represent a minority. But
when, as it appears now, the majority excuse themselves from responsibility by
accepting corruption as natural to society ("They all do it"), this society is bordering
on total confusion. If the line between right and wrong is finally erased, there is no
defense against the power of evil.

Before this happens—and it is by no means far away—it might be well for the 15
schools of the nation to substitute for the much-argued issue of prayer a daily lesson
in ethics, law, and responsibility to society that would strengthen the conscience
as exercise strengthens muscles. And it would be even better if parents were forced
to attend it. For corruption is not something you read about in the papers and leave
to courts. We are all involved.

■ Reading Comprehension Questions

1. Which of the following would be a good alternative title for this selection?
   a. The Loss of Heroes
   b. Dishonesty in the Workplace
   c. The Power of Evil
   d. The Growth of Corruption

2. Which sentence best expresses the main idea of the selection?
   a. Police officers are becoming cynical about crime.
   b. The distinction between right and wrong is becoming blurred.
   c. People are blaming society for their problems.
   d. Most juvenile offenders come from middle-class homes.

3. The author blames the wrongdoing of many middle-class children on
   a. indulgent parents.
   b. the schools.
   c. broken homes.
   d. peer pressures.

4. *True or false?* _____ The author says that a minority of people are corrupt.

5. *True or false?* _____ The author believes that one way to stop corruption
   is for schools to teach daily lessons in ethics.

6. The author implies that
   a. some petty crime is justifiable.
   b. blaming racial discrimination for criminal behavior is just an excuse.
   c. space explorers are not heroic.
   d. the line between right and wrong can never be completely erased.

7. The author implies that
   a. those who fail to get involved when crime occurs can be excused.
   b. celebrity does not always mean intelligence or talent.
   c. psychiatrists can help us distinguish between right and wrong.
   d. corrupt parents are usually strict with their children.

8. The author implies that
   a. prayer in the schools would discourage corruption.
   b. a person from a broken home is not responsible for his or her actions.
   c. payoffs and corruption will never change.
   d. novelists, sociologists, and playwrights are among those to blame for corruption.

9. The word *impotence* in "instead of . . . fighting indignation . . . , we have the admission of impotence" (paragraph 5) means
   a. powerlessness.
   b. importance.
   c. oppression.
   d. unpleasantness.

10. The word *reprisal* in "fear of reprisal, fear of 'trouble'" (paragraph 6) means
    a. recognition.
    b. destruction.
    c. murder.
    d. retaliation.

■ **Discussion Questions**

About Content

1. In paragraph 6, Mannes writes that "failure to uphold the law is no less corrupt than violation of the law." Explain what she means. Do you agree with her?

2. What answer or answers does Mannes provide for her question in paragraph 7, "How did we get this way?"

About Structure

3. In which paragraph does Mannes state her thesis?
   a. Paragraph 1
   b. Paragraph 5
   c. Paragraph 11

4. Mannes uses examples as a form of paragraph development (see paragraph 1; paragraph 4; paragraphs 8–10). Find two other paragraphs in Mannes' essay that are supported with examples, and write the numbers of those paragraphs here: ＿＿＿＿   ＿＿＿＿

5. What key word does Mannes repeat in each of the five final paragraphs of her essay? ＿＿＿＿＿＿＿＿＿＿

6. What conclusion technique does she use?
    a. Recommendation
    b. Quotation
    c. Summary

About Style and Tone

7. How would you characterize the tone of paragraph 13, especially the section beginning, ''A fellow commits a crime . . .''?
    a. Humorous
    b. Sad
    c. Disbelieving

■ Writing Assignments

Assignment 1

Mannes says that ''law, ethics, and the dictation of conscience have broken down.'' What signs do you see that this has happened? Give examples of small dishonesties that you, your family, or people you know about practice. You may want to divide the examples into groups:

> Those committed at school
>
> Those committed on the job
>
> Those committed against the government
>
> Those committed against friends and neighbors

or any other groupings you can think of.

   If you decide to write about cheating on the job, that supporting paragraph might begin, ''At the department store where I work, many of the employees practice small dishonesties. For one thing, punching in a late or absent friend's time card is very common. . . .''

Assignment 2

Describe practical steps that we could take to put an end to three particular kinds of cheating or petty corruption, such as

Cheating on school assignments and tests

Lying on tax forms

Lying on job applications

Shoplifting

"Fixing" traffic tickets

Avoiding paying tolls, parking fees

Pick three of these areas (or any other you might come up with) and write about specific actions that could be taken to prevent such cheating. For instance, if you decide to write about how to stop students from cheating on assignments and tests, you might begin that particular supporting paragraph with the topic sentence, "Some practical steps could be taken immediately that would almost eliminate cheating on assignments and tests." You might begin to develop your ideas by saying, "No teacher, first of all, should be permitted to give out the same exams and term paper assignments semester after semester. . . . " Then you would continue to develop the paragraph with other specific suggestions.

Assignment 3

Is it ever all right to commit a minor crime or to be dishonest? Is it all right to do such things if a person feels that a greater good will come out of the action? Consider, for instance, honest people who deliberately withhold some of their income taxes because they believe the weapons the money will be used to buy are immoral. Or consider a person who steals money to buy medicine for a sick child.

Write an essay supporting the thesis that, in some cases, a dishonest action may be justified. Create three situations with fictional people. (See the section in this book on hypothetical examples on page 92.) Use these situations to support your thesis.

Advertising Claims

Jeffrey Schrank

Why do you buy the shampoos, soaps, clothes, and cars that you do? Do you go by price, by your friends' recommendations, or by the latest ratings in *Consumer Reports?* More likely—whether you realize it or not—you are persuaded by advertisers to buy certain products. Even if you peer into the refrigerator during televised ads, close your eyes when you drive past billboards, or use newspaper ads for cat litter, commercials are working on you. In the following selection, Jeffrey Schrank analyzes the claims—often false or misleading—that advertisers use to make us buy.

. . . Students, and many teachers, are notorious believers in their own immunity to advertising. These naive inhabitants of consumerland believe that advertising is childish, dumb, a bunch of lies, and influences only the vast hordes of the less sophisticated. Their own purchases, they think, are made purely on the basis of value and desire, with advertising playing only a minor supporting role. They know about Vance Packard and his "hidden persuaders" and the adman's psychosell and bag of persuasive magic. They are not impressed. 1

Advertisers know better. Although few people admit to being greatly influenced by ads, surveys and sales figures show that a well-designed advertising campaign has dramatic effects. A logical conclusion is that advertising works below the level of conscious awareness and it works even on those who claim immunity to its message. Ads are designed to have an effect while being laughed at, belittled, and all but ignored. 2

A person unaware of advertising's claim on him is precisely the one most vulnerable to the adman's attack. Advertisers delight in an audience that believes ads to be harmless nonsense, for such an audience is rendered defenseless by its belief that there is no attack taking place. The purpose of classroom study of advertising is to raise the level of awareness about the persuasive techniques used in ads. One way to do this is to analyze ads in microscopic detail. Ads can be studied to detect their psychological hooks, how they are used to gauge values and hidden desires of the common man. They can be studied for their use of symbols, color, and imagery. But perhaps the simplest and most direct way to study ads is through an analysis of the language of the advertising claim. 3

The "claim" is the verbal or print part of an ad that makes some claim of superiority for the product being advertised. After studying claims, students should be able to recognize those that are misleading and accept as useful information those that are true. A few of these claims are downright lies, some are honest statements about a truly superior product, but most fit into the category of neither bold lies nor helpful consumer information. They balance on the narrow line between truth and falsehood by a careful choice of words. 4

The reason so many ad claims fall into this category of pseudoinformation is that they are applied to parity products, those in which all or most of the brands available are nearly identical. Since no one superior product exists, advertising is used to create the illusion of superiority. The largest advertising budgets are devoted to parity products such as gasoline, cigarettes, beer, soft drinks, soaps, and various headache and cold remedies. 5

The first rule of parity claims involves the Alice in Wonderland use of the words "better" and "best." In parity claims, "better" means "best" but "best" only means "equal to." If all the brands are identical, they must all be equally good, the legal minds have decided. So "best" means that the product is as good as the other superior products in its category. When Bing Crosby declared Minute Maid Orange Juice "the best there is," he meant it was only as good as the other orange juices you can buy. 6

The word "better," however, as grammarians will be pleased to hear, is legally as well as logically comparative and therefore becomes a clear claim to superiority. Bing could not have said that Minute Maid was "better than any other orange juice." "Better" is a claim to superiority. The only time "better" can be used is when a product does indeed have superiority over other products in its category or when the "better" is used to compare the product with something other than competing brands. An orange juice could make the claim to be "better than a vitamin pill," or even that it was "the better breakfast drink." 7

The second rule of ad claim analysis is simply that if any product is truly superior, the ad will say so very clearly and will offer some kind of convincing evidence of the superiority. If an ad hedges the least about a product's advantage over the competition, you can strongly suspect it is not superior—maybe equal to but not better. You will probably never hear a gasoline company say, "We will give you four miles per gallon more in your car than any other brand." They would love to make such a claim, but it would not be true. Gasoline is a parity product, and, in spite of some very clever and sometimes deceptive ads of a few years ago, no one has yet claimed one brand of gasoline better than—and therefore superior to—any other brand. 8

To create the necessary illusion of superiority, advertisers usually resort to one or more of the following ten basic techniques. Each is common and easy to identify. 9

■ 1 The Weasel Claim

A weasel word is a modifier that practically negates the claim that follows. The expression "weasel word" is aptly named after the egg-eating habits of weasels. A weasel will suck out the inside of an egg, leaving it to appear intact to the casual reader. Upon closer examination, the egg is discovered to be hollow. Words or claims that appear substantial upon first glance but disintegrate into hollow meaninglessness on analysis are weasels. Commonly used weasel words include "helps" (the champion weasel), "like" (used in a comparative sense), "virtual" or "virtually," "acts" or "works," "can be," "up to," "as much as," "refreshes," "comforts," "tackles," "fights," "comes on," "the feel of," "the look of," "looks like," "fortified," "enriched," and "strengthened." 10

Samples of Weasel Claims

"Helps Control dandruff *symptoms* with *regular use"*
The weasels include "helps control," and possibly even "symptoms," and "regular use." The claim is not "stops dandruff.".

"Leaves dishes virtually spotless"
We have seen so many ad claims that we have learned to tune out weasels. You are supposed to think "spotless," rather than "virtually" spotless.

"Only half the price of many color sets"
"Many" is the weasel. The claim is supposed to give the impression that the set is inexpensive.

"Tests confirm one mouthwash best against mouth odor."
"Hot Nestle's cocoa is the very best."
Remember the "best" and "better" routine.

"Listerine fights bad breath."
"Fights," not "stops."

"Lots of things have changed, but Hershey's goodness hasn't."
The claim does not say that Hershey's chocolate hasn't changed.

"Bacos, the crispy garnish that tastes just like its name"

■ 2 The Unfinished Claim

The unfinished claim is one in which the ad claims the product is better, or has   11
more of something but does not finish the comparison.

Samples of Unfinished Claims

"Magnavox gives you more."
More what?

"Anacin: Twice as much of the pain reliever doctors recommend most"
This claim fits in a number of categories; as an unfinished claim it does not say twice as much of what pain reliever.

"Supergloss does it with more color, more shine, more sizzle, more!"
"Coffee-mate gives coffee more body, more flavor."
Also note that "body" and "flavor" are weasels.

"You can be sure if it's Westinghouse."
Sure of what?

"Scott makes it better for you."
Makes what better? How is it better?

"Ford LTD—700 percent quieter"

When the Federal Trade Commission asked Ford to substantiate this last claim, Ford   12
revealed that they meant the inside of the Ford was 700 percent quieter than the outside.

■ 3   The "We're Different and Unique" Claim

This kind of claim states simply that there is nothing else quite like the product   13
advertised. For example, if Schlitz were to add pink food coloring to their beer,
they could say, "There's nothing like new pink Schlitz." The uniqueness claim is
supposed to be interpreted by readers as a claim to superiority.

Samples of "We're Different and Unique" Claims

"There's no other mascara like it."

"Only Doral has this unique filter system."

"Cougar is like nobody else's car."

"Either way, liquid or spray, there's nothing else like it."

"If it doesn't say Goodyear, it can't be Polyglas."
"Polyglas" is a trade name copyrighted by Goodyear. Goodrich or Firestone
could make a tire exactly identical to the Goodyear one and yet couldn't
call it "Polyglas"—a name for fiberglass belts.

"Only Zenith has Chromacolor."
Same as the "Polyglas" gambit. Admiral has Solarcolor and RCA has
Accucolor.

■ 4   The "Water Is Wet" Claim

"Water is wet" claims say something about the product that is true for any brand   14
in that product category (e.g., "Schrank's water is really wet"). The claim is usually
a statement of fact, but not a real advantage over the competition.

Samples of "Water Is Wet" Claims

"Mobil: the Detergent Gasoline"
Any gasoline acts as a cleaning agent.

"Great Lash greatly increases the diameter of every lash."

"Rheingold: the natural beer"
Made from grains and water as are other beers.

"SKIN smells differently on everyone."
As do many perfumes.

■ 5   The "So What" Claim

This is the kind of claim to which the careful reader will react by saying, "So   15
what?" A claim is made that is true but gives no real advantage to the product.
This is similar to the "water is wet" claim except that it claims an advantage that
is not shared by most of the other brands in the product category.

Samples of "So What" Claims

"Geritol has more than twice the iron of ordinary supplements."
  But is it twice as beneficial to the body?

"Campbell's gives you tasty pieces of chicken and not one but two chicken stocks."
  Does the presence of two stocks improve the taste?

"Strong enough for a man but made for a woman"
  This deodorant claim says only that the product is aimed at the female market.

■ 6 The Vague Claim

The vague claim is simply not clear. This category often overlaps with others. The 16
key to the vague claim is the use of words that are colorful but meaningless, as
well as the use of subjective and emotional opinions that defy verification. Most
contain weasels.

Samples of Vague Claims

"Lips have never looked so luscious."
  Can you imagine trying to either prove or disprove such a claim?

"Lipsavers are fun—they taste good, smell good, and feel good."

"Its deep rich lather makes hair feel new again."

"For skin like peaches and cream"

"The end of meatloaf boredom"

"Take a bite and you'll think you're eating on the Champs Elysées."

"Winston tastes good like a cigarette should."

"The perfect little portable for all-around viewing with all the features of higher-priced sets"

"Fleischmann's makes sensible eating delicious."

■ 7 The Endorsement or Testimonial

A celebrity or authority appears in an ad to lend his or her stellar qualities to the 17
product. Sometimes the people will actually claim to use the product, but very
often they don't. There are agencies surviving on providing products with testimonials.

Samples of Endorsements or Testimonials

"Joan Fontaine throws a shot-in-the-dark party and her friends learn a thing or two."

"Darling, have you discovered Masterpiece? The most exciting men I know are smoking it." (Eva Gabor)

"Vega is the best-handling car ever made in the U.S."
   This claim was challenged by the FTC, but GM answered that the claim is a direct quote from *Road and Track* magazine.

■ **8   The Scientific or Statistical Claim**

This kind of ad uses some sort of scientific proof or experiment, very specific   18 numbers, or an impressive-sounding mystery ingredient.

Samples of Scientific or Statistical Claims

"Wonder Bread helps build strong bodies twelve ways."
   Even the weasel "helps" did not prevent the FTC from demanding this ad be withdrawn. But note that the use of the number "twelve" makes the claim far more believable than if it were taken out.

"Easy-Off has 33 percent more cleaning power than another popular brand."
   "Another popular brand" often translates as some other kind of oven cleaner sold somewhere. Also, the claim does not say Easy-Off works 33 percent better.

"Special Morning—33 percent more nutrition"
   Also an unfinished claim.

"Certs contains a sparkling drop of Retsyn."

"ESSO with HTA"

"Sinarest: created by a research scientist who actually gets sinus headaches"

■ **9   The "Compliment the Consumer" Claim**

This kind of claim butters up the consumer by some form of flattery.   19

Samples of "Compliment the Consumer" Claims

"If you do what is right for you, no matter what others do, then RC Cola is right for you."

"We think a cigar smoker is someone special."

"You pride yourself on your good home cooking. . . ."

"The lady has taste."

"You've come a long way, baby."

■ 10 The Rhetorical Question

This technique demands a response from the audience. A question is asked and 20 the viewer or listener is supposed to answer in such a way as to affirm the product's goodness.

Samples of Rhetorical Questions

"Plymouth—isn't that the kind of car America wants?"

"Shouldn't your family be drinking Hawaiian Punch?"

"What do you want most from coffee? That's what you get most from Hills."

"Touch of Sweden: could your hands use a small miracle?"

Teaching someone how to build a log cabin or how to make yogurt is more exciting 21 (or at least "different") than teaching the complexities of processed food deceptions, or the ins and outs of misleading ads from banks and savings and loan associations. But for 205 million Americans learning to stalk wild asparagus is far less important than learning to stalk honest value for hard-earned money in the neon neatness of the grocery store.

■ Reading Comprehension Questions

1. Which of the following would be a good alternative title for this selection?
   a. Studying Ads in the Classroom
   b. Illegal Gimmicks in Ads
   c. Analyzing the Language of Advertising Claims
   d. How Companies Promote Their Products
2. Which sentence best expresses the main idea of the selection?
   a. Parity products are those in which all brands are identical.
   b. Weasel claims in ads have been upheld in court.
   c. Creating the illusion of superiority is the reason that advertisers use vague claims.
   d. Analyzing the language of an advertising claim can reduce an ad's influence on us.
3. The slogan ''the only laxative of its kind'' is an example of
   a. the testimonial.
   b. the scientific claim.
   c. the ''water is wet'' claim.
   d. the ''we're unique'' claim.
4. *True or false?* _____ In an ad, a celebrity must claim that he or she uses the product.

5. The slogan ''L'eggs pantyhose have the feel of silk'' would be an example
   of
   a. a ''so what'' claim.
   b. a weasel claim.
   c. a ''we're unique'' claim.
   d. an unfinished claim.

6. The author implies that
   a. studying ads for their use of symbols and imagery is ineffective.
   b. ads do not work when they are ignored.
   c. many teachers and students do not really know how advertising works.
   d. ads use the values and hidden desires of the upper class.

7. *True or false?* _____ The author implies that *better* is a word that advertisers
   avoid.

8. The author implies that
   a. if a product is unique, then it is superior.
   b. subjective opinions are valid claims of product superiority.
   c. most advertising claims are ineffective.
   d. most people underestimate the influence of advertising on their purchases.

9. The word *parity* in ''parity products, those in which all . . . are nearly
   identical'' (paragraph 5) means
   a. valuable.
   b. economical.
   c. equality.
   d. advertised.

10. The word *stellar* in ''to lend his or her stellar qualities'' (paragraph 16)
    means
    a. honest.
    b. outstanding.
    c. expensive.
    d. inner.

■ **Discussion Questions**

About Content

1. Schrank maintains that a person unaware of advertising's influence ''is
    precisely the one most vulnerable to the adman's attack.'' Why is this true,
    according to Schrank?

2. Why can advertisers say a product is ''best'' but not ''better''?

3. Why are testimonials by celebrities such effective advertising techniques?

About Structure

4. In his introductory section, the author begins by stating how sure teachers and students are that advertising has no effect on them. Then he states, ''Advertisers know better.'' What method of introduction is Schrank using?
   a. Beginning with an opposite
   b. Broad to narrow
   c. Anecdote

5. The author divides the selection into ten parts, each one dealing with a particular kind of advertising claim. What, according to the author, are all these claims supposed to create? Where is this stated?

About Style and Tone

6. For what kind of audience do you think this selection was written?
   a. General public
   b. Teachers and students
   c. Advertisers
   Give reasons for your answer.

7. Schrank uses the term *pseudoinformation* (meaning ''false information'') in paragraph 5 to show his negative feelings about advertising claims. What other words and phrases does he use that reveal his negative attitude? Find three and list them below:

   _____   _____   _____

■ Writing Assignments

Assignment 1

Pick three ads currently used on television or in print. Show that each ad uses one or more of the advertising claims discussed in Schrank's article. Be sure that you are specific about product names, what the ad looks like, the kinds of characters in the ad, and so on. Don't forget that all your specific details concerning the ad should back up your point that the ad uses a certain kind of claim (or claims) to sell a product.

Assignment 2

Imagine that you work for an ad agency and have been asked to come up with at least three possible campaigns for a new product (for example, a kind of car, perfume, detergent, jeans, beer, toothpaste, deodorant, or appliance). Write an essay in which you describe three different claims that might be made for the product and how these claims could convince the public to buy.

Assignment 3

Do some informal "market research" on why people buy the products they do. Begin by asking at least ten people why they bought a particular brand-name item. You might question them about something they're wearing (designer jeans, for example). Or you might ask them what toothpaste they use, what car they drive, what pain reliever they take, or what chicken they eat—or ask about any other product people use. Take notes on the reasons people give for their purchases.

Then write an essay with the thesis, "On the basis of my research, _____, _____, and _____ influence people to buy particular products." Fill in the blanks with three reasons that were the ones mentioned most often by the people you interviewed. Develop your supporting paragraphs with examples drawn from the interviews; use quotations from the people you spoke with as part of your support.

Five Parenting Styles

Mary Ann Lamanna and Agnes Reidmann

Parenting has been called "the biggest on-the-job training program ever." Parents have to raise children without much guidance or advance instruction, and sometimes this results in a "parenting style" that causes problems. In the following textbook selection, the authors discuss five parenting styles. See if you can identify your parents—or yourself—in one of the classifications.

Considering the lack of consensus about how to raise children today, it may seem 1 difficult to single out styles of parenting. From one point of view there are as many parenting styles as there are parents. . . . Yet certain elements in relating to children can be broadly classified. One helpful grouping is provided in E. E. LeMasters's listing of five parenting styles: the martyr, the pal, the police officer, the teacher-counselor, and the athletic coach. . . . We will discuss each of these.

The Parent as Martyr. Martyring parents believe "I would do anything for 2 my child." . . . Some common examples of martyring are parents who habitually wait on their children or pick up after them; parents who nag children rather than letting them remember things for themselves; parents who buy virtually anything the child asks for; and parents who always do what the children want to do.

This parenting style presents some problems. First, the goals the martyring parent sets are impossible to carry out, and so the parent must always feel guilty. Also, . . . martyring tends to be reciprocated by manipulating. In addition, it is useful to ask if persons who consistently deny their own needs can enjoy the role of parenting and if closeness between parent and child is possible under these conditions.

The Parent as Pal. Some modern parents, mainly those of older children and adolescents, feel that they should be pals to their children. They adopt a **laissez-faire** policy, *letting their children set their own goals, rules, and limits,* with little or no guidance from parents. . . . According to LeMasters, "pal" parents apparently believe that they can avoid the conflict caused by the generation gap in this way.

Pal parenting is unrealistic. For one thing, parents in our society *are* responsible for guiding their children's development. Children deserve to benefit from the greater knowledge and experience of their parents, and at all ages they need some rules and limits, although these change as children grow older. Much research points to the conclusion that laissez-faire parenting is related to juvenile delinquency, heavy drug use, and runaway behavior in children. . . .

LeMasters points out that there are also relationship risks in the pal-parent model. If things don't go well, parents may want to retreat to a more formal, authoritarian style of parenting. But once they've established a buddy relationship, it is difficult to regain authority. . . .

The Parent as Police Officer. The police officer (or drill sergeant) model is just the opposite of the pal. These parents make sure the child obeys all the rules at all times, and they punish their children for even minor offenses. Being a police officer doesn't work very well today, however, and **autocratic discipline,** *which places the entire power of determining rules and limits in the parents' hands*—like laissez-faire parenting—has been associated with juvenile delinquency, drug use, and runaway teen-agers. . . .

There are several reasons for this. First, Americans have tended to resist anything that smacks of tyranny ever since the days of the Boston Tea Party. Hence, children are socialized to demand a share of independence at an early age.

A second reason why policing children doesn't work well today is that rapid social change gives the old and the young different values and points of view and even different knowledge. In our complex culture, youth learn attitudes from specialized professionals, such as teachers and school counselors, who often "widen the intellectual gap between parent and child." . . . For example, many young people today may advocate Judy Blume's novel for teens, *Forever* (1975), which is explicit about and accepting of premarital sex. Many parents, however, disapprove of the book.

A third reason why the police officer role doesn't work is that children, who find support from their adolescent peers, will eventually confront and challenge their parents. LeMasters points out that the adolescent peer group is "a formidable opponent" to any cop who insists on strict allegiance to autocratic authority. . . .

A fourth reason is that autocratic policing just isn't very effective in molding   11
children's values. One study of 451 college freshmen and sophomores at a large
western university found that adolescents were far more likely to be influenced by
their parents' referent or expert power . . . than by coercive or legitimate power.
The key was respect and a close relationship; habitual punishment or the "policing"
of adolescents were far less effective modes of socialization. . . .

The Parent as Teacher-Counselor. The parent as teacher-counselor acts in   12
accord with the **developmental model of child rearing,** *in which the child is viewed
as an extremely plastic organism with virtually unlimited potential for growth and
development.* The limits to this rich potential are seen as encompassed in the limits
of the parent to tap and encourage it. . . . This model conceptualizes the parent(s)
as almost omnipotent in guiding children's development. . . . If they do the right
things at the right time, their children will more than likely be happy, intelligent,
and successful.

Particularly during the 1960s and 1970s, authorities have stressed the ability of   13
parents to influence their children's intellectual growth. Psychologist J. McVicker
Hunt, for example, stated that he believes "you could raise a middle-class child's
I.Q. by twenty points with what we know about child-rearing." . . .

The teacher-counselor approach has many fine features, and children do benefit   14
from environmental stimulation. Yet this parenting style also poses problems. First,
it puts the needs of the child above the parents' needs. It may be unrealistic for
most parents to always be there, ready to stimulate the child's intellect or to act as
a sounding board. Also, parents who respond as if each of their child's discoveries
is wonderful may give the child the mistaken impression that he or she is the center
of everyone's universe. . . .

A second difficulty is that this approach expects parents to be experts—an   15
expectation that can easily produce guilt. Parents can never learn all that psychologists, sociologists, and specialized educators know. Yet if anything goes wrong,
teacher-counselor parents are likely to feel they have only themselves to blame.
. . .

Finally, contemporary research suggests more and more that this view greatly   16
exaggerates the power of the parent and the passivity of children. Children also
have inherited intellectual capacities and needs. Recent observers point instead to
an **interactive perspective,** *which regards the influence between parent and child
as mutual and reciprocal,* not just a "one-way street." . . .

The "athletic coach" model proceeds from this perspective.   17

The Parent as Athletic Coach. Athletic-coach parenting incorporates aspects   18
of the developmental point of view. The coach (parent) is expected to have sufficient
ability and knowledge of the game (life) and to be prepared and confident to lead
players (children) to do their best and, it is hoped, to succeed.

This parenting style recognizes that parents, like coaches, have their own   19
personalities and needs. They establish team rules, or *house rules* (and this can be
done somewhat democratically with help from the players), and teach these rules

to their children. They enforce the appropriate penalties when rules are broken, but policing is not their primary concern. Children, like team members, must be willing to accept discipline and, at least sometimes, to subordinate their own interests to the needs of the family team.

Coaching parents encourage their children to practice and to work hard to develop their own talents. But they realize that they can not play the game for their players. LeMasters says: 20

> The coach's position here is quite analogous to that of parents; once the game has begun it is up to the players to win or lose it. . . .[He] faces the same prospect as parents of sitting on the sidelines and watching players make mistakes that may prove disastrous.

LeMasters also points out that coaches can put uncooperative players off the team or even quit, but no such option is available to parents. 21

■ Reading Comprehension Questions

1. Which of the following would be a good alternative title for this selection?
   a. Mistakes Parents Make
   b. How to Be a Good Parent
   c. Kinds of Parents
   d. Parents as Coaches

2. Which sentence best expresses the main idea of the selection?
   a. There are as many parenting styles as there are parents.
   b. Styles of parenting can be broadly classified into five groups.
   c. The "police officer" parenting approach can lead to delinquency.
   d. The influence between parent and child must be mutual.

3. Martyr parents
   a. act as buddies to their children.
   b. buy anything the child asks for.
   c. insist on strict obedience.
   d. establish house rules.

4. *True or false?* _____ The athletic-coach approach regards the parent-child relationship as a one-way street.

5. Teacher-counselor parents
   a. often blame themselves if something goes wrong.
   b. use autocratic discipline.
   c. adopt a laissez-faire policy.
   d. let their children set their own limits.

6. The authors imply that
    a.   the teacher-counselor style of parenting is most effective.
    b.   the athletic coach style of parenting is most effective.
    c.   ''pal'' parents have solved the problem of the generation gap.
    d.   parents should set all the rules for the household.

7. *True or false?* _____ Sometimes children learn different values at school.

8. We might conclude from this selection that
    a.   parenting is a complex and difficult role.
    b.   the best parents are unsophisticated ones.
    c.   different parenting styles are appropriate at different stages of growth.
    d.   the authors favor the parent as teacher-counselor.

9. The word *plastic* in ''an extremely plastic organism'' (paragraph 12) means
    a.   sickly.
    b.   stiff.
    c.   transparent.
    d.   pliable.

10. The word *autocratic* in ''autocratic discipline, which places the entire power . . . in the parents' hands'' (paragraph 7) means
    a.   unfocused.
    b.   independent.
    c.   dictatorial.
    d.   generous.

■ Discussion Questions

About Content

1.   What reasons do the authors give for saying that parents cannot be pals to their children? Do you agree?
2.   Which parenting style do you think the authors prefer? How can you tell?
3.   Why is it difficult for parents to act as teacher-counselors? Give examples from your own experience.

About Structure

4.   What method of development is used in the section ''The Parent as Police Officer''?
    a.   Reasons
    b.   Contrast
    c.   Narrative

5. Analyze the third paragraph of ''The Parent as Teacher-Counselor.'' Where is the topic sentence? What kind of support is given for this topic sentence?

6. What are three transition words used in paragraph 3?

    _____   _____   _____

7. Find at least four terms that are defined in the selection. Write the terms in the spaces below:

    _____   _____

    _____   _____

About Style and Tone

8. Below are aids to understanding often used in textbooks. Which *three* appear in this selection?
    a. Preview and summary
    b. Charts
    c. Heads and subheads
    d. Definitions and examples
    e. Boldface and italic type
    f. Graphs

■ Writing Assignments

Assignment 1

Write a description of ''Three Childing Styles.'' In other words, write an essay similar to ''Five Parenting Styles'' in which you discuss three different behavior patterns of being a child in a family. Choose from the following behavior patterns or others that may occur to you. The child as:

Prima donna or spoiled brat

Miniature adult

Helpless baby

''Daddy's girl'' or ''mama's boy''

Tough kid

Rebel

Showoff

Carbon copy of parent

Little angel

In separate supporting paragraphs, describe in detail how each of your three types behaves.

Assignment 2

Write an essay that uses the following thesis statement:

> My parents were (tried to be) _____.
>
> Fill in the blank with one of the five parenting styles described in the article (or with another one that you think up). Then present three different incidents that show your parents acting according to that style. (You may, of course, choose to write about only one parent.)

Assignment 3

Write an essay in which you argue that ''a _____ (name a particular parenting style described in the selection) is the ideal parent.'' Develop the essay by giving three reasons why such parents are best.

Feel free to use any of the styles the authors describe; you could, for example, come up with a convincing argument that ''police officer'' parents are best, based on your own experience or reasoning.

CONFRONTING PROBLEMS

How to Make It in College, Now That You're Here

Brian O'Keeney

The author of this selection presents a compact guide to being a successful student. He will show you how to pass tests, how to avoid becoming a student zombie, how to find time to fit in everything you want to do, and how to deal with personal problems while keeping up with your studies. These and other helpful tips have been culled from the author's own experience and his candid interviews with fellow students.

Today is your first day on campus. You were a high school senior three months 1 ago. Or maybe you've been at home with your children for the last ten years. Or maybe you work full time and you're coming to school to start the process that leads to a better job. Whatever your background is, you're probably not too concerned today with staying in college. After all, you just got over the hurdle (and the paperwork) of applying to this place and organizing your life so that you could attend. And today, you're confused and tired. Everything is a hassle, from finding the classrooms to standing in line at the bookstore. But read my advice anyway. And if you don't read it today, clip and save this article. You might want to look at it a little further down the road.

By the way, if this isn't your very first day, don't skip this article. Maybe you **2**
haven't been doing as well in your studies as you'd hoped. Or perhaps you've had
problems juggling your work schedule, your class schedule, and your social life.
If so, read on. You're about to get the inside story on making it in college. On the
basis of my own experience as a final-year student, and on dozens of interviews
with successful students, I've worked out a no-fail system for coping with college.
These are the inside tips every student needs to do well in school. I've put myself
in your place, and I'm going to answer the questions that will cross (or have already
crossed) your mind during your stay here.

■ What's the Secret of Getting Good Grades?

It all comes down to getting those grades, doesn't it? After all, you came here for **3**
some reason, and you're going to need passing grades to get the credits or degree
you want. Many of us never did much studying in high school; most of the learning
we did took place in the classroom. College, however, is a lot different. You're
really on your own when it comes to passing courses. In fact, sometimes you'll
feel as if nobody cares if you make it or not. Therefore, you've got to figure out a
study system that gets results. Sooner or later, you'll be alone with those books.
After that, you'll be sitting in a classroom with an exam sheet on your desk. Whether
you stare at that exam with a queasy stomach or whip through it fairly confidently
depends on your study techniques. Most of the successful students I talked to agreed
that the following eight study tips deliver solid results.

1   Set Up a Study Place. Those students you see "studying" in the cafeteria **4**
or game room aren't learning much. You just can't learn when you're distracted
by people and noise. Even the library can be a bad place to study if you constantly
find yourself watching the clouds outside or the students walking through the stacks.
It takes guts to sit, alone, in a quiet place in order to study. But you have to do it.
Find a room at home or a spot in the library that's relatively quiet—and boring.
When you sit there, you won't have much to do except study.

2   Get into a Study Frame of Mind. When you sit down, do it with the **5**
attitude that you're going to get this studying done. You're not going to doodle in
your notebook or make a list for the supermarket. Decide that you're going to study
and learn *now,* so that you can move on to more interesting things as soon as
possible.

3   Give Yourself Rewards. If you sweat out a block of study time, and do **6**
a good job on it, treat yourself. You deserve it. You can "psych" yourself up for
studying by promising to reward yourself afterwards. A present for yourself can be
anything from a favorite TV show to a relaxing bath to a dish of double chocolate
ice cream.

4   Skim the Textbook First. Lots of students sit down with an assignment   7
like "read chapter five, pages 125–150" and do just that. They turn to page 125
and start to read. After a while, they find that they have no idea what they just
read. For the last ten minutes, they've been thinking about their five-year-old or
what they're going to eat for dinner. Eventually, they plod through all the pages but
don't remember much afterwards.

In order to prevent this problem, skim the textbook chapter first. This means: 8
look at the title, the subtitles, the headings, the pictures, the first and last paragraphs.
Try to find out what the person who wrote the book had in mind when he or she
organized the chapter. What was important enough to set off as a title or in bold
type? After skimming, you should be able to explain to yourself what the main
points of the chapter are. Unless you're the kind of person who would step into an
empty elevator shaft without looking first, you'll soon discover the value of skimming.

5   Take Notes on What You're Studying. This sounds like a hassle, but it   9
works. Go back over the material after you've read it, and jot down key words and
phrases in the margins. When you review the chapter for a test, you'll have handy
little things like "definition of rationalization" or "example of assimilation" in the
margins. If the material is especially tough, organize a separate sheet of notes.
Write down definitions, examples, lists, and main ideas. The idea is to have a single
sheet that boils the entire chapter down to a digestible lump.

6   Review after You've Read and Taken Notes. Some people swear that   10
talking to yourself works. Tell yourself about the most important points in the
chapter. Once you've said them out loud, they seem to stick better in your mind.
If you can't talk to yourself about the material after reading it, that's a sure sign you
don't really know it.

7   Give Up. This may sound contradictory, but give up when you've had   11
enough. You should try to make it through at least an hour, though. Ten minutes
here and there are useless. When your head starts to pound and your eyes develop
spidery red lines, quit. You won't do much learning when you're exhausted.

8   Take a College Skills Course If You Need It. Don't hesitate or feel   12
embarrassed about enrolling in a study skills course. Many students say they wouldn't
have made it without one.

■ How Can I Keep Up with All My Responsibilities without Going Crazy?

You've got a class schedule. You're supposed to study. You've got a family. You've   13
got a husband, wife, boyfriend, girlfriend, child. You've got a job. How are you
possibly going to cover all the bases in your life and maintain your sanity? This is
one of the toughest problems students face. Even if they start the semester with the

best of intentions, they eventually find themselves tearing their hair out trying to do everything they're supposed to do. Believe it or not, though, it is possible to meet all your responsibilities. And you don't have to turn into a hermit or give up your loved ones to do it.

The secret here is to organize your time. But don't just sit around half the 14
semester planning to get everything together soon. Before you know it, you'll be confronted with midterms, papers, family, and work all at once. Don't let yourself reach that breaking point. Instead, try these three tactics.

1 Monthly Calendar. Get one of those calendars with big blocks around 15
the dates. Give yourself an overview of the whole term by marking down the due dates for papers and projects. Circle test and exam days. This way those days don't sneak up on you unexpectedly.

2 Study Schedule. Sit down during the first few days of this semester and 16
make up a sheet listing the days and hours of the week. Fill in your work and class hours first. Then try to block out some study hours. It's better to study a little every day than to create a huge once-or-twice-a-week marathon session. Schedule study hours for your hardest classes for the times when you feel most energetic. For example, I battled my tax law textbook in the mornings; when I looked at it after 7:00 P. M., I may as well have been reading Chinese. The usual proportion, by the way, is one hour of study time for every class hour.

In case you're one of those people who get carried away, remember to leave 17
blocks of free time, too. You won't be any good to yourself or anyone else if you don't relax and pack in the studying once in a while.

3 A "To-Do" List. This is the secret that single-handedly got me through 18
college. Once a week (or every day if you want to), write a list of what you have to do. Write down everything from "write English paper" to "buy cold cuts for lunches." The best thing about a "to do" list is that it seems to tame all those stray "I have to" thoughts that nag at your mind. Just making the list seems to make the tasks "doable." After you finish something on the list, cross it off. Don't be compulsive about finishing everything; you're not Superman or Wonder Woman. Get the important things done first. The secondary things you don't finish can simply be moved to your next "to do" list.

■ **What Can I Do If Personal Problems Get in the Way of My Studies?**

One student, Roger, told me this story: 19

> Everything was going OK for me until the middle of the spring semester. I went through a terrible time when I broke up with my girlfriend and started seeing her best friend. I was trying to deal with my ex-girlfriend's hurt and anger, my new girlfriend's guilt, and my own worries and anxieties at the same time. In addition

to this, my mother was sick and on a medication that made her really irritable. I hated to go home because the atmosphere was so uncomfortable. Soon, I started missing classes because I couldn't deal with the academic pressures as well as my own personal problems. It seemed easier to hang around my girlfriend's apartment than to face all my problems at home and at school.

Another student, Marian, told me: 20

I'd been married for eight years and the relationship wasn't going too well. I saw the handwriting on the wall, and I decided to prepare for the future. I enrolled in college, because I knew I'd need a decent job to support myself. Well, my husband had a fit because I was going to school. We were arguing a lot anyway, and he made it almost impossible for me to study at home. I think he was angry and almost jealous because I was drawing away from him. It got so bad that I thought about quitting college for a while. I wasn't getting any support at home and it was just too hard to go on.

Personal troubles like these are overwhelming when you're going through them.   21
School seems like the least important thing in your life. The two students above are perfect examples of this. But if you think about it, quitting or failing school would be the worst thing for these two students. Roger's problems, at least with his girlfriends, would simmer down eventually, and then he'd regret having left school. Marian had to finish college if she wanted to be able to live independently. Sometimes, you've just got to hang tough.

But what do you do while you're trying to live through a lousy time? First of   22
all, do something difficult. Ask yourself, honestly, if you're exaggerating small problems as an excuse to avoid classes and studying. It takes strength to admit this, but there's no sense in kidding yourself. If your problems are serious, and real, try to make some human contacts at school. Lots of students hide inside a miserable shell made of their own troubles and feel isolated and lonely. Believe me, there are plenty of students with problems. Not everyone is getting A's and having a fabulous social and home life at the same time. As you go through the term, you'll pick up some vibrations about the students in your classes. Perhaps someone strikes you as a compatible person. Why not speak to that person after class? Share a cup of coffee in the cafeteria or walk to the parking lot together. You're not looking for a best friend or the love of your life. You just want to build a little network of support for yourself. Sharing your difficulties, questions, and complaints with a friendly person on campus can make a world of difference in how you feel.

Finally, if your problems are overwhelming, get some professional help. Why   23
do you think colleges spend countless dollars on counseling departments and campus psychiatric services? More than ever, students all over the country are taking advantage of the help offered by support groups and therapy sessions. There's no shame attached to asking for help, either; in fact, almost 40 percent of college students (according to one survey) will use counseling services during their time in school. Just walk into a student center or counseling office and ask for an appointment. You wouldn't think twice about asking a dentist to help you get rid of your toothache. Counselors are paid—and want—to help you with your problems.

■ Why Do Some People Make It and Some Drop Out?

Anyone who spends at least one semester in college notices that some students   24
give up on their classes. The person who sits behind you in accounting, for example,
begins to miss a lot of class meetings and eventually vanishes. Or another student
comes to class without the assignment, doodles in his notebook during the lecture,
and leaves during the break. What's the difference between students like this and
the ones who succeed in school? My survey may be nonscientific, but everyone I
asked said the same thing: attitude. A positive attitude is the key to everything
else—good study habits, smart time scheduling, and coping with personal difficulties.

What does "a positive attitude" mean? Well, for one thing, it means avoiding   25
the zombie syndrome. It means not only showing up for your classes, but also doing
something while you're there. Really listen. Take notes. Ask a question if you want
to. Don't just walk into a class, put your mind in neutral, and drift away to never-
never land.

Having a positive attitude goes deeper than this, though. It means being mature   26
about college as an institution. Too many students approach college classes like
six-year-olds who expect first grade to be as much fun as *Sesame Street*. First grade,
as we all know, isn't as much fun as *Sesame Street*. And college classes can
sometimes be downright dull and boring. If you let a boring class discourage you
so much that you want to leave school, you'll lose in the long run. Look at your
priorities. You want a degree, or a certificate, or a career. If you have to, you can
make it through a less-than-interesting class in order to achieve what you want.
Get whatever you can out of every class. But if you simply can't stand a certain
class, be determined to fulfill its requirements and be done with it once and for all.

After the initial high of starting school, you have to settle in for the long haul.   27
If you follow the advice here, you'll be prepared to face the academic crunch.
You'll also live through the semester without giving up your family, your job, or
Monday Night Football. Finally, going to college can be an exciting time. You do
learn. And when you learn things, the world becomes a more interesting place.

■ Reading Comprehension Questions

1. Which of the following would be a good alternative title for this selection?
    a. Your First Day on Campus
    b. Coping with College
    c. How to Budget Your Time
    d. The Benefits of College Skills Courses

2. Which sentence expresses the main idea of the selection?
    a. In high school, most of us did little homework.
    b. You should give yourself rewards for studying well.
    c. Sometimes personal problems interfere with studying.
    d. You can succeed in college by following certain guide'

3. According to the author, "making it" in college means
   a. studying whenever you have any free time.
   b. getting a degree by barely passing your courses.
   c. quitting school until you solve your personal problems.
   d. getting good grades without making your life miserable.

4. If your personal problems seem overwhelming, you should
   a. drop out for a while.
   b. try to ignore them.
   c. tell another student.
   d. seek professional help.

5. Which of the following is *not* described by the author as a means of time control?
   a. Monthly calendar
   b. To-do list
   c. Study schedule
   d. Flexible job hours

6. We might infer that the author
   a. is a writer for the school newspaper.
   b. is president of his class.
   c. has taken a study skills course.
   d. was not a successful student in his first year of college.

7. From the selection we can conclude that
   a. college textbooks are very expensive.
   b. it is a good practice to write notes in your textbook.
   c. taking notes on your reading takes too much time.
   d. a student should never mark up an expensive textbook.

8. The author implies that
   a. fewer people than before are attending college.
   b. most students think that college is easy.
   c. most students dislike college.
   d. coping with college is difficult.

9. The word *queasy* in "with a queasy stomach" (paragraph 3) means
   a. intelligent.
   b. healthy.
   c. full.
   d. nervous.

10. The word *tactics* in "try these three tactics" (paragraph 14) means
    a. proofs.
    b. problems.
    c. methods.
    d. questions.

■ Discussion Questions

About Content

1. What pitfalls does O'Keeney think are waiting for students just starting college? Are there other pitfalls not mentioned in the article?
2. What is the secret that the author says got him through college? What do you think is the most helpful or important suggestion the author makes in the selection?
3. Do you agree with the author that Roger and Marian should stay in school? Are there any situations where it would be better for students to quit school or leave temporarily?

About Structure

4. What is the thesis of the selection? Write here the number of the paragraph in which it is stated: _____
5. Why does the article begin with the first day on campus?
6. What method of introduction does the author use in the section on personal problems (starting on page 427)? What is the value of using this method?

About Style and Tone

7. This essay is obviously written for college students. Can you guess where an essay like this one would appear? (*Hint:* Reread the first paragraph.)

■ Writing Assignments

Assignment 1

Write a process essay similar to the one you've just read that explains how to succeed in some other field—for example, a job, a sport, marriage, child rearing. First, brainstorm the three or four problem areas a newcomer to this experience might encounter. Then jot down some helpful hints and techniques for overcoming these problems under each area you have listed. For example, a process paper on "How to Succeed as a Waitress" might describe the following problem areas in this kind of job:

Developing a good memory
Learning to do tasks quickly
Coping with troublesome customers

Each supporting paragraph in this particular paper would discuss specific techniques for dealing with these problems. Be sure that the advice you give is detailed and specific enough to really help a person in such a situation.

You may find it helpful to look over the process essays on pages 138–141.

Assignment 2

Write a letter to Roger or Marian advising him or her on how to deal with the personal problem mentioned in the article. You could recommend any or all of the following:

Face the problem realistically. (By doing what?)

Make other contacts at school. (How? Where?)

See a counselor. (Where? What should this person be told?)

Realize that the problem is not so serious. (Why not?)

Ignore the problem. (How? By doing what instead?)

In your introductory paragraph, explain why you are writing the letter. Include a thesis statement that says what plan of action you are recommending. Then, in the rest of the paper, explain the plan of action (or plans of action) in detail.

Assignment 3

Write an essay contrasting college *as you thought it would be* with college *as it is*. You can organize the essay by focusing on three specific things that are different from what you expected. Or you can cover three areas of difference. For instance, you may decide to contrast your expectations of (1) a college dorm room, (2) your roommate, and (3) dining hall food with reality. Or, you could contrast your expectations of (1) fellow students, (2) college professors, and (3) college courses with reality.

Refer to the section on comparison and contrast essays in this book (pages 147–163) to review point-by-point and one-side-at-a-time methods of development. Be sure to make an outline of your essay before you begin to write.

Drugs and Alcohol:
A Continuing Threat to Health

George Gallup, Jr.

The destructive effects of drugs and alcohol confront us every day. We hear of a celebrity—an entertainer, perhaps, or an athlete—who has been arrested or has checked into a treatment center. Or we read in our local paper about another drunken driving accident or a raid where a variety of drugs have been seized. At such times we question whether enough is being done in our country to fight this problem. In this selection, the pollster George Gallup, Jr., gives and supports his answer, which is based on the findings of recent Gallup polls.

1   A dozen women gathered in the dressing room of a fashionable health club in a great American metropolis after their Saturday morning exercise class. Exhilarated after their brisk workout, they exuded a general sense of well-being and offered each other mutual encouragement about the physical progress they were making.

2   "You're getting much stronger, Sue," one said. "Your ring work was really good today!"

3   "Who's going to lunch?" another asked.

4   "Me! The usual place?"

5   The "usual place" was a diet-oriented health food shop where the menu included salads and low-calorie breads.

6   "I can't make it today," one of the other women responded. "I have to leave early for the weekend—a date with a guy I just met. He's managed to get some really good stuff, and we're going to turn on until Sunday night."

7   The "good stuff" was cocaine, and in this actual conversation, the irony of American attitudes toward physical health appears in stark relief. We desperately want trim, strong, healthy bodies, and we're willing to agonize through whatever exercise and diet programs are deemed necessary to reach that goal. Yet we're making little if any headway in conquering the destructive habits that seriously threaten our health. I'm referring in particular to our addiction to drugs and alcohol.

■ Self-Improvement or Self-Abuse?

8   A concern about these contradictory trends emerges from the answers of the national opinion leaders whom we polled. Nearly 30 percent of their responses indicate a belief that drugs and alcohol addiction are among the most serious problems in the

United States today. These opinion leaders believe that the greater emphasis being placed on health—as shown in the above health-club illustration—is one of the most encouraging trends in our society. They're sufficiently optimistic about the future that a significantly lower number—16 percent—feel that alcohol and drugs will be a major problem in the year 2000. Yet for the situation to improve, something must be done.

For example, take the life-styles of our typical teenagers. The bright side of the 9 picture they present us is that three-fourths of American teenagers, or 74 percent of those questioned in a recent poll, claim that they do something every day to keep physically fit. That means something *in addition to* exercise in their gym class at school. Also, 74 percent of all our teenagers are concerned about their weight, with 24 percent wanting to gain and 50 percent wanting to lose. The majority are also concerned enough to *do* something to reach their ideal weight through actual exercise or diet.

But despite this concern with physical fitness, the teenagers told us in a 1980 10 survey that pot smoking was the number one student problem. Moreover, the percentage of teenagers who thought that the use of marijuana among their peers was a serious problem increased from 26 percent in 1978 to 38 percent by 1980. Also, teenagers viewed with increasing alarm the use of alcohol and hard drugs in their ranks.

But young people are by no means the only offenders. Marijuana is the illegal 11 drug most commonly used by people of all ages, according to the 1982 National Household Survey on Drug Abuse. The use of marijuana has become so widespread that law enforcement agencies and representatives have been applying pressure to ease the legal punishments. Some states now have laws that make it illegal to possess or sell marijuana only in large amounts. Also, many "establishment" groups have come out for the "decriminalization" of marijuana, including the American Bar Association, the National Education Association, the National Council of Churches, and the governing board of the American Medical Association. One of their basic arguments is that smoking marijuana is a victimless crime, in that there is no danger to third parties. Also, many advocates of decriminalization say there's no clear-cut evidence showing that marijuana is harmful to the health.

But is this really true? A major study, sponsored by the National Academy of 12 Sciences' Institute of Medicine, states that marijuana "has a broad range of psychological and biological effects, some of which, at least under certain conditions, are harmful to human health."

In the same cautionary tone, Dr. Arnold Relman, editor of the prestigious *New* 13 *England Journal of Medicine,* has warned, "What little we know for certain about the effects of marijuana on human health—and all that we have reason to suspect— justifies serious national concern" (*The Wall Street Journal,* March 1, 1982).

Of course, the problems with marijuana are just the tip of the iceberg. Many 14 drug-abuse experts are raising their voices against the growing social tolerance of all sorts of drugs.

"Society is giving all of us a double message," says Dr. Robert E. Gould, 15
professor of psychiatry and associate director of the Family Life Division of New
York Medical College. "On the one hand, we are told, 'Don't take illegal drugs.'
At the same time, this is a drug-taking culture and a drug-encouraging culture.
Look in anyone's medicine chest and see how many drugs Americans rely on.
Drug-taking is often portrayed in the media as glamorous and chic. And the message
the commercials give is: If you have a problem, take a pill" (*The New York Times,*
March 21 and 22, 1983).

One of our main problems is that "the selection in the delicatessen of drugs is 16
much greater than it's ever been," according to Dr. M. Duncan Stanton, the director
of research for the Addicts and Families Program at the University of Pennsylvania
School of Medicine. Perhaps the biggest threat to Americans today is that we have
access to many intoxicants and drugs from many societies—and we don't know
how to control them. "This can be very dangerous to those who are at risk: the
young, the psychologically disturbed, and the disadvantaged," warns Dr. Robert
B. Millman, director of the Alcohol and Drug Abuse Service at the Payne Whitney
Psychiatric Clinic in New York.

The trends in drug abuse are more depressing than encouraging. In 1962 less 17
than 4 percent of the population had ever used an illegal drug. But two decades
later, 33 percent of Americans age twelve and older reported having used marijuana,
hallucinogens, cocaine, heroin, or psychotherapeutic drugs for nonmedical purposes (*The New York Times,* March 21, 1983).

One bright note in the statistics is that the number of people under the age of 18
twenty-six who have used an illegal drug has dropped significantly. But at the same
time, the number of those above twenty-six who have used drugs has risen.

■ The Other Drug

Narcotics abuse is only half of the threat to our health that we will face during the 19
next two decades. The other big challenge to our physical well-being is alcohol,
and that may prove to be an ever greater source of destruction.

As they turn away from the drug culture, some young people are turning to 20
liquor. Alcohol is used more widely than any other drug and has almost complete
social acceptance, in contrast to the shady reputation that accompanies most of
the others. The number of young people who have acquired this habit already
suggests that alcohol will continue to be a problem well into the future.

As might be expected, parents have a strong influence over whether or not 21
their children drink, according to our Gallup Youth Polls. Teenagers whose parents
drink are almost twice as likely to drink themselves, compared with those youngsters
whose parents are nondrinkers. Moreover, if a youngster's parents are drinkers, that
fact has an important bearing on whether alcohol is served at the teen's parties. In
29 percent of homes where parents drink, alcoholic beverages are likely to be
served, while this is true in the homes of only 13 percent of teens whose parents
are abstainers.

Predictably, the age of the teenager makes a big difference in his or her drinking 22
habits. Alcoholic beverages are served at 34 percent of parties involving those who
are sixteen to eighteen years old, whereas the figure for younger teens, thirteen to
fifteen years old, is 10 percent. Another important factor is the type of alcoholic
beverage served. Our surveys have found beer to be the most popular: It's served
at almost nine out of ten teen parties. Also, wine or hard liquor may be offered as
well as beer at 25 percent of the teen parties that are held in homes where alcoholic
beverages are served.

So it's apparent that drinking has become socially acceptable among even the 23
youngest members of our society. But is there really any reason to get worried about
this trend? Excessive use of alcohol, of course, can have a devastating effect on
the body, but what's the problem with moderate social drinking?

The biggest fear is that moderate social drinking will move gradually into heavy 24
drinking for increasing numbers of people. When this occurs, the heavy drinkers
can expect serious physical debilitation:

- The body's ability to use vitamins and produce disease-fighting white blood
  cells, which counter the effects of hostile bacteria, is impaired.
- As the liver becomes fatty, there's at least a one-in-ten chance of developing
  cirrhosis.
- Chronic indigestion may result from a damaged liver.
- Gastritis, caused by irritation of the sensitive linings of the stomach and small
  intestine, may appear.
- Heavy drinkers may experience damage to the central nervous system and also
  a hormonal imbalance that can cause impotence in males.

But perhaps the most serious physical problems that alcohol causes occur on 25
the nation's highways. It's been estimated that about 25,000 lives are lost each year
in alcohol-related accidents, and 650,000 more people are seriously injured in
such crashes. Moreover, alcohol is a factor in about 55 percent of all fatal
automobile accidents. To counter this trend, citizens' action groups such as MADD
(Mothers Against Drunk Drivers) in California and RID (Remove Intoxicated Drivers)
in New York have worked for stiffer penalties for driving while intoxicated.

Alcohol abuse has also done enormous damage to our family relationships. 26
Nearly one-fourth of Americans whom we've polled say that liquor has actually
been a cause of trouble in their homes; and one person in seven says that alcohol
abuse currently ranks as one of the top three problems facing his or her family.

With the continued problems with teenaged drinking and the general social 27
acceptability of this practice among all age groups, it's unlikely that alcohol abuse
will disappear in the next twenty years.

Yet our opinion leaders are surprisingly optimistic. Only 4 percent think that 28
alcoholism will be a major problem in the year 2000. Their optimism finds support
in the growing number of companies that have established programs and counseling
for employees who have trouble controlling their drinking. Also, the increased

public awareness of the problems connected with consuming alcohol should help somewhat. But clearly, much, much more must be done to solve this problem if this optimism is to prove justified.

■ Reading Comprehension Questions

1. Which of the following would be a good alternative title for this selection?
   a. Why Drugs Are Harmful
   b. The Future of Drug and Alcohol Addiction
   c. Physical Signs of Drug and Alcohol Abuse
   d. How Drugs and Alcohol Are Used

2. Which sentence best expresses the main idea of the selection?
   a. Drugs and alcohol are glamorous.
   b. We must do more to conquer drug and alcohol abuse.
   c. Physical fitness prevents addiction.
   d. Drugs and alcohol have psychological and biological effects.

3. One reason ''establishment'' groups favor legalizing marijuana is that
   a. users don't hurt anybody else.
   b. alcohol is worse.
   c. too many people are already in jail.
   d. use of cocaine is increasing.

4. Conditions that show society's toleration of drugs include
   a. the increased interest in physical fitness.
   b. teenagers' concern with weight and diet.
   c. broad support for legalizing marijuana.
   d. optimism about drugs in the year 2000.

5. *True or false?* _____ Teenagers don't think that widespread use of drugs and alcohol is a problem.

6. From the article we might conclude that
   a. most drug users are teenagers.
   b. more people over twenty-six are experimenting with drugs.
   c. fewer people use illegal drugs now than did twenty years ago.
   d. many more ways have been found to control drug use.

7. The author implies that social acceptance of drugs and alcohol
   a. is unlikely.
   b. will soon decrease.
   c. is necessary for improvement.
   d. shows we're not doing enough to combat them.

8. From the article we might conclude that moderate drinkers
   a. are rare.
   b. are no threat to society.
   c. sometimes become heavy drinkers.
   d. eventually suffer great physical harm.

9. The word *advocates* in ". . . many advocates of decriminalization say there's no clear-cut evidence showing that marijuana is harmful . . ." (paragraph 11) means
   a. users.
   b. supporters.
   c. opponents.
   d. investigators.

10. The word *debilitation* in ". . . heavy drinkers can expect . . . serious physical debilitation" (paragraph 26) means
    a. weakness.
    b. fitness.
    c. improvement.
    d. inspiration.

■ **Discussion Questions**

About Content

1. Gallup begins his article by discussing the "contradictory trends" of exercise and addiction to drugs and alcohol. Why do you think people might choose to exercise to keep fit and abuse their bodies with drugs and alcohol at the same time?

2. Alcohol, writes Gallup, "may prove to be an even greater source of destruction" than drugs. In what ways might alcohol pose a greater threat than drugs?

3. In this article, Gallup expresses the opinion that "more must be done" to fight drug and alcohol abuse, but he doesn't go into much detail as to how we might do that. What are some ways that we could fight drug and alcohol abuse?

About Structure

4. What type of introduction is used in paragraphs 1–7?
   a. Statistics
   b. Quotations from experts
   c. An anecdote
   d. A definition

5. The author uses numerous transition words and phrases to help his readers follow his thoughts. For example, look at paragraphs 9 and 10. Find four transition words or phrases used to begin sentences in these paragraphs and write them here.

_____   _____   _____

About Style and Tone

6. To support his point of view, Gallup relies most heavily on
   a. anecdotes.
   b. statistics and experts.
   c. humor.
   d. personal experiences.
7. Does Gallup include only the pessimistic aspects of society's addiction problems? Or does he also include points about society's progress with drugs and alcohol? Why do you think he has written his article in this way?
8. One of the boldface headings in this article refers to alcohol as "the other drug." Why do you think Gallup refers to alcohol this way?

■ Writing Assignments

Assignment 1

Drugs and alcohol are so prevalent that most of us know someone who has been hurt in some way by their use. Write an essay about someone you know whose life has been affected by alcohol or drugs (legal or illegal). Include such details as how that person began to use drugs or alcohol and how they eventually affected his or her life. If you don't know of such a person, write about how you think drug or alcohol abuse might affect someone's life.

Assignment 2

Gallup writes that some influential "establishment" groups have supported the decriminalization of marijuana. What do you think about this? Write an essay of several paragraphs giving and supporting your point of view on this issue. Your central point for this essay will be either that marijuana should remain illegal or that it should be legalized.

Once you've decided on your main point, jot down a list of reasons that will support it. For your essay, select a few of the most persuasive reasons on your list. Then you will have enough information to write out a broad outline that includes your thesis and supporting points. On the next page are some factors you might consider:

Possible overuse

Health problems

Difficulties of law enforcement

Whether or not smoking marijuana is a victimless act

How legalization will affect other drugs

Individual freedom versus society's concerns about health and safety

Each of your reasons will provide the meat for a topic sentence of a paragraph of its own. Here is a possible topic sentence for this assignment: "If marijuana were legal, pot smoking would be an even greater problem in high schools than it now is." You can develop each paragraph by using what you know from experience and from reading to explain your supporting point. You may find Gallup's article useful as a source of statistics and quotations.

Assignment 3

Why do you think people use drugs and alcohol? Write an essay on the temptations of drugs and alcohol. Use anecdotes (real or imagined) to support your points. You may use any of the following as supporting points for your essay:

Social pressure

Personal problems

Tempting effects of drugs and alcohol

Ignorance (or ignoring) of negative effects of drugs and alcohol

College Lectures: Is Anybody Listening?

David Daniels

 College students are doodling in their notebooks or gazing off into space as their instructor lectures for fifty minutes. What is wrong with this picture? Many would say that what is wrong is the students. However, the educator and author David Daniels would say that the lecture itself is the problem. As you read this article, see if you agree with his analysis of lectures and their place in a college education.

A former teacher of mine, Robert A. Fowkes of New York University, likes to tell   1
the story of a class he took in Old Welsh while studying in Germany during the
1930s. On the first day the professor strode up to the podium, shuffled his notes,
coughed, and began, *"Guten Tag, Meine Damen und Herren"* ("Good day, ladies
and gentlemen"). Fowkes glanced around uneasily. He was the only student in the
course.

Toward the middle of the semester, Fowkes fell ill and missed a class. When   2
he returned, the professor nodded vaguely and, to Fowkes's astonishment, began
to deliver not the next lecture in the sequence but the one after. Had he, in fact,
lectured to an empty hall in the absence of his solitary student? Fowkes thought it
perfectly possible.

Today, American colleges and universities (originally modeled on German   3
ones) are under strong attack from many quarters. Teachers, it is charged, are not
doing a good job of teaching, and students are not doing a good job of learning.
American businesses and industries suffer from unenterprising, uncreative executives
educated not to think for themselves but to mouth outdated truisms the rest of the
world has long discarded. College graduates lack both basic skills and general
culture. Studies are conducted and reports are issued on the status of higher
education, but any changes that result either are largely cosmetic or make a bad
situation worse.

One aspect of American education too seldom challenged is the lecture system.   4
Professors continue to lecture and students to take notes much as they did in the
thirteenth century, when books were so scarce and expensive that few students
could own them. The time is long overdue for us to abandon the lecture system
and turn to methods that really work.

To understand the inadequacy of the present system, it is enough to follow a   5
single imaginary first-year student—let's call her Mary—through a term of lectures
on, say, introductory psychology (although any other subject would do as well).
She arrives on the first day and looks around the huge lecture hall, taken a little
aback to see how large the class is. Once the hundred or more students enrolled
in the course discover that the professor never takes attendance (how can he?—
calling the role would take far too much time), the class shrinks to a less imposing
size.

Some days Mary sits in the front row, from where she can watch the professor   6
read from a stack of yellowed notes that seem nearly as old as he is. She is bored
by the lectures, and so are most of the other students, to judge by the way they are
nodding off or doodling in their notebooks. Gradually she realizes the professor is
as bored as his audience. At the end of each lecture he asks, "Are there any
questions?" in a tone of voice that makes it plain he would much rather there
weren't. He needn't worry—the students are as relieved as he is that the class is
over.

Mary knows very well she should read an assignment before every lecture.   7
However, as the professor gives no quizzes and asks no questions, she soon realizes
she needn't prepare. At the end of the term she catches up by skimming her notes
and memorizing a list of facts and dates. After the final exam, she promptly forgets

much of what she has memorized. Some of her fellow students, disappointed at the impersonality of it all, drop out of college altogether. Others, like Mary, stick it out, grow resigned to the system and await better days when, as juniors and seniors, they will attend smaller classes and at last get the kind of personal attention real learning requires.

I admit this picture is overdrawn—most universities supplement lecture courses with discussion groups, usually led by graduate students, and some classes, such as first-year English, are always relatively small. Nevertheless, far too many courses rely principally or entirely on lectures, an arrangement much loved by faculty and administrators but scarcely designed to benefit the students. 8

One problem with lectures is that listening intelligently is hard work. Reading the same material in a textbook is a more efficient way to learn because students can proceed as slowly as they need to until the subject matter becomes clear to them. Even simply paying attention is very difficult: people can listen at a rate of four hundred to six hundred words a minute, while the most impassioned professor talks at scarcely a third of that speed. This time lag between speech and comprehension leads to daydreaming. Many students believe years of watching television have sabotaged their attention span, but their real problem is that listening attentively is much harder than they think. 9

Worse still, attending lectures is passive learning, at least for inexperienced listeners. Active learning, in which students write essays or perform experiments and then have their work evaluated by an instructor, is far more beneficial for those who have not yet fully learned how to learn. While it's true that techniques of active listening, such as trying to anticipate the speaker's next point or taking notes selectively, can enhance the value of a lecture, few students possess such skills at the beginning of their college careers. More commonly, students try to write everything down and even bring tape recorders to class in a clumsy effort to capture every word. 10

Students need to question their professors and to have their ideas taken seriously. Only then will they develop the analytical skills required to think intelligently and creatively. Most students learn best by engaging in frequent and even heated debate, not by scribbling down a professor's often unsatisfactory summary of complicated issues. They need small discussion classes that demand the common labors of teacher and students rather than classes in which one person, however learned, propounds his or her own ideas. 11

The lecture system ultimately harms professors as well. It reduces feedback to a minimum, so that the lecturer can neither judge how well students understand the material nor benefit from their questions or comments. Questions that require the speaker to clarify obscure points and comments that challenge sloppily constructed arguments are indispensable to scholarship. Without them, the liveliest mind can atrophy. Undergraduates may not be able to make telling contributions very often, but lecturing insulates a professor even from the beginner's naive question that could have triggered a fruitful line of thought. 12

If lectures make so little sense, why have they been allowed to continue?   **13**
Administrators love them, of course. They can cram far more students into a lecture
hall than into a discussion class, and for many administrators that is almost the end
of the story. But the truth is that faculty members, and even students, conspire with
them to keep the lecture system alive and well. Lectures are easier on everyone
than debates. Professors can pretend to teach by lecturing just as students can
pretend to learn by attending lectures, with no one the wiser, including the
participants. Moreover, if lectures afford some students an opportunity to sit back
and let the professor run the show, they offer some professors an irresistible forum
for showing off. In a classroom where everyone contributes, students are less able
to hide and professors less tempted to engage in intellectual exhibitionism.

Smaller classes in which students are required to involve themselves in discussion   **14**
put an end to students' passivity. Students become actively involved when forced
to question their own ideas as well as their instructor's. Their listening skills improve
dramatically in the excitement of intellectual give and take with their instructors
and fellow students. Such interchanges help professors do their job better because
they allow them to discover who knows what—before final exams, not after. When
exams are given in this type of course, they can require analysis and synthesis from
the students, not empty memorization. Classes like this require energy, imagination,
and commitment from professors, all of which can be exhausting. But they compel
students to share responsibility for their own intellectual growth.

Lectures will never entirely disappear from the university scene both because   **15**
they seem to be economically necessary and because they spring from a long
tradition in a setting that rightly values tradition for its own sake. But the lectures
too frequently come at the wrong end of the students' educational careers—during
the first two years, when they most need close, even individual, instruction. If
lecture classes were restricted to junior and senior undergraduates and to graduate
students, who are less in need of scholarly nurturing and more able to prepare work
on their own, they would be far less destructive of students' interests and enthusiasms
than the present system. After all, students must learn to listen before they can listen
to learn.

■ Reading Comprehension Questions

1. Which of the following would be a good alternative title for this selection?
   a. How to Benefit From Lecture Classes
   b. Passive Learning
   c. The Problems with Lecture Classes
   d. Lectures: An Academic Tradition

2. Which sentence best expresses the main idea of the selection?
   a. American colleges and universities are being attacked from many sides.
   b. Colleges and universities should offer interactive, not lecture, classes
      to first-year and second-year students.
   c. College graduates lack basic skills and general culture.
   d. American colleges and universities are modeled on German ones.

3. The lecture system
   a. encourages efficient learning.
   b. encourages students to ask questions.
   c. helps professors teach better.
   d. discourages students' attendance and preparation.

4. An example of passive learning is
   a. attending lectures.
   b. writing essays.
   c. doing experiments.
   d. debating a point.

5. To develop their thinking skills, students do *not* need to
   a. bring tape recorders to class.
   b. question professors.
   c. debate.
   d. attend small discussion classes.

6. The author implies that large lecture classes
   a. require that students have well-developed listening skills.
   b. encourage participation.
   c. are more harmful for juniors and seniors than for first-year students.
   d. are a modern invention.

7. *True or false?* _____ Daniels suggests that small classes demand greater effort from both faculty and students.

8. The author implies that administrators love lectures because
   a. students learn better in lectures.
   b. professors teach better through lecturing.
   c. schools make more money on lecture classes.
   d. professors can show off in lectures.

9. The word *enhance* in ''techniques of active listening . . . can enhance the value of a lecture'' (paragraph 10) means
   a. ruin.
   b. ignore.
   c. increase.
   d. claim.

10. The word *atrophy* in ''Without [questions and comments], the liveliest mind can atrophy'' (paragraph 12) means
    a. waste away.
    b. be unchanged.
    c. compete.
    d. strengthen.

■ Discussion Questions

About Content

1. How do your experiences in lecture classes and smaller classes compare with Daniels' descriptions of such classes?
2. What reasons are given for lectures being "much loved by faculty and administrators"?
3. What are the disadvantages of lectures, according to the author?

About Structure

4. In which early paragraph does the thesis of this selection appear? Paragraph

   ———

5. What method of introduction does the author use in his essay?

About Style and Tone

6. The author supports his main point with
   a. research and statistics.
   b. experts' opinions.
   c. students' opinions.
   d. personal observations.
7. What is the tone of Daniels' comments on administrators, professors, and students in paragraph 13? Back up your choice with details from the paragraph.
   a. Peaceful
   b. Critical
   c. Affectionate
   d. Humorous

■ Writing Assignments

Assignment 1

Write an essay in which you contrast a lecture class with a smaller, more interactive class. First make a list of the differences between the two classes. Here are some possible areas of difference you might consider:

Interest level

Demands on students

Opportunities for asking questions

Opportunities for discussions

Quality of teacher feedback

Choose three of the differences you have found, and then decide which class you learned more in. You will then have the basis for a thesis statement and three supporting topic sentences. An example of a thesis statement for this essay is:

Because of the different approaches to students' questions, class discussion, and feedback from the instructor in grading papers, I learned a lot more in my first-year English class than in my business lecture class.

That thesis statement could be shortened to:

I learned a lot more in my first-year English class than in my business lecture class.

The three supporting points for this thesis statement are about:

Different approaches to student questions
Class discussion
Personal feedback on assignments

Change each of the points listed above into a sentence, and you have your three topic sentences. A topic sentence based on the last point above might be: "While my English teacher gave me a lot of useful feedback on my assignments, my business teacher put only a grade on papers." Use specific details from your experience to develop your supporting paragraphs.

Here is another possible thesis for this assignment:

While my business principles class was a large lecture class, I learned a lot more in it than in my American literature class because of the quality of the instructor's presentations, time set aside for attention to individual students, and use of audiovisual and computer materials.

If you haven't as yet taken any lecture classes, compare any two classes in college or high school.

Assignment 2

In this selection, Daniels has given some disadvantages of lectures. Write an essay on the advantages of lectures. Use examples from your personal experience and the experience of others to support your points. Begin by jotting down a list of advantages. Then choose the ones you have the most to say about and develop those advantages in your essay.

Assignment 3

Which teachers have you had who were not in a rut, who conducted classes that made you glad to learn? Write a description of your idea of a very good teacher. Your description may be of a teacher you really have had, or it may be of a fictional teacher who combines all the traits you have enjoyed (or missed) in your teachers through the years. Be sure to include plenty of specific examples of classroom activities and their effects on students. Following is a list of various aspects of teachers and teaching methods that you may wish to use in your description.

Mastery of subject matter
Ability to excite students about subject
Types of activities used
Relationships with students
Feedback to students
Homework and tests

Seven Ways to Keep the Peace at Home

Daniel A. Sugarman

We like to think of our homes as havens of peace and security, but they more often resemble battlegrounds. Living together in close quarters, family members must cope with each other's moods, problems, worries, and pressures. The author of this selection presents several helpful suggestions for defusing tense situations in the home. You may discover the underlying reasons for some of your own recurring family quarrels.

Not long ago, the parents of a seven-year-old girl consulted me because their daughter was on her way to becoming a full-fledged hypochondriac. The girl's father was a physician, and both parents were busy, involved people. During an early session with the family, the reasons behind the girl's problems became clear.   1

Dad arrived late and was preoccupied and worried. He started to speak to me when his daughter interrupted: "My throat hurts a lot. I feel sick." Automatically he produced a tongue depressor and looked into her throat. As he reassured her about her health, I realized the girl's complaints represented the *only* way that she could engage her father's full attention.

When I pointed out that it was *he* who was unconsciously turning his daughter into a chronic complainer, the father altered his behavior. He began giving her more attention when she was *not* complaining about her health, and treating her physical complaints very lightly when they did occur. The girl began to improve. Soon, she hardly complained about her health at all.

In the course of my clinical practice, I have seen hundreds of families in conflict, and I am astounded at how frequently families unwittingly perpetuate tension-causing behavior. Explosions just seem to happen again and again, until family members can be helped to understand their interactions and learn to meet their mutual needs in less destructive ways.

Although conflicts may be so ingrained for some families that outside professional help is needed, certain principles of Family First Aid can go a long way in reducing friction for most families. Here are seven steps that I have found to be helpful for diminishing family tension.

1   Give Up the Myth of the Perfect Family. A couple of years ago, an unhappy teen-ager came to my office with her family and announced, "Well, here we are! The *Shady,* not the *Brady* Bunch!" I find that many people, like this girl, resent their own families for not living up to some romanticized notion of family life that can be found only on television. In contrast to TV, *real* families go through periods of crisis that strain everyone's nerves. During these trying times, most families' feelings and actions bear little resemblance to the sanitized, prepackaged, half-hour comedy routines on TV.

Some months ago, for example, Grace and Lew Martin* brought their sixteen-year-old son to me. Frank was an angry, sullen boy who had been doing poorly in school and been caught smoking pot there. When Frank took his father's car out and was caught speeding at ninety miles per hour, his parents insisted he come for treatment.

During our first session, it became evident that Frank's problem was certainly not the only one in the family. Mr. Martin had been consistently passed over for promotion at work. Mrs. Martin worked long hours trying to sell real estate, but because of high mortgage rates she was having little success. Frank's fourteen-year-old sister had fractured her leg the previous winter, and several operations had been required before it was set properly. Mr. Martin had become angry and withdrawn, and was criticizing Mrs. Martin's ability to manage the household. She, in turn, spent more time away from home and began to drink heavily. Family fights became more and more frequent. Everyone tried to bolster his or her own tottering sense of self-esteem by shattering the self-esteem of a loved one.

---

*All names in this article have been changed to protect patients' privacy.

As I listened to this troubled family, I became aware that it wasn't the real **8** problems that were about to do them in. It was their self-hate. Mr. Martin was furious at himself for not having gotten his promotion and because his wife had to work. Mrs. Martin was furious with herself because she wasn't selling houses and because she couldn't stay at home and care for her daughter. Frank was angry at them all, and so guilty about his angry feelings that I suspect his ninety-mile-per-hour ride partially represented an attempt at self-execution.

Once the Martin family understood how they were punishing themselves for **9** not being a perfect family, they began to show compassion toward themselves. They rapidly began to solve the real problems.

The idea of the typical, happy family is becoming an anachronism. As the **10** national divorce rate approaches 50 percent, increasing numbers of people will live in single-parent families. Should these people hate themselves because they aren't part of a typical family? Unfortunately, too many do just that. As high interest rates nibble away at the American dream of owning one's own home, should people hate themselves because they don't have a "typical" single-family dwelling—or because everyone in the family has to work to support this home? Unfortunately, too many do that, too.

I often wonder if the perfect American family ever did exist. If it did, I haven't **11** met it often in the past few years. As a matter of fact, research suggests that growing up in a perfectly happy family is not as important as psychologists once thought. In one continuing study of 248 children, Jean Macfarlane at the University of California Institute of Human Development has found that children who grew up in troubled homes do *not* necessarily grow up to be troubled adults. Children who grew up in happy homes are *not* necessarily better adjusted by the age of thirty.

When you give up the myth of the perfect family and deal with your real **12** problems in a spirit of compassion, psychological growth begins to take place.

2   Tell It Like You Feel It. Have you heard the story of the fifteen-year-old **13** boy who had never said a word in his whole life? He came to breakfast one day and suddenly yelled, "This oatmeal is cold!" His astounded mother replied, "You can *talk!* Why haven't you spoken before?" The boy shrugged and said, "Before this, everything was okay."

Funny story. Not so funny when situations like this occur in real families. And **14** they do. All too frequently I encounter people in families who, for one reason or another, feel they must hide their feelings.

A few months ago, I saw an unhappy couple. Mrs. Raymond was almost always **15** depressed. Sometimes she couldn't even take care of her home and children. Mr. Raymond was quite protective of his wife—but at the same time he was having an affair.

Together in my office, the Raymonds had little to say to each other. Each was **16** very solicitous, but wary of saying something that might upset the other. By not saying what they felt, they managed to upset each other more than if they had communicated their feelings directly.

It's odd how many people believe that when they stop verbalizing, communi- 17
cation ceases. Nothing, of course, is further from the truth, because communication consists of much more than words. Angry silence, sighs, headaches, impotence and arrests for drunken driving can often be forms of distorted communication.

For his vacation, Mr. Raymond made plans to take his family on a two-week 18
camping trip. Mrs. Raymond told me she *dreaded* the idea of camping. When I urged her to express her displeasure so a mutually satisfying vacation could be arranged, she replied, "But he works so hard. He deserves to go where he wants for vacation." Once at the campsite, however, she developed headaches and nausea. After two days of misery, she went to a local doctor, who failed to find any physical reason for her discomfort. During the rest of the vacation she tortured both herself and her husband with her physical complaints. It would have been much kinder had she told him how she felt before they left home.

Each time we conceal something from someone close to us, the relationship 19
becomes poorer. So, if you want to reduce family tensions, one of the most important ways to start is to send honest communications to those you love.

3   Don't Play Telephone. Do you remember the game "Telephone"? A 20
message gets passed from person to person, and everyone laughs at how distorted it becomes. As a game, telephone can be fun. In real life, sending messages through third parties fouls things up. It's important for family members who have "business" with other family members to take it up *directly*.

When tension mounts in a relationship between two people, a frequent way of 21
dealing with this is to send messages through a third person. Family therapists refer to the process as "triangulation." Following a spat, a mother may say to her son, "Tell your father to pass the salt," which may be answered by, "Tell your mother to get her own salt." In many chronic cases of triangulation, the middleman becomes severely disturbed.

Two years ago, Ruth and Ralph Gordon brought their seventeen-year-old 22
daughter for treatment. Lucille was not doing well in school, using drugs heavily and becoming blatantly promiscuous. When I began to work with her, she was uncommunicative and hostile. After some time, however, she opened up and told me her parents rarely talked to each other—but both used her as a confidante. Mrs. Gordon was sexually unsatisfied and suggested to Lucille that she ask her father to go for marital counseling. Mr. Gordon told Lucille that he was seeing another woman, and he urged Lucille to speak to her mother about improving her grooming. Caught in this tangle of feelings, Lucille became more and more troubled. It wasn't until she refused to play middleman that she began to improve. When either parent began to send a message through her, she learned to say, "Tell him/her yourself!"

You'll find that when family members learn to dial each other directly, there's 23
rarely a busy signal or wrong number. With direct dealing, a sense of freshness is engendered.

4   Make Your Blueprints Flexible. Almost all parents have a secret master   24
plan for their children. Sometimes this calls for a child to grow up exactly like a
parent—or, more often, for the child to become an improved version of the parent.
In our culture, with its emphasis on getting ahead and self-fulfillment, it's tempting
to hope that our children will realize many of our own desires. Whether we like it
or not, though, children have a habit of spinning their own dreams. When a child's
plans become different from his parents' blueprint, the family is on a collision
course that can be avoided only by understanding and flexibility.

Most parents don't even realize how much they push and pull. I think you   25
would be surprised, too, at how frequently children will say things to their parents
only to placate them.

One teenage girl assured her parents that she was going to study harder and   26
prepare for college. This girl told me, "I don't plan to go to college, but I can't tell
them yet. They are disappointed enough, and I don't want to rip up any more of
their dreams for me." Caught in a web of parental expectations, this girl was
miserable, and didn't feel free enough to explore her own potential and channel
her abilities into realistic vocational goals.

An experienced parent knows that different children require different handling.   27
When we become wise and willing enough to revise our blueprints so that they
incorporate the child's realistic needs and aptitudes, we are on the road to a less
tension-filled family life.

5   Learn to Use Contracts. Psychologists say that when two people marry,   28
they agree to a contract. Sometimes, a couple has a strong emotional investment
in keeping the not-so-pretty clauses of the contract hidden from everyone—including
themselves. Gina and Tom Butler were married twenty-five years before their hidden
contract caused problems.

When Tom met Gina, he was a skinny kid from a poor family who had a   29
burning desire to become financially successful. He was, under his bravado,
painfully anxious and felt very inadequate. Gina was the prettiest girl in town. She
was also desperately unhappy at home and couldn't wait to get away from the
constant bickering there. When she was sixteen, she had an abortion. At seventeen,
she met Tom. As they dated they unwittingly began to draft their contract. Gina,
unconsciously, agreed to make Tom feel adequate to reduce his anxieties. Tom,
for his part, agreed never to discuss Gina's abortion, and to remove her from her
hostile home situation by marrying her.

For many years their contract worked well. Gina massaged Tom's ego. She   30
encouraged, reassured, supported him. When the children went off to college,
however, she felt she needed to grow. She attended a local college, graduated with
honors and accepted a position with a well-known company. As Gina became
successful, Tom became irritable and angry. He accused her of not being interested
in the family. Eventually, he accused her of having a lover and of being "a tramp,
like you were when I met you and like you'll always be." With these words, their
contract was breached, and both sought the services of attorneys. Fortunately,
Gina's lawyer suggested counseling before divorce. Once in treatment, the hidden
aspects of Gina and Tom's contract were uncovered, and they negotiated a more
mature contract based upon mutual respect.

Many family contracts, like the Butlers', tend to disintegrate when one member   31
of the family begins to grow. And that's really all right, if the family can use the
anxiety that inevitably results as a catalyst to foster healthy mutual growth.

I find it helps a lot if you can face up to your hidden contracts and then update   32
them. It's also fruitful when you set clear provisions for the many minor vicissitudes
of daily living that can vex the family. Coats not hung up in the closet, hedges left
untrimmed—these are the raw materials that fuel family explosions. Frequently, an
annoying, persistent source of tension can be cleared away by drafting a new
contract, whose terms are clearly understood by all parties.

One teenager agreed to wash the dishes in exchange for transportation to   33
cheerleading practice. One husband agreed not to smoke when he was with his
wife, in exchange for her maintaining her weight loss. In these cases, all involved
felt they had gotten a good deal, and niggling sources of family tension were
eliminated by negotiation.

6   Stop the "Good Guy"–"Bad Guy" Routine. Sometimes, the greatest   34
problems in families arise when people classify children as Good Guys and Bad
Guys. These families tend to make a scapegoat of one of their members, who from
that point on becomes "it" in a never-ending game of tag.

The Freemonts had four children. Brett, the third child, resembled Mrs.   35
Freemont's uncle Mark, who was serving time for embezzlement. "He's just like
Uncle Mark," the Freemonts proclaimed when Brett came home from nursery
school with a toy giraffe that he had taken, and again when Brett was eight and
got into a fight with another third-grader. By the time Brett was fifteen, he had far
more serious problems. "I'm just like my uncle Mark," he told me: the label had
become a self-fulfilling prophecy. Brett felt doomed to replicate his uncle's life.
But once you realize that no two people are exactly alike, you can free members
of your family to be themselves.

Curiously, sometimes the Bad Guy of the family really serves to hold that family   36
together. I once worked with an eighteen-year-old girl who was constantly involved
in mischief. As I began to understand her family situation, I realized that this girl's
parents were emotionally estranged and the constant turmoil her behavior produced
was an attempt to get her parents to form a united front. Indeed, she was partially
successful. Her bizarre antics were at times so extreme that her parents barely had
time to examine their own problems.

The next time you're in the midst of a family problem, resist your natural urge   37
to think in terms of *right* and *wrong*. Rather, ask yourself, "What is going on here
and why?" In our era of no-fault car insurance and no-fault divorce, it makes
increasing sense to have no-fault (or all-fault) family problems.

7   Get Rid of Old Emotional Baggage. When people enter into any new   38
relationship, they come to the new with a lot of old fears and unhealed emotional
wounds. Unless you look at your own history honestly, you're likely to unwittingly
re-create the same unhappy mess that gave you so much pain in the past.

Rachel Dorton grew up in an unhappy household in which her father frequently   39
had affairs. When *she* married, with fidelity her top priority, Rachel chose Mal, a
hard-working, earnest accountant. For a time, all went well. After several months
of marriage, however, Rachel became increasingly suspicious when Mal did audits
in distant cities. She made his life miserable with constant suspicion and pleas for
reassurance. After several sessions of counseling, Rachel came to realize that,
without conscious intent, she was recreating the very experiences she had hated
so much as a child. As she faced her feelings squarely, she was able to become
less provocative, and she came to understand that *some* men—particularly Mal—
could indeed be trusted.

During periods of severe stress, it's astounding how people may treat others the   40
same way they were treated by their parents. Ed Richardson had had a rough
childhood. His father, a hard-working train conductor, would often take abuse from
passengers and arrive home irritable and tense. Sometimes he would beat Ed
severely. "You're no good," his father would proclaim. "You're a nothing."

Ed resolved that he would never hit his own children or call them names. For   41
years his resolve held, but then Ed's company went bankrupt and he was forced to
take a job he despised. The family had to retrench and move to a smaller home.
During this crisis, Ed's oldest boy cut school and was caught shoplifting. Ed brought
the boy home and began to beat him. To his horror he found himself yelling,
"You're no good . . . you're a nothing." Shaken by this experience, Ed got
professional help. It took him a while to put things back together, but it helped
when he realized that, when the chips are down, most people do unto others what
has been done unto them.

At its best, a nourishing family serves as a safe haven enclosed by invisible   42
walls of love and concern. In such a family, individuals can replenish diminished
feelings of self-esteem.

At its worst, a family can become a red-hot crucible in which ancient conflicts   43
brew and boil and are reenacted again and again. Most frequently, however, families
just seem to bumble along with little emotional insight into how the family itself
may be responsible for intensifying or perpetuating a family member's problem.

Solving family problems has never been easy. As a practicing psychologist, I   44
know that good intentions alone are usually not enough. Effective action most often
follows accurate understanding. With a little practice, care and use of these seven
steps, the chances are good that you'll be able to lower the tension level in the best
family of all—your own.

■ **Reading Comprehension Questions**

1. Which of the following would be a good alternative title for this selection?
    a.   Creating Family Blueprints
    b.   How to Reduce Family Tension
    c.   Hidden Contracts
    d.   Troubled Families

2. Which sentence best expresses the main idea of the selection?
   a. Believing myths about the perfect family can cause problems.
   b. When people marry, they agree to a contract.
   c. Following certain steps can help keep peace in a family.
   d. Family members play psychological games with each other.

3. One way for a family to stop playing "telephone" would be to
   a. get rid of old emotional baggage.
   b. negotiate better contracts.
   c. communicate directly.
   d. create flexible blueprints.

4. *True or false?* _____ Children who grow up in happy homes are not necessarily better adjusted as adults.

5. The "Good Guy/Bad Guy" routine means that
   a. family members feel they must be perfect.
   b. family members refuse to communicate with each other directly.
   c. families make scapegoats of one of their members.
   d. parents create secret master plans for their children.

6. The author implies that
   a. "triangulation" can be a helpful way for family members to communicate.
   b. making a scapegoat of a family member can unite a family.
   c. people need to identify their problems before they can act to help themselves.
   d. fidelity is essential in marriage.

7. The author implies that
   a. the perfect American family existed until fairly recently.
   b. creating family contracts inevitably leads to problems.
   c. how a parent treats a child can affect the following generations.
   d. families need "middlemen" to pass along communications.

8. *True or false?* _____ The author implies that all families need professional help at times.

9. The word *anachronism* in "The idea of the typical, happy family is becoming an anachronism" (paragraph 10) means
   a. ideal.
   b. injustice.
   c. disease.
   d. something out of its time.

10. The word *catalyst* in "the family can use the anxiety . . . as a catalyst to foster healthy mutual growth" (paragraph 31) means
    a. something which brings about change.
    b. an unfortunate accident.
    c. criticism.
    d. form of destruction.

■ Discussion Questions

About Content

1. According to Sugarman, who is more to blame for family problems, the parents or the children? Give examples from the selection to prove your point. Do you agree with him?
2. What are some ways, according to the selection, that family members take out their frustrations on each other? Can you think of any other ways?
3. At the end of the third section of the selection, Sugarman writes, "You'll find that when family members learn to dial each other directly, there's rarely a busy signal or wrong number." What does he mean? Do you think he is correct?
4. What does Sugarman mean by a "hidden contract" in a relationship? Give examples of such contracts from the article or from your own knowledge.

About Structure

5. What method of introduction does the author use?
    a. Broad to narrow
    b. Anecdote
    c. Questions
6. Which method of introduction does the author use to begin the section on step 1?
    a. Beginning with an opposite
    b. Anecdote
    c. Broad to narrow
    Which method does he use to begin the section on step 3?
    a. Question
    b. Anecdote
    c. Quotation

About Style and Tone

7. In the concluding three paragraphs, the author compares a nourishing family to a "haven enclosed by invisible walls of love and concern." He compares a tension-filled family to a "red-hot crucible in which ancient conflicts brew and boil." See if you can think of two other comparisons that could be used to describe a loving family and a fighting family.

■ Writing Assignments

Assignment 1

Write about the three ways that would be most appropriate for keeping peace at your home. Here are examples of how the three supporting paragraphs in your essay might begin:

First supporting paragraph: One way our family would benefit is if we would stop playing the game of telephone. All too often, one family member uses another to . . .

Second supporting paragraph: Another step our family should take is to "Tell it like you feel it." My mother, for example, sometimes hides her true feelings about . . .

Third supporting paragraph: Perhaps most important, our family needs to stop the "Good-Guy/Bad-Guy" routine. Two people in my family seem to have been cast in these roles . . .

Develop the ways you choose with specific examples that involve the actual members of your family.

Assignment 2

Sugarman tells us seven ways to keep the peace at home. However, there are other places where it is important to keep the peace—for instance, at school, at the workplace, in the dormitory room. Pick one of these other places and write your own guide to how to keep the peace there. Use three rules discussed in the article or think of other rules, and develop each paragraph by giving specific examples of the rule you are suggesting. Try to include appropriate stories, as Sugarman does, to show what you mean.

Assignment 3

Write an essay-length summary of the selection. Your goal is to write a shortened and condensed—but accurate—version of the selection in about five hundred words. To do this, you should do the following:

Cover two or three of the peace-keeping methods in each supporting paragraph.

Include only *key* ideas.

Shorten examples (or eliminate extra examples).

Eliminate dialog and repeated ideas.

Most important, remember that a summary should be *in your own words*, not the original author's. Therefore, don't simply copy material from the selection. You should, instead, put the author's ideas into your own words.

Below is an introduction that you can use to begin the essay:

A Summary of "Seven Ways to Keep the Peace at Home"

"Family" is a word associated with warmth, affection, caring, love, and peace. In reality, though, family life can be very different. Tension, anger, and frustration take over, at times, in almost every household. In his article, "Seven Ways to Keep the Peace at Home," Daniel A. Sugarman describes several techniques people can use to prevent or resolve family conflicts.

The Plug-In Drug

Marie Winn

What effect has television had on American family life? In the following selection, Marie Winn argues that TV is the most significant—and possibly most damaging—influence in children's lives today. If you have ever seen a family sitting hypnotized in front of the TV set, eyes glazed, unable to communicate with each other, you may agree with her. After you read the selection, you might also think twice before you use TV as a baby-sitter.

A quarter of a century after the introduction of television into American society, a   1 period that has seen the medium become so deeply ingrained in American life that in at least one state the television set has attained the rank of a legal necessity, safe from repossession in case of debt along with clothes, cooking utensils, and the like, television viewing has become an inevitable and ordinary part of daily life. Only in the early years of television did writers and commentators have sufficient perspective to separate the activity of watching television from the actual content it offers the viewer. In those early days writers frequently discussed the effects of television on family life. However, a curious myopia afflicted those early observers: almost without exception they regarded television as a favorable, beneficial, indeed, wondrous influence upon the family.

"Television is going to be a real asset in every home where there are children," 2 predicts a writer in 1949.

"Television will take over your way of living and change your children's habits, 3 but this change can be a wonderful improvement," claims another commentator.

"No survey's needed, of course, to establish that television has brought the 4 family together in one room," writes *The New York Times* television critic in 1949.

Each of the early articles about television is invariably accompanied by a 5 photograph or illustration showing a family cozily sitting together before the television set, Sis on Mom's lap, Buddy perched on the arm of Dad's chair, Dad with his arm around Mom's shoulder. Who could have guessed that twenty or so years later Mom would be watching a drama in the kitchen, the kids would be looking at cartoons in their rooms, while Dad would be taking in the ball game in the living room?

Of course television sets were enormously expensive in those early days. The 6 idea that by 1975 more than 60 percent of American families would own two or more sets was preposterous. The splintering of the multiple-set family was something the early writers could not foresee. Nor did anyone imagine the number of hours children would eventually devote to television, the common use of television by parents as a child pacifier, the changes television would effect upon child-rearing methods, the increasing domination of family schedules by children's viewing requirements—in short, the *power* of the new medium to dominate family life.

After the first years, as children's consumption of the new medium increased, 7 together with parental concern about the possible effects of so much television viewing, a steady refrain helped to soothe and reassure anxious parents. "Television always enters a pattern of influences that already exist: the home, the peer group, the school, the church and culture generally," write the authors of an early and influential study of television's effects on children. In other words, if the child's home life is all right, parents need not worry about the effects of all that television watching.

But television does not merely influence the child; it deeply influences that 8 "pattern of influences" that is meant to ameliorate its effects. Home and family life have changed in important ways since the advent of television. The peer group has become television-oriented, and much of the time children spend together is occupied by television viewing. Culture generally has been transformed by television. Therefore it is improper to assign to television the subsidiary role its many apologists (too often members of the television industry) insist it plays. Television is not merely one of a number of important influences upon today's child. Through the changes it has made in family life, television emerges as *the* important influence in children's lives today.

Television's contribution to family life has been an equivocal one. For while it has, indeed, kept the members of the family from dispersing, it has not served to bring them *together*. By its domination of the time families spend together, it destroys the special quality that distinguishes one family from another, a quality that depends to a great extent on what a family *does,* what special rituals, games, recurrent jokes, familiar songs, and shared activities it accumulates. . . . [9]

Yet parents have accepted a television-dominated family so completely that they cannot see how the medium is involved in whatever problems they might be having. A first-grade teacher reports: [10]

"I have one child in the group who's an only child. I wanted to find out more about her family life because this little girl was quite isolated from the group, didn't make friends, so I talked to her mother. Well, they don't have time to do anything in the evening, the mother said. The parents come home after picking up the child at the baby-sitter's. Then the mother fixes dinner while the child watches TV. Then they have dinner and the child goes to bed. I said to this mother, 'Well, couldn't she help you fix dinner? That would be a nice time for the two of you to talk,' and the mother said, 'Oh, but I'd hate to have her miss *Zoom*. It's such a good program!' " [11]

Even when families make efforts to control television, too often its very presence counterbalances the positive features of family life. A writer and mother of two boys aged three and seven described her family's television schedule in an article in *The New York Times*: [12]

> We were in the midst of a full-scale War. Every day was a new battle and every program was a major skirmish. We agreed it was a bad scene all around and were ready to enter diplomatic negotiations. . . . In principle we have agreed on 2½ hours of TV a day, *Sesame Street, Electric Company* (with dinner gobbled up in between) and two half-hour shows between 7 and 8:30 which enables the grown-ups to eat in peace and prevents the two boys from destroying one another. Their pre-bedtime choice is dreadful, because, as Josh recently admitted, "There's nothing much on I really like." So . . . it's *What's My Line* or *To Tell the Truth*. . . . Clearly there is a need for first-rate children's shows at this time. . . .

Consider the "family life" described here: Presumably the father comes home from work during the *Sesame Street—Electric Company* stint. The children are either watching television, gobbling their dinner, or both. While the parents eat their dinner in peaceful privacy, the children watch another hour of television. Then there is only a half-hour left before bedtime, just enough time for baths, getting pajamas on, brushing teeth, and so on. The children's evening is regimented with an almost military precision. They watch their favorite programs, and when there is "nothing much on I really like," they watch whatever else is on—because *watching* is the important thing. Their mother does not see anything amiss with watching programs just for the sake of watching; she only wishes there were some first-rate children's shows on at those times. [13]

Without conjuring up memories of the Victorian era with family games and long, leisurely meals, and large families, the question arises: isn't there a better family life available than this dismal, mechanized arrangement of children watching television for however long is allowed them, evening after evening? [14]

Of course, families today still do *special* things together at times: go camping 15
in the summer, go to the zoo on a nice Sunday, take various trips and expeditions.
But their *ordinary* daily life together is diminished—that sitting around at the dinner
table, that spontaneous taking up of an activity, those little games invented by
children on the spur of the moment when there is nothing else to do, the scribbling,
the chatting, and even the quarreling, all the things that form the fabric of a family,
that define a childhood. Instead, the children have their regular schedule of
television programs and bedtime, and the parents have their peaceful dinner
together.

The author of the article in *The Times* notes that "keeping a family sane means 16
mediating between the needs of both children and adults." But surely the needs of
adults are being better met than the needs of the children, who are effectively
shunted away and rendered untroublesome, while their parents enjoy a life as
undemanding as that of any childless couple. In reality, it is those very demands
that young children make upon a family that lead to growth, and it is the way
parents accede to those demands that builds the relationships upon which the future
of the family depends. If the family does not accumulate its backlog of shared
experiences, shared *everyday* experiences that occur and recur and change and
develop, then it is not likely to survive as anything other than a caretaking institution.

■ Family Rituals

Ritual is defined by sociologists as "that part of family life that the family likes about 17
itself, is proud of and wants formally to continue." Another text notes that "the
development of a ritual by a family is an index of the common interest of its
members in the family as a group."

What has happened to family rituals, those regular, dependable, recurrent 18
happenings that gave members of a family a feeling of *belonging* to a home rather
than living in it merely for the sake of convenience, those experiences that act as
the adhesive of family unity far more than any material advantages?

Mealtime rituals, going-to-bed rituals, illness rituals, holiday rituals, how many 19
of these have survived the inroads of the television set?

A young woman who grew up near Chicago reminisces about her childhood 20
and gives an idea of the effects of television upon family rituals:

"As a child I had millions of relatives around—my parents both come from 21
relatively large families. My father had nine brothers and sisters. And so every
holiday there was this great swoop-down of aunts, uncles, and millions of cousins.
I just remember how wonderful it used to be. These thousands of cousins would
come and everyone would play and ultimately, after dinner, all the women would
be in the front of the house, drinking coffee and talking, all the men would be in
the back of the house, drinking and smoking, and all the kids would be all over
the place, playing hide and seek. Christmas time was particularly nice because
everyone always brought all their toys and games. Our house had a couple of
rooms with go-through closets, so there were always kids running in a great circle
route. I remember it was just wonderful.

"And then all of a sudden one year I remember becoming suddenly aware of   22
how different everything had become. The kids were no longer playing Monopoly
or Clue or the other games we used to play together. It was because we had a
television set which had been turned on for a football game. All of that socializing
that had gone on previously had ended. Now everyone was sitting in front of the
television set, on a holiday, at a family party! I remember being stunned by how
awful that was. Somehow the television had become more attractive."

As families have come to spend more and more of their time together engaged   23
in the single activity of television watching, those rituals and pastimes that once
gave family life its special quality have become more and more uncommon. Not
since prehistoric times when cave families hunted, gathered, ate, and slept, with
little time remaining to accumulate a culture of any significance, have families
been reduced to such a sameness.

■ Real People

It is not only the activities that a family might engage in together that are diminished   24
by the powerful presence of television in the home. The relationships of the family
members to each other are also affected, in both obvious and subtle ways. The
hours that the young child spends in a one-way relationship with television people,
an involvement that allows for no communication or interaction, surely affect his
relationships with real-life people.

Studies show the importance of eye-to-eye contact, for instance, in real-life   25
relationships, and indicate that the nature of a person's eye-contact patterns, whether
he looks another squarely in the eye or looks to the side or shifts his gaze from side
to side, may play a significant role in his success or failure in human relationships.
But no eye contact is possible in the child-television relationship, although in
certain children's programs people purport to speak directly to the child and the
camera fosters this illusion by focusing directly upon the person being filmed. (Mr.
Rogers is an example, telling the child "I like you, you're special," etc.) How might
such a distortion of real-life relationships affect a child's development of trust, of
openness, of an ability to relate well to other *real* people? . . .

A family therapist discusses the use of television as an avoidance mechanism: 26
"In a family I know the father comes home from work and turns on the television
set. The children come and watch with him and the wife serves them their meal
in front of the set. He then goes and takes a shower, or works on the car or
something. She then goes and has her own dinner in front of the television set. It's
a symptom of a deeper-rooted problem, sure. But it would help them all to get rid
of the set. It would be far easier to work on what the symptom really means without
the television. This television simply encourages a double avoidance of each other.
They'd find out more quickly what was going on if they weren't able to hide behind
the TV. Things wouldn't necessarily be better, of course, but they wouldn't be
anesthetized." . . .

A number of research studies substantiate the assumption that television interferes 27
with family activities and the formation of family relationships. One survey shows
that 78 percent of the respondents indicated no conversation taking place during
viewing except at specified times such as commercials. The study notes: "The
television atmosphere in most households is one of quiet absorption on the part of
family members who are present. The nature of the family social life during a
program could be described as 'parallel' rather than interactive, and the set does
seem to dominate family life when it is on." Thirty-six percent of the respondents
in another study indicated that television viewing was the only family activity
participated in during the week. . . .

■ Undermining the Family

In its effect on family relationships, in its facilitation of parental withdrawal from 28
an active role in the socialization of their children, and in its replacement of family
rituals and special events, television has played an important role in the disintegration
of the American family. But of course it has not been the only contributing factor,
perhaps not even the most important one. The steadily rising divorce rate, the
increase in the number of working mothers, the decline of the extended family, the
breakdown of neighborhoods and communities, the growing isolation of the nuclear
family—all have seriously affected the family. . . .

And so the American family muddles on, dimly aware that something is amiss 29
but distracted from an understanding of its plight by an endless stream of television
images. As family ties grow weaker and vaguer, as children's lives become more
separate from their parents', as parents' educational role in their children's lives is
taken over by television and schools, family life becomes increasingly more
unsatisfying for both parents and children. All that seems to be left is Love, an
abstraction that family members *know* is necessary but find great difficulty giving
each other because the traditional opportunities for expressing love within the
family have been reduced or destroyed.

For contemporary parents, love toward each other has increasingly come to 30
mean successful sexual relations, as witnessed by the proliferation of sex manuals
and sex therapists. The opportunities for manifesting other forms of love through
mutual support, understanding, nurturing, even, to use an unpopular word, *serving*
each other, are less and less available as mothers and fathers seek their independent
destinies outside the family.

As for love of children, this love is increasingly expressed through supplying 31
material comforts, amusements, and educational opportunities. Parents show their
love for their children by sending them to good schools and camps, by providing
them with good food and good doctors, by buying them toys, books, games, and a
television set of their very own. Parents will even go further and express their love
by attending PTA meetings to improve their children's schools, or by joining groups
that are acting to improve the quality of their children's television programs.

But this is love at a remove, and is rarely understood by children. The more 32
direct forms of parental love require time and patience, steady, dependable,
ungrudgingly given time actually spent *with* a child, reading to him, comforting
him, playing, joking, and working with him. But even if a parent were eager and
willing to demonstrate that sort of direct love to his children today, the opportunities
are diminished. What with school and Little League and piano lessons and, of
course, the inevitable television programs, a day seems to offer just enough time
for a good-night kiss.

■ Reading Comprehension Questions

1. Which of the following would be a good alternative title for this selection?
   a. Television's Influence on America
   b. How Television Changes People
   c. Children and Television
   d. Television's Harmful Influence on the Family

2. Which sentence best expresses the main idea of the selection?
   a. Modern parents are using television as a baby-sitter.
   b. The domination of television has led to a breakdown in family relation-
      ships.
   c. Family rituals have been destroyed by TV.
   d. Parents can fight TV's influence by giving children strong values.

3. According to the author, the demands that young children make on their
   parents
   a. can tear a family apart.
   b. add to a stressful atmosphere.
   c. are caused by watching TV.
   d. can lead to growth.

4. *True or false?* _____ Research studies show that families talk about TV
   shows while they are watching them.

5. According to the author, parents can best show their love for children by
   a. providing good food and good doctors.
   b. sending them to good schools.
   c. spending time with children in activities other than watching TV.
   d. improving the quality of children's TV programs.

6. The author implies that
   a. the influence of TV can be effectively offset by limiting children to two
      hours or less of TV a day.
   b. peers, not TV, are the most important influence on a child's life.
   c. Mister Rogers is an example of TV's positive influence.
   d. today's parents are more selfish about their need for private time.

7. The author implies that
   a. teachers should use TV in the classroom.
   b. TV prevents families from expressing their love for each other.
   c. watching TV can help children settle their quarrels.
   d. TV is the most important factor in the disintegration of the American family.

8. The author implies that
   a. by watching quality TV shows, children can learn to handle real-life relationships.
   b. TV cannot influence a child who already has strong values.
   c. parents are dangerously unaware of the effect of TV on their children.
   d. it is all right to allow children to watch TV so that parents can enjoy a peaceful dinner.

9. The word *ameliorate* in "that pattern . . . that is meant to ameliorate its effects" (paragraph 8) means
   a. improve.
   b. process.
   c. begin.
   d. model.

10. The word *equivocal* in "television's contribution . . . has been an equivocal one" (paragraph 9) means
    a. temporary.
    b. equal.
    c. uncertain.
    d. unusual.

■ **Discussion Questions**

About Content

1. Why were early observers of television's effect on the family wrong in their conclusions?
2. How has television destroyed the "special quality that distinguishes one family from another"?
3. How do hours of watching TV affect a child's interactions with real-life people?

About Structure

4. What method of development is used in paragraph 5?
   a. Contrast
   b. Reasons
   c. Classification

About Style and Tone

5. Why do you think Winn titled her selection "The Plug-In Drug"? What does her title imply about her attitude toward television?

6. Reread the last paragraph of the selection. In the last sentence, the author talks about piano lessons and Little League. How does she feel about these activities?
   a. They are necessary to a child's growth.
   b. They are a waste of time.
   c. They are not as important as things families do together.

   On the basis of your answer, what would you say is the tone of this sentence?
   a. Slightly sarcastic
   b. Straightforward
   c. Humorous

7. The author uses the words *domination, destroy, danger*, and *dismal*, among others, to describe television. What is the effect of these words on the reader? Pick out three additional negative words the author uses to describe TV and list them here:

   _____   _____   _____

■ Writing Assignments

Assignment 1

In paragraph 3 of "The Plug-In Drug," Marie Winn quotes an early prediction: "Television will take over your way of living and change your children's habits." Is this true? Think about some ways in which television has taken over your way of living and affected your (or your children's) habits. Then organize your thoughts into an essay of several paragraphs. You might want to use as your thesis a sentence similar to the one below:

   Television has affected my life in several ways.

Then devote a paragraph to each way, supporting your points with details and examples.

Assignment 2

Winn devotes her essay to discussing the negative effects of television on family life. Can you think of any positive effects television can have (or has had) on your family life—or on families in general? Make a list of these positive effects. Then pick out the best ones and arrange them in order of importance, saving the most important one for last. Develop each one in its own paragraph in your essay. The following list will give you some ideas of possible *good* things about television:

Educational value

Moral value—some programs do teach lessons

Role model—we see people on television we admire

Eases loneliness

Keeps us up-to-date on current events

Takes us to places we would never be able to visit; allows us to see events we couldn't eyewitness

Visual impact—beautiful or exciting to watch

Assignment 3

Write an essay contrasting how one of your family rituals is conducted *with television* and how it might be *without television*. You might write about:

A family celebration

A holiday

Saturday mornings or Sunday afternoons

Getting ready for school or work

Bedtime

Dinnertime

Organize the essay into two supporting paragraphs using a one-side-at-a-time method of development (see pages 152–153). In the first supporting paragraph, describe your particular ritual as it is with television. Then, in the second supporting paragraph, imagine how it would be without TV. Be sure that each detail in the first supporting paragraph is covered in the second supporting paragraph; for example, if you state that the first thing you do in the morning now is turn on the *Today* show, you should describe in the second supporting paragraph what you *could* do instead—play soft music to start the day, perhaps.

Why Do Bad Things Happen to Good People?

Harold S. Kushner

The nice family next door suffers a tragic fire. Your little brother contracts bone cancer, or your friend's mother is killed in a car accident. Why do such terrible things happen? All of us have wondered why good people have to suffer. We have all felt cheated and angry over life's injustices. How can we deal with such horrible, senseless events? Do we become bitter? Do we put our faith in God? In this selection, a rabbi tells of his own personal tragedy and the conclusions he has drawn about why bad things happen to good people.

1   Our son, Aaron, a bright and happy child who could identify a dozen varieties of dinosaur, had just passed his third birthday. My wife and I had been concerned about his health because he stopped gaining weight at the age of eight months, and a few months later his hair started falling out. Yet prominent doctors had told us that while Aaron would be very short as an adult, he would be normal in all other ways.

2   When we moved from New York to a Boston suburb, we discovered a pediatrician who was doing research in problems of children's growth. We introduced him to Aaron. Two months later he told us that our son's condition was called progeria, rapid aging. He said that Aaron would never grow much beyond three feet in height, would have no hair on his head or body, would look like a little old man while he was still a child, and would die in his early teens.

3   How does one handle such news? What I felt was a deep, aching sense of unfairness. I had been a good person. I had tried to do what was right. I was living a more religiously committed life than most people I knew. How could this happen to me?

4   Even if I deserved this punishment, on what grounds did an innocent child have to suffer? Why should he have to endure physical and psychological pain every day of this life? Why should he be condemned to grow into adolescence, see other boys and girls dating, and realize that he would never know marriage or fatherhood? It simply didn't make sense.

5   Why do bad things happen to good people? Virtually every conversation I have had on the subject of God and religion has gotten around to this question. The misfortunes of good people are a problem to everyone who wants to believe in a just and fair world.

I try to help my congregation of 2,500 through the wrenching pain of their   6
divorces, their business failures, their unhappiness with their children. But time and
again, I have seen the wrong people get sick, the wrong people be hurt, the wrong
people die young.

I was once called on to help a family through an almost unbearable tragedy.   7
This middle-aged couple had one daughter, a bright nineteen-year-old college
freshman. One morning they received a phone call from the university infirmary:
"We have bad news. Your daughter collapsed while walking to class. A blood
vessel burst in her brain, and she died before we could do anything. We're terribly
sorry. . . ."

I went over to see them that same day, I expected anger, shock, grief, but I   8
didn't anticipate their first words: "You know, Rabbi, we didn't fast last Yom
Kippur."

Why did they think that they were somehow responsible for this tragedy? Who   9
taught them to believe in a God who would strike down a gifted young woman as
punishment for someone else's ritual infraction?

Assuming that somehow our misfortunes come as punishment for our misdeeds   10
is one way to make sense of the world's suffering. But such an answer has serious
limitations. It creates guilt where there is no basis for guilt.

Often, victims of misfortune try to console themselves with the idea that God   11
has reasons that they are in no position to judge. I think of a woman I know named
Helen.

She noticed herself getting tired easily. She chalked it up to getting older. Then   12
one night, she stumbled over the threshold of her front door. The following morning,
Helen made an appointment to see a doctor.

The diagnosis was multiple sclerosis, a degenerative nerve disease. The doctor   13
explained that Helen might find it progressively harder to walk without support.
Eventually she might be confined to a wheelchair, and become more and more of
an invalid until she died.

Upon hearing the news, Helen broke down and cried: "I have a husband and   14
young children who need me. I have tried to be a good person. I don't deserve
this."

Her husband attempted to console her: "God must have his reasons for doing   15
this, and it's not for us to question him. You have to believe that if he wants you
to get better, you will, and if he doesn't, there has to be some purpose to it."

Helen wanted to be comforted by the knowledge that there was some purpose   16
to her suffering, but her husband's words only made her feel more abandoned and
more bewildered. What kind of higher purpose could possibly justify what she
would have to face?

We have all read stories of little children who were left unwatched for just a   17
moment and fell from a window or into a swimming pool and died. Why does God
permit such things to happen? Is it to teach parents to be more careful? That is too
trivial a lesson to be purchased at the price of a child's life. Is it to make the parents
more sensitive, more compassionate people? The price is still too high.

Well, then, is tragedy a test? I was the parent of a handicapped child for 18
fourteen years, until his death. I was not comforted by the notion that God had
singled me out because he recognized some special spiritual strength within me. I
may be a more effective pastor, a more sympathetic counselor than I would ever
have been without Aaron's death, but I would give up all those gains in a moment
if I could have my son back.

Does God then "temper the wind to the shorn lamb"? Does he never ask more 19
of us than we can endure? My experience has been otherwise. I have seen people
crack under the strain of tragedy. I have seen marriages break up after the death of
a child. I have seen people made noble and sensitive through suffering, but I have
also seen people grow cynical and bitter. If God is testing us, he must know by
now that many of us fail the test.

These various responses to tragedy all assume that God is the cause of our 20
suffering. But maybe our suffering happens for some reason other than the will of
God. The Psalmist writes, "I will lift up mine eyes unto the hills, from whence
cometh my help. My help cometh from the Lord, which made heaven and earth."
He does not say "My tragedy comes from the Lord."

Could it be that God does not cause the bad things that happen to us? Could it 21
be that he does not decide which families shall give birth to handicapped children
but, rather, that he stands ready to help us cope with our tragedies?

One day, a year and a half after Aaron's death, I realized that I had gone 22
beyond self-pity to accepting what had happened. I knew that no one ever promised
us a life free from disappointment. The most anyone promised was that we would
not be alone in our pain, that we would be able to draw upon a source outside
ourselves for strength and courage.

I now recognize that God does not cause our misfortunes, but helps us—by 23
inspiring other people to help. We were sustained in Aaron's illness by people who
made a point of showing that they cared: the man who made Aaron a scaled-down
tennis racket; the woman who gave him a small handmade violin; the friend who
got him a baseball autographed by the Boston Red Sox; the children who overlooked
his limitations to play stickball with him. These people were God's way of telling
our family that we were not alone.

In the same way, I believe that Aaron served God's purposes, not by being sick 24
but by facing up so bravely to his illness. Aaron's friends and schoolmates were
affected by his courage and by the way he managed to live a full life despite his
limitations. Others who knew our family were moved to handle the difficult times
of their own lives with more hope and courage by our example.

Let me suggest that the bad things that happen to us in our lives do not have a 25
meaning when they happen. But we can redeem these tragedies from senselessness
by imposing meaning on them. In the final analysis, the question is not why bad
things happen to good people, but how we respond when such things happen. Are
we capable of accepting a world that has disappointed us by not being perfect, a
world in which there is so much unfairness and cruelty, disease and crime,
earthquake and accident? Are we capable of forgiving and loving the people around
us, even if they have let us down? Are we capable of forgiving and loving God
despite his limitations?

If we can do these things, we will be able to recognize that forgiveness and love are the weapons God has given to enable us to live fully and bravely in this less-than-perfect world.   26

I think of Aaron and all that his life taught me, and I realize how much I have lost and how much I have gained. Yesterday seems less painful, and I am not afraid of tomorrow.   27

■ Reading Comprehension Questions

1. Which of the following would be a good alternative title for this selection?
   a. Why God Punishes Us
   b. Coping with Tragedy
   c. One Father's Story
   d. Illness, Death, and Other Misfortunes

2. Which sentence best expresses the main idea of the selection?
   a. Some people think life's tragedies are tests.
   b. Aaron faced up bravely to his illness.
   c. We can never learn to deal with sickness and death.
   d. God does not cause our sufferings but can help us endure them.

3. Aaron died of
   a. premature aging.
   b. a burst blood vessel in the brain.
   c. multiple ˙sclerosis.
   d. unknown causes.

4. When the author learned of his son's condition, he
   a. blamed himself.
   b. temporarily lost his faith.
   c. felt resigned.
   d. felt an aching sense of unfairness.

5. According to the selection, God helps us
   a. only if we pray.
   b. through other people.
   c. by punishing us for our sins.
   d. whenever we ask for help.

6. The author implies that
   a. tragedies are God's way of punishing us for our sins.
   b. we can cope with tragedies as soon as they occur.
   c. we are incapable of coping with our tragedies.
   d. we can cope with our tragedies a while after they happen.

7. The author implies that
   a. Aaron's problems were more tragic than other people's.
   b. suffering may improve a person.
   c. Helen's husband helped her cope with her illness.
   d. most people lose their faith in God after a tragedy.

8. The author implies that
   a. God does not control who will or will not suffer a tragic event.
   b. good people suffer fewer tragedies than bad people.
   c. sometimes God does cause misfortunes.
   d. God never asks more of us than we can endure.

9. The word *cynical* in "grow cynical and bitter" (paragraph 19) means
   a. young.
   b. happy.
   c. pessimistic.
   d. sympathetic.

10. The word *infraction* in "punishment for someone else's . . . infraction" (paragraph 9) means
    a. understanding.
    b. violation.
    c. improvement.
    d. injury.

■ Discussion Questions

About Content

1. In paragraph 6, Kushner writes that he has often seen "the wrong people get sick, the wrong people be hurt, the wrong people die young." Whom does he mean by the "wrong people"? Give examples.
2. Why is it wrong to assume that our troubles are punishments for our misdeeds?
3. According to the author, how did God inspire other people to help him endure his son's illness? Give examples.

About Structure

4. What method of introduction does the author use in his first two paragraphs?
   a. Anecdote
   b. Quotation
   c. Questions

5. Before the author states what he feels is the right answer to the question of why bad things happen to good people, he discusses several wrong answers. One is that misfortune is a punishment for mistakes. List three other responses to tragedy that the author discusses as incorrect ones:

_____

_____

_____

About Style and Tone

6. Why might the author have chosen to write this selection in the first person?
7. Why are so many of the sentences in the selection in the form of questions?

■ Writing Assignments

Assignment 1

All of us have at times had to wrestle in a personal way with the problems of evil and injustice in the world. Write about three experiences you have had where you were not treated fairly—where the fates seemed to be against you. Your thesis might be similar to this one:

> On several occasions, I have experienced the feeling that life just isn't fair.

Then, in each supporting paragraph, describe such a time. Use specific details to help your readers see and experience the bewilderment and frustration you felt at the time. Close with a concluding paragraph in which you offer some thought or thoughts on the significance of your experiences.

Alternatively, write about unfair experiences of one or more people you know.

Assignment 2

Each of us, at some point, has probably learned from misfortune. Think of a time in your life when you felt that everything was hopeless. Then, after a while, you managed to survive and learned something in the process. Tell about this event—and what lesson you learned from it—in an essay. You might want to organize your supporting paragraphs in the following way: (1) Describe the event or situations in your life that made you feel hopeless. (2) Explain what you did to change the situation or how it eventually resolved itself. (3) Discuss the lesson you learned from living through such a time.

Alternatively, you might want to write about someone you know who has learned from misfortune.

Assignment 3

Write an essay that attempts, like Kushner's, to answer a baffling question. In addition, structure the essay so that, in your supporting paragraphs, you discuss (*a*) an answer you believe is incorrect, (*b*) another answer you believe is incorrect, and (*c*) the right answer—in your opinion. The essay can have a serious or humorous tone. Here are two thesis statements and brief outlines for two such essays:

> Thesis: I have finally figured out why my little brother is such a complete slob.
> a. My mother thinks he's immature.
> b. My older sister says he's just lazy.
> c. I am positive he actually likes dirt.
>
> Thesis: I believe there is one major reason why some people are so cruel to animals.
> a. It's not that humans have a sadistic streak.
> b. It's not that we are simply unthinking.
> c. Most of us are not educated about animals.

Can Society Banish Cruelty?

J. H. Plumb

 Every day, newspapers and TV news shows bombard us with reports of unspeakable cruelty. A woman burns her children with lighted cigarettes to punish them; baby seals are skinned alive while their mothers watch; soldiers massacre innocent civilians. At times like these we may ask ourselves, "What makes humans so cruel? Why do we have such a capacity for violence?" In this selection, J. H. Plumb presents a brief history of cruelty and ponders the answers to these questions. Be warned: You may be shocked by what you will read. More important, though, the selection will make you think.

No one can doubt that cruelty is a major obscenity of modern life. A woman of 1
eighty is thrown over a railing in Central Park and raped; a small girl is murdered
for sexual pleasure; an old man is bayoneted to death for the sake of five dollars.
"Snuff films," which progress from mass sex to the deliberate murder and dismemberment of the "actress," are rumored to be displayed in New York City for two
hundred dollars a seat. Leaving aside the organized violence of war, are we as
individuals more cruel than our ancestors? Are we more wanton in our infliction
of pain?

In January, 1757, Robert François Damiens made a feeble attempt to assassinate 2
Louis XV of France. Though his small knife barely penetrated the king's thick winter
clothes, causing little more than a four-inch scratch, Damiens was caught and
tortured to make him name his accomplices. He had none. Then he became the
centerpiece of a theatre of cruelty. The philosopher La Condamine, for one, was
so fascinated by the prospect of such an extravagant spectacle that he got himself
a place on the scaffold to watch the victim. He was part of a huge audience that
paid exorbitant prices to see Damiens's flesh pulled off with red-hot pincers and
his battered body pulled apart by horses. After that the Parisians—aristocrats,
bourgeoisie, and workingmen alike—went back to their dinners.

True, this execution was rather more elaborately staged than most in the 3
eighteenth century, but it was highly traditional. Damiens's executioners had
carefully copied, with scrupulous attention to detail, the way François Ravaillac,
the assassin of Henry IV, had been put to death in 1610. The French, however,
must not be regarded as peculiarly ferocious. The treatment of traitors in England,
a method of execution that had first been used against Catholic priests in Queen
Elizabeth's reign, was particularly horrifying. Before a vast crowd in a carnival-like
atmosphere, the traitor was hanged, but taken down while still alive; then his
genitals were cut off and stuffed in his mouth, he was disembowled, and finally his
head was cut off and his trunk quartered. The head, stuck on a pike, would festoon
Temple Bar for years; sometimes the quarters were sent to decorate provincial
cities.

These were but upsurges in an ocean of cruelty. Several times a year huge 4
crowds swarmed to Tyburn (near Marble Arch in London) to watch and enjoy the
executions by hanging of men and women, youths and girls, turned off the ladder
into eternity for minor robberies and petty pilfering, as well as murder and mayhem.
Such sadism was not merely an occasional visual thrill, for cruelty had been deeply
embedded in western European society for centuries and was still to be for a century
or so more. It was a constant theme of everyday life, a continuing event of family
experience.

Cruelty to animals was widespread—one might say total. Cocks fought each 5
other to the death, bulls and bears were baited by specially trained dogs; cats were
sewn up in effigies of the pope to create realistic howls when they were burned.
Oxen and horses were driven and flogged until they died. And yet animals were
not treated much worse than infants or small children.

The callous behavior of parents and adults to infants in seventeenth-century 6
England or eighteenth-century France is scarcely credible. The women of the poor
suckled for a trade, getting as many babies to a meager breast as they could.
Naturally their own child was fed first; often the other sucklings were half starved,
and frequently hand fed on an appalling diet of pap—a little flour and water. The
broken-down hovels to which babies were consigned for wet-nursing were as dirty
as they were pitiable. Often there was a dung heap at the door to give warmth, and
the floor was strewn with filth of every kind.

Swaddling was universal. Newborn babies were stretched out on a board, a 7
piece of diaper stuck between their thighs, and then were strapped down so tight
that they could not move. Swaddled infants were frequently hung up on pegs on
the wall and left there, and, of course, they lived in their own feces and urine until
they were reswaddled. It is not surprising, therefore, that the death of an infant was
an event of small consequence and of exceptional frequency—50 percent of all
infants died before they were a year old.

Childhood was little better. Children were remorselessly flogged. A middle- 8
class child in England was required to stand whenever he was in the presence of
his parents and would be savagely punished if he did not. The children of the poor
were expected to work as soon as they could walk and were often driven from
home to work when little more than seven or eight. Born and bred in a world of
callous brutality, the men and women of those days took torture and dismemberment
in their stride, were indifferent to the horrors of slavery and the slave trade, and
thought nothing of tormenting an idiot or an animal or throwing a witch onto a
bonfire.

And then, about 1700, attitudes among the prosperous commercial classes in 9
England began to change, for reasons that are difficult to comprehend. John Locke
protested against swaddling and child beating and argued powerfully that mothers
should suckle their own children. Hogarth's satirical prints show that by 1750
hatred of cruelty had a market. Take a long look at his bitter satire *The Four Stages
of Cruelty,* in which animals are being flogged to death or tortured, or children
casually killed. One print in this series, *Cruelty in Perfection,* depicts a savage and
murderous rape. The very fact that Hogarth satirized cruelty shows that there were
some flickers of sensitivity to horror.

Men and women formed societies to prevent the worst exploitation of child 10
labor—the young chimney sweeps; they banded together against the slave trade;
they helped suppress the most savage type of blood sports. In children's books after
1740, the horrors of cruelty to birds and animals, to fellow human beings, are
stressed over and over again. Children were taught to regard cruelty as evil, as
sinful. The result was the great wave of humanitarianism that swept Europe and
America in the nineteenth century. Wherever we look we find a positive gain over
cruelty: public executions largely vanished, torture was stopped. Of course, and
this must be stressed, a great tide of cruelty remained, but it was steadily diminishing.

The fight against cruelty was long and arduous; it was largely the campaign of 11
a social and cultural elite whose greatest success may have been in conditioning
their own children in the horrors of cruelty. This attitude never permeated the

whole of society or restrained the behavior of governments. Its influence was always fragile, and in this century cruelty has been widespread and growing toward individuals and toward classes of men and women. True, in previous centuries there would not have been the twentieth-century storms of protest against the more outrageous forms of government cruelty; neither are the worst excesses of personal cruelty allowed to flourish unchecked. But we have no cause to congratulate ourselves, for the position is insecure, and permitting the pornography of violence, which stirs deep and dangerous emotions, is a risk that society can ill afford.

And yet, maybe we should worry more about children's books, which seem   12
singularly devoid of overt morality. Perhaps we are too concerned with the happiness of the child, rather than with the community's happiness with him. Most children are instinctively cruel to animals, and sensitivity toward pain and suffering must be taught. At the same time, the adult world should take a far sterner view of cruelty than it currently does. We need to think clearly about it; we ought to think more carefully about what ought to be forbidden and what not. Surely, there would be no greater folly than to suppress all pornography simply because some of it extols violence. But certainly a good place to start would be the prohibition of *wanton* infliction of pain on another human being.

■ Reading Comprehension Questions

1. Which of the following would be a good alternative title for this selection?
   a.   Cruelty: Past and Present
   b.   The End of Cruelty
   c.   Torture in the Eighteenth Century
   d.   Modern-Day Cruelty

2. Which sentence best expresses the main idea of the selection?
   a.   Cruelty has been reduced, but has not vanished, in society.
   b.   Capital punishment should be banned.
   c.   Executions in the past were horrifying.
   d.   Cruelty is part of human nature and cannot be eliminated.

3. The infant mortality rate in seventeenth-century France and eighteenth-century England was
   a.   5 percent.
   b.   10 percent.
   c.   25 percent.
   d.   50 percent.

4. The greatest success of the movement against cruelty was
   a.   conditioning children to the horrors of cruelty.
   b.   reducing cruelty to animals.
   c.   condemning rape.
   d.   banning public executions.

5. The fight against cruelty was
   a.   a campaign by the common people.
   b.   a restraint on the behavior of government.
   c.   the concern of an elite class.
   d.   all of the above.

6. The author implies that
   a.   historians do not know why attitudes toward cruelty began to change.
   b.   children were deliberately killed because parents couldn't afford them.
   c.   we must abolish pornography.
   d.   cruelty to animals was not as widespread as cruelty to children.

7. The author implies that
   a.   we have almost abolished cruelty in our time.
   b.   children's books should teach children strong values.
   c.   forming societies to prevent cruelty did little good.
   d.   there has been almost no protest against modern cruelty.

8. The author implies that
   a.   humankind should be pleased at the progress against cruelty.
   b.   violence is still a strong tendency in human nature.
   c.   all pornography is violent.
   d.   most governments are now less violent.

9. The word *exorbitant* in "audience that paid exorbitant prices" (paragraph 2) means
   a.   foreign.
   b.   thrifty.
   c.   low.
   d.   excessive.

10. The word *scrupulous* in "had carefully copied, with scrupulous attention to detail" (paragraph 3) means
    a.   dishonest.
    b.   conscientious.
    c.   careless.
    d.   false.

■ Discussion Questions

About Content

1. In paragraphs 6 and 7, Plumb details cruelty to infants in Europe several hundred years ago. Why do you think parents swaddled their children? Why didn't mothers feed their infants themselves?

2. What do you think the author means by "*wanton* infliction of pain on another human being" (final paragraph)? How is this different from other kinds of cruelty?

3. The author says that a feeling of revulsion against cruelty never affected the whole of society or the behavior of governments. Can you think of examples of segments of society or of governments that condone or practice cruelty?

About Structure

4. How does Plumb develop paragraphs 5, 6, and 7?
   a. Contrast
   b. Examples
   c. Reasons

5. What is the transition sentence in paragraph 5 that tells the reader the topic of the following paragraph?

About Style and Tone

6. Why does the author devote so much of the essay to a history of cruelty? What effect do all the horrible examples of cruelty have on his audience?

7. The author uses the words *savage* and *savagery* several times in the essay. One meaning of *savage* is "cruel," but another is "uncivilized." Why are both of these meanings appropriate in the context of Plumb's essay?

■ Writing Assignments

Assignment 1

The author asks a question in the title of the article: "Can Society Banish Cruelty?" Write an essay of your own in which you answer this question, giving several reasons why society *can* or *cannot* get rid of cruelty (to people, animals, criminals—whatever). Use *either* of the following as your thesis statement:

- Society could banish cruelty if it really wanted to.
- Society will never be able to banish cruelty.

Then think of several reasons to support your thesis statement, and develop each in its own paragraph. Remember to make your paragraphs convincing by including vivid and specific examples, just as Plumb does.

Assignment 2

What does the word *cruelty* mean to you? For example, can a person be cruel to another person without threatening that person's life or health? Can cruelty be mental or verbal as well as physical? Can we be cruel to ourselves as well as to other people or animals? Write an essay in which you define the word *cruelty,* thinking of at least three different ways in which this word could be defined. For example, here are the three topic sentences from an essay defining cruelty:

Topic sentence 1: Cruelty can be an assault on a person's body.

Topic sentence 2: Cruelty can also be an assault on a person's emotional well-being.

Topic sentence 3: Perhaps worse than these, however, cruelty can be self-inflicted mental anguish.

For each form of cruelty, explain what you mean by giving your own examples of cruel behavior—either real ones of cruelty you have seen or read about or imaginary examples you invent. You may find it helpful to look at the essay written on this topic on page 114. You should also look at the three definition essays on pages 164–167.

Assignment 3

In his conclusion, Plumb recommends that we should teach our children to be sensitive to pain and suffering. What are some actions parents could take to raise children who are *not* cruel?

You might want to think about areas such as:

The kinds of books children should read

Controlling the shows children watch on TV

How to deal with the cruelties children hear about on the news

Punishment

Teaching children strong values

Organize your essay by deciding on the three techniques that would be most important for parents to use. In each supporting paragraph, give specific examples of how one of the techniques could be put into practice. For example, if you state that parents should control children's TV viewing, you should (1) name the shows children should watch, (2) name the shows children shouldn't watch, and (3) explain exactly how viewing could be controlled. In other words, give *specific,* not general, advice.

A Fable
for Tomorrow

Rachel Carson

The astronauts who first landed on the moon sent back some famous photographs of Earth. The pictures showed a beautiful blue-and-white world hanging like a bright jewel against the empty blackness of space. The more we discover about the universe around us, the more we realize what a precious, fragile world Earth really is—a world of water, air, and light in a solar system of freezing, burning, barren planets. In the following selection, author Rachel Carson writes vividly and movingly about the possible destruction of our unique and beautiful Earth.

There was once a town in the heart of America where all life seemed to live in 1
harmony with its surroundings. The town lay in the midst of a checkerboard of prosperous farms, with fields of grain and hillsides of orchards where, in spring, white clouds of bloom drifted above the green fields. In autumn, oak and maple and birch set up a blaze of color that flamed and flickered across a backdrop of pines. Then foxes barked in the hills and deer silently crossed the fields, half hidden in the mists of the fall mornings.

Along the roads, laurel, viburnum and alder, great ferns and wildflowers 2
delighted the traveler's eye through much of the year. Even in winter the roadsides were places of beauty, where countless birds came to feed on the berries and on the seed heads of the dried weeds rising above the snow. The countryside was, in fact, famous for the abundance and variety of its bird life, and when the flood of migrants was pouring through in spring and fall people traveled from great distances to observe them. Others came to fish the streams, which flowed clear and cold out of the hills and contained shady pools where trout lay. So it had been from the days many years ago when the first settlers raised their houses, sank their wells, and built their barns.

Then a strange blight crept over the area and everything began to change. Some 3
evil spell had settled on the community: mysterious maladies swept the flocks of chickens; the cattle and sheep sickened and died. Everywhere was a shadow of death. The farmers spoke of much illness among their families. In the town the doctors had become more and more puzzled by new kinds of sickness appearing among their patients. There had been several sudden and unexplained deaths not only among adults but even among children, who would be stricken suddenly while at play and die within a few hours.

There was a strange stillness. The birds, for example—where had they gone? 4
Many people spoke of them, puzzled and disturbed. The feeding stations in the
backyards were deserted. The few birds seen anywhere were moribund; they
trembled violently and could not fly. It was a spring without voices. On the mornings
that had once throbbed with the dawn chorus of robins, catbirds, doves, jays,
wrens, and scores of other bird voices there was now no sound; only silence lay
over the fields and woods and marsh.

On the farms the hens brooded, but no chicks hatched. The farmers complained 5
that they were unable to raise any pigs—the litters were small and the young
survived only a few days. The apple trees were coming into bloom but no bees
droned among the blossoms, so there was no pollination and there would be no
fruit.

The roadsides, once so attractive, were now lined with browned and withered 6
vegetation as though swept by fire. These, too, were silent, deserted by all living
things. Even the streams were now lifeless. Anglers no longer visited them, for all
the fish had died.

In the gutters under the eaves and between the shingles of the roofs, a white 7
granular powder still showed a few patches; some weeks before it had fallen like
snow upon the roofs and the lawns, the fields and streams.

No witchcraft, no enemy action had silenced the rebirth of new life in this 8
stricken world. The people had done it themselves.

This town does not actually exist, but it might easily have a thousand counterparts 9
in America or elsewhere in the world. I know of no community that has experienced
all the misfortunes I describe. Yet every one of these disasters has actually happened
somewhere, and many real communities have already suffered a substantial number
of them. A grim specter has crept upon us almost unnoticed, and this imagined
tragedy may easily become a stark reality we all shall know.

■ **Reading Comprehension Questions**

1. Which of the following would be a good alternative title for this selection?
   a. No More Birds
   b. A True Story
   c. Bleak Farming
   d. Paradise Lost

2. Which sentence best expresses the main idea of the selection?
   a. Humans are destroying their environment.
   b. Farmers depend on the weather for their livelihood.
   c. Everything must die.
   d. Disasters can happen without due cause.

3. *True or false?* _____ After the white powder fell, all the animals died.

4. The author states that
   a.   some of the disasters never occurred in real life.
   b.   all of the disasters occurred in one town.
   c.   all of the disasters occurred in one place or another.
   d.   the town has a real name.

5. *True or false?* _____ The people in the town expected the disaster to happen.

6. The author implies that
   a.   farmers are more destructive than city dwellers.
   b.   establishing communities leads to disaster.
   c.   a town like this could never exist.
   d.   all nature will be destroyed.

7. The author implies that
   a.   Americans are more destructive than other peoples.
   b.   children in disasters die more quickly than adults.
   c.   such disasters result from pollution.
   d.   a drought had destroyed the town.

8. From the article we can conclude that
   a.   people are often unaware that they destroy nature.
   b.   a forest fire had swept through the area.
   c.   birds are the weakest creatures.
   d.   people are learning to preserve their surroundings.

9. The word *moribund* in "the few birds seen anywhere were moribund" (paragraph 4) means
   a.   hiding.
   b.   numerous.
   c.   dying.
   d.   fat.

10. The word *counterparts* in "it might easily have a thousand counterparts" (paragraph 9) means
   a.   equivalents.
   b.   opposites.
   c.   myths.
   d.   differences.

■ Discussion Questions

About Content

1. How many different kinds of trees, birds, and animals does Rachel Carson mention in her narrative? Why do you think she emphasizes how many there are?
2. What do you think the "white granular powder" in paragraph 7 is? Why is it important?
3. In paragraph 4, Carson writes, "There was a strange stillness." What does she mean? What sounds, in particular, can no longer be heard?
4. Carson's essay is an example of development by contrast. Which method of contrast (see also page 152) does Carson use in her essay?
    a. One side at a time
    b. Point by point

    In which paragraph does the contrast begin? _____

About Structure

5. What words are used as synonyms for *illness* in paragraph 3?

    _____   _____

About Style and Tone

6. What significance does the title have? (*Hint:* A fable is a story designed to teach a lesson.)
7. Rachel Carson says that "no witchcraft, no enemy action" caused the disaster. She mentions only the "white granular powder." Why doesn't she name the powder or state specifically who or what was responsible for the disaster? In the same way, why doesn't she name the town (or at least give it a fictional name)?

■ Writing Assignments

Assignment 1

Write an essay describing three ways you, your family, or your neighbors are currently contributing to pollution problems. You might want to consider the following causes of various kinds of pollution:

Using chemical pesticides on lawns and gardens

Dumping motor oil, detergents, or chemicals onto the ground

Throwing away nonbiodegradable plastic products

Using cars for unnecessary trips and chores

Burning wood, coal, or leaves

Dumping trash or unwanted furniture on the roadside

Tampering with pollution-control devices on your car to get better performance

Buying products with wasteful packaging

In each supporting paragraph, give examples of times you (or your family or neighbors) polluted the environment in that particular way. For instance, if you decide to write about the wasteful packaging your family buys, you might discuss

The cardboard boxes, plastic bags, cellophane wrappers, and paper coverings that go directly into the trash after a trip to the supermarket

The heavy paper supermarket bags that are used once and discarded

The cardboard cartons from larger purchases that are thrown away

and any other examples you can think of.

In your conclusion, you might make some recommendations about how you or the people you know could stop polluting in the future.

Assignment 2

In paragraph 8, Carson tells us, "The people had done it themselves." This is her explanation of the tragedy. Is she correct? Are we destroying our planet—even now—through our own thoughtless actions? Decide if you agree with Rachel Carson's opinion. Then write a persuasive essay using *either* of the thesis statements below:

- "A Fable for Tomorrow" will probably come true for a number of reasons.
- There are several reasons why "A Fable for Tomorrow" will never come true.

Discuss each of your reasons in detail in its own paragraph. Be sure to use specifics, not generalities, in your paragraphs. If you feel it is necessary, be prepared to do some research to obtain facts and statistics to back up your reasons.

Assignment 3

How do you think the world will end (if it does)? Write your own version of the end of the world. You might organize the essay as a narrative, showing what would happen *first, next, after that,* and so on. Use vivid, descriptive language to make the experience as real as possible for your readers.

This essay presents an opportunity for you to let your imagination take flight; the fate of the earth is up to you! (You might try, though, to base your vision on current trends and problems, such as war, overpopulation, and pollution.)

READING COMPREHENSION CHART

Put an X through the numbers of any questions you missed while answering the comprehension questions for each selection in Part Five, Readings for Writing. Then write in your comprehension score. The chart will make clear any skill question you get wrong repeatedly, so that you can pay special attention to that skill in the future.

Selection	Subject or Title	Thesis or Main Idea	Key Details			Inferences			Vocabulary in Context		Comprehension Score
Haley	1	2	3	4	5	6	7	8	9	10	%
Gregory	1	2	3	4	5	6	7	8	9	10	%
Ames	1	2	3	4	5	6	7	8	9	10	%
Francke	1	2	3	4	5	6	7	8	9	10	%
Hughes	1	2	3	4	5	6	7	8	9	10	%
Adler	1	2	3	4	5	6	7	8	9	10	%
McMurtry	1	2	3	4	5	6	7	8	9	10	%
Orwell	1	2	3	4	5	6	7	8	9	10	%
Lopez	1	2	3	4	5	6	7	8	9	10	%
Herndon	1	2	3	4	5	6	7	8	9	10	%

Selection	Subject or Title	Thesis or Main Idea	Key Details			Inferences			Vocabulary in Context		Comprehension Score
Terkel	1	2	3	4	5	6	7	8	9	10	%
Adler	1	2	3	4	5	6	7	8	9	10	%
Bernard	1	2	3	4	5	6	7	8	9	10	%
Banas	1	2	3	4	5	6	7	8	9	10	%
Mannes	1	2	3	4	5	6	7	8	9	10	%
Schrank	1	2	3	4	5	6	7	8	9	10	%
Lamanna	1	2	3	4	5	6	7	8	9	10	%
O'Keeney	1	2	3	4	5	6	7	8	9	10	%
Gallup	1	2	3	4	5	6	7	8	9	10	%
Daniels	1	2	3	4	5	6	7	8	9	10	%
Sugarman	1	2	3	4	5	6	7	8	9	10	%
Winn	1	2	3	4	5	6	7	8	9	10	%
Kushner	1	2	3	4	5	6	7	8	9	10	%
Plumb	1	2	3	4	5	6	7	8	9	10	%
Carson	1	2	3	4	5	6	7	8	9	10	%

ACKNOWLEDGMENTS

"An Adventure in the City." Steve Lopez. Reprinted with permission from *The Philadelphia Inquirer*, September 9, 1987. Selection on pages 365–367.

"Advertising Claims." Jeffrey Schrank, adapted from *Deception Detection*. Copyright © 1975 by Jeffrey Schrank. Reprinted by permission of Beacon Press. Selection on pages 408–414.

"The Ambivalence of Abortion." Linda Bird Francke, from *The New York Times,* May 1976. Copyright © 1976 by The New York Times Company. Reprinted by permission of the author's agent. Selection on pages 332–334.

"Brett Hauser: Supermarket Box Boy." Studs Terkel, from *Working: People Talk about What They Do All Day and How They Feel about What They Do.* Copyright © 1972, 1974 by Studs Terkel. Reprinted by permission of Pantheon Books, a division of Random House, Inc. Selection on pages 377–379.

"Can Society Banish Cruelty?" Sir John Plumb, F. B. A. Reprinted by permission of the author. Selection on pages 473–476.

"College Lectures: Is Anybody Listening?" David Daniels. Reprinted with permission from *Trend* magazine, November, 1987. Selection on pages 440–443.

"Defense Mechanisms." Ronald B. Adler and Neil Towne, abridged from *Looking Out/ Looking In,* 3d ed. Copyright © 1981 by Holt, Rinehart and Winston. Reprinted by permission of Holt, Rinehart and Winston, CBS College Publishing. Selection on pages 383–387.

"Drugs and Alcohol: A Continuing Threat to Health." George Gallup, Jr., with William Proctor, from "The High Hope for Good Health" (pp. 124–130) in *Forecast 2000.* Copyright © 1984 by George Gallup, Jr. By permission of William Morrow and Company, Inc. Selection on pages 433–437.

"A Fable for Tomorrow." Rachel Carson, from *Silent Spring.* Copyright © 1962 by Rachel L. Carson. Reprinted by permission of Houghton Mifflin Company. Selection on pages 480–481.

"The First Step to the Cemetery." Kenneth Bernard. *Newsweek,* 1982. Copyright © 1982 by Newsweek, Inc. All rights reserved, reprinted by permission. Selection on pages 390–392.

"Five Parenting Styles." Mary Ann Lamanna and Agnes Reidmann, from *Marriages and Families: Making Choices throughout the Life Cycle.* Copyright © 1981 by Wadsworth, Inc. Reprinted by permission of Wadsworth Publishing Company, Belmont, California 94004. Selection on pages 417–420.

"A Hanging." George Orwell, from *Shooting an Elephant and Other Essays.* Copyright © 1945, 1946, 1949, 1950 by Sonia Brownell Orwell; renewed 1973, 1974 by Sonia Orwell. Reprinted by permission of Harcourt Brace Jovanovich, Inc. Selection on pages 357–360.

INDEX

CORRECTION SYMBOLS

Here is a list of symbols your instructor may use when marking papers. The numbers in parentheses refer to the pages that explain the skill involved.

Agr	Correct the mistake in agreement of subject and verb (234–246) or pronoun and the word the pronoun refers to (257–260).
Apos	Correct the apostrophe mistake (266–271).
Bal	Balance the parts of the sentence so they have the same (parallel) form (255–256).
Cap	Correct the mistake in capital letters (261–265).
Coh	Revise to improve coherence (39–48; 69–72).
Comma	Add a comma (272–279).
CS	Correct the comma splice (231–235).
DM	Correct the dangling modifier (253).
Det	Support or develop the topic more fully by adding details (17–20; 30–34; 67–69).
Frag	Attach the fragment to a sentence or make it a sentence (224–230).
lc	Use a lowercase (small) letter rather than a capital (261–263).
MM	Correct the misplaced modifier (252).
¶	Indent for a new paragraph.
No ¶	Do not indent for a new paragraph.
Pro	Correct the pronoun mistake (257–260).
Quot	Correct the mistake in quotation marks (269–271).
R-O	Correct the run-on (231–235).
Sp	Correct the spelling error.
Trans	Supply or improve a transition (42–46).
Und	Underline (270).
Verb	Correct the verb or verb form (236–242; 247–251).
Wordy	Omit needless words (284–285).
WW	Replace the marked word with a more accurate one.
?	Write the illegible word clearly.
/	Eliminate the word, letter, or punctuation mark so slashed.
∧	Add the omitted word or words.
;/:/-/—/	Add the semicolon (281) or colon (280) or hyphen (281) or dash (281).
√	You have something fine or good here: an expression, a detail, an idea.